Lecture Notes in Computer Science 8706

Commenced Publication in 1973
Founding and Former Series Editors:
Gerhard Goos, Juris Hartmanis, and Jan van Leeuwen

T0212948

Benoît Combemale   David J. Pearce
Olivier Barais   Jurgen J. Vinju (Eds.)

Software Language Engineering

7th International Conference, SLE 2014
Västerås, Sweden, September 15-16, 2014
Proceedings

 Springer

Volume Editors

Benoît Combemale
Olivier Barais
IRISA
Campus de Beaulieu
Rennes, France
E-mail:{benoit.combemale, barais}@irisa.fr

David J. Pearce
Victoria University of Wellington
School of Engineering and Computer Science
Wellington, New Zealand
E-mail: david.pearce@ecs.vuw.ac.nz

Jurgen J. Vinju
University of Amsterdam
Science Park 123
Amsterdam, The Netherlands
E-mail: jurgen.vinju@cwi.nl

ISSN 0302-9743   e-ISSN 1611-3349
ISBN 978-3-319-11244-2   e-ISBN 978-3-319-11245-9
DOI 10.1007/978-3-319-11245-9
Springer Cham Heidelberg New York Dordrecht London

Library of Congress Control Number: 2014947963

LNCS Sublibrary: SL 2 – Programming and Software Engineering

Typesetting: Camera-ready by author, data conversion by Scientific Publishing Services, Chennai, India

Printed on acid-free paper

Springer is part of Springer Science+Business Media (www.springer.com)

Preface

We cheerfully welcome you to SLE 2014, the 7th International Conference on Software Language Engineering, September 15–16, 2014 in Västerås, Sweden! We have worked to put together a program that has broad appeal to researchers, industrial practitioners, students, and educators in the field of software language engineering. The conference was also co-located with the 29th IEEE/ACM International Conference on Automated Software Engineering (ASE 2014) and the 13th International Conference on Generative Programming and Component Engineering (GPCE 2014), along with two workshops: the Industry Track on Software Language Engineering (ITSLE) and the Parsing@SLE workshop.

The SLE conference series is devoted to a wide range of topics related primarily to the use of artificial languages in software engineering. SLE brings together several communities that have traditionally looked at software languages from different and yet complementary perspectives: programming languages, model driven engineering, domain specific languages, and semantic web. Furthermore, SLE crosses a number of different technological spaces, including: context-free grammars, object-oriented modeling frameworks, rich data, structured data, object-oriented programming, functional programming, logic programming, term-rewriting, attribute grammars, algebraic specification, etc. Supporting these communities in learning from each other, and transferring knowledge is the guiding principle behind the organization of SLE.

The conference program included a keynote presentation, 16 technical paper presentations, and 3 tool paper demonstrations. The invited speaker was Prof. Colin Atkinson (University of Mannheim, Germany), with a talk entitled "From Language Engineering to Viewpoint Engineering". An extended abstract of the keynote presentation is also included in the conference proceedings.

We received 64 full submissions from 75 abstract submissions. From these submissions, the Program Committee (PC) eventually selected 19 papers: 16 out of 53 research papers (for an acceptance rate of 30%), and 3 out of 8 tool papers (for an acceptance rate of 37%). Each submitted paper was reviewed by at least three PC members and discussed in detailed during the electronic discussion period. Awards were also given out as part of the program for the overall best paper, the overall best student paper and the best reviewer.

SLE 2014 would not have been possible without the significant contributions of many individuals and organizations. The SLE Steering Committee provided invaluable assistance and guidance, whilst the Program Committee (and additional reviewers) undertook with dedication the critical task of reviewing and discussing the submissions. We are also grateful to members of the Organizing Committee for making the necessary arrangements and helping to publicize the conference and prepare the proceedings. We thank the authors for their efforts in writing and revising their papers in accordance with feedback from the reviewers. We would also like to thank our sponsors: Google (main sponsor), the GEMOC initiative, and Itemis. Finally, we would also like to thank the hosting organization, Mälardalen University.

We hope you enjoy the conference!

August 2014   Benoit Combemale
                                                                David J. Pearce
                                                                Olivier Barais
                                                                Jurgen Vinju

Organization

Program Committee

Emilie Balland	Inria, France
Tony Clark	Middlesex University, UK
Zinovy Diskin	McMaster University/University of Waterloo, Canada
Martin Erwig	Oregon State University, USA
Anne Etien	University of Lille, France
Joerg Evermann	Memorial University of Newfoundland, Canada
Jean-Marie Favre	University of Grenoble, France
Robert France	Colorado State University, USA
Andy Gill	University of Kansas, USA
Martin Gogolla	University of Bremen, Germany
Pieter Van Gorp	Eindhoven University of Technology, The Netherlands
Giancarlo Guizzardi	Federal University of Espirito Santo, Brazil
Gorel Hedin	Lund University, Sweden
Markus Herrmannsdoerfer	Technische Universität München, Germany
Jean-Marc Jézéquel	University of Rennes, France
Thomas Kuehne	Victoria University of Wellington, New Zealand
Ralf Laemmel	Universität Koblenz-Landau, Germany
Peter Mosses	Swansea University, UK
Sean Mcdirmid	Microsoft, China
Kim Mens	Université catholique de Louvain, Belgium
Marjan Mernik	University of Maribor, Slovenia
Pierre-Alain Muller	University of Haute-Alsace, France
Nathaniel Nystrom	University of Lugano, Switzerland
Klaus Ostermann	University of Marburg, Germany
Oscar Nierstrasz	University of Bern, Switzerland
Richard Paige	University of York, UK
Fiona Polack	University of York, UK
Arnd Poetzsch-Heffter	University of Kaiserslautern, Germany
Davide Di Ruscio	Università degli Studi dell'Aquila, Italy
João Saraiva	Universidade do Minho, Portugal
Bran Selic	Malina Software Corp., Canada
Jim Steel	University of Queensland, Australia
Tijs Van der Storm	Centrum Wiskunde & Informatica, The Netherlands
Juha-Pekka Tolvanen	MetaCase, Finland

Michael Whalen   University of Minnesota, USA
Eric Van Wyk   University of Minnesota, USA
Steffen Zschaler   King's College London, UK

Additional Reviewers

Al Lail, Mustafa
Al-Refai, Mohammed
Allen, Wyatt
Barais, Olivier
Bennett, Phillipa
Bieniusa, Annette
Brauner, Paul
Brunnlieb, Malte
Büttner, Fabian
Chen, Sheng
Chis, Andrei
Degueule, Thomas
Feller, Christoph
Fernandes, Joao
Fors, Niklas
Hamann, Lars
Hilken, Frank
Inostroza, Pablo
Kuhlmann, Mirco
Kurnia, Ilham
Kurs, Jan
Lukyanenko, Roman

Martins, Pedro
Mendez, David
Milojković, Nevena
Mukkamala, Raghava Rao
Nan, Shan
Osman, Haidar
Oumarou, Hayatou
Passos, Leo
Pereira, Rui
Pierantonio, Alfonso
Polito, Guillermo
Santos, Gustavo
Smeltzer, Karl
Sun, Wuliang
Teruel, Camille
van der Ploeg, Atze
van Rozen, Riemer
Vinju, Jurgen
Vojtisek, Didier
Walkingshaw, Eric
Weber, Mathias

From Language Engineering
to Viewpoint Engineering
(Invited Talk)

Colin Atkinson

University of Mannheim
B6, Mannheim, Germany

Abstract. As software systems increase in size and complexity, and are
expected to cope with ever more quantities of information from ever more
sources, there is an urgent and growing need for a more view-oriented
approach to software engineering. Views allow stakeholders to see exactly the right information, at exactly the right time, in a way that best
matches their capabilities and goals. However, this is only possible if the
information is represented in the optimal languages (i.e. domain- and
purpose-specific), with the necessary context information and the optimal manipulation/editing features - that is, if information is viewed
from the optimal viewpoints. Rather than merely engineering languages,
therefore, software engineers in the future will need to engineer viewpoints, which augment language definitions (e.g. meta-models, syntax ...)
with context information (e.g. elision, location, perspective ...) and user-
interaction information (e.g. editing pallets, view manipulation services
...). In this talk Colin Atkinson will outline the issues faced in supporting
the flexible and efficient engineering of viewpoints and will present some
key foundations of a fundamentally view-oriented approach to software
engineering.

Keywords: Viewpoint engineering, separation of concerns

As software systems increase in size and complexity, and are expected to cope
with ever more quantities of information from ever more sources, there is an
urgent and growing need for a more view-oriented approach to software engineering. Views allow stakeholders to see exactly the right information, at exactly
the right time, in a way that best matches their capabilities and goals. Domain-
specific languages are a key foundation for supporting views by allowing them
to display their contents in a customized way, but the current generation of
software language engineering technologies do not go far enough. In particular,
they currently lack the ability to convey the precise relationship between the
information shown in a view and the information it is a view of. They also focus
on describing how model elements should be visualized but provide little or no
support for describing how stakeholders should edit and interact with them.

The premise of this talk is that software language engineering technologies
need to evolve to support an enhanced approach to modeling in which model
content can be set in context relative to the underlying source from which it is de-

rived – an approach we refer to as "contextualized modeling". These technologies would then be more accurately characterized as "view engineering" technologies rather than "language engineering"'" technologies since they would support all aspects of view definition, including the context in which the content is to be interpreted and the mechanisms by which model elements are to be visualized and edited. Some of the key additional capabilities that the current generation of language engineering technologies need to support in order to become viewpoint engineering languages include -

Enriched Designation. The most important context information in a view is its model elements' location in the three key hierarchies of the underlying information model – the classification hierarchy, the inheritance hierarchy and the containment (i.e. ownership) hierarchy. These are supported to various degrees in today's language engineering technologies through a mix of explicit symbolism and location-defining designators (a.k.a. headers) in model elements. However, they are not supported in a uniform and consistent way, and are often severely limited in what they can express. In particular most contemporary language engineering technologies only allow one level of classification to be expressed at a time. Fully contextualized modeling requires a comprehensive, systematic and deep designation notation which allows a model element's exact location in each hierarchy to be expressed in its designator.

Explicit Elision Symbolism. Since views almost always convey only a subset of the information contained in the underlying model, an important requirement in viewpoint engineering is to support the description of what things are not included in a view, as well as the description of what things are. This is a challenging task since it involves subtle interactions between explicit omission statements (e.g. "..." in UML generalization sets), explicit completeness statements (e.g. complete and disjoint in UML generalization sets) and background "world" assumptions (e.g. "open world" versus "closed world" assumption). Fully contextualized modeling therefore requires comprehensive and systematic support for elision, both in the form of explicit elision symbols and elided model element designators.

Explicit Derivation Symbolism. As well as omitting information from the underlying subject of a view it is possible to derive new information that the subject does not explicitly contain. Such derivation operations can be driven by the application of basic characterization relationships such as inheritance and classification (e.g. subsumption) or by more complex inference operations based on the principles of logic. In both cases, contextualized modeling must incorporate the ability to express what information in a view has been derived and what information has been explicitly asserted by a human modeller. This is important for resolving conflicts and signalling the weight that should be given to the information represented within views.

Language Symbiosis. Domain-specific representations of information have the advantage that they are optimized for particular classes of stakeholders or communities of experts, whereas general-purpose languages have the advantage that they are widely known and can represent information in quasi-standard ways. In order to enjoy both benefits simultaneously, contextualized models should be represented by highly flexible, symbiotic languages that allow different visualizations of model elements to be mixed and interchanged at will.

Viewpoint Environment Definition. A user's experience of a view is determined not only by the way in which its contents are displayed, but also by the way in which the user can interact with the model and, when it is editable, input information. This impacts all aspects of the environment in which the view is displayed, including the menu items, the pallets of predefined types and models elements and the range of operations that can be applied to the content (e.g. checking, printing, persisting etc.). The engineering of viewpoints therefore involves much more than just the engineering of languages it also involves the definition of the associated interaction experience.

In this talk Colin Atkinson will introduce the vision of contextualized modeling and explain these key ingredients needed to turn the current generation of software language engineering technologies into fully fledged viewpoint-engineering technologies

Biography

Colin Atkinson has been the leader of the Software Engineering Group at the University of Mannheim since April 2003. Before that he has held positions at the University of Kaiserslautern, the Fraunhofer Institute for Experimental Software Engineering and the University of Houston - Clear Lake. His research interests are focused on the use of model-driven and component based approaches in the development of dependable and adaptable computing systems. He was a contributor to the original UML development process and is one of the original developers of the deep (multi-level) approach to conceptual modelling. He received his Ph.D. and M.Sc. in computer science from Imperial College, London, in 1990 and 1985 respectively, and his B.Sc. in Mathematical Physics from the University of Nottingham 1983.

Table of Contents

ProMoBox: A Framework for Generating Domain-Specific Property Languages

Bart Meyers[1], Romuald Deshayes[2], Levi Lucio[3], Eugene Syriani[4],
Hans Vangheluwe[1,3], and Manuel Wimmer[5]

[1] Modeling, Simulation and Design Lab (MSDL), University of Antwerp, Belgium
{bart.meyers,hans.vangheluwe}@uantwerp.be
[2] Institut d'Informatique, Universit de Mons, Mons, Belgium
romuald.deshayes@umons.ac.be
[3] Modeling, Simulation and Design Lab (MSDL), McGill University, Canada
{levi,hv}@cs.mcgill.ca
[4] Software Engineering Research Group (SERG), University of Alabama, United States
esyriani@cs.ua.edu
[5] Business Informatics Group (BIG), Vienna University of Technology, Austria
wimmer@big.tuwien.ac.at

Abstract. Specifying and verifying properties of the modelled system has been mostly neglected by domain-specific modelling (DSM) approaches. At best, this is only partially supported by translating models to formal representations on which properties are specified and evaluated based on logic-based formalisms, such as linear temporal logic. This contradicts the DSM philosophy as domain experts are usually not familiar with the logics space. To overcome this shortcoming, we propose to shift property specification and verification tasks up to the domain-specific level. The *ProMoBox* framework consists of (i) generic languages for modelling properties and representing verification results, (ii) a fully automated method to specialize and integrate these generic languages to a given DSM language, and (iii) a verification backbone based model checking directly plug-able to DSM environments. In its current state, *ProMoBox* offers the designer modelling support for defining temporal properties, and for visualizing verification results, all based on a given DSM language. We report results of applying *ProMoBox* to a case study of an elevator controller.

1 Introduction

Domain-specific modelling (DSM) advocates that, providing languages that are specific to the problem space rather than to the solution space, systems are designable by domain experts while model transformations are taking care of achieving the transition to the solution space [1]. An essential activity in DSM is the specification and verification of properties to ensure the high quality of the designed systems [2]. Thus, supporting these tasks by DSM is necessary to provide a holistic DSM experience to domain engineers. However, specifying and verifying properties of systems has been mostly neglected by DSM approaches. At best, this is only partially supported by translating models to formal representations on which properties are specified and evaluated with logic-based formalisms [3], such as Linear Temporal Logic (LTL). This contradicts the DSM philosophy as domain experts are usually not familiar with temporal logic. The need

B. Combemale et al. (Eds.): SLE 2014, LNCS 8706, pp. 1–20, 2014.

to raise the level of abstraction for specification and verification tasks is also recently raised in [4]. The authors emphasize that domain engineers should be shielded from the underlying verification technologies. In this sense, DSM includes not only the design of the system-under-study, but also the properties themselves, the representation of the run-time state of a system, the behaviour of the environment, and a visualisation of a counter-example, all at the domain-specific level. In the spirit of DSM, they should each be defined in their own domain-specific modelling language (DSML).

To overcome this shortcoming, we propose to shift property specification and verification tasks up to the DSM level, resulting in the generation and execution of *ProMoBox*. The contribution of the *ProMoBox* framework consists of (i) generic languages for modelling all artefacts that are needed for specifying and verifying temporal properties with the expressive power of LTL, (ii) a fully automated method to specialise and integrate these generic languages to a given DSML, and (iii) a verification backbone based on model checking with LTL that is directly plug-able to DSM environments.

In the following section, we introduce the running example of an elevator controller. Section 3 introduces our approach *ProMoBox* from a language engineering point of view and explains how properties are defined and verified based on a model checking backbone. Section 4 is dedicated to implementation and evaluation of *ProMoBox*. Section 5 elaborates on assumptions that are made in the current state of the approach while discussing the limitations of the approach. In Section 6 we discuss related work and conclude in Section 7.

2   Running Example

Our running example is an elevator controller modeled by a graphical DSL. This DSL enables modelling a building with floors, elevators and buttons, and defines the stepwise behaviour of this model.

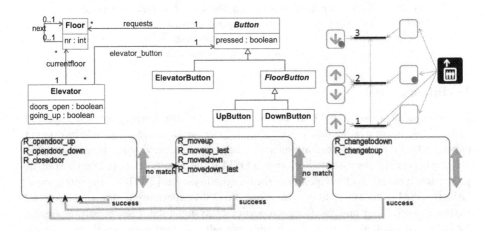

Fig. 1. The meta-model E of the Elevator DSL (top left), an instance e of the Elevator DSL representing an elevator that serves three floors (top right), and the transformation model $E_{[[.]]}$ that schedules all the operational rules (bottom)

The left of Fig. 1 shows the meta-model which we will denote by *E*. *Button*s can request an *Elevator* to go to a particular *Floor*. Floors are ordered by the *next* association and a derived attribute *nr* representing the *Floor* number. An *Elevator* is at exactly one *Floor*, modelled by the *currentfloor* association. An *ElevatorButton* is a button inside an *Elevator*, requesting a certain *Floor*. At every floor, there can be an *UpButton* to request to go up and a *DownButton* to request to go down. An Elevator can have its doors open (it cannot move) and has a direction (up or down).

The top right of Fig. 1 shows an instance *e* with three floors, one elevator and seven buttons, depicting the concrete syntax. Pressed buttons are annotated with red dots, and are connected to the floor they request. At the top floor a button is pressed by someone who requested to go down, and inside the elevator the button to go to floor 2 has been pressed. The elevator is currently at the bottom level.

The bottom of Fig. 1 shows the transformation model $E_{[[\cdot]]}$ of the operational semantics. The model shows how different rules are scheduled. Rounded rectangles refer to a set of rules where at most one is randomly chosen to be applied. Execution starts at the left rectangle. Grey arrows annotated with "no match" are followed when none of the rules in the source rectangle can be applied, green arrows annotated with "success" are followed when a rule was applied. Inspired from a realistic elevator controller, the rules implement how the elevator changes floors (one at a time), and opens and closes its door to serve the requests of users (modelled as pressed buttons). The elevator passes all floors that are requested on its path (which is either up or down), and opens its door when the elevator's direction corresponds to the requested direction. Pressed buttons are turned off (released) when the door opens at a requested floor and the elevator goes in that direction. When a request for a floor is made for a different floor than the elevator's current floor, the doors close and the elevator starts moving. The elevator only changes its direction when there are no more requests on its path. Note that, if the elevator is at a lower floor, it can pass by a floor where one has requested to go down without stopping, as the elevator is going in the opposite direction. The rules are not shown in Fig. 1 because of space constraint, but later in the paper, one of the rules is shown in Fig. 7.

When designing the elevator software system, we would like to verify the *ReachesFloor* property: whenever a request for any floor is made, the elevator will eventually open its doors at the latest the second time it passes by that floor.

3   The ProMoBox

Based on preliminary ideas outlined in our previous work [5, 6], the *ProMoBox* framework consists of the following three parts.

Generic languages for modelling all artefacts that are needed for specifying and verifying properties. For a given DSML, *ProMoBox* defines a family of five sub-languages [5] that are required to modularly support property verification, covering (*i*) design modelling as supported by traditional DSMLs, (*ii*) run-time state representation, (*iii*) event-based input modelling (to model the behaviour of an environment), (*iv*) state-based output representation (to model an execution trace of the system or verification results), and (*v*) property specification. Property languages generated by *ProMoBox* are specifically tailored to ease the development of temporal patterns as well as structural patterns needed to describe the desired properties of the system's design by domain engineers in the DSML's concrete syntax. To allow to formulate temporal properties at a high-level of abstraction, we formalise Dwyer's specification patterns [7] for defining temporal patterns as a DSML. With the help of this DSML, domain engineers are able to express temporal properties for finite state verification such as absence, existence, or universality. To ease the development of structural patterns to be checked on snapshots of the system's execution states, we propose an automated technique based on [8,9] that is able to produce a specialised language from a given DSML tailored to express structural patterns. The language for defining structural patterns is inspired by *PaMoMo* [10, 11], a language supporting several pattern kinds such as enabling, positive, and negative patterns. Finally, we introduce the possibility to define quantifiers for temporal properties to express complex properties in a more concise manner, *e.g., every* element of a certain type has to fulfil a certain property.

A **fully automated method** to specialise and integrate these generic languages to a given DSML. We extend meta-modelling and model transformation languages with annotations, to add necessary information for every language construct and semantic step. This additional information enables the fully automatic generation of the five sub-languages and necessary transformations between the sub-languages, thus minimising the effort of the language engineer. Because of their generative definition, consistency between the languages and their models is guaranteed by construction. We use templates that describe the generic part of each language, and that are subsequently woven with the DSML. By using templates, we allow the *ProMoBox* framework to be configurable for different types of DSMLs.

A **verification backbone** based model checking directly plug-able to DSM environments. Properties in *ProMoBox* are translated to LTL and a Promela system is generated that includes a translation of the system, the environment, and the rule-based operational semantics of the system. The properties are checked by SPIN [12]. The verification results (in case of a counter-example) are translated back to the DSM level.

The *ProMoBox* approach is illustrated in Fig. 2 using the elevator example presented in Section 2. When using the *ProMoBox* approach, only the grey models in Fig. 2 need to be modelled by hand, the white models are generated. This is done in two parts: first, we define how meta-models can be annotated (E' in Fig. 2) and how the five sub-languages (*i.e.,* the design, run-time, input, output and properties languages) are generated (upper part of Fig. 2). Second, we define how mappings are generated that allow a given property to be verified on a given system, and how the results can be visualised in a domain specific way (steps 1 to 5 of Fig. 2).

3.1 The Annotated Meta-model

The abstract syntax of the sub-languages is generated from the *annotated meta-model* that provides additional information on which parts are static (never change at run-time), dynamic (change at run-time) and which parts can be input into the system.

First, we present a formal definition of a meta-model. The complete formalisation can be found in [5]. We define Σ as the alphabet of all possible names. For simplicity, all class, association, and attribute names are globally unique and are from here on referred to as the classes, associations or attributes themselves. A meta-model is defined by:

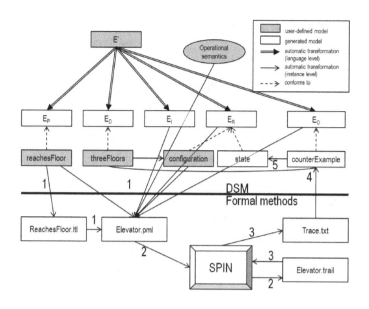

Fig. 2. Property verification with ProMoBox and SPIN

$$\mathcal{M} = (C, D, A, \alpha, \iota, P, \pi), \tag{1}$$

with

$C \subseteq \Sigma$	the set of all classes,
$D \subseteq C$	the set of all abstract classes,
$A \subseteq \Sigma$	the set of all associations,
$\alpha : A \to C \times C$	the association mapping, a total function,
$\iota : C \times C$	the set of inheritance relations,
$P \subseteq \Sigma$	the set of all attributes,
$\pi : P \to C$	the attribute mapping, a total function.

ι^+ is the set of relations of ι under transitive closure. This means that $x, y, z \in C \mid (x, y) \in \iota^+ \wedge (y, z) \in \iota^+ \implies (x, z) \in \iota^+$, and specifically, $x \in C \implies (x, x) \in \iota^+$. Note that attributes are considered to be nothing more than names. Their types are abstracted away from because of space constraints and they are not essential to explain the approach. Similarly, cardinalities of associations are not modelled in this definition.

All incoming associations defined by inheritance $in^* : C \to \mathcal{P}(A)$ are the set of incoming associations of the class or its parents:

$$in^*(c) = \big\{ a \in A \mid \exists x, y \in C, \alpha(a) = (x, y) \wedge (c, y) \in \iota^+ \big\}$$

All outgoing associations defined by inheritance $out^* : C \to \mathcal{P}(A)$ are the set of outgoing associations of the class or its parents:

$$out^*(c) = \big\{ a \in A \mid \exists x, y \in C, \alpha(a) = (x, y) \wedge (c, x) \in \iota^+ \big\}$$

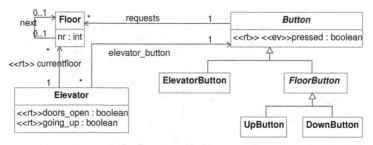

Fig. 3. The annotated metamodel E'

All classes defined by inheritance that have an attribute $\pi^* : P \rightarrow \mathcal{P}(C)$ are the property-containing class and its subclasses:

$$\pi^*(p) = \left\{ c \in C \mid \exists x \in C, \pi(p) = x \wedge (c, x) \in \iota^+ \right\}$$

For example, the meta-model E in Fig. 1 can be described as:

$$\mathcal{M}_e = (C_e, D_e, A_e, \alpha_e, \iota_e, P_e, \pi_e),$$

where

$$C_e = \{Elevator, Floor, Button, ElevatorButton, FloorButton,$$
$$UpButton, DownButton\}$$

$$D_e = \{Button, FloorButton\}$$

$$A_e = \{currentfloor, requests, elevator\_button\}$$

$$\alpha_e(a) = \begin{cases} (Elevator, Floor) & \text{if } a = currentfloor \\ (Button, Floor) & \text{if } a = requests \\ (Elevator, ElevatorButton) & \text{if } a = elevator\_button \end{cases}$$

$$\iota_e = \{(ElevatorButton, Button), (FloorButton, Button),$$
$$(UpButton, FloorButton), (DownButton, FloorButton)\}$$

$$P_e = \{nr, doors\_open, going\_up, pressed\}$$

$$\pi_e(p) = \begin{cases} Floor & \text{if } p = nr \\ Elevator & \text{if } p \in \{doors\_open, going\_up\} \\ Button & \text{if } p = pressed \end{cases}$$

An annotated meta-model is an extension of a meta-model as defined in Formula 1:

$$\mathcal{M}' = (C, D, A, \alpha, \iota, P, \pi, S, \sigma), \tag{2}$$

where

$S \subseteq \{rt, ev\}$ the set of all supported annotations

$\sigma : C \cup A \cup P \rightarrow \mathcal{P}(S) \{rt, ev, tr\}$ the annotation mapping.

All concepts (classes, associations and attributes) can be annotated with:

- *rt*: run-time, annotates a dynamic concept that serves as output (*e.g.*, a state variable);
- *ev*: an event, annotates a dynamic concept that serves as input only (*e.g.*, a marking).

More annotations are possible, but the generation of the sub-languages currently only supports those two. For example, the annotated meta-model of an elevator control DSML, shown in Fig. 3 can be described as:

$$E' = (C_e, D_e, A_e, \alpha_e, \iota_e, P_e, \pi_e, S_e, \sigma_e), \tag{3}$$

where

$$S_e = \{rt, ev\}$$

$$\sigma_e(x) = \begin{cases} \{rt\} & \text{if } x \in \{doors\_open, going\_up, current\_floor\} \\ \{ev, rt\} & \text{if } x = pressed \end{cases}$$

In this meta-model, the language engineer specifies that *Floor*, *Elevator* and *Button*, the associations *requests* and *elevator_button* and the attribute *nr* are static as they are not annotated. A button press is an input event, and *going_up*, *doors_open*, *currentfloor* and *pressed* are dynamic.

3.2 Generation of Sub-languages

The annotated meta-model E' includes enough detail to generate the five sub-languages as shown in Fig. 2. The generated sub-languages are each expressive enough to serve their intent. At the same time they maximally constrain the modeller so that they are maximally domain-specific. The result of this generation process with E' as input (see Fig. 3) is shown in Fig. 4. Templates are used in the generation process, shown with grey classes. These templates consist of generic language constructs, that can be instantiated to create a sub-language. The meta-models of sub-languages are generated by a function that operates on E' so that only relevant elements are used and no more annotations are present so that the result is a regular meta-model.

We formalise the approach so that the definition of the sub-languages is precise and unambiguous. For every language, there is a language mapping function $f : \mathcal{M}' \times \mathcal{M}_t \rightarrow \mathcal{M}$ that returns the sub-language meta-model $\mathcal{M}_x = (C_x, D_x, A_x, \alpha_x, \iota_x, P_x, \pi_x)$ of an annotated meta-model $\mathcal{M}' = (C, D, A, \alpha, \iota, P, \pi, S, \sigma)$ and a template $\mathcal{M}_t = (C_t, D_t, A_t, \alpha_t, \iota_t, P_t, \pi_t)$. This template $\mathcal{M}_t$ is different for every sub-language. By default, a sub-language will simply consist of $\mathcal{M}'$ without annotations, but preserving all elements. We define this default mapping function as the function $weave : \mathcal{M}' \times \mathcal{M} \times \Sigma \rightarrow \mathcal{M}$. The result of $weave$ is defined as follows:

$$\mathcal{M}_x = (C_x, D_x, A_x, \alpha_x, \iota_x, P_x, \pi_x),$$

where the components of $\mathcal{M}_x$ are defined by $weave(\mathcal{M}', \mathcal{M}_t, Element)$ under the condition that $Element \in C_t$: $X_x = X \cup X_t$ for $X \in \{C, D, A, \alpha, P, \pi\}$ and $\iota_x = \iota \cup \iota_t \cup \{(c, Element) \mid c \in C \wedge \nexists s \in C, (c, s) \in \iota\}$.

In case of the elevator DSML, meta-model $\mathcal{M}_x$ is the union of E' and a given template $\mathcal{M}_t$, and a all elements of E' that do not have a superclass (in this case *Floor*, *Button* and *Elevator*), become a subclass of a given *Element* class in the template $\mathcal{M}_t$.

The meta-models of all five sub-languages are defined below, and their intent is explained. We explain the approach using the elevator control DSML of which the abstract syntax is defined by E'.

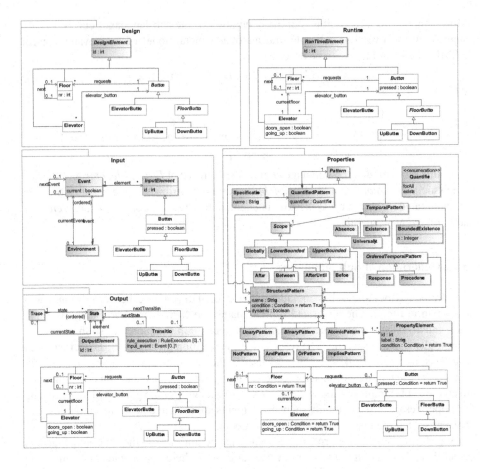

Fig. 4. The meta-models of the five sub-languages of E'

The Design Language E_d. The design language allows modellers to design systems in a general way. The static system (*i.e.,* its structure) is defined, and state or configuration information is not taken into account in this language. Its generated meta-model is shown in the top left of Fig. 4. In the generation process, all constructs (classes, associations and attributes) of E' annotated with *rt* and *ev* are removed. The template consists of a single *DesignElement* class with an *id* that has to be unique. This id will be used to refer to link class instances of the DSML. No dynamic constructs are available in E_d, so the modeller can only model the structure of a system (*e.g.,* how *Floor*s and *Button*s are linked), not its state.

$$\mathcal{M}_d = (C_d, D_d, A_d, \alpha_d, \iota_d, P_d, \pi_d),$$

where the components of $\mathcal{M}_d$ are defined by $design(\mathcal{M}', \mathcal{M}_t)$:

$C_d = \{c \mid c \in C \cup C_t \wedge rt, ev \notin \sigma(c)\}$

$D_d = D \cup D_t \cap C_d$

$A_d = \{a \mid a \in A \cup A_t \wedge rt, ev \notin \sigma(a)\}$

$$\alpha_d = \alpha \cup \alpha_t$$
$$\iota_d = (C_d, p_2(\iota) \cup p_2(\iota_t) \cup \{(c, DesignElement) \mid c \in C \wedge \nexists s \in C, (c, s) \in \iota\})$$
$$P_d = \{p \mid p \in P \cup P_t \wedge rt, ev \notin \sigma(p)\}$$
$$\pi_d = \pi \cup \pi_t$$

where p is the projection operation and $p_i(x)$ denotes the element of x with index i.

The Run-Time Language E_r. The run-time language enables modellers to define a state of the system, *e.g.*, an initial state as input of a simulation. It can also be used to visualise a "snapshot" or state of a system, during run-time. Its generated meta-model is shown in the top right of Fig. 4. In the generation process, all constructs of E' are preserved. The template consists of a single *RunTimeElement* class with an *id*. In E_r, all information, but structure and state (*e.g., currentfloor*), is available. As all constructs of the annotated meta-model are preserved, the meta-model of a run-time language can be defined as $\mathcal{M}_r = weave(\mathcal{M}', \mathcal{M}_t, RunTimeElement)$ with $\mathcal{M}_t$ the template described above.

The Input Language E_i. The input language lets the modeller model the environment of a system, by *e.g.*, modelling an input scenario. Its generated meta-model is shown in the middle left of Fig. 4. In the generation process, all constructs of E' that are not annotated with *ev* are removed. This means that classes that are not annotated with *ev* are removed if they do not inherit an association or attribute that is annotated with *ev*. The template models an *Environment* as an *Event* list containing *InputElements*. In E_i, a series of inputs can consist of button presses. For now, we assume that at most one button can be pressed in the same event, meaning that an event should not contain two unattached elements. If the language engineer decides that more than one or exactly one button can be pressed at the same time, he can create a variant of this template.

$$\mathcal{M}_i = (C_i, D_i, A_i, \alpha_i, \iota_i, P_i, \pi_i),$$

where the components of $\mathcal{M}_i$ are defined by $input(\mathcal{M}', \mathcal{M}_t)$:

$$C_i = \{c \mid c \in C \wedge ((ev \in \sigma(c))$$
$$\vee (\exists p \in P, ev \in \sigma(p) \wedge c \in \pi^*(p))$$
$$\vee (\exists a \in in^*(c) \cup out^*(c), ev \in \sigma(a)))\} \cup C_t$$
$$D_i = D \cup D_t \cap C_i$$
$$A_i = \{a \mid a \in A \wedge ev \in \sigma(a)\} \cup A_t$$
$$\alpha_i = \alpha \cup \alpha_t$$
$$\iota_i = \iota \cup \iota_t \cup \{(c, InputElement) \mid c \in C \wedge \nexists s \in C, (c, s) \in \iota\}$$
$$P_i = \{p \mid p \in P \wedge ev \in \sigma(p)\} \cup P_t$$
$$\pi_i = \pi \cup \pi_t$$

The Output Language E_o. The output language can be used to represent execution traces of a simulation. An output model is usually generated by a simulator or as a counter-example by a verification tool, but can be generated manually as well for *e.g.*, modelling an oracle for a test case. Its generated meta-model is shown in the bottom left of Fig. 4. In the generation process, all constructs of E' are preserved. The template consists of a *Trace* of *States* and *Transitions*. This language is able to express a sequence of system states and the intermediate operations that caused the state change (a rule application in the operational semantics $E_{[[.]]}$, and/or an input event). The output of $E_{[[.]]}$, or the counter-example in verification are instances of E_o. Due to the possibly large number of elements in such an execution trace, an instance of E_o is stored more implicitly as text, and can be interpreted or "played out" by showing step-by-step an instance of the run-time language E_r. The meta-model of a output language can be defined as $\mathcal{M}_o = weave(\mathcal{M}', \mathcal{M}_t, OutputElement)$ with $\mathcal{M}_t$ the template described above.

The Properties Language E_p. The properties language allows the user to define temporal properties, which are properties on the behaviour of systems. Its generated meta-model is shown in the bottom right of Fig. 4, is constructed from four components.

[A] The quantification of the formula by (i) *forAll* or *exists* clause(s), and (ii) corresponding structural pattern(s). The modeller can choose to model a property for all elements that match the associated structural pattern. This structural pattern is evaluated on the design model, and can thus not refer to run-time concepts. Consequently, the property must be satisfied for all, or for one (depending on the quantifier) match(es) of the structural pattern. The resulting matches can be re-used as bound variables in the property, if they have the same label. Quantification patterns can be nested, or can contain a temporal or structural pattern.

[B] The temporal pattern, based on Dwyer's specification patterns [7]. The temporal pattern allows the user to specify a pattern over a given scope, *e.g.,* "the absence of P, after the occurrence of Q", or "P is responded by S, between occurrences of Q and R" (with proposition variables P, S, Q and R). Over 90% of the properties that were investigated by Dwyer et al. can be expressed in this simple framework [7]. Six patterns are supported, to express the absence, existence, bounded existence, universality response or precedence for given proposition(s). Additionally a scope can be defined: must the pattern be valid globally, or after, before, in between or after until the occurrence of given proposition(s). In total up to four proposition variables can be used in a temporal pattern, and we implement them as structural patterns, that represent patterns on the state of the system at run-time.

[C] The structural pattern, based on PaMoMo [11], for both static (when used in a quantification pattern) as well as dynamic (when used in a temporal pattern) models. Using a structural pattern, a query can be defined on a model. If the pattern is static, it returns all bound variables in found matches, and if it is dynamic it returns *true* if at least one match is found or *false* when no match is found. In our current approach, we use simple patterns (*e.g.,* the elevator is at a given floor) and an ad-hoc matching

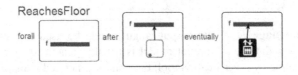

Fig. 5. The *reachesFloor* property as an instance of E_p

algorithm, but we intend to re-use the matching algorithm presented in [9]. Only a small part of PaMoMo's expressiveness is included in the property language, but this suffices for defining most properties. A *StructuralPattern*, and a *PropertiesElement* can hold a condition, which returns *true* by default and is in our current approach modelled as a string.

[D] The pattern elements, based on the RAM process [8,9]. The elements of a structural pattern are based on E' but need to be changed in several ways in order to allow the modeller to specify patterns that are match in model fragments. A similar problem exists when constructing a pattern language for creating a meta-model for transformation rules, and is formalized by the RAM process. In this process, all classes are subclasses of *ModelElement* and have a label (for binding variables) and a condition, attribute types are now conditions, no more classes are abstract classes, and all lower bounds of association multiplicities are set to 0. Pattern elements are compiled to their corresponding Promela variable names, which can be used in the Promela boolean expression of the structural pattern.

The properties pattern is composed of parts A, B and C, which are generic. Only component D, depends on E' that is subjected to the RAM process for left-hand side patterns [9]. Let us define the function $RAM : \mathcal{M}' - \mathcal{M}' \rightarrow$ that performs the RAM process for left-hand side patterns on an annotated meta-model $\mathcal{M}'$, resulting in a RAM-ified meta-model $\mathcal{M}_{RAM}$:

$$RAM(\mathcal{M}') = (C_{RAM}, \varnothing, A_{RAM}, \alpha_{RAM}, \iota_{RAM}, P_{RAM}, \pi_{RAM}, S, \sigma),$$

then the meta-model of a properties language can be defined as:

$$\mathcal{M}_p = weave(RAM(\mathcal{M}'), \mathcal{M}_t, PropertiesElement),$$

with $\mathcal{M}_t$ the template described above.

Generation of Concrete Syntax of the Sublanguages. The concrete syntax of each of the sub-languages is defined by the union of the concrete syntax of E' of which an example is shown in the top right of Fig. 1 (possibly leaving out removed concepts in case of the design and input language) and the predefined concrete syntax for the template $\mathcal{M}_t$.

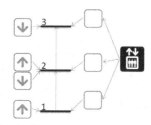

Fig. 6. The system from Fig. 1 modelled in the design language, without run-time information

An instance of the design language looks like the traditional instance of the DSML but without run-time concepts. In the case of E_d, it is impossible to model whether buttons are pressed, on which floor the elevator is, whether its doors are open and in what direction it is going. The system-under-study of Fig. 1, now modelled in E_d, is shown in Fig. 6. An example instance of the run-time language E_r looks the same as the traditional instance of the DSML, shown at the top right in Fig. 1.

An instance of the input language is not used in the context of verification by model checking. Its concrete syntax is a sequence of connected events represented as green circles containing the events visualised using the concrete syntax as shown in the top right of Fig. 1. Each step of an instance of the output language can be visualised as a run-time instance. Alternatively, it can be visualised completely at once as red circles containing the states, connected by arrows with the transition event(s) as label. An instance of the property language E_p is shown in Fig. 5. It uses a combination of text and domain-specific patterns.

3.3 Generation of Mappings for Model Checking With the SPIN Environment

Verification is automated in five steps, as depicted in Fig. 2.

Step 1: Transformation to LTL and Promela. As shown in Fig. 2, a generic transformation generates the LTL formula and the Promela model by means of a model-to-text transformation. The operation results in a *.pml* file, in the example called *Elevator.pml*, that serves as input for the SPIN verification tool. The *.pml* file is generated from a number of models, and its overall structure is shown in Listing 1.1, where code snippets are referenced between < and >. The role of each model in the compilation process is discussed below.

The design meta-model (line 3 in Listing 1.1): The design meta-model, in our case E_d is translated to a number of Promela `typedefs`. Only the three classes on top of the inheritance hierarchy become Promela types. Their instances are stored as static arrays, and instances are accessed by indexing that array. Since Promela is not an object-oriented language, inheritance and associations has to be encoded in a particular way as shown in Listing 1.2). For the types on line 1-21, inheritance is implemented by the `__subtype` attribute, that refer to any class in the design meta-model. Associations are implemented with bidirectional accessibility by `shorts`, that refer to the index of the target, rather than an object. For instance, if the `currentfloor_out` of an `Elevator` is 1, its target is the `Floor` with index 1. If a target is the *null* object, its index is set to -1. The Promela `typedefs` are also influenced by the model of the initial configuration of system-under-study (modelled as a run-time instance), which is modelled as a `__System` type on line 22-26, with static arrays of 7 Buttons, 1 Elevator and 3 Floors. These numbers are extracted from the run-time instance and are predetermined, as the number of buttons, elevators and floors are static. Suppose they are not static, then a maximum number must be set because SPIN requires the state to be bounded. On line 27 the system is created, and values should be filled in (see below).

The output meta-model (line 4 in Listing 1.1): A function called `print_state` (not shown) is defined that prints the current state of the system in a predefined encoding. Only run-time concepts are printed. This, in combination with printing the input events and the applied rule (done in the rule schedule code, which is not shown), provides all the necessary information to construct an output trace.

A run-time instance (line 5-6 in Listing 1.1): After all type, variable and function declarations, the process declaration starts on line 5. Only one process is used. It starts with the initial configuration of the system (line 6, not shown in detail), by setting all values of s (declared in Listing 1.2 on line 27). This results in the initial state of s.

The operational semantics (line 7-14 in Listing 1.1): At line 7, the initial rule, in our case *opendoor_up*, is scheduled using a *go to* statement that jumps to one of the rules at line 10-13 (one of which is shown in Listing 1.5). This rule schedule is generated from the operational semantics model of Fig. 1. Upon evaluation of the rule, a boolean variable will be set that denotes whether the rule was successfully applied or failed to match. If the rule was applied, execution is continued at the environment section (line 15) and the next rule is scheduled by setting a variable according to the operational semantics model. If the rule fails, the rule schedule decides to try the next rule according to the operational semantics model. If all rules fail, code continues execution at the SKIP_RULE label on line 14, printing the state and subsequently continuing to the environment section. Fig. 7 shows the *movedown_last* rule of the schedule at the bottom of Fig. 1. Its Promela code resides in the overall structure of Listing 1.1 at one of the rules that are referenced at line 10-13, and is fully shown in Listing 1.5. For performance, the generated code uses a d_step to calculate the rule matching as an atomic step. The code generator traverses the left-hand side pattern of Fig. 7 element by element by following associations in the pattern. In Promela, the match candidates are represented by indices of s (line 4). The code consists of nested for loops, where match candidates are traversed checked that (1) they are not *null* (*i.e.,* the match candidate is not -1), (2) if applicable, they are not the same as a previously matched item, (3) if applicable, their dynamic type, represented by the _subtype attribute, is correct, and (4) if applicable, node conditions that are specified are satisfied (in case of the *movedown_last* rule the elevator should have its doors open and should go down - line 12-13, not visual in Fig. 7). When a match for the pattern is found, the right-hand side (RHS) of the rule is applied (line 26-29), which is generated from the difference between the RHS and the left-hand side of the rule. The rule is flagged successful, the state of the LTL propositions is updated (see below), and the rule is exited on line 30-32. Finally at line 43, the execution jumps back to the rule schedule, which will decide the next step.

The input meta-model (line 15-17 in Listing 1.1): At line 15, a model of the environment like Listing 1.3. It consists of an atomic block containing an if-statement. The if-statement in Promela non-deterministically chooses an option for which the guard (in this case "1") is true. This environment model thus selects a possible event that will be input for the system (lines 3-9), or none (line 10). For each event, a print statement is generated. The numbers on the left side of the dot are the node id attributes of the node as presented in Fig. 4, and can be used to denote a specific node. In this case, the *Elevator* instance has an id value of 0, the *Floor*s have id values of 1 to 3 and the *Button*s have id values between 4 and 10. Finally a jump to the LOOP label is generated (line 16 in Listing 1.1), so that the rule schedule can decide the next step.

A property instance (line 1-2 in Listing 1.1): The property instance, in our case *reachesFloor*, is translated to the LTL formula at line 1-3 of Listing 1.4. The LTL formula is composed by concatenating three times an Eventually pattern $\Box(!Q \lor \Diamond(Q \land \Diamond P))$ [7], as the property must hold for all (in this case three) floors. In Promela, it is only allowed to specify LTL formulas without boolean expressions. Therefore, proposition variables are used in the LTL formula, and they are updated boolean expressions using when the update_state function is called (line 4-13). $Q0$, $Q1$ and $Q2$ represent the possible button presses at floors 0, 1 and 2, as defined by the middle pattern in Fig. 5. Note how the bound floor f is used in the boolean expressions to select the correct s.button_ indices that match f. On line 9-11 $P0$, $P1$ and $P2$ represent the right pattern in Fig. 5, where it is checked whether the elevator is at floor f and its doors are open. The function update_state will need to be called every time the state of the system changes.

```
1  <LTL FORMULA>
2  <UPDATE STATE FUNCTION DEFINITION>
3  <METAMODEL>
4  <PRINT STATE FUNCTION DEFINITION>
5  active proctype instance() {
6     <INSTANCE>
7     <SET INITIAL RULE>
8  LOOP:
9     <RULE SCHEDULE>
10    <RULE 1>
11    <RULE 2>
12    ...
13    <RULE N>
14 SKIP_RULE: print_state();
15    <ENVIRONMENT>
16    goto LOOP;
17 }
```

Listing 1.1. The overall structure of the generated Promela model

```
1  typedef Button {
2     short __subtype;
3     bit pressed;
4     short requests_out;
5     short elevator_button_in;
6  }
7  typedef Elevator {
8     short __subtype;
9     bit doors_open;
10    bit going_up;
11    short currentfloor_out;
12    short elevator_button_out[3];
13 }
14 typedef Floor {
15    short __subtype;
16    short nr;
17    short next_out;
18    short next_in;
19    short currentfloor_in;
20    short requests_in[3];
21 }
22 typedef __System {
23    Button button_[7];
24    Elevator elevator_[1];
25    Floor floor_[3];
26 }
27 __System s;
```

Listing 1.2. The compiled bounded meta-model

```
1  atomic {
2  if
3  :: 1 -> s.button_[0].pressed=1; printf("4.
           pressed=1\n");
4  :: 1 -> s.button_[1].pressed=1; printf("5.
           pressed=1\n");
5  :: 1 -> s.button_[2].pressed=1; printf("6.
           pressed=1\n");
6  :: 1 -> s.button_[3].pressed=1; printf("7.
           pressed=1\n");
7  :: 1 -> s.button_[4].pressed=1; printf("8.
           pressed=1\n");
8  :: 1 -> s.button_[5].pressed=1; printf("9.
           pressed=1\n");
9  :: 1 -> s.button_[6].pressed=1; printf("10.
           pressed=1\n");
10 :: 1 -> skip;
11 fi;
12 }
```

Listing 1.3. The compiled environment model

```
1  ltl reachesFloor {
2     []((!Q0 || <>(Q0 && <>P0)) && []((!Q1 || <>(Q1 && <>P1)) && []((!Q2 || <>(Q2
       && <>P2))
3  }
4  inline updatestate() { // called after the evaluation of a RHS
5     d_step {
6        Q0 = (s.button_[0].pressed == 1 || s.button_[3].pressed == 1);
7        Q1 = (s.button_[1].pressed == 1 || s.button_[4].pressed == 1 || s.button_
           [5].pressed == 1);
8        Q2 = (s.button_[2].pressed == 1 || s.button_[6].pressed == 1);
9        P0 = (s.elevator_[0].currentfloor_out == 0 && s.elevator_[0].doors_open ==
           1);
10       P1 = (s.elevator_[0].currentfloor_out == 1 && s.elevator_[0].doors_open ==
           1);
11       P2 = (s.elevator_[0].currentfloor_out == 2 && s.elevator_[0].doors_open ==
           1);
12    }
13 }
```

Listing 1.4. The compiled LTL formula

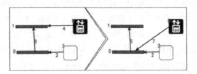

Fig. 7. The *movedown_last* rule

```
1  MOVEDOWN_LAST:
2  MOVEDOWN_LAST_success = 0;
3  d_step {
4     short elevator5, floor1, floor0, button3, button3_candidate;
5     floor1 = 0;
6     do          // look for floor1 match
7     :: (MOVEDOWN_LAST_success == 0 && floor1 < 3) ->
8        if       // check floor1 conditions
9        :: (floor1 >= 0) ->
10          elevator5 = s.floor_[floor1].currentfloor_in;
11          if     // check elevator5 conditions
12          :: (elevator5 >= 0 && s.elevator_[elevator5].doors_open == 0
13             && s.elevator_[elevator5].going_up == 0) ->
14             floor0 = s.floor_[floor1].next_in;
15             if     // check floor0 conditions
16             :: (floor0 >= 0 && floor0 != floor1) ->
17                button3_candidate = 0;
18                do          // look for button3 match
19                :: (MOVEDOWN_LAST_success == 0 && button3_candidate < 3) ->
20                   button3 = s.floor_[floor0].requests_in[button3_candidate];
21                   if     // check button3 conditions
22                   :: (button3 >= 0 && s.button_[button3].pressed == 1) ->
23                      if     // global condition
24                      :: (s.floor_[floor0].nr < s.floor_[floor1].nr) ->
25                         // apply right-hand side
26                         s.elevator_[elevator5].currentfloor_out = -1;
27                         s.floor_[floor1].currentfloor_in = -1;
28                         s.elevator_[elevator5].currentfloor_out = floor0;
29                         s.floor_[floor0].currentfloor_in = elevator5;
30                         MOVEDOWN_LAST_success = 1; // for multi-loop break
31                         update_state();
32                         break;
33                      :: else -> skip; fi;
34                   :: else -> skip; fi;
35                   button3_candidate++;
36                :: else -> break; od;
37             :: else -> skip; fi;
38          :: else -> skip; fi;
39       :: else -> skip; fi;
40       floor1++;
41    :: else -> break; od;
42 }
43 goto MOVEDOWN_LAST_schedule;
```

Listing 1.5. The compiled *movedown_last* rule

Step 2: Verification with SPIN. Step 2 of the verification process shown in Fig. 2 is the automatic verification by SPIN on the Promela model (using the -a option). The LTL formula is checked on all possible execution traces. In this process, printing is suppressed. If the Promela model satisfies the LTL property, the verification is completed, and steps 3-5 are not followed. If the SPIN encounters a counter-example during verification, the verification process is terminated and a *.trail* file is generated, as shown in Fig. 2.

Step 3: Trace generation by SPIN. In case of a counter-example, SPIN is used to perform a guided simulation using the trail on the Promela model (-t option). In this step, the print statements in the Promela model are executed, so that all relevant information about the counter-example is written to *Trace.txt*. In our example, one line in *Trace.txt* may look like: "`0.going_up=1; 0.doors_open=1; 0.currentfloor_out= 2; 4.pressed=0; 5.pressed=0; 6.pressed=1; 7.pressed=1; 8.p ressed=0; 9.pressed=0; 10.pressed=0;`". Other lines can show the transformation rule that is applied (*e.g.,* "`movedown_last`"), or the input that was generated by the environment model, as discussed before (*e.g.,* "`6.pressed=1`"). On the left side of each dot, the ids for model elements as presented in Fig. 4 are used to refer to the node in question. Depending on the type of the attribute/association, the value behind the equal sign is interpreted as boolean, integer or id. In case of class that can be created or deleted at run-time, all instances are printed out using newly assigned ids. For conciseness, associations are printed in one direction only.

Step 4: Transformation of the counter-example to the domain-specific level. As shown in Fig. 2, the *Trace.txt* is transformed to an output model, making use of the design model to map corresponding ids. This results in an output model, that sequentially shows all the system states of the counter-example.

Step 5: Animation of the counter-example. The output model can be "played" out step-by-step by visualising each state. As described in [6], one state is visualised as a run-time model, which may look like the instance model on the top right of Fig. 1.

To conclude, as shown in Fig. 2 *ProMoBox* enables the modelling and verification of properties while the user only has to provide the bare minimum of models: an annotated meta-model, the concrete syntax (implicit in Fig. 2), the operational semantics, the system he wants to verify, a configuration of the system, and the property.

4   Example and Evaluation

We implemented the *ProMoBox* framework in AToMPM [13], and the compiler that compiles models to and from Promela or text were written in Python.

   We verified three properties on the modelled system with the configuration at the top right of Fig. 1:

- *reachesFloor*: when a button that requests the elevator to go to a certain floor is pressed, the elevator will eventually open its doors at that floor;
- *skipFloorOnce*: when a button that requests the elevator to go to a certain floor is pressed, the elevator will open its doors at that floor at the latest the second time it passes that floor;

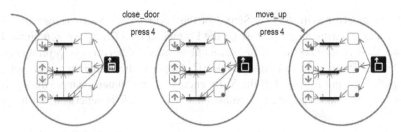

Fig. 8. The counter-example of the *staysAtSecondFloor* property

- *staysAtSecondFloor*: when the elevator is at a certain floor, it stays at that floor. The system will not satisfy this property, and this it should yield a counter-example.

The properties are checked with SPIN [12] version 6.2.6 on a 64-bit Windows 7 SP1 PC with an Intel(R) Core(TM) i7 Q 720 CPU at 1.60 GHz 8 GB of DDR3 memory. The results are shown in Table 1. The properties *reachesFloor* and *skipFloorOnce* take more than a minute to evaluate, and use up to almost 2GB of memory as the depth of the search tree is more than 5×10^4. We can conclude that the performance of the approach in terms of time and memory consumption is acceptable but poor, as this can be considered to be a small example. Alternatively it is possible to evaluate up to a given search tree depth (using the -m option in SPIN) to obtain a fair confidence in the correctness of the modelled system.

As expected, the *staysAtSecondFloor* property yields a counter example. In that case, the verification only takes a very limited amount of time and memory. This turns out to by exemplary due to the relative simplicity of the LTL formula in comparison with the Promela system: if there is a counter-example, it is relatively quickly found. This raises the confidence of using a maximum depth for the SPIN verification.

Table 1. Verification results of the system with initial state as shown at the top right of Fig. 1

property	counter-example	depth	# states	memory	time taken
reachesFloor	no	54422	8×10^6	1934 MB	104s
skipFloorOnce	no	54518	8×10^6	1934 MB	172s
staysAtSecondFloor	yes	255	127	0.226 MB	0.037s

5   Assumptions and Limitations

We now discuss the assumptions and current limitations of the *ProMoBox* approach.

Format of the DSL. It is assumed that we can express the abstract syntax of the DSML as a meta-model, its concrete syntax is defined graphically by icons for every abstract syntax concept and its semantics are given by a transformation model with a rule schedule supporting control flow.

Boundedness. The rule-based nature of the operational semantics ensure a step-wise, state-based semantics. In its current state, *ProMoBox* supports DSMLs that have a notion of state. Since we apply model checking, the possible number of states must be bounded. In the example, this is assured by the limited cardinality of the run-time elements (especially the *currentfloor* association). If such boundedness is not achieved in the meta-model because of an infinite cardinality value, this value must be bounded in order to allow model checking. Such abstraction operations (including decreasing state spaces that are bounded but too large) are nonetheless key to modelling in SPIN, and are beyond the scope of this paper.

Format of the Properties. The only type of properties that is currently supported is based on LTL. However, properties language also supports quantification and structural patterns, so the approach can be considered representative for a wide range of properties. Although we cannot provide any proof, we feel that the *ProMoBox* approach described in this paper can be reused for different kinds of properties by defining generic mappers to tools supporting model checking with OCL and CTL, real time properties, or properties using distributions. The target tool has to be expressive enough so that a correct structure and operational semantics can be defined, *i.e.,* all elements can be queried, variables can be stored and throughout the evaluation of the temporal formula (context-dependency), etc. The key of the approach is that it is defined on the meta-level formalisms (class diagrams, concrete syntax definitions, and rule-based transformation with scheduling), in combination with pre-defined, generic templates.

Scalability. Scalability remains the main concern however. On the one hand, model checking as a technique is a cause of scalability limitations, on the other hand generates the Promela code generator generic code, which could be optimised. A radically different solution to the problem of scalability would be not to map to a model checking approach, but instead use test case generation techniques to generate relevant test cases in the form of input models and output models (oracles). Tests are executed by using the input models as initial state, applying the operational semantics transformation, and comparing (by using model comparison, *e.g.,* the DSMDiff algorithm [14]) the resulting trace with the oracle. This illustrates how *ProMoBox* benefits from its modelling approach, because mappings to different semantic domains can be implemented. However, this research direction is not investigated for the *ProMoBox* approach.

6   Related Work

With respect to the contribution of this paper, we distinguish two threads of related work. First, we consider approaches that translate models to formal representations to specify and verify properties that are created specifically for one modelling language. Second, we discuss approaches that have a more general view on providing specification and verification support for different modelling languages.

Specific Solutions. In the last decade, a plethora of language-specific approaches have been presented to define properties and verification results for different kinds of design-oriented languages. For instance, Cimatti et al. [15] have proposed to verify component-based systems by using scenarios specified as Message Sequence Charts (MSCs). Li et al. [16] also apply MSCs for specifying scenarios for verifying concurrent systems. The CHARMY approach [17] offers amongst other features, verification support for architectural models described in UML. Collaboration and sequence diagrams have been applied to check the behaviour of systems described in terms of state machines [18–20].

Rivera et al. [21] map the operational semantics of DSMLs to Maude, and thus, benefit from analysing methods provided out-of-the-box of Maude environments such as checking of temporal properties specified in LTL. These mentioned approaches are just a few examples that aim at specifying temporal properties for models and verifying them by model checkers (see [22] for a survey). They have in common that they offer language-specific property languages or LTL properties have to be defined directly on the formal representation. Thus, these approaches are not aiming to support DSMLs engineers in the task of building domain-specific property languages.

Generic Solutions. There are some approaches that aim to shift the specification and verification tasks to the model level in a more generalized manner. First of all, there are approaches that propose OCL extensions, often referred to Temporal OCL (TOCL), for defining temporal properties on models [23–25]. As OCL may be combined with any modelling language, TOCL can be seen as a generic model-based property language as well. In [26, 27] the authors discuss and apply a pattern to extend modelling languages with events, traces, and further runtime concepts to represent the state of a model's execution and to use TOCL for defining properties that are verified by mapping the design models as well as the properties expressed in TOCL to formal domains that provide verification support. In addition, not only the input for model checkers is automatically produced, but also the output, *i.e.,* the verification results, is translated back to the model level. The authors explain the choice of using TOCL to be able to express properties at the domain level, because TOCL is close to OCL and should be therefore familiar to domain engineers. However, they also state that early feedback of applying their approach has shown that TOCL is still not well suited to many domain engineers and they state in future work that more tailored languages may be of help for the domain engineers. The work presented in this paper goes directly in this direction by enabling domain engineers to use their familiar notation for defining properties and exploring the verification results.

Another approach that aims to define properties on the model level in a generic way is presented in [28]. The authors extend a language for defining structural patterns based on Story Diagrams [29] to allow for modelling temporal patterns as well. The resulting language allows to define conditionally timed scenarios stating the partial order of structural patterns. The authors argue that their language is more accessible for domain engineers, because their language allow decomposition of complex temporal properties into smaller ones by if-then-else decomposition and quantification over free variables. Their approach is tailored to engineers that are familiar to work with UML class diagrams and UML object diagrams as their notation is heavily based on the concepts of these two languages. Furthermore, they explain how the specification patterns of Dwyer et al. [7] are encoded in their language, but there is no language-inherent support to explicitly apply them. In our work, we tackle these two issues in the context of DSM by reusing the notation of domain engineers for specifying properties and providing explicit language support for specification patterns.

Finally, [30] present specification patterns for describing properties over reachable states of graph grammars. These specification patterns are purely defined on graph structures (*i.e.,* nodes and edges) and thus are reusable for any modelling language. However, the authors do not discuss integration with current modelling languages to use such specification patterns for specific properties. A possible line of future work may aim to integrate such specification patterns to our generic meta-model.

7   Conclusion and Future Work

We presented the *ProMoBox* approach, in which a minimum number of models is required as input to specify and check properties with SPIN and visualise possible counter-examples, while the user is shielded from the underlying formal methods. This is made possible by using annotations on the DSML meta-model to generate five sub-languages, and by compiling models to Promela and back. The key of the approach is that all information of the DSML is explicitly modelled. We presented the approach on a state-based DSML for elevator control. The process of evaluating properties using *ProMoBox* is described in detail, including a formal description of the generation of the sub-languages, and a compiler to Promela. Our results show that *ProMoBox* is applicable for current DSMLs and the resulting specification languages are usable by domain engineers.

For future work, we intend to use *ProMoBox* in a case study for gestural interaction [31]. In this case study, we plan to do more research on the performance of model checking using *ProMoBox*. Moreover, we plan to investigate how different property languages can be supported using different templates, and how these templates can be re-used, *e.g.,* an existing template for structural properties could be re-used in the properties template that is presented in this paper. We are also interested in broadening the types of languages that are supported by ProMoBox, *e.g.,* languages that explicitly include time. We expect that this would typically result in investigating associated templates for real-time properties.

References

1. Gray, J., Tolvanen, J.P., Kelly, S., Gokhale, A., Neema, S., Sprinkle, J.: Domain-specific modeling. In: Handbook of Dynamic System Modeling (2007)
2. France, R., Rumpe, B.: Model-driven development of complex software: A research roadmap. In: ICSE (2007)
3. Risoldi, M.: A Methodology For The Development Of Complex Domain Specific Languages. PhD thesis, University of Geneva (2010)
4. Visser, W., Dwyer, M., Whalen, M.: The hidden models of model checking. SoSym 11, 541–555 (2012)
5. Meyers, B., Deshayes, R., Lucio, L., Syriani, E., Wimmer, M., Vangheluwe, H.: The ProMoBox approach to language modelling. Technical Report SOCS-TR-2014.3, School of Computer Science, McGill University (2014)
6. Meyers, B., Wimmer, M., Vangheluwe, H.: Towards domain-specific property languages: The ProMoBox approach. In: DSM (2013)
7. Dwyer, M.B., Avrunin, G.S., Corbett, J.C.: Patterns in Property Specifications for Finite-State Verification. In: ICSE (1999)
8. Kühne, T., Mezei, G., Syriani, E., Vangheluwe, H., Wimmer, M.: Explicit transformation modeling. In: Ghosh, S. (ed.) MODELS 2009. LNCS, vol. 6002, pp. 240–255. Springer, Heidelberg (2010)
9. Syriani, E.: A Multi-Paradigm Foundation for Model Transformation Language Engineering. PhD thesis, McGill University Montreal, Canada (2011)

10. Guerra, E., de Lara, J., Kolovos, D.S., Paige, R.F.: A Visual Specification Language for Model-to-Model Transformations. In: VL/HCC (2010)
11. Guerra, E., de Lara, J., Wimmer, M., et al.: Automated verification of model transformations based on visual contracts. ASE 20, 5–46 (2013)
12. Holzmann, G.J.: The Model Checker SPIN. TSE 23, 279–295 (1997)
13. Syriani, E., Vangheluwe, H., Mannadiar, R., Hansen, C., Mierlo, S.V., Ergin, H.: AToMPM: A Web-based Modeling Environment. In: MoDELS Demonstrations (2013)
14. Lin, Y., Gray, J., Jouault, F.: DSMDiff: A Differentiation Tool for Domain-Specific Models. European Journal of Information Systems 16 (2007)
15. Cimatti, A., Mover, S., Tonetta, S.: Proving and Explaining the Unfeasibility of Message Sequence Charts for Hybrid Systems. In: FMCAD (2011)
16. Li, X., Hu, J., Bu, L., Zhao, J., Zheng, G.: Consistency Checking of Concurrent Models for Scenario-Based Specifications. In: Prinz, A., Reed, R., Reed, J. (eds.) SDL 2005. LNCS, vol. 3530, pp. 298–312. Springer, Heidelberg (2005)
17. Pelliccione, P., Inverardi, P., Muccini, H.: CHARMY: A Framework for Designing and Verifying Architectural Specifications. TSE 35, 325–346 (2008)
18. Brosch, P., Egly, U., Gabmeyer, S., Kappel, G., Seidl, M., Tompits, H., Widl, M., Wimmer, M.: Towards Scenario-Based Testing of UML Diagrams. In: Brucker, A.D., Julliand, J. (eds.) TAP 2012. LNCS, vol. 7305, pp. 149–155. Springer, Heidelberg (2012)
19. Knapp, A., Wuttke, J.: Model checking of UML 2.0 interactions. In: Kühne, T. (ed.) MoDELS 2006. LNCS, vol. 4364, pp. 42–51. Springer, Heidelberg (2007)
20. Schäfer, T., Knapp, A., Merz, S.: Model Checking UML State Machines and Collaborations. ENTCS 55, 357–369 (2001)
21. Rivera, J.E., Guerra, E., de Lara, J., Vallecillo, A.: Analyzing Rule-Based Behavioral Semantics of Visual Modeling Languages with Maude. In: Gašević, D., Lämmel, R., Van Wyk, E. (eds.) SLE 2008. LNCS, vol. 5452, pp. 54–73. Springer, Heidelberg (2009)
22. Gabmeyer, S., Kaufmann, P., Seidl, M.: A classification of model checking-based verification approaches for software models. In: VOLT (2013)
23. Ziemann, P., Gogolla, M.: OCL Extended with Temporal Logic. In: Broy, M., Zamulin, A.V. (eds.) PSI 2003. LNCS, vol. 2890, pp. 351–357. Springer, Heidelberg (2004)
24. Kanso, B., Taha, S.: Temporal Constraint Support for OCL. In: Czarnecki, K., Hedin, G. (eds.) SLE 2012. LNCS, vol. 7745, pp. 83–103. Springer, Heidelberg (2013)
25. Bill, R., Gabmeyer, S., Kaufmann, P., Seidl, M.: OCL meets CTL: Towards CTL-Extended OCL Model Checking. In: OCL Workshop (2013)
26. Zalila, F., Crégut, X., Pantel, M.: Leveraging Formal Verification Tools for DSML Users: A Process Modeling Case Study. In: Margaria, T., Steffen, B. (eds.) ISoLA 2012, Part II. LNCS, vol. 7610, pp. 329–343. Springer, Heidelberg (2012)
27. Combemale, B., Crégut, X., Pantel, M.: A Design Pattern to Build Executable DSMLs and Associated V&V Tools. In: APSEC (2012)
28. Klein, F., Giese, H.: Joint structural and temporal property specification using timed story scenario diagrams. In: Dwyer, M.B., Lopes, A. (eds.) FASE 2007. LNCS, vol. 4422, pp. 185–199. Springer, Heidelberg (2007)
29. Fischer, T., Niere, J., Torunski, L., Zündorf, A.: Story Diagrams: A New Graph Rewrite Language Based on the Unified Modeling Language and Java. In: Ehrig, H., Engels, G., Kreowski, H.-J., Rozenberg, G. (eds.) TAGT 1998. LNCS, vol. 1764, pp. 296–309. Springer, Heidelberg (2000)
30. da Costa Cavalheiro, S.A., Foss, L., Ribeiro, L.: Specification Patterns for Properties over Reachable States of Graph Grammars. In: Gheyi, R., Naumann, D. (eds.) SBMF 2012. LNCS, vol. 7498, pp. 83–98. Springer, Heidelberg (2012)
31. Deshayes, R., Palanque, P.A., Mens, T.: A generic framework for executable gestural interaction models. In: VL/HCC (2013)

A SAT-Based Debugging Tool for State Machines and Sequence Diagrams[*]

Petra Kaufmann[1], Martin Kronegger[2], Andreas Pfandler[2],
Martina Seidl[1,3], and Magdalena Widl[4]

[1] Business Informatics Group, TU Wien, Austria
[2] Database and Artificial Intelligence Group, TU Wien, Austria
[3] Institute for Formal Models and Verification, JKU Linz, Austria
[4] Knowledge-Based Systems Group, TU Wien, Austria
{firstname.lastname@tuwien.ac.at}

Abstract. An effective way to model message exchange in complex settings is to use UML sequence diagrams in combination with state machine diagrams. A natural question that arises in this context is whether these two views are consistent, i.e., whether a desired or forbidden scenario modeled in the sequence diagram can be or cannot be executed by the state machines. In case of an inconsistency, a concrete communication trace of the state machines can give valuable information for debugging purposes on the model level. This trace either hints to a message in the sequence diagram where the communication between the state machines fails, or describes a concrete forbidden communication trace between the state machines. To detect and explain such inconsistencies, we propose a novel SAT-based formalization which can be solved automatically by an off-the-shelf SAT solver. To this end, we present the formal and technical foundations needed for the SAT-encoding, and an implementation inside the Eclipse Modeling Framework (EMF). We evaluate the effectiveness of our approach using grammar-based fuzzing.

1 Introduction

The abstraction power of multi-view modeling languages like UML comes along with the possibility of inconsistencies in the description of the system under development [18]. On the one hand, different diagram types lower the complexity of describing and understanding large software systems by providing focused views on specific aspects like, for example, interprocess communication [2]. On the other hand, performing modifications on one diagram may require changes in other diagrams. If these changes are not implemented carefully in the other diagrams as well, the model can contain inconsistent information which, in the worst case, might propagate up to the running application. Hence, if the diagrams do not complement one another in a consistent manner, then the benefits of

---

[*] This work was partially funded by the Vienna Science and Technology Fund (WWTF) under grant ICT10-018 and by the Austrian Science Fund (FWF) under grants P25518-N23, S11408-N23, and S11409-N23.

B. Combemale et al. (Eds.): SLE 2014, LNCS 8706, pp. 21–40, 2014.

multi-view modeling are rendered void [23]. Especially when the models are not directly executable or when no simulation environment is available, then testing and debugging is difficult.

Therefore, mechanisms are required which support the *evolution* of a model [10] and ensure consistency. In this paper, we are concerned with the consistency between state machines and sequence diagrams. State machines describe the internal behavior of objects and sequence diagrams focus on interaction scenarios between different instances of the objects. These scenarios model either required or forbidden message exchange. Our approach verifies whether the communication described by a sequence diagram can be executed by a given set of state machines. If a sequence of messages can be executed although it is forbidden by the sequence diagram, then a concrete communication trace is returned. If a sequence of messages is not possible although according to the sequence diagram it should be, then a reason for the failure is given. On this basis, inconsistencies introduced during the evolution of a model cannot only be discovered easily, but also be corrected immediately. Hence, sequence diagrams are test cases describing desired or undesired behavior of the state machines. With our approach the test cases can be evaluated even if no execution environment for the state machines is available.

For solving this consistency checking problem, we propose to use an approach based on the satisfiability problem of propositional logic (SAT) [3]. For SAT powerful solvers are available which are successfully used out of the box in many verification applications. For instance, we have made very positive experiences with using SAT encodings to solve the merging problem in the context of optimistic model versioning [30] as well as for reachability checking of composite state machines [14]. Based on these experiences, we developed the consistency checking encoding presented in this paper. This considerably improves our previous work on consistency checking using the model checker Spin [4,5]. Spin offers the high level input language Promela which seems to be very appealing for formulating the consistency checking problem. However, due to the semantic differences of Promela and UML-like languages the encoding becomes rather complicated. In SAT, however, we do not have any semantical restrictions. With a concise problem formulation together with encoding techniques borrowed from planning applications [21] the SAT encoding turns out intuitive and flexible. Further, the SAT-based approach integrates smoothly into our model evolution framework FAME[1].

This paper is structured as follows. First, we review related approaches in Section 2. Then we motivate this work with a concrete example in Section 3 and informally explain the modeling language concepts relevant for this work. In Section 4 we give a concise formal problem definition. To this end, we formally describe the sequence diagram and the state machine along with their interplay. Further, we introduce the notion of lifeline consistency, which is what we want to check. This problem definition directly allows us to derive a problem encoding to SAT which can be handed to a SAT solver (Section 5). Section 6 discusses

---

[1] http://www.modelevolution.org/

the implementation based on the Eclipse Modeling Framework and Section 7 presents a detailed evaluation of our approach based on grammar-based white-box fuzzing. Finally, we conclude this paper with an outlook on future work.

2   Related Work

The problem tackled in this paper is a typical model checking problem. There-fore, it is not surprising that different works [5,13,15,20,22] propose a formulation in languages like Promela, the input language of the popular model checker Spin. Due to semantical differences of state machines and Promela, it turns out that an equivalence preserving translation capturing all language concepts is chal-lenging. For example, in our previous work [4,5], we employed Spin to ensure that given traces do not occur during the execution of a set of state machines, but with this encoding we could not ensure that a given message sequence is possible.

In the past, many other formal approaches have been presented, but most of the implementations do not seem to have gone beyond a proof of concept state and are either not updated to UML 2 or are not available at all. We summa-rize the approaches most related to our work in the following. For a detailed discussion we refer the interested reader to specific surveys like [18]. Lam and Vitus [16] present an algebraic approach to express the consistency checking problem in the π-calculus. The practical realizability of the approach is not dis-cussed. Van der Straeten et al. [27] propose to use description logics to formally describe the consistency between class diagrams, sequence diagrams, and state machines. Compared to SAT, description logics are more expressive in general, but their satisfiability checking problem is located in higher complexity classes than NP. Bernardi et al. propose to use petri nets for checking the consistency between different diagrams [1]. Communication, however, is only considered at the class level and not at the object level. Engels et al. [8] propose to check consistency by evaluating dedicated consistency constraints represented in form of collaborations. Therefore, an interpreter is provided. Egyed [7] applies instant consistency validation by rules formulated in OCL which shows to be very effi-cient on large models. For capturing the same kind of inconsistency, which we deal with in this paper, however, a temporal extension of OCL is necessary.

A different approach for consistency checking is presented by Graaf and Van Deursen [12] who suggest to synthesize a state machine from the given sequence diagram as in [28] and then compare the automatically generated state ma-chine to the given state machine. Therefore, they realize normalization, trans-formation, and comparison steps, respectively. In [12], however, the comparison requires manual intervention. Feng and Vangheluwe propose to use a simulation-based approach for consistency checking [9].

Besides checking the consistency between state machine diagrams and se-quence diagrams, a lot of effort has been spent for consistency checking between other diagrams like class diagrams, collaboration diagrams, activity diagrams, etc. We refer to [11,26] for detailed surveys.

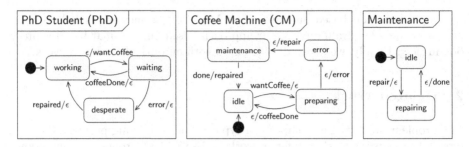

Fig. 1. Three state machines modeling a PhD student, a coffee machine, and a maintenance unit

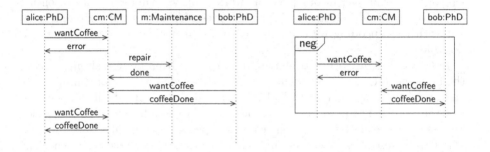

Fig. 2. (Left) A sequence diagram depicting a desired scenario that is inconsistent with the state machines of Fig. 1. The state machines have to be changed in order to allow the scenario. (Right) A sequence diagram depicting a forbidden scenarios that is inconsistent with the state machines of Fig. 1. No changes are required.

3   A Motivating Example

To motivate our work and to illustrate useful application scenarios we present the following example. Fig. 1 shows three state machines that describe the behaviors of a PhD student, a coffee machine, and a maintenance unit for the coffee machine. As typical for the UML state machine view, rectangles with rounded corners present *states* which are connected by *transitions*. Each transition carries a label consisting of a *trigger* on the left side of the "/" and an *effect* on the right side. The special symbol ϵ on the left side of the "/" indicates that no trigger is necessary for the transition to fire. The initial state is indicated by an incoming arc from a black dot.

Instances of state machines communicate with each other by message passing. They change states according to messages that are sent and received. A state change is initiated by the receipt of a symbol indicated as trigger in one of the outgoing transitions of the current state. An outgoing transition carrying the special symbol ϵ as trigger can be initiated without receiving any symbol.

The transition is fully executed only if the effect can be sent successfully, i.e., if it also can be received by another instance of a state machine.

Fig. 2 shows two sequence diagrams that describe communication scenarios between instances of the state machines in Fig. 1. A state machine is instantiated by one or more *lifelines*. Similar as in UML, they are shown as rectangles with a dashed vertical line underneath. Each lifeline's name is shown inside the rectangle before the ":", followed by the name of the state machine it instantiates after the ":". For space reasons, we have abbreviated these names. Along the lifelines, a sequence of messages is shown. A message is depicted as an arrow from the sender lifeline to the receiver lifeline labeled with the symbol being sent. The set of symbols used in the sequence diagrams is the same as the set of symbols used in the state machines.

In order to be *consistent* with the state machines, the message sequence of a sequence diagram must be executable from some global state of the lifelines which is reachable from the global initial state, where a global state is a tuple of states of the state machines instantiated by the lifelines. More precisely, from such a global state it must be possible for each message after another to be a trigger in the sending lifeline's state machine instantiation and to be an effect in the receiving lifeline's state machine instantiation.

We present two possible application scenarios for checking a set of state machine diagrams and a sequence diagram for consistency. (1) A desired scenario is depicted in the sequence diagram. If the sequence diagram is consistent with the state machines, then we know that the state machines fulfill the scenario. Otherwise, we can obtain information about the global state of the state machines where the sequence first fails, which helps to discover erroneous or missing transitions in the state machines view. (2) An unwanted scenario is depicted in the sequence diagram. If a sequence diagram is consistent with the state machines, then we know that there is a bug in the state machines and we can obtain a counter-trace, namely a sequence of global states which follows from the application of the message sequence.

In Fig. 2 an example for each scenario is depicted. The left sequence diagram shows a desired scenario. However, it is inconsistent with the state machines for the following reason: The PhD student "alice" changes into state "desperate" after receiving the symbol "error" from the coffee machine. She must remain there until the symbol "repaired" is received. According to the sequence diagram, the coffee machine never sends this symbol. This also means, that the coffee machine never returns to state "idle" and therefore cannot receive the symbol "wantCoffee" from PhD student "bob". Therefore, the message sequence of the sequence diagram can only be executed up to and including the fourth message, "done". In this case, our tool returns the sequence of messages up to the message that cannot be sent or received, in this case, up to and including "done" from "m:Maintenance" to "cm:CM". A possible fix for this broken scenario would be to remove the state "desperate" from the PhD student and to connect the transition with trigger "error" from the state "waiting" directly to state "working".

Further, in the coffee machine the effect of the transition with trigger "done" from state "maintenance" to state "idle" would have to be replaced by ϵ.

Similarly to the "neg" fragment used in UML sequence diagrams, we mark the negative scenario in the right diagram of Fig. 2 using this notation. Note that we refer to a complete application scenario rather than to a subsequence of a sequence diagram. Hence, the second diagram shows an unwanted scenario. It allows the coffee machine to prepare coffee while being in the error state. This scenario is not implemented in the state machines, so no bug can be found. If it was implemented, the tool would return a sequence of global states of the instances of the state machines representing this message sequence.

4 Problem Definition

Given a sequence diagram and a set of communicating state machines modeling the behavior of the sequence diagram's lifelines, the *Multiview Sequence Consistency Problem* (MSCP) asks whether the communication sequence modeled in the sequence diagram is executable by the state machines. If this is the case, then we call the two views *consistent*. The desired outcome of a positive scenario (no "neg" label) depicted in a sequence diagram is to be consistent with the state machine view, i.e., the desired scenario is indeed implemented in the state machines. The desired outcome of a negative scenario ("neg" label) is to be inconsistent with the state machine view, which means, that the state machines do not implement the undesired trace. In the following, we present a precise definition of the semantics of the state machine view and of the sequence view in order to present the formal definition of MSCP.

The core elements for defining state machines, sequence diagrams, and their interaction are the symbols of the alphabets Σ_A and Σ_L where the special symbol ϵ is in Σ_A. The alphabet Σ_A contains symbols which label messages in the sequence diagrams and which trigger transitions and occur as effects in the state machines. The special symbol ϵ is the "empty symbol" used for transitions triggered by on-completion-events and for empty events on transitions. The alphabet Σ_L contains names for the instances of the state machines, also called lifelines. Based on Σ_A we define state machines as follows.

Definition 1 (State Machine). *Given an alphabet Σ_A, a state machine M is a quadruple (S, ι, A, T), where*

- *S is a finite set of states,*
- *$\iota \in S$ is a designated initial state,*
- *$A \subseteq \Sigma_A$ with $\epsilon \in A$ is the alphabet of M, and*
- *$T \subseteq S \times A \times A \times S$ is a transition relation such that for all $s, s' \in S$ there is no transition $(s, \epsilon, \epsilon, s') \in T$.*

A state machine consists of a set of states, a designated initial state, an alphabet, and a transition relation which connects the states. The rightmost state machine shown in Fig. 1 which is called Maintenance, contains the set

$S = \{\mathsf{idle}, \mathsf{repairing}\}$ of states, the initial state $\iota = \mathsf{idle}$, and the alphabet $A = \{\epsilon, \mathsf{repair}, \mathsf{done}\}$. For a transition $t \in T$ with $t = (s, tr, \mathit{eff}, s')$, s is the source state of the transition, s' is the target state, tr is a symbol (trigger) which upon receipt triggers the execution of transition t, and eff is a symbol (effect) that is sent and has to be received by another state machine when the transition is executed. The state machine Maintenance in Fig. 1 has two transitions: $(\mathsf{idle}, \mathsf{repair}, \epsilon, \mathsf{repairing}), (\mathsf{repairing}, \epsilon, \mathsf{done}, \mathsf{idle}) \in T$.

For a transition to be executed in a state machine M, the trigger symbol of the transition must be received by M from a state machine different to M and the effect symbol must be received by a state machine different to M. Either trigger or effect can be the special symbol ϵ which stands for an empty trigger or effect. A transition containing ϵ as trigger is triggered without receiving any symbol, e.g., by an on-completion-event, and the execution of a transition containing ϵ as effect can be finished without sending any symbol. We assume that no transition of a state machine contains ϵ as both trigger and effect. Such transitions can be eliminated by contracting the connected states. Furthermore notice that the requirement of having a single effect does not impose a strong restriction as multiple effects can be simulated by a state machine that sends a predefined sequence of effects upon receiving a designated trigger symbol.

In order to give a precise semantics to the interaction between state machines, we introduce the notion of an *extended* state machine.

Definition 2 (Extended State Machine). *Given a state machine M, the extended state machine M^* of $M = (S, \iota, A, T)$ is a quadruple $(S \cup S^*, \iota, A, T^*)$ where*

- *$S^* = \{s_t^* \mid t \in T\}$ and*
- *$T^* = \{(s, tr, \epsilon, s_t^*), (s_t^*, \epsilon, \mathit{eff}, s') \mid t = (s, tr, \mathit{eff}, s') \in T\}$*

An extended state machine introduces an *intermediate state* s_t^* for each transition t. This intermediate state has exactly one incoming transition, which is triggered by the trigger of t and contains the effect ϵ, i.e., has no effect. It also has exactly one outgoing transition, which leads to the target state of t with ϵ as trigger and the effect of t. We call S the *original states* and S^* the *intermediate states*.

The extended state machine helps to distinguish between the event of having received the trigger and the event of being able to send the effect. Note that any state machine can be translated to exactly one extended state machine and vice versa. Fig. 3 depicts the extended state machine of the state machine PhD Student. The intermediate states are represented by black diamonds with rounded corners.

Next we formally define sequence diagrams, starting with the concept of lifelines.

Definition 3 (Lifeline). *Given a set $\mathcal{M}$ of extended state machines and the alphabet Σ_L, a lifeline is a pair $L = (l, M^*)$ where $l \in \Sigma_L$ is the name of the lifeline and $M^* \in \mathcal{M}$ is associated with the lifeline.*

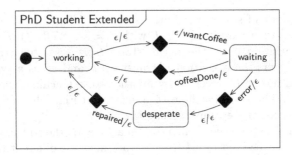

Fig. 3. Extended state machine corresponding to the state machine "PhD student"

A lifeline is an instance of an extended state machine. The name l of a lifeline is used to distinguish different instances of the same state machine and M^* is the extended state machine the lifelines refers to. In the sequel, we refer to M^* of a lifeline L by $\mathsf{sm}(L)$. The communication between lifelines takes place through *messages*, which are defined as follows.

Definition 4 (Message). *Given an alphabet Σ_A and a set $\mathcal{L}$ of lifelines such that each lifeline's extended state machine is defined over Σ_A, a message is a triple (σ, a, ρ) where*

- *$\sigma \in \mathcal{L} \cup \{\varepsilon\}$ is the sending lifeline,*
- *$a \in \Sigma_A$ is the message symbol, and*
- *$\rho \in \mathcal{L} \setminus \{\sigma\}$ is the receiving lifeline*

such that $\sigma = \varepsilon$ if and only if $a = \epsilon$.

For a message (σ, a, ρ), the sender lifeline σ either refers to an extended state machine or is the empty sender ε when the empty symbol ϵ is received. Note that for better readability, we do not show empty messages in the concrete syntax of the sequence diagrams. The receiver lifeline ρ refers to an extended state machine.

Based on the definition of a lifeline and of a message, we can now formally define a sequence diagram.

Definition 5 (Sequence Diagram). *Given the alphabets Σ_A and Σ_L, and a set $\mathcal{M}$ of extended state machines over Σ_A, a sequence diagram is a pair $(\mathcal{L}, \mu)$ where*

- *$\mathcal{L}$ is a set of lifelines over $\mathcal{M}$ and Σ_L*
- *the names of the lifelines are pairwise distinct*
- *$\mu = [m_1, \ldots, m_n]$ is a sequence of messages such that for each $(\sigma, a, \rho) \in \mu$ it holds that $\sigma, \rho \in \mathcal{L}$ and $a \in \Sigma_A$.*

The right-hand sequence diagram of Fig. 2 contains the set $\mathcal{L} = \{(\mathsf{alice}, \mathsf{PhD}), (\mathsf{cm}, \mathsf{CM}), (\mathsf{bob}, \mathsf{PhD})\}$ of lifelines and the sequence $\mu = [((\mathsf{alice}, \mathsf{PhD}), \mathsf{wantCoffee}, (\mathsf{cm}, \mathsf{CM})), \ldots, ((\mathsf{cm}, \mathsf{CM}), \mathsf{coffeeDone}, (\mathsf{bob}, \mathsf{PhD}))]$.

To describe the interaction between lifelines via messages we define a *global state* which captures a configuration of a set of lifelines.

Definition 6 (Global State). *Given a set $\mathcal{L} = \{L_1, \ldots, L_l\}$ of lifelines, let* $\mathsf{sm}(L_i) = (S_i, \iota_i, A_i, T_i)$ *be the extended state machine of lifeline L_i, for $1 \leq i \leq l$. Then a global state $\hat{s}$ is a tuple $(s_1, \ldots, s_l) \in S_1 \times \cdots \times S_l$.*

For three lifelines instantiating the three state machines of Fig. 1, an example for a global state is (desperate, <maintenance/done/repaired/idle>, idle) where the second state refers to the intermediate state on the transition from maintenance to idle in state machine CM.

In each global state, there exists a (possibly empty) set of messages that can be sent and a set of messages that can be received. After sending or receiving a message out of these sets, a different global state is reached. This semantics is described in the following definition.

Definition 7 (Admissibility and Application of a Message). *Given the alphabet Σ_A, a set $\mathcal{L} = \{L_1, \ldots, L_l\}$ of lifelines with $\mathsf{sm}(L_i) = (S_i, \iota_i, A_i, T_i)$, and a global state $\hat{s} = (s_1, \ldots, s_l) \in S_1 \times \cdots \times S_l$, the message $m = (L_s, a, L_r)$ with $L_s \in \mathcal{L} \cup \{\varepsilon\}$, $L_r \in \mathcal{L}$, $L_s \neq L_r$, and $a \in \Sigma_A$ is admissible in $\hat{s}$ if the following holds: If $L_s \neq \varepsilon$, then*

1. $(s_s, \epsilon, a, s_s') \in T_s$, *and*
2. $(s_r, a, \epsilon, s_r') \in T_r$.

Otherwise, i. e., if $m = (\varepsilon, \epsilon, L_r)$, then $(s_r, \epsilon, \epsilon, s_r') \in T_r$.
By applying the admissible message m in the global state $\hat{s}$, a global successor state $\hat{s}' = (s_1, \ldots, s_s', \ldots, s_r' \ldots, s_l) \in S_1 \times \cdots \times S_l$ is reached.

A message is *admissible* in some global state if (1) (for $L_s \neq \varepsilon$) the state of the sender lifeline is an intermediate state whose outgoing transition has the message symbol a as effect and (2) unless $L_s = \varepsilon$, the state of the receiver lifeline is an original state which has as least one outgoing transition with the message symbol a as trigger. If $L_s = \varepsilon$, the receiver can also be in an intermediate state.

In the global state $s =$ (desperate, <maintenance/done/repaired/idle>, idle) of the lifelines (alice, PhD), (cm, CM), (m, Maintenance) the set of applicable messages contains only one message, namely $\{m = ((cm, CM), repaired, (alice, PhD))\}$.

Note that lifelines refer to extended state machines, which means that a transition cannot carry a trigger symbol other than ϵ together with an effect other than ϵ. Therefore, it can never happen that a receiver lifeline sends any effect while executing a transition triggered by a symbol other than ϵ.

The global successor state $\hat{s}'$ is reached by applying a message. Then, $\hat{s}'$ differs from $\hat{s}$ in the states of the sender and the receiver lifeline: The sender's state changes from an intermediate state to its only successor state, and the receiver's state changes accordingly to the received symbol into an intermediate state. Applying the above message m to the global state $\hat{s}$ reaches the global successor state (<desperate/repaired/ϵ/working>, idle, idle).

The set of admissible messages in a global state can contain a subset of messages that are *independent*, i.e., that have no sender or receiver in common. The messages in such a set can be executed simultaneously. We call a set of independent messages a *transaction*. It is defined as follows.

Definition 8 (Transaction). *Let* $\mathcal{L} = \{L_1, \ldots, L_l\}$ *be a set of lifelines. A transaction is a nonempty set* $m = \{m_1, \ldots, m_t\}$ *of messages such that for distinct* $i, j \in \{1, \ldots, t\}$, $m_i = (\sigma_i, a_i, \rho_i)$, *and* $m_j = (\sigma_j, a_j, \rho_j)$ *it holds that all* σ_i, σ_j, ρ_i, *and* ρ_j *are pairwise distinct.*

A transaction is admissible if all its messages are admissible. The global state reached by applying a transaction is the global state reached by applying each of the transaction's messages. Note that a sequence of messages can also be seen as a sequence of transactions that are singletons, i.e., each transaction contains a single message. A sequence of messages, such as depicted in a sequence diagram, can therefore be seen as a sequence of singleton transactions.

We further define a path as a sequence of transactions connecting global states as follows.

Definition 9 (Path). *A path* μ *from a global state* $\hat{s}_0$ *to a global state* $\hat{s}_k$ *is a sequence* $\mu = [m_1, \ldots, m_k]$ *of transactions such that there exists a sequence* $[\hat{s}_0, \ldots, \hat{s}_k]$ *of global states where for all* $1 \leq i \leq k$, m_i *is admissible in state* $\hat{s}_{i-1}$ *and* $\hat{s}_i$ *is the global successor state of* $\hat{s}_{i-1}$ *after applying* m_i.

A global state $\hat{s}_j$ *is reachable from* $\hat{s}_i$ if there is a path from $\hat{s}_i$ to $\hat{s}_j$. The *length* of a path is the number of its transactions.

The *Multiview Sequence Consistency Problem* (MSCP) deals with the question whether from some global state that is reachable from the global initial state, i.e., $\hat{s}_\iota = (\iota_1, \ldots, \iota_l)$ for the initial states of the state machines of l lifelines, there is a path representing the sequence of messages described in the sequence diagram. In order to be able to express this problem as a propositional formula of polynomial size with respect to the input, we have to bound the length of the path leading to the beginning of the sequence. This bound is included in the *k-Multiview Sequence Consistency Problem* (k-MSCP).

Definition 10 (k-Multiview Sequence Consistency). *Given a sequence diagram* $SD = (\mathcal{L}, \mu)$ *with* $\mathcal{L} = \{L_1, \ldots, L_l\}$ *and* $\mathsf{sm}(L_i) = (S_i, \iota_i, A_i, T_i)$ *for* $1 \leq i \leq l$ *over a set* $\mathcal{M}$ *of extended state machines and the alphabets* Σ_A *and* Σ_L, *SD and* $\mathcal{M}$ *are k-consistent if there exists a path of length at most k starting at* $\hat{s} = (\iota_1, \ldots, \iota_l)$ *and leading to a global state* $\hat{s}'$ *such that a global state* $\hat{s}''$ *is reachable from* $\hat{s}'$ *by applying the sequence of messages* μ.

Finally, the *k-Multiview Sequence Consistency Problem* is defined as follows.

---

k-Multiview Sequence Consistency Problem (k-MSCP)

Instance: A sequence diagram $SD = (\mathcal{L}, \mu)$ over a set $\mathcal{M}$ of state machines and the alphabets Σ_A and Σ_L.

Question: Are SD and $\mathcal{M}$ k-consistent?

---

5 Encoding

To solve the k-MSCP problem we propose to encode it to the satisfiability problem of propositional logic (SAT). We assume the reader to be familiar with the basics of propositional logic and SAT-solvers (for details we refer to [3,19]). To this end, we build a propositional formula representing an instance of the k-MSCP problem and hand it to a SAT solver. The solver returns SAT and a logical model if the sequence diagram of the k-MSCP problem instance can be executed after at most k transactions between the lifelines. The logical model can then be translated back into a concrete sequence of transactions between the lifelines as well as to the state transitions triggered by the application of the messages. The solver returns UNSAT if the sequence diagram cannot be executed by the lifelines after at most k message exchanges. In this case, we remove trailing messages one after another from the sequence diagram and call the solver again until the first failing message is found. The encoding presented below is an extension of the encoding discussed in [14, Section 4] where we check the reachability of a global state regardless of a particular message sequence.

We encode an instance of the k-MSCP as the propositional formula φ over a set of variables representing original states, intermediate states, transitions, and alphabet symbols. We assume that all states of all lifelines are pairwise distinct. This natural assumption can be achieved by indexing the states with the name of the respective lifeline. Observe that this also ensures that all transitions of all lifelines are pairwise distinct. Let $\mathcal{M}$ be a set of extended state machines over the alphabet Σ_A, let $SD = (\mathcal{L}, \mu)$ be a sequence diagram over $\mathcal{M}$ with $\mathcal{L} = \{L_1, \ldots, L_l\}$ and $\mu = [m_1, \ldots, m_n]$, let $\mathcal{T} := \bigcup_{1 \le i \le l} T_i$ be the set of all transitions in all extended state machines, let $\mathcal{S} := \bigcup_{1 \le i \le l} S_i$ be the set of all original states of all lifelines (all instances of extended state machines), let $\mathcal{S}^* := \bigcup_{1 \le i \le l} S_i^*$ be the set of all intermediate states of all lifelines, and let $\mathcal{A} := \Sigma_A \setminus \{\epsilon\}$. Recall that k is an integer defining the maximum length of the path leading to a global state from which the message sequence in SD is executed. Further, let $k' := k + 4n$ be the maximum number of timesteps needed to apply n messages after a path of a maximum length of k. The factor 4 is necessary because moving forward on a transition with the empty symbol ϵ as trigger or effect requires additional timesteps. Then the set of variables occurring in the encoding is given by $\{v^i \mid v \in (\mathcal{T} \cup \mathcal{A} \cup \mathcal{S} \cup \mathcal{S}^*), 0 \le i \le k'\}$. That is, each transition, symbol, original state, and intermediate state together with an index up to k' is represented by a variable. We refer to this index as *timestep*.

We further use the following functions to simplify the presentation of the formula. Let $L = (S, \iota, A, T)$ be a lifeline, (s, tr, ϵ, s_t^*) and $(s_t^*, \epsilon, eff, s')$ be transitions of the extended state machine $\mathsf{sm}(L)$. Recall that the states of $\mathsf{sm}(L)$ are made distinct by indexing as described above. The two transitions correspond to a transition $t = (s, tr, eff, s')$ of a non-extended state machine. Additionally, let $m = (\sigma, a, \rho)$ be a message. Then $\mathsf{trans}(L) = T$, $\mathsf{src}(t) := s$, $\mathsf{int}(t) := s_t^*$, $\mathsf{trg}(t) := tr$, $\mathsf{eff}(t) := eff$, $\mathsf{tgt}(t) := s'$, $\mathsf{snd}(m) := \sigma$, $\mathsf{rec}(m) := \rho$, and $\mathsf{symb}(m) := a$.

The formula φ is given by a conjunction of the following subformulas.

$$\varphi_{\text{init}} := \bigwedge_{i=1}^{l} \left(\iota_i^0 \wedge \bigwedge_{s \in S_i \cup S_i^*, s \neq \iota_i} \overline{s}^0 \right) \wedge \bigwedge_{a \in \mathcal{A}} \overline{a}^0$$

$$\varphi_1 := \bigwedge_{i=0}^{k'-1} \bigwedge_{t \in \mathcal{T}} \left[t^i \to \left(\text{src}(t)^i \wedge \text{int}(t)^{i+1} \wedge \right. \right.$$
$$\left(\text{trg}(t)^i \neq \epsilon \to \left(\text{trg}(t)^i \wedge \overline{\text{trg}(t)}^{i+1} \right) \right) \wedge$$
$$\left. \left. \left(\text{eff}(t)^i \neq \epsilon \to \left(\overline{\text{eff}(t)}^i \wedge \text{eff}(t)^{i+1} \right) \right) \right) \right]$$

$$\varphi_2 := \bigwedge_{i=0}^{k'-1} \bigwedge_{trg \in \mathcal{A}} \left[trg^i \wedge \overline{trg}^{i+1} \to \left(\bigvee_{\substack{t \in \mathcal{T}, \\ \text{trg}(t)=trg}} t^i \bigwedge_{\substack{t_1,t_2 \in \mathcal{T}, \\ \text{trg}(t_1)=\text{trg}(t_2)=trg}} \left(\overline{t_1}^i \vee \overline{t_2}^i \right) \right) \right]$$

$$\varphi_3 := \bigwedge_{i=0}^{k'-1} \bigwedge_{eff \in \mathcal{A}} \left[\overline{eff}^i \wedge eff^{i+1} \to \left(\bigvee_{\substack{t \in \mathcal{T}, \\ eff=\text{eff}(t)}} t^i \bigwedge_{\substack{t_1,t_2 \in \mathcal{T}, \\ \text{eff}(t_1)=\text{eff}(t_2)=eff}} \left(\overline{t_1}^i \vee \overline{t_2}^i \right) \right) \right]$$

$$\varphi_4 := \bigwedge_{i=0}^{k'-1} \bigwedge_{s \in S} \left[s^i \wedge \overline{s}^{i+1} \to \bigvee_{t \in \mathcal{T}, s=\text{src}(t)} t^i \right]$$

$$\varphi_5 := \bigwedge_{i=0}^{k'-1} \bigwedge_{t \in \mathcal{T}, \text{eff}(t) \neq \epsilon} \left[\left(\text{int}(t)^i \wedge \text{int}(t)^{i+1} \right) \to \text{eff}(t)^{i+1} \right]$$

$$\varphi_6 := \bigwedge_{i=0}^{k'-1} \bigwedge_{t \in \mathcal{T}, \text{eff}(t) \neq \epsilon} \left[\left(\text{int}(t)^i \wedge \overline{\text{int}(t)}^{i+1} \right) \to \overline{\text{eff}(t)}^{i+1} \right]$$

$$\varphi_7 := \bigwedge_{i=0}^{k'-1} \bigwedge_{t \in \mathcal{T}} \left[\left(\text{int}(t)^i \wedge \left(\text{eff}(t)^{i+1} \neq \epsilon \to \overline{\text{eff}(t)}^{i+1} \right) \right) \to \left(\overline{\text{int}(t)}^{i+1} \wedge \text{tgt}(t)^{i+1} \right) \right]$$

$$\varphi_8 := \bigwedge_{i=0}^{k'-1} \bigwedge_{j=1}^{l} \left[\bigvee_{s \in (S_j \cup S_j^*)} s^i \wedge \bigwedge_{\substack{s_1,s_2 \in (S_j \cup S_j^*), \\ s_1 \neq s_2}} \left(\overline{s_1}^i \vee \overline{s_2}^i \right) \right]$$

$$\varphi_{\text{seq}} := \bigwedge_{\substack{i \in [1,\dots,n], \\ j \in [k, k+4, \dots, k+4n]}} \left[\text{symb}(m_i)^j \wedge \overline{\text{symb}(m_i)}^{j+1} \wedge \right.$$
$$\bigvee_{\substack{t \in \text{trans}(\text{snd}(m_i)), \\ \text{eff}(t)=m_i}} \left(\text{int}(t)^j \wedge \overline{\text{int}(t)}^{j+1} \right) \wedge$$
$$\left. \bigwedge_{\substack{a \in \mathcal{A} \\ a \neq m_i}} \left(\left(a^j \to a^{j+1} \right) \wedge \left(a^{j+1} \to a^{j+2} \right) \wedge \left(a^{j+2} \to a^{j+3} \right) \right) \right]$$

The formula φ is satisfiable if and only if a state $\hat{s}$ is reachable by a path of length at most k starting at the global initial state such that starting from $\hat{s}$, the messages in μ are applicable one after another, i.e., there exists a solution to the k-MSCP instance. The intuition behind the encoding can be explained as follows: A state $s \in S$ is active at timestep i if s^i is *true*. A symbol $a \in \mathcal{A}$

is waiting to be received at timestep i if a^i is *true*. This way, when a transition with a as an effect is triggered at timestep i, then a^i is set to *true*. A state machine which is currently in a state with an outgoing transition with a as a trigger, can consume a in the same or a following timestep $j \geq i$. By doing so, a^j is set to *false*, i.e., it cannot be consumed anymore. Then the subformulas can be understood as follows.

- φ_{init} sets the global state at timestep 0 to the initial states of the lifelines. All other variables representing states and symbols are set to *false*.
- φ_1 ensures that whenever a transition is triggered, the corresponding lifeline changes to the respective intermediate state. Then the trigger symbol is set to *false* and the effect symbol is set to *true*.
- The subformulas φ_i with $i \in \{2, \ldots, 6\}$ are also called *framing axioms*. They ensure that each change of a symbol or of a state has a cause.
  - φ_2 and φ_3 make sure that whenever the polarity of a symbol is changed, there has also been a transition causing this change.
  - φ_4 ensures that a state is only left if a transition causes the change.
  - φ_5 and φ_6 encode that whenever a lifeline leaves an intermediate state, the corresponding symbol is consumed; otherwise the symbol stays available.
- φ_7 forces a lifeline to move to the target state if the effect symbol has been consumed.
- φ_8 ensures that each lifeline is in exactly one state at each timestep.
- Finally, φ_{seq} forces the sequence of messages μ to be executed after the preparation phase.

In formulas φ_1 and φ_7, the expressions $\mathsf{trg}(t)^i \neq \epsilon$ and $\mathsf{eff}(t)^i \neq \epsilon$ occurring in the formula are replaced by the corresponding logical constants ($\top$ and $\bot$) during generation of the formula. The formula is converted to conjunctive normal form, the input format of most SAT solvers. To this end, we apply the Tseitin transformation [25] where necessary.

Note that the encoding allows that nothing happens, i.e., no transaction takes place at a timestep. It is ensured by the framing axioms that in this case, the global state remains the same. This relaxation implicitly encodes the "at most k" steps formulation. If at x indices nothing happens and the execution of the message sequence starts at index k, it means that the length of the transaction sequence executed before the message sequence of the sequence diagram is of length $k - x$. The framing axioms also ensure that lifelines not participating in a transaction do not change.

A solution returned by the SAT solver consists of a set of positive and negative literals representing variables set to *true* or *false*. By extracting the positive literals whose variables represent states and transitions (sets $\mathcal{S}$, $\mathcal{S}^*$, and $\mathcal{T}$) we obtain the path of at most k steps leading to the execution of the sequence diagram, as well as the state changes of the lifelines during the execution of the sequence diagram. If the length of the path is less than k, then for some consecutive indices the state variables represent identical states.

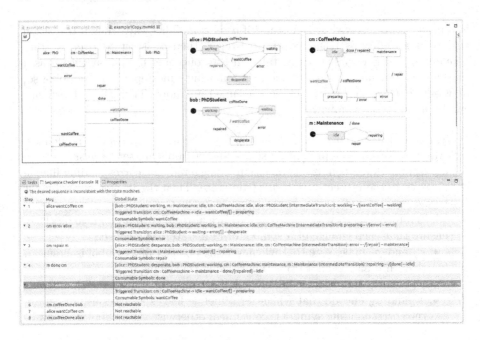

Fig. 4. Screenshot of the graphical user interface

In order to simplify the encoding, we assume that after applying a transaction each symbol can be consumable only once at a timestep. Allowing a symbol to be consumable multiple times requires the integration of counters, which can be realized, e.g., by building upon ideas presented in [24].

6   Implementation

We implemented a tool to solve k-MSCP instances based on the SAT encoding presented above as plugin for the Eclipse framework[2]. It can be downloaded from

http://modelevolution.org/updatesite/

To define the input language of our tool, i.e., the language of state machines and sequence diagrams, we formulated a metamodel in Ecore, the modeling language of the Eclipse modeling framework (EMF)[3]. This metamodel contains all language concepts discussed in this paper. Strongly inspired by the UML metamodel, it is designed for the easy integration of future language extensions.

The input models provided by the user of our tool are automatically translated to propositional logic using the encoding described above. After the encoding phase, the obtained formula is passed to the solver Sat4j [17], a Java-based SAT solver integrated in our tool.

---

[2] http://www.eclipse.org/
[3] http://www.eclipse.org/emf/

If the SAT solver returns SAT, then at least one execution path in the state machines exists which conforms to the message sequence in the sequence diagram. If the SAT solver returns UNSAT then the state machines and the sequence diagram are inconsistent. In this case, the last message is removed, and the SAT solver is called again, until it eventually returns SAT. The remaining sequence diagram is consistent with the state machines, and the information about the removed messages can be used for debugging purposes.

Then the solution returned by the SAT solver is mapped back to the model elements and visualized in the graphical user interface as shown in Fig. 4. Our user interface allows the user to step through a whole trace by coloring the current messages, transitions, and states. This visualization is very useful to understand the interplay and the behavior of the different state machines and provides valuable debugging assistance.

7 Evaluation

We thoroughly tested our tool using a grammar-based white-box fuzzing approach [29]. This method generates random input models based on a grammar provided by an EMF metamodel. We employed a random input model generator based on the tool presented in [29] but using a different definition of consistency between sequence diagrams and state machines. Other than taking into account only the receive event of a message exchange as is the case in [29], we consider both the send and the receive events. The tool consists of two components, a *generator* to build syntactically correct diagrams, and a *simulator* to ensure that a message sequence can be executed after a certain number of steps.

We applied white-box fuzzing for both debugging and performance evaluation purposes of our SAT encoding of k-MSCP. In the following we describe the random generation of instances and the results of the evaluation of our SAT-based k-MSCP solving tool.

7.1 Random Instance Generation

The instance generation tool first builds a set of state machines and then generates a sequence diagram consistent with these state machines. Consistency is ensured by the simulator following the generated sequence and proposing subsequent messages. In order to also generate inconsistent diagrams, messages are removed at random from an already generated message sequence. Further, if the considered bound for the generation of the diagrams is higher than the bound set in the encoding, the SAT solver may return UNSAT even though the message sequence is executable. The tool takes the following parameters to define the two views:

- nrStateMachines: Number of state machines to be created.
- minNrStates and maxNrStates: Bounds on the number of states per state machine. The actual number of states is chosen randomly between and including these bounds for each state machine.

- minNrTrans and maxNrTrans: Bounds on the number of transitions per state machine. The actual number of transitions is chosen randomly between and including these bounds for each state machine.
- nrSymbols: The size of the alphabet the state machines are defined over.
- probTrigger: The probability of a transition to contain a trigger symbol other than ϵ.
- probEff: The probability of a transition to contain an effect symbol other than ϵ.
- nrLifelines: The number of lifelines to be contained in the sequence view.
- nrMessages: The number of messages to be contained in the sequence view.

For each state machine, the algorithm randomly chooses a number of states and transitions in between the bounds minNrStates, maxNrStates, minNrTrans, and maxNrTrans, and connects the states by transitions randomly in a way such that no state is isolated. To at least one outgoing transition of the initial state, the trigger ϵ is added, and to all other transitions, a trigger other than ϵ is added with probability probTrigger. To each transition containing ϵ as trigger an effect other than ϵ is added, and to all other transitions an effect other than ϵ is added with probability probEff. Each time a trigger or an effect is added, a fresh symbol is created and added to the alphabet until the alphabet has reached size nrSymbols. After that, the trigger and effect symbols are chosen randomly.

Then a sequence diagram consistent with the state machine view is created according to the two parameters nrLifelines and nrMessages. In order to ensure the consistency, a model simulator keeps track of the global state of the lifelines' state machines. For each lifeline, a state machine is chosen at random from the state machine view. If nrLifelines > nrStateMachines then it is ensured that each state machine is instantiated at least once. The main data structure in the simulator represents possible global states as a hashmap with lifelines as keys and a set of states of the state machine instanced by the lifeline as value. For each lifeline, the hashmap is initialized with all original and intermediate states of the respective state machine. All admissible messages are calculated according to the current global state stored in the simulator. One message is chosen at random and the simulator is updated according to all possible successor states with respect to the application of the chosen message. Note that the state machines are non-deterministic, and therefore the number of possible states and admissible messages can become very large.

To obtain unsatisfiable instances, we generate one more message than required and remove one message at random among all messages except the first one. This procedure, however, still results in a satisfiable instance in many cases because a different path than the one followed by the simulator might be possible.

7.2   Testing Environment and Results

We selected a set of parameter values for the parameters described in Section 7.1 in order to generate sets of instances. The parameter values influence each other to a great extent, and it can easily happen that no or only a small message sequence can be generated for the sequence diagram. For example, a high value for

Table 1. Parameter settings

	small	medium	large
minNrStates	2	4	7
maxNrStates	3	6	10
minNrTrans	4	8	21
maxNrTrans	6	12	30
nrLifelines	3	5	8
nrMessages	4	10	20

probTrigger along with a high value for nrSymbols results in transitions containing different triggers and effects, making the generation of a consistent communication sequence difficult.

We grouped instances created according to different parameter sets into three different groups according to their size. Table 1 describes the parameter settings for each group. The following parameters have been set to the same values for all instances. nrStateMachines has been set to 3 for all instances because the size of the instance is regulated by the nrLifelines, i.e., the number of instantiations of the state machines, nrSymbols has been set to minNrStates, probTrigger and probEff have been set to 0.9, and k has been set to maxNrStates.

The experiments were executed on a computer with an Intel Core i5-540M CPU with 2.53GHz and 8GB of RAM. Table 2 describes the results of our experiments over 1,000 randomly generated instances in each category. We distinguish both encoding and solving time by UNSAT and SAT instances. The time required to determine the failing message in an UNSAT instance is significantly longer than the time required to determine satisfiability and to return a model. This is the case because unsatisfiable instances are modified by removing the last message and are sent back to the SAT solver until the failing message is found. The numbers of clauses and numbers of variables refer to the initial encoding of each instance, not taking into account the modified instances after unsatisfiability is detected, as the re-encoding results in less variables and clauses than the initial encoding.

Table 2. Average results over 1,000 runs for each category

	small	medium	large
Encoding time SAT (ms)	11	180	2,543
Solving time SAT (ms)	4	201	9,476
Encoding time UNSAT (ms)	34	970	27,848
Solving time UNSAT (ms)	8	727	179,914
Nr variables	1,802	12,746	88,560
Nr clauses	9,652	118,245	1,700,101
Nr instances SAT	837	750	803
Nr instances UNSAT	163	250	197

The difference in numbers of SAT instances and UNSAT instances can be explained by the way instances are created. In order to generate a sequence diagram at random without too much overhead, the state machines need many transitions with not too many symbols. However, in this case, when a valid sequence is found and a message removed, chances are high, that this "cropped" sequence can still be found by a path other than the one followed by the simulator, because of the previous requirement to have many transitions and few symbols.

It can be seen that the overall runtimes are acceptable even if executed on an standard hardware. As can be expected, the solving time scales worse than the encoding time. The overall runtime for UNSAT instances could probably be improved by implementing a binary search to find the failing message, instead of removing trailing messages one after another. This way, the SAT solver has to be called less often.

8   Conclusion and Future Work

We presented a novel SAT-based approach to check the consistency between state machines and sequence diagrams. To this end, we concisely formulated a formal semantics of the considered modeling language concepts. On this basis we were able to obtain an exact formal description of the consistency checking problem which was then directly mapped to SAT. The encoding reuses ideas and techniques well established for formulating planning problems. We obtained an encoding which is extremely flexible, efficiently processable, and still keeps the information necessary to map the solutions obtained from the SAT solver back to the modeling environment.

With our current solution we have a powerful tool for checking the consistency between different views in UML models. In combination with our other SAT-based encodings [14,30] we have now the means to establish a uniform framework supporting safe model evolution.

In future work, we plan to consider additional modeling language concepts like hierarchical states in the state machines or combined fragments in the sequence diagrams. Especially for the latter case which introduces programming language constructs like loops into the diagram, techniques applied in software verification must be considered. Also it is possible to apply ideas from this encoding to other diagram types like the UML activity diagram. Further, we plan to extend our approach for automatic repair. In particular, the encoding can be modified such that missing messages in the sequence diagram can be filled. This scenario can happen in automated merging environments as, for instance, in model versioning systems [6].

References

1. Bernardi, S., Donatelli, S., Merseguer, J.: From UML sequence diagrams and statecharts to analysable Petri net models. In: 3rd International Workshop on Software and Performance, pp. 35–45. ACM (2002)

2. Bézivin, J.: On the unification power of models. Software & Systems Modeling 4(2), 171–188 (2005)
3. Biere, A., Heule, M., van Maaren, H., Walsh, T. (eds.): Handbook of Satisfiability. FAIA, vol. 185. IOS Press (2009)
4. Brosch, P., Egly, U., Gabmeyer, S., Kappel, G., Seidl, M., Tompits, H., Widl, M., Wimmer, M.: Towards semantics-aware merge support in optimistic model versioning. In: Kienzle, J. (ed.) MODELS 2011 Workshops. LNCS, vol. 7167, pp. 246–256. Springer, Heidelberg (2012)
5. Brosch, P., Egly, U., Gabmeyer, S., Kappel, G., Seidl, M., Tompits, H., Widl, M., Wimmer, M.: Towards Scenario-Based Testing of UML Diagrams. In: Brucker, A.D., Julliand, J. (eds.) TAP 2012. LNCS, vol. 7305, pp. 149–155. Springer, Heidelberg (2012)
6. Brosch, P., Kappel, G., Langer, P., Seidl, M., Wieland, K., Wimmer, M.: An introduction to model versioning. In: Bernardo, M., Cortellessa, V., Pierantonio, A. (eds.) SFM 2012. LNCS, vol. 7320, pp. 336–398. Springer, Heidelberg (2012)
7. Egyed, A.: Instant consistency checking for the UML. In: 28th International Conference on Software Engineering (ICSE), pp. 381–390. ACM (2006)
8. Engels, G., Hausmann, J.H., Heckel, R., Sauer, S.: Testing the consistency of dynamic UML diagrams. In: 6th International Conference on Integrated Design and Process Technology (IDPT) (2002)
9. Feng, T.H., Vangheluwe, H.: Case study: Consistency problems in a UML model of a chat room. In: Workshop on Consistency Problems in UML-based Software Development, p. 18 (2003)
10. France, R., Rumpe, B.: Model-driven development of complex software: A research roadmap. In: Future of Software Engineering (FOSE), pp. 37–54. IEEE Computer Society (2007)
11. Gabmeyer, S., Kaufmann, P., Seidl, M.: A classification of model checking-based verification approaches for software models. In: STAF Workshop on Verification of Model Transformations (VOLT), pp. 1–7 (2013)
12. Graaf, B., van Deursen, A.: Model-driven consistency checking of behavioural specifications. In: 4th International Workshop on Model-Based Methodologies for Pervasive and Embedded Software (MOMPES), pp. 115–126 (2007)
13. Inverardi, P., Muccini, H., Pelliccione, P.: Automated check of architectural models consistency using SPIN. In: 16th Annual International Conference on Automated Software Engineering (ASE), pp. 346–349. IEEE Computer Society (2001)
14. Kaufmann, P., Kronegger, M., Pfandler, A., Seidl, M., Widl, M.: Global state checker: Towards SAT-based reachability analysis of communicating state machines. In: 10th Workshop on Model-Driven Engineering, Verification, and Validation (MoDeVVa). CEUR Workshop Proceedings, vol. 1069, pp. 31–40 (2013)
15. Knapp, A., Wuttke, J.: Model checking of UML 2.0 interactions. In: Kühne, T. (ed.) MoDELS 2006. LNCS, vol. 4364, pp. 42–51. Springer, Heidelberg (2007)
16. Lam, V.S.W., Padget, J.: Consistency Checking of Sequence Diagrams and Statechart Diagrams Using the π-Calculus. In: Romijn, J.M.T., Smith, G.P., van de Pol, J. (eds.) IFM 2005. LNCS, vol. 3771, pp. 347–365. Springer, Heidelberg (2005)
17. Le Berre, D., Parrain, A.: The Sat4j Library, Release 2.2, System Description. Journal on Satisfiability, Boolean Modeling and Computation 7, 59–64 (2010)
18. Lucas, F.J., Molina, F., Toval, A.: A systematic review of UML model consistency management. Information and Software Technology 51(12), 1631–1645 (2009)
19. Papadimitriou, C.H.: Computational complexity. Addison-Wesley (1994)

20. Pelliccione, P., Inverardi, P., Muccini, H.: CHARMY: A Framework for Designing and Verifying Architectural Specifications. IEEE Transactions on Software Engineering 35(3), 325–346 (2008)
21. Rintanen, J.: Planning and SAT. In: Handbook of Satisfiability. FAIA, vol. 185, pp. 483–504. IOS Press (2009)
22. Schäfer, T., Knapp, A., Merz, S.: Model Checking UML State Machines and Collaborations. Electronic Notes in Theoretical Computer Science 55(3), 357–369 (2001)
23. Selic, B.: What will it take? A view on adoption of model-based methods in practice. Software & Systems Modeling 11(4), 513–526 (2012)
24. Sinz, C.: Towards an Optimal CNF Encoding of Boolean Cardinality Constraints. In: van Beek, P. (ed.) CP 2005. LNCS, vol. 3709, pp. 827–831. Springer, Heidelberg (2005)
25. Tseitin, G.S.: On the complexity of derivations in the propositional calculus. Studies in Mathematics and Mathematical Logic, Part II, 115–125 (1968)
26. Usman, M., Nadeem, A., Kim, T., Cho, E.: A survey of consistency checking techniques for UML models. In: Advanced Software Engineering and Its Applications (ASEA), pp. 57–62. IEEE Computer Society (2008)
27. Van Der Straeten, R., Mens, T., Simmonds, J., Jonckers, V.: Using description logic to maintain consistency between UML models. In: Stevens, P., Whittle, J., Booch, G. (eds.) UML 2003. LNCS, vol. 2863, pp. 326–340. Springer, Heidelberg (2003)
28. Whittle, J., Schumann, J.: Generating statechart designs from scenarios. In: 22nd International Conference on Software Engineering (ICSE), pp. 314–323. ACM (2000)
29. Widl, M.: Test Case Generation by Grammar-Based Fuzzing for Model-Driven Engineering. In: Biere, A., Nahir, A., Vos, T. (eds.) HVC 2013. LNCS, vol. 7857, pp. 278–279. Springer, Heidelberg (2013)
30. Widl, M., Biere, A., Brosch, P., Egly, U., Heule, M., Kappel, G., Seidl, M., Tompits, H.: Guided Merging of Sequence Diagrams. In: Czarnecki, K., Hedin, G. (eds.) SLE 2012. LNCS, vol. 7745, pp. 164–183. Springer, Heidelberg (2013)

Towards User-Friendly Projectional Editors

Markus Voelter[1], Janet Siegmund[2], Thorsten Berger[3], and Bernd Kolb[4]

[1] independent/itemis, Stuttgart, Germany
voelter@acm.org
[2] Universität Passau, Passau, Germany
Janet.Siegmund@uni-passau.de
[3] University of Waterloo, Waterloo, Canada
tberger@gsd.uwaterloo.ca
[4] itemis AG, Stuttgart, Germany
kolb@itemis.de

Abstract. Today's challenges for language development include language extension and composition, as well as the use of diverse notations. A promising approach is projectional editing, a technique to directly manipulate the abstract syntax tree of a program, without relying on parsers. Its potential lies in the ability to combine diverse notational styles – such as text, symbols, tables, and graphics – and the support for a wide range of composition techniques. However, projectional editing is often perceived as problematic for developers. Expressed drawbacks include the unfamiliar editing experience and challenges in the integration with existing infrastructure. In this paper we investigate the usability of projectional editors. We systematically identify usability issues resulting from the architecture. We use JetBrains Meta Programming System (MPS) as a case study. The case study discusses the concepts that MPS incorporates to address the identified issues, evaluates effectiveness of these concepts by surveying professional developers, and reports industrial experiences from realizing large-scale systems. Our results show that the benefits of flexible language composition and diverse notations come at the cost of serious usability issues – which, however, can be effectively mitigated with facilities that emulate editing experience of parser-based editors.

1   Introduction

As expressed by *closeness of mapping* in the cognitive dimensions of notations [1], the degree to which we can effectively express facts in a given domain is heavily influenced by the alignment of the used language with that domain. This applies to programming languages, but also to domain-specific languages (DSLs) used in a wide range of technical and business domains. However, a language must also use a suitable notation. Imagine mathematics represented as a linear sequence of characters, without integral symbols, fraction bars or superscripts: it would be much harder to read, making mathematics as a language less useful – more *hard mental operations* [1] would be due to the syntax and not the underlying semantics. DSLs are often targeted at non-programmers. While the suitability of a

B. Combemale et al. (Eds.): SLE 2014, LNCS 8706, pp. 41–61, 2014.

language for its target audience is guided by many criteria (as discussed in [1]), our experience tells us that that the notation is especially important for languages targeted at non-programmers. Another important concern in languages is their composability (approximated by *juxtaposability* in [1]). Software systems are often expressed with a set of languages (some used by programmers, some by other stakeholders), and these languages must be integrated in terms of syntax, semantics, and their development environments: today, IDEs are essential to languages since users increasingly rely on IDEs to efficiently edit programs.

Traditionally, languages use either textual or graphical notations. Each kind of notation comes with its own editor architecture. Textual notations are typically edited with text buffers, grammars and parsers. The supported notations are essentially linear sequences of characters and – depending on the grammar class – in their ability to compose independently developed languages. Graphical notations use direct manipulation instead of parsers. But purely graphical notations are only suitable for a limited set of languages, and many real-world languages require a mix of graphical, textual, tabular and symbolic/mathematical notations. Projectional editors (ProjEs) support this approach. They generalize the approach used in graphical editors to arbitrary notations. Editing gestures directly change the abstract syntax tree (AST). Users see and interact with a rendering of the AST called a projection. There is no transformation (that is, parsing) from the concrete syntax to the AST. This allows non-textual notations, as demonstrated by intentional programming [2,3], which relies on projectional editing. ProjEs also avoid the problems with compositionality known from grammar-based systems: ambiguities cannot arise since no grammars are used.

However, ProjEs have traditionally had two problems. First, for notations that look textual, users expect that the editing behavior resembles classical text editing as much as possible. Historically, ProjEs have not been good at this; users had to be aware of the AST when editing programs, leading to usability problems. For example, when entering 2+3, users first had to enter the + and then enter the two arguments. Second, ProjEs cannot store programs in the concrete syntax – otherwise, this syntax would have to be parsed when programs are loaded into the editor. Instead, programs are stored as a serialized AST, often as XML. This makes the integration with existing infrastructures, such as version control systems (VCS) or diff/merge tools, a challenge.

Hypothesis.   Although ProjEs have been around for a long time (see Section 2.2), and despite their demonstrated advantages in terms of notational flexibility and support for language composition and extension, ProjE have not seen much adoption in practice.   We hypothesize that this is mainly because of the drawbacks regarding editor usability and infrastructure integration discussed above.

Goals, Methods, and Contributions.   Our goal is to evaluate the usability of projectional editors. To this end, we first systematically identify and categorize usability issues arising from the architectural peculiarities of projectional editors. We then provide a case study of a state-of-the-art projectional editor – the JetBrains Meta Programming System (MPS). In the case study, we discuss the techniques used by MPS to mitigate the identified issues, and evaluate their effectiveness by surveying professional developers. We finally report industrial experiences from realizing large-scale systems. We contribute: (i) a taxonomy of usability issues that projectional editors face, (ii) a mapping of concrete mitigation techniques for the issues, and (iii) empirical data on how professional developers perceive effectiveness of projectional editing.

Results. We identify 14 usability issues related to efficiently entering code (e.g., non-linear typing), selection and modification of code (e.g., introducing cross-tree parentheses), and integration with existing infrastructure (e.g., version control systems). Half of these issues can be addressed sufficiently, for instance, using code completion or expression-tree-refactoring support. Others require language- or notation-specific implementations, or cannot be mitigated conceptually. Results of the survey show that developers perceive projectional editing as an efficient technique applicable in every-day work, while the effort of getting used to it is high. However, the survey also reveals weaknesses, such as the support for commenting, which is currently not addressed sufficiently in MPS.

2 Background

2.1 Parsing vs. Projection

In parser-based editors (ParEs), users type characters into a text buffer. The buffer is then parsed to check whether a sequence of characters conforms to a grammar. The parser builds a parse tree, and ultimately, an abstract syntax tree (AST), which contains the relevant structure of the program, but omits syntactic details. Subsequent processing (such as linking, type checks, and transformation) is based on the AST. Modern IDEs (re-)parse the concrete syntax while the user edits the code, maintaining an up-to-date AST in the background that reflects the code in the editor's text buffer. However, even in this case, this AST is created by a parser-driven transformation from the source text.

A ProjE does not rely on parsers. As a user edits a program, the AST is modified *directly*. A projection engine uses projection rules to create a representation of the AST with which the user interacts, and which reflects the resulting changes. No parser-based transformation from concrete to abstract syntax involved here. Fig. 1 shows the difference. This approach is well-known from graphical editors: when editing a UML diagram, users do not draw pixels onto a

Fig. 1. In ParEs (left), users see and modify the concrete syntax. A parser constructs the AST. In ProjEs, users see and interact with the concrete syntax, but changes *directly* affect the AST. The concrete syntax is projected from the changing AST.

canvas, and a "pixel parser" then creates the AST. Rather, the editor creates an instance of `uml.Class` when a user drops a class onto the canvas. A projection engine renders the diagram by drawing a rectangle for the class. Programs are stored using a generic tree persistence format (such as XML). As the user edits the program, program nodes are created as instances of language concepts. This approach can be generalized to work with any notation, including textual. A code-completion menu lets users create instances based on a text string entered in the editor called the *alias*. The concepts available for instantiation (and, thus, the valid text strings/aliases) depend on the language definition. Importantly, *every next text string is recognized as it is entered*, so there is never any parsing of a sequence of text strings. In contrast to ParEs, where disambiguation is performed by the parser after a (potentially) complete program has been entered, in ProjEs, disambiguation is performed by the user as he selects a concept from the code-completion menu. Once a node is created, it is *never* ambiguous what it represents, *irrespective of its syntax*: every node points to its defining concept. Every program node has a unique ID, and references between program elements are represented as references to the ID. These references are established during program editing by directly selecting reference targets from the code-completion menu; the references are persistent. This is in contrast to ParEs, where a reference is expressed as a string in the source text, and a separate name resolution phase resolves the target AST element after the text has been parsed.

2.2   Related Work in Projectional Editing

An early example of a ProjE is the Incremental Programming Environment (IPE) [4]. It supports the definition of several notations for a language as well as partial projections, where parts of the AST are not shown. However, IPE suffers from the problem with editing expressions introduced earlier: to enter 2+3, users first have to enter the + and then fill in the two arguments. This is tedious and forces users to be aware of the language structure at all times. IPE also does not address language modularity; it comes with a fixed, C-like language and does not have a built-in facility for defining new languages. Another early example is GANDALF [5], which generates a ProjE from a language specification. Even though [6] does not report on a systematic study, the authors expect the same usability problems as IPE: "Program editing will be considerably slower than normal keyboard entry, although actual time spent programming non-trivial programs should be reduced due to reduced error rates." The Synthesizer Generator [7] is also a ProjE. However, at the fine-grained expression level, textual input and parsing is used. While this improves usability, it destroys many of the advantages of projectional editing in the first place, because language composition *at the expression level* is limited. In fact, extension of expressions is particularly important to tightly integrate an embedded language with its host language [8].

The Intentional Programming [2,3] project has gained widespread visibility and has popularized projectional editing; the Intentional Domain Workbench (IDW) is the contemporary implementation of the approach. IDW supports diverse notations [9,10]. However, we are not aware of any studies regarding its usability, and since it is a commercial system, we cannot evaluate it. Our understanding is that the IDW has not found widespread adoption so far.

Language boxes [11] rely on explicitly delineating the boundaries between different languages used in a single program (e.g., the user could change the box with `Ctrl-Space`). Each language box may use parsing or projection. This way, textual notations can be edited naturally, solving the usability issues associated with editing text in a ProjE. However, it is not clear whether fine-grained mixing between different boxes will work in terms of usability. For example, consider a projectional editor for a mathematical notation embedded (in its own box) inside an otherwise textual editor for C code. As part of the mathematical expression, users would like to use (textual) references to C variables. Providing an integrated user experience, as well as integrated symbol tables, may not be a trivial problem. In addition, language boxes address *only* the usability problem: the approach still requires a specialized IDE (that knows about the boxes) plus non-concrete syntax storage (because the boxes must be represented somehow).

Hybrid editors are another alternative of solving the usability problems of ProjEs by on-demand parsing. Unlike in a ParE, the editor content consists of atomic tokens, not characters. These tokens have normal projectional editors. This makes it possible to embed complex tokens, such as diagrams or math symbols, and still edit sequences of such tokens linearly. A prototype is currently being explored by a team at JetBrains (available at `http://jb-proj-demo.appspot.com/index.html`). It is not clear at this point what the trade-offs are regarding language composability, notational freedom, and usability.

2.3 Case Study: MPS and mbeddr

JetBrains MPS (`http://jetbrains.com/mps`) is an open-source language workbench that uses projectional editing. It is a comprehensive environment for language engineering, supporting language aspects such as concrete and abstract syntax, type systems and transformations, as well as IDE aspects, such as syntax highlighting, code-completion, find-usages, diff and merge, refactoring, and debugging. It also supports language modularization and composition [8].

We have chosen MPS as our case study for three reasons. (1) MPS is currently the most widely used ProjE. It is used for various projects, including JetBrains YouTrack, mbeddr (discussed below), computational biology [12], web applications (`http://codeorchestra.com/ide/`), requirements engineering [13], and insurance DSLs. (2) Some of the authors of this paper have significant industry experience with MPS. (3) MPS is open-source, which fosters replicability of our results.

MPS relies on a meta meta model very similar to EMOF and EMF Ecore [14]. Language concepts (corresponding to meta classes) declare children (single or lists), references and primitive properties. Concepts can extend other concepts or implement concept interfaces. Subconcepts can be used where a superconcept is expected (polymorphism). Programs are represented as instances of concepts, called nodes. Each concept also defines one or more editors. These are the projection rules that determine the notation of instance nodes in the program. The editor also defines intentions, little in-place program transformations that can be triggered by the user as he edits the program.

mbeddr (http://mbeddr.com) is an extensible set of integrated languages for embedded software engineering [15], developed with MPS. mbeddr is also open source. It is primarily used for implementing embedded systems, ranging from relatively small examples (such as Lego Mindstorm robots) to non-trivial commercial applications (e.g., a smart meter [16]). mbeddr has been chosen by Siemens PLM Software (formerly LMS) as the basis of a new controls engineering tool, which is currently being developed as a set of mbeddr extensions.

The core of mbeddr is an extensible version of C99 and a set of extensions for embedded software, such as interfaces and components, state machines or physical units. mbeddr provides multi-paradigm programming for C [17], in which different abstractions can be used and mixed in the same program. mbeddr also supports languages for cross-cutting concerns, such as documentation, requirements management, and traceability, as well as product-line engineering. Several formal verification techniques are also directly integrated with the languages.

3   Advantages and Drawbacks of Projectional Editing

We now systematically analyze the usability challenges traditionally associated with ProjEs. We have identified three categories: efficiently entering (textual) code (EE), selecting and modifying code (SM), as well as infrastructure integration (II). These categories reflect anecdotal evidence on usability challenges of ProjEs. They are also obviously relevant for productively using an editor. For each of the categories, we identify and explain specific challenges in the following sections.

3.1   Efficiently Entering (Textual) Code

Most grammars used in practice by ParEs are not freely composable, because the composed grammar may become ambiguous. The details depend on the grammar class used by the parser, and various disambiguation approaches are used to address the issue. We mention two examples below; an extensive discussion can be found in [8]. Formalisms that implement full context-free grammars compose much better, depending on the modularity of the grammar language [18]. An example of a grammar formalism that supports only limited composition is ANTLR [19]. In contrast, SDF2 [20] supports full context-free grammars based on a scannerless generalized LR parser, and composition support is much better: As an example, [21] demonstrates embedding SQL into Java. Disambiguation is necessary if the same syntactic form is used in the same location to represent different language concepts (i.e., must be parsed differently). SDF2 performs disambiguation via quotations, and SILVER/COPPER [22] uses disambiguation functions. In ProjEs, since no grammars are used, language composition is unlimited (discussed systematically in [8]). Situations which would lead to an ambiguity in ParEs are resolved by **asking the user to manually disambiguate (EE.1)** at the time of entering the potentially ambiguous code. As an example of composition and extension, the mbeddr system currently has over 30 modular extensions to C; all of them can be used in the same program. Many of them are illustrated in [15].

The manual disambiguation also includes references: Targets are picked from the code-completion menu. This means that users **cannot establish references to non-existing nodes (EE.2)**, because, if they do not exist yet, the code-completion menu cannot offer them to the user. In ParEs, a user can just type i++ even though i has not yet been declared. The user can go back later, and add a declaration of i before its use. This works because the i in i++ is just a symbol, and its resolution happens later – it is marked as an error as long as no declaration for i is in scope. In a ProjE, every reference is an actual pointer to its target. If the target does not exist, the reference cannot be entered.

Textual projections require the AST to be projected linearly. As discussed in Section 2.2, ProjEs have traditionally forced the tree structure on the user even when the notation was linear, i.e., they **required structure-aware typing (EE.3)**. 2+3 must be entered by first typing the + and then entering its two children, instead of just linearly typing 2+3.

ParEs extract structure from characters in a text buffer based on a grammar. Mainstream grammars work on linear sequences of characters. This severely limits non-linear notations, such as math/symbols (because they are two-dimensional) or graphics, and limits tabular notations to simple cases where the vertical bar (|) is used to separate columns and rows (as shown by Jnario (http://jnario.org), a language for behavior-driven development) or simple, non-recursive fraction bar-like notations (used for type system rules in [23]). Coordinate grammars [24] have been proposed to parse two-dimensional mathematics structures. Parsers for visual notations have been proposed as well; for example, [25] discusses parsing of hand-inputted shapes on tablet computers based on a formalism called set grammars. More general discussions on parsing visual languages are provided in [26] and [27]. However, these grammars use different formalisms and so do not easily integrate with traditional grammars for linear text. None of these approaches has found its way into industry-strength language tooling.

Since ProjEs never parse the concrete syntax, they can use notations that are not parseable, or use two-dimensional layout. Examples include tables, mathematical symbols (fraction bars, superscript or $\sum$) or diagrams. This is discussed for IDW in[9,10] and for MPS/mbeddr in [15]. ProjEs can also mix different notational styles. For example, tables can contain textual expressions and mathematical symbols (as in mbeddr's decision tables), and textual programs can embed graphics. This works because all notational styles are implemented using the same projectional architecture. In contrast, maintaining an integrated overall model created with editors that combine parsing and diagram editing is challenging for a number of technical reasons [28]. These include that parser-based editors use (qualified) names to represent program node identity, whereas graphical editors natively use IDs for this purpose or that references in ParEs are created via name binding, and graphical editors use the unique ID.

This notational flexibility leads to drawbacks. In a ParE, a program can always be typed exactly the way it looks by typing the sequence of characters one by one. In a ProjE, it is possible to project program nodes in arbitrary ways, including tables or mathematical symbols; these cannot just be typed. For example, the $\sum$ is not available on the keyboard. Thus, it cannot be deduced from just looking at a program (e.g., in a presentation or a book) how to enter it: **What you see is not what you type (EE.4)**. More generally, the different notational styles may **require notation-specific editor support (EE.5)**, each potentially with their own idiosyncrasies.

Many ProjEs support the definition of multiple editable notations for the same language structure. A program's representation can be switched on the fly by selecting another set of projection rules. This is not practical for ParEs, since most useful changes in representation also lead to changes in the underlying structure. As an example, mbeddr supports editing state machines either as text, or as tables, and a graphical notation is currently being added. Also, in a ProjE, a program can contain data that is not shown in the projection, and partial projections or views are possible. This is because the program is stored as the AST, which contains all data, even when it is not shown. For example, mbeddr stores requirements traces [29] in programs. In contrast, a ParE must always contain all data in the concrete syntax, because this is the persistent representation. It is possible to hide some parts, but this requires specific, language-aware support in the editor. The Jnario editor can optionally hide the formal aspects of tests. However, this flexibility means that programs cannot be stored in their concrete syntax, requiring persisting programs as a generic tree structure. This leads to challenges with infrastructure integration (discussed below).

3.2 Selecting and Modifying Code (SM)

In ParEs, selection happens in the text buffer: any character, word, line (or sequences thereof) can be selected and subsequently changed, cut, copied or pasted. In a ProjE, **selection is based on the tree structure (SM.1)**: nodes, parent nodes, or siblings in lists can be selected. This also makes it **hard to perform cross-tree modifications (SM.2)**, i.e., editing structures that are not aligned with the tree. Consider the expression 1 + 2*3. To change this into (1+2) * 3, parentheses have to be inserted in places that cross-cut the tree structure: most ProjEs do not support this, and the expression has to be retyped. Finally, **copy and paste is structure-aware (SM.3)**, and not just based on the syntax. If a user wants to paste something in a location where it may fit syntactically, but the underlying AST uses a different language concept, this will not work. An example is pasting a C `Function` into a C++ class, where it needs to be a `Method` instead, even though it has essentially the same syntax.

In ParEs, it is sometimes hard to detect semantic associations between program elements, since such associations are expressed by "geographical proximity". For example, comments are typically located above the program element they

Table 1. Mapping of identified usability issues to mitigation techniques

	Issue	Mitigation Technique used by MPS
Efficiently Entering (Textual) Code	EE.1 Requires manual, user-based disambiguation	code completion, aliases, context constraints
	EE.2 Cannot establish references to non-existing nodes	intentions to create missing targets
	EE.3 Requires structure-aware typing	side transforms, delete actions, smart references, wrappers, smart delimiters
	EE.4 What you see is not what you type	–
	EE.5 Requires notation-specific editor support	– (but editors share common aspects)
Selecting and Modifying Code	SM.1 Selection is based on the tree structure	–
	SM.2 Hard to perform cross-tree modifications	expression tree restructuring
	SM.3 Requires structure-aware copy/paste	paste handlers
	SM.4 Does not support free-floating comments	– (partly addressed by metamodel extension in mbeddr)
	SM.5 Requires dedicated support for commenting code	– (partly addressed by metamodel extension in mbeddr)
	SM.6 Does not support custom layout	–
Infrastructure Integration	II.1 Requires tool support for diff/merge	node-by-node revert, merge driver, diff/merge tool using projection rules
	II.2 Text-based shell-scripting tools cannot be used	– (build system support for generating and testing models)
	II.3 Requires tool support to export/import textual syntax	copy/paste, parser hooks, generic node (de-)serialization

belong to. In a ProjE, the relationship between program nodes is typically designed to be explicit: for example, comments would be children of the element they are associated to, even though they may still be projected above it. This results in more robust merging and refactoring, but also means that a ProjE has **no support for free-floating comments (SM.4)**.

In a ParE, code that is temporarily not needed can be commented out. It is then ignored by the compiler, type checker, and other IDE services; it is treated as plain text. When the code is needed again, it can be uncommented: the parser parses the text and (re-)creates the AST. In a ProjE, commenting is not so easy, since the commented code must retain its structure so it can be uncommented later when it is needed again. Hence, **dedicated support for commenting code is required (SM.5)**.

Whitespace is typically ignored by ParEs, and not explicitly described in grammars. To be able to pretty-print a program after an automated modification, an additional pretty-printing specification is typically required. In a ProjE, this is not required, since the projection rules already contain layout information. On the flip side, a ProjE **does not support custom layout (SM.6)** – the representation is determined completely by the projection rules.

3.3   Infrastructure Integration (II)

Today's development infrastructure is geared towards text files, and ParEs integrate seamlessly. The diff/merge facilities of VCS rely on showing the file contents. This works well for concrete syntax storage, but it does not work for AST-based storage. Special **tool support for diff/merge is needed (II.1)**.

Tools such as `grep` assume concrete syntax storage. While ProjEs store names as strings (so they can be `grep`'ed), more complex structures are represented as several nodes and `grep`'ing for their concrete syntax representation will not work. **Text-based shell scripting tools cannot be used (II.2)**. A ProjE will typically support searching on the projected syntax, but the ProjE must be used for the purpose; generic text-search tools are not enough.

Code written in a ParE can trivially be pasted to and copied from another text-based application. For a ProjE, this is not necessarily so simple; **tool support is required to export/import textual syntax (II.3)**. Non-textual notations, such as tables or symbols, cannot be pasted to a text editor at all.

4   Addressing the Drawbacks in Projectional Editors

In this section, we revisit the problems associated with ProjEs introduced in Section 3 and illustrate the mechanisms (typeset in *italic*) used by MPS to address them. Some of these approaches have already been introduced in [15]. Table 1 summarizes the issues and MPS' mitigation techniques where applicable.

4.1   Efficiently Entering (Textual) Code (EE)

EE.1 Requires Manual, User-Based Disambiguation.   Disambiguation in MPS relies on the user selecting the correct language concept from the *code-completion* menu, whose contents are driven by the language structure. Language concepts define an *alias*, the string used to pick the concept from the code-completion menu. By making the alias the same as the leading keyword (e.g. `if` for an `IfStatement`), users can "just type" the code. MPS also supports *context constraints* that restrict the locations where concepts can be used based on arbitrary conditions. For example, mbeddr has different `assert` keywords, each with different translation to C. To avoid confusing the user by requiring manual disambiguation between them, context constraints ensure that each of these `assert` statements is available only in disjoint contexts.

EE.2: Cannot Establish References to Non-existing Nodes.   MPS supports *intentions to create the missing targets* in a context-dependent way. For example, if a user enters a global variable in mbeddr C as `int32 global = someName`, where `someName` does not exist, MPS provides two intentions: one to create a global variable `someName`, and one to create a global constant. If a user enters a local variable (in a function) as `int32 local = someName`, there are two more intentions that support creation of a local variable and a function argument.

EE.3: Requires Structure-Aware Typing.   Consider an expression 2 that should be changed to 2 + 3. MPS supports *side transforms* to allow users to simply type + on the right side of the 2. The transform replaces the 2 with the +, puts the 2 in the left slot, and then puts the cursor into the right slot so the user can enter the second argument. Side transforms also reshuffle the tree to ensure it reflects operator precedence: higher precedence means the operator is further down in the tree. Precedence is typically specified by a number associated with each operator. *Delete actions* are used for a similar effect when elements are deleted. Pressing `Backspace` on the 3 in 2 + 3 keeps the 2 +, with an empty right slot. Pressing `Backspace` on the + replaces it with its left argument, the 2.

References are also established via code-completion. Consider pressing `Ctrl-Space` after the + in 2 + 3. If local variables are in scope, these should be available in the code-completion menu. However, technically, a `VarRef` has to be instantiated first, whose `variable` slot is then made to point to a variable. This is tedious, and *smart references* solve the problem: If a `VarRef` is allowed in a given context, the editor first finds the possible targets and puts those targets into the code-completion menu. Only after the user has selected a target, then the `VarRef` is created, and the selected element is put into its `variable` slot. This makes the reference object invisible in terms of the editing experience.

Consider a local variable declaration `int a;` represented by the concept `LocalVarDecl`, a subconcept of `Statement` so it can be used in function bodies. Users expect to be able to enter a local variable by typing `int`. However, `int` is a `Type`, and a `Type` is not legal in a statements list – a statement list expects instances of `Statement` – and hence cannot be entered. *Wrappers* solve this problem: if a `Type` is entered in `Statement` context, the wrapper creates a `LocalVarDecl`, puts the `Type` into its `type` slot, and moves the cursor into the `name` slot. This way, a local variable declaration `int a;` can be entered by starting to type the `int` type, as expected.

Finally, *smart delimiters* are used to simplify inputting lists that are separated with a separator symbol (such as the arguments in a function). Typing the separator (e.g., comma), automatically adds a new node to the list.

EE.4: What You See is Not What You Type. The problem that some concepts (such as $\sum$) cannot be entered just by typing what is projected cannot be solved; it is a consequence of allowing notations that are not on the keyboard.

EE.5: Requires Notation-Specific Editor Support. The editors used for the different notations share common aspects: code completion and intentions work everywhere, selection is always based on the tree structure, and pressing `Backspace` on a program element always deletes it. Still, notation-specific gestures have to be learned. For instance, the table editors offer special gestures to create new rows, and graphical editors require the mouse to move elements.

4.2 Selecting and Modifying Code (SM)

SM.1: Selection is Based on the Tree Structure. MPS provides no solution to this problem. `Ctrl-Up/Down` selects along the tree structure. `Shift-Up/Down` selects siblings in child lists. This works independent of the notations. For example, if a tree is projected as a table, `Ctrl-Up` will select the current row if that row represents the parent node, and then `Shift-Down` selects rows under the current one if the corresponding nodes are siblings. As this example illustrates, selection based on the tree structure is not always bad, because programs are highly structured. This is also illustrated by the fact that some ParEs (such as Eclipse) support tree-based selection in addition to character-based selection.

SM.2: Hard to Perform Cross-Tree Modifications. Cross-tree editing, as in changing 1 + 2*3 to (1+2) * 3 is solved as follows: a separate opening parenthesis can be entered anywhere in the tree, and its position is remembered temporarily. Upon entering a corresponding closing parenthesis, the *expression tree is restructured* to reflect the new structure indicated by the inserted parentheses.

SM.3: Requires Structure-Aware Copy/Paste. To address the problem of not being able to paste an instance of concept A in a program location where an instance of B is expected, MPS supports *paste handlers*. These are callbacks that transform an instance of B to an instance of A if the paste context requires it.

SM.4: No Support for Free-Floating Comments. Free-floating comments remain unsupported in MPS. mbeddr supports attaching comments to all program elements that implement an interface `IDocumentable`. All top-level mbeddr C constructs and all statements implement this interface, so essentially everything except expressions or types can be commented. In addition, mbeddr support a `CommentStatement`, which means that procedural code (such as function bodies) can contain comments that are not associated with any particular element.

SM.5: Requires Dedicated Support for Commenting Code. Unfortunately, MPS provides no generic support for (temporarily) commenting out code. mbeddr uses the following approach: If instances of some concept should be commentable, a subconcept is defined that implements an interface `ICommentedCode`. The subconcept stores the commented code and is marked to suppress errors. It also overrides the editor styles to use a uniformly gray text color. Using this approach, it is relatively simple to make statements or module contents commentable. However, the approach does not work for commenting out parts of expressions, as in 1 + 2 * (4 /*+7*/).

SM.6: Does Not Support Custom Layout. MPS does not support user-defined layout. However, the projection rules can be defined with conditional projections so that, for example, a statement list that contains only one statement is rendered on one line (as in if (..) { return x; }) instead of over several lines. Conditional projections can also be used to implement user-definable preferences, such as whether the opening curly brace should be on a new line or not. More generally, it is not clear whether predefined layout is actually a problem: many organizations mandate formatters that enforce a predefined layout.

4.3 Infrastructure Integration (II)

II.1: Requires Tool Support for Diff/Merge. The fact that MPS stores its models in XML files (and not in a database) means that MPS can be integrated with file-based development infrastructures. More specifically, the VCS integration involves the following ingredients. First, the editor highlights those parts of programs that have changed since the last update, shows diffs of these parts, and supports reverting changes on a *node-by-node basis*. Second, while diff/merge is performed by the underlying VCS, MPS ships with a *merge driver* that makes sure the merging process respects the idiosyncrasies of MPS' XML format. Finally, any diff or merge that requires manual user intervention is performed in an internal *diff/merge tool that uses the projection rules.* It works for any notation, and for textual languages, diff/merge works exactly as in text-based merge tools.

II.2: Text-Based Shell-Scripting Tools Cannot Be Used. The problem that text-oriented console tools cannot directly work with MPS models is not solved generically. However, the most important one, checking and generating models, is supported. First, MPS models can be generated with an `ant` task. It transforms all models in a specified project, enabling subsequent compilation, test, and packaging of generated artifacts. Second, MPS supports a headless mode for executing type-system tests. These verify that error messages appear at locations in programs where, according to the type system rules, they should appear.

II.3: Requires Tool Support to Export/Import Textual Syntax. By default, all *textual notations can be copy-pasted* to a text editor. The other way, from text to MPS, requires integrating a parser that creates the MPS tree from the textual source. MPS provides *hooks to integrate such parsers.* In mbeddr, we have developed more utilities for dealing with MPS code in the context of a text-based collaboration infrastructure. First, a node's ID can be represented as a text string, which can then be used by other developers to select the node in MPS. Second, a node can be copied as XML and then be transported via a text-based infrastructure. When the XML is pasted into MPS, the original node is reconstructed. This works independent of the notation.

5 Evaluation

We now evaluate the degree to which MPS' solutions of the drawbacks of ProjEs work in practice. The first two dimensions (Efficiently Entering (Textual) Code, Selecting and Modifying Code) are evaluated in Section 5.1 based on a survey; the questionnaire and anonymized results are available in [30]. Infrastructure Integration is discussed based on project experience in Section 5.2.

5.1 Editor Usability

Survey Setup. Our survey addresses the following research question: *Does MPS solve known usability issues of projectional editors?* To answer it, we designed a questionnaire that assesses how developers work with MPS and how they perceive its usability. For each question, developers should estimate their opinion on a five-point Likert [31] scale, ranging from *strongly agree (1)* over *neutral (3)* to *strongly disagree (5)*. An example statements for developers to rate is: *I can work productively with MPS*. To help us understand the rating, we also asked users to elaborate on their rating in a text field. The survey questions are aligned with some of Nielsen's heuristic [32] to make sure the results are relevant for usability.

All participants are professional developers who are using or have used MPS for non-trivial tasks. We targeted professionals to obtain a controlled sample, excluding developers who have just experimented with MPS. We contacted each developer personally via e-mail. The contacted developers included users of mbeddr as well as other professional MPS users. Our contactees were allowed to forward the survey to other users. This led to one beginner in our sample, and we decided to not exclude the data so we can get an impression of the obstacles beginners face (to be explored further in future work). We piloted the questionnaire with one developer to rule out any misunderstandings in the questions: no adaptations were necessary, so we included the results from this developer in the analysis. To put the answers into context, we also assessed their general programming experience and how experienced they are with MPS and its underlying concepts (e.g., DSLs, AST, meta model, model transformation).

We used SurveyGizmo (`http://www.surveygizmo.com`) to present the questionnaire to developers. Completion took about 25 minutes, and developers were not compensated for their time. There are no deviations to report.

Participants. We received responses from 21 developers, originating primarily from Europe (mostly Germany, the Netherlands, and Austria) and the US, plus one response from India. All have at least moderate experience with MPS. Eight of them have been using it between one and six months; only two just started, but three have used it for more than two years. The remaining seven developers report experience between half a year and two years. Most of the participants use MPS daily (13 developers), or at least multiple times a week (4); three less than once a week. 43% of developers estimate that they have written between 1,000 and 10,000 lines of code, only few (5%) less than 1,000, and many (29%) even more than 10,000 lines. Thus, our sample represents sufficient experience to establish an informed opinion about MPS.

Our participants have significant programming experience. Two thirds report more than ten years, with only one having less than two years. The experience as professional developer is also high (more than a third of participants report over ten years), but slightly lower on average, with five developers being beginners in professional development. Our most experienced participants were a managing director and a director of research and development with 24 years of experience. All but five participants have used a ParE-based IDE before, mostly Eclipse (62%) and Visual Studio (48%). The participants also have significant experience with model-driven development (MDD) and language engineering; this is not necessarily surprising, since MPS is a language engineering tool. For each of the

nine MDD concepts (meta model, AST, grammar, DSL, textual DSL, graphical
DSL, model transformation, M2T, and M2M), the majority reported being *very
familiar*. The highest familiarity could be seen for meta model, AST, and textual
DSL, while it was lower (but still on a high level) for graphical DSL and model
transformation. Two thirds of all participants have used or designed a DSL
before.

Usage. Our participants report using MPS in a variety of domains – mostly
automotive and embedded systems (these are the mbeddr users), but also the
web, mobile, insurance, and enterprise resource planning. The majority of participants uses MPS as a programmer, while half of these also develop language
extensions for mbeddr, indicating some more in-depth experience and language-
design knowledge. One of them reported using it for his Master's thesis. Only
three participants exclusively develop language extensions.

We now show the answers to how developers perceive various aspects of MPS,
as assessed by the Likert-scale questions, shown in Fig. 2.

Efficiently Entering (Textual) Code (EE).   Regarding Efficiency, most
developers agree that they can write code as fast as with a ParE (median: 2;
min/max: 1/5). Only one developer strongly disagrees, but explains that he is a
proficient Emacs user ("Years of investment in Emacs are hard to beat."). One
user also disagrees, but indicates that this is because he is a novice MPS user. A
second developer who disagrees states that while code entering may not be that
efficient, it is less error-prone, increasing overall efficiency. The remaining participants state that after getting used to the different style of entering code, there is
no difference in efficiency to ParEs. We also asked about the general perception
of Productivity with MPS. Most developers are positive in this respect (median:
2; min/max: 1/5). While 28% express a neutral opinion, 40% agree, and 28%
even strongly agree. Only one participant expressed strong disagreement. This
participant also faced intensive learning effort and stated that becoming familiar with the environment was difficult, mainly since all of MPS' concepts were
completely new to him. In contrast, he strongly agrees that he can write code
as fast as with a ParE, arguing that the code-completion facilities significantly
contribute to the productivity. We conclude that after a learning phase, MPS
lets developers work efficiently and productively.

Selecting and Modifying Code (SM).   We asked developers what they
think about producing correct programs with MPS (Correctness) and that they
can produce only valid ASTs (CorrectAST). Most developers agree that these
are supported well with MPS (median for both: 2). Many developers state that
compared to a ParE, MPS does neither provide an advantage nor a disadvantage,
because "the main type of errors are logical errors, which are not influenced by
the IDE." Those who agree state that the error prevention in MPS is related
to the fact that they can produce only valid ASTs. However, this enforcement
of valid ASTs is also perceived as a drawback, because it reduces flexibility
during programming: "Sometimes though, it would be nice to introduce classes,

interfaces etc. by just using them, and then let the development environment generate the appropriate types if ordered so by the user via a quickfix".[1]

All participants agree that they benefit from the modular language support of MPS (median: 1, min/max: 1/2), confirming one of the key benefits of MPS. One developer states: "Language composition is the main strength of MPS." Regarding the support for different notations, the flexible notations provide a considerable benefit for developers (median: 2, min/max: 1/3), especially for integrating stakeholders from different domains ("My DSL users are business

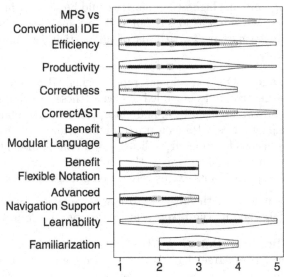

Fig. 2. Overview of Survey Answers

people, not IT people. Being able to use mathematical notations for Sum and Product expressions, fraction bars for division, tabular notations for test cases is crucial."). No problems were reported with the usability of these non-text editors.

Developers are often not satisfied with the commenting support of MPS, which is consistent with the shortcomings of the commenting facilities discussed earlier (Section 4.2). Developers complain about two main issues. The first one is the problems with (temporarily) commenting code ("You always have to use some workarounds, like cutting out program fragments ..."). The other one is the convenience of free text editing[2] inside documentation comments ("The editing of text is not straight forward ..."). We conclude that, except for supporting comments, MPS addresses the issue of selecting and modifying code quite well.

General Usability. In addition to the three dimensions, we asked about the general usability of MPS. In general, developers like the advanced navigation support of MPS (median: 2; min/max: 1/3). Especially the direct navigation on the AST is a key advantage. This is especially true for the language engineers, as one user expresses: "Because of the direct navigation of the AST many features (refactoring, quick fixes, etc.) are easy to build." Participants expressed mixed feelings about learnability and familiarization. When asked whether MPS and its facilities are easy to learn and getting used to, more than half of our participants

---

[1] mbeddr C provides such quick fixes (see Section 4, EE.2), but MPS' Java does not. This was a Java user.

[2] The plugin that supports unstructured free text editing for documentation and comments is a recent addition to MPS. Since the time of the survey, it has been improved significantly. It is now used to write the complete mbeddr user guide.

express a negative or neutral opinion, only few agree or strongly agree. Interestingly, the results become slightly more negative if we only consider participants who are both language users and language engineers (median: 4; min/max: 1/5). Thus, we conjecture that their perception was biased by the language development facilities in MPS, which require mastery of more advanced concepts than just *using* MPS languages to write programs. In fact, in the comment field, the respective participants reported only about issues related to language development. Just considering language users yields a more positive result (median: 3; min/max: 2/4, for both learnability and familiarization). One language engineer explained his positive attitude: "I have much experience and knowledge in language development, and given this background, MPS is rather logically structured. From this point of view, learning how to use MPS to build a new language [...] is not hard." Thus, with sufficient experience in language development, the learnability of MPS seems not to be a problem. Looking at more inexperienced programmers, we found that one problem of learning MPS is insufficient documentation, as stated by the same developer: "However, for certain specialist areas within MPS, there is a lack of good or enough documentation."

Since documentation is not a conceptual issue, we believe that learnability of MPS can be considerably improved with sufficient documentation. To address this, the MPS developers can build on the results of this survey.

Summary. In general, the perception of MPS is positive. While the majority agrees that working with MPS can be productive, developers see some difficulty in learning (Learnability) and getting used to MPS (Familiarization). The overarching opinion regarding usability can be summarized in one sentence: MPS takes a while to get used to, but then its usability is comparable to ParEs. The stated advantages of ProjE, such as the flexible notations and modular languages, are also confirmed by our participants. However, there is also room for improvement: the hotspots expressed by the participants are in line with those problems identified in Section 3, for which MPS does not yet have satisfactory answers.

Threats to Validity. To increase *external validity*, we ensured that all participants have significant prior experience with MDD. Thus, our survey results and conclusions about usability primarily apply to such developers. However, we had one beginner in our survey (participants were allowed to forward the survey to other MPS users). Thus, our results are slightly biased by this beginner, but at the same time give us valuable insights into the struggles that new MPS users face. We are currently planning a controlled experiment with students to further explore how beginners learn MPS. Regarding the results, we can carefully generalize beyond MPS based on the assumption that other ProjE can adopt MPS' usability-improving techniques, but further studies would improve the external validity. A threat to *internal validity* is that the results may be influenced by specific technical issues with MPS (or bugs), and are unrelated to the conceptual usability issues, as identified in Section 3. We mitigate this threat by targeting experienced developers, and cross-checking the experience with multiple questions in the survey questionnaire. To minimize biasing our participants, we asked them explicitly for the advantages and disadvangtes of MPS. By replicating our study, these threats can be reduced further. *construct validity*, i.e, to ensure that our survey measures usability correctly, we consulted the usability heuristics by Nielsen [32] before creating the questionnaire.

5.2   Infrastructure Integration

We now report on industrial experiences to evaluate the effectiveness of MPS infrastructure-integration support.

Version Control.   Since 06/2011, a team growing from five to eight people has been developing mbeddr based on MPS. Starting 07/2013, Siemens PLM has started developing a commercial tool on top of mbeddr, adding an additional four people to the team. Some of the mbeddr languages are also used in different domains, and two more developers are now working on the code base. This leads to a total of fourteen people. The work is spread over four git repositories[3]. In addition, two developers from BMW Car IT (plus two from mbeddr) worked on an SVN repository to develop an AUTOSAR extension for mbeddr.

In 2011 there were a few problems with merging; some changes just disappeared. This has since been fixed, and since 2012 no more problems have occurred with the VCS integration (git and SVN). Two aspects have to be kept on mind for it to work. First, diff and merge has to be done within MPS. Since all team members work with MPS anyway, this is not a problem. Second, if an update contains changes to languages as well programs that use these languages, users have to make sure to first merge and rebuild the languages. Otherwise MPS cannot correctly show the diff of programs written with these languages.

Continuous Integration.   mbeddr, as well as the projects built with it, use Jet-Brains Teamcity as an integration server[4]. It generates and compiles languages, runs tests, and packages the mbeddr system as MPS plugins. Even though Teamcity is also developed by JetBrains, there is no specific integration: it simply calls `ant` which in turn use MPS-provided `ant` tasks for building and testing.

Summary.   VCS integration and building on the server are the two most important concerns in terms of infrastructure integration. As discussed above, they are supported well. Used together with the mbeddr utilities for interoperability with textual environments discussed in Section 4.3, we conclude that infrastructure integration is addressed well enough to make MPS usable in practice. The mbeddr-specific extensions should be integrated directly into MPS, though.

6   Remaining Issues and Further Improvement

Automatically Deriving Actions   The editor usability facilities have to be implemented manually for each language. While MPS provides DSLs to do this efficiently (and to a degree, generically), this is still tedious and error-prone. It

---

[3] including the open source repo at https://github.com/mbeddr/mbeddr.core

[4] The CI server is at https://build.mbeddr.com; log in as guest.

is easy to forget some of the facilities for some language concepts, leading to an inconsistent user experience. One approach of addressing this problem is to describe textual-looking languages with a more grammar-like formalism from which many of the necessary editor facilities can be derived automatically. Both the MPS and mbeddr teams are currently experimenting with this approach.

Automatic Rebinding.   Consider a reference to a global variable v. If v is deleted, references to it break. Consider further that later, a new node named v is created, possibly a global variable or a function. The old references should now be bound to the new v. Currently, this is not supported; all reference sites have to be manually rebound by selecting the target from the code-completion menu. MPS 3.1 will support automatic rebinding of references based on target names stored in the (broken) references and existing scoping rules.

Legacy Import.   One use case of a ProjE is providing state-of-the-art IDE support and language extension and composition facilities for existing programming languages. To make this possible, the language must be reimplemented in MPS. The effort to do this is limited; it took the mbeddr team about five person months to implement C. However, in this scenario, interoperability with textual C code is necessary. Currently, a parser that creates MPS trees from text has to be implemented manually. If the aforementioned grammar-like formalisms were available, the necessary parser could potentially be automatically derived as well.

Command-Line Support.   While MPS supports command-line integration for building and testing models, it is not possible to simply `grep` MPS models for text strings (beyond simple names). This is because programs are not stored in their concrete syntax notation. To address this problem, a textual representation of the program could be stored along with the AST-based persistence.

What You See Is Not What You Type.   We are currently experimenting with two ideas for entering notations that are not on the keyboard. The first one simply shows the alias in a tooltip over the respective symbol. The second alternative uses a palette that contains buttons to enter those special notations.

Generic Commenting.   As confirmed by the survey, generic support for commenting (documentation as well as commenting out code) is necessary. Most likely this requires specific support by MPS' projectional editor. The MPS and mbeddr teams are currently discussing various approaches to the problem.

7   Conclusion

We have analyzed the usability of projectional editors, discussed mitigation techniques, and evaluated them by surveying professional developers. Our results show that the benefits of better language composition and notational flexibility are impaired by significant usability issues, but that the majority of those can be sufficiently mitigated with the facilities provided by MPS and discussed in this paper. In fact, the surveyed professional developers confirm the effectiveness of these mitigations in their every-day work, while the learning curve is high, requiring additional training. Further, our industrial experiences indicate MPS' usefulness for large-scale development projects. Thus, we believe that projectional editing can be efficient in projects that benefit from language composition and diverse syntax – outweighing the remaining usability issues. We believe this generalization is justified in the sense that MPS establishes a minimum viable set of techniques for improving editor usability that can be adopted by other ProjEs.

Our results can be used in various ways. The categorization of usability issues allows us to characterize ProjEs in general. The discussed mitigation techniques establish a minimal baseline for usability of ProjEs. Our empirical survey data indicates the cost (training and learning investment) to benefit (language composition, notational diversity, and potentially fewer errors) ratio, which can be used to assess the applicability of ProjEs in concrete projects.

Our future work is two-fold. First, we will investigate the remaining usability issues not currently addressed in MPS. Second, we aim at understanding adoption challenges, problem solving patterns, and efficiency with editing operations using a controlled experiment. It will comprise both beginning and professional developers (subset of survey participants), whose behavior when using a ProjE is compared to developers relying on a ParE. This experiment will complement our present work by providing an in-depth behavior analysis.

Acknowledgements. We thank Alexander Shatalin, Vaclav Pech and Konstantin Solomatov for clarifying details about MPS and feedback to this paper.

References

1. Green, T.R.: Cognitive dimensions of notations. People and Computers V, 443–460 (1989)
2. Simonyi, C.: The death of computer languages, the birth of intentional programming. In: NATO Science Committee Conference (1995)
3. Czarnecki, K., Ulrich, E.: Generative Programming: Methods, Tools, and Applications. Addison-Wesley, Reading (2000)
4. Medina-Mora, R., Feiler, P.H.: An Incremental Programming Environment. IEEE Trans. Software Eng. 7(5) (1981)
5. Notkin, D.: The GANDALF project. Journal of Systems and Software 5(2) (1985)
6. Porter, S.W.: Design of a syntax directed editor for psdl (prototype systems design language). Master's thesis, Naval Postgraduate School, Monterey, CA, USA (1988)
7. Reps, T.W., Teitelbaum, T.: The Synthesizer Generator. In: First ACM SIGSOFT-/SIGPLAN Software Engineering Symposium on Practical Software Development Environments. ACM (1984)
8. Voelter, M.: Language and IDE Modularization and Composition with MPS. In: Lämmel, R., Saraiva, J., Visser, J. (eds.) GTTSE 2011. LNCS, vol. 7680, pp. 383–430. Springer, Heidelberg (2013)
9. Simonyi, C., Christerson, M., Clifford, S.: Intentional Software. In: OOPSLA 2006. ACM (2006)

10. Christerson, M., Kolk, H.: Domain expert DSLs (2009) talk at QCon London 2009 (2009), http://www.infoq.com/presentations/DSL-Magnus-Christerson-Henk-Kolk

11. Diekmann, L., Tratt, L.: Parsing composed grammars with language boxes. In: Workshop on Scalable Language Specifications (2013)

12. Simi, M., Campagne, F.: Composable Languages for Bioinformatics: The NYoSh experiment. PeerJ PrePrints 1:e112v2 (2013)

13. Voelter, M., Ratiu, D., Tomassetti, F.: Requirements as first-class citizens. In: Proceedings of ACES-MB Workshop (2013)

14. Steinberg, D., Budinsky, F., Merks, E., Paternostro, M.: EMF: eclipse modeling framework. Pearson Education (2008)

15. Voelter, M., Ratiu, D., Kolb, B., Schaetz, B.: mbeddr: instantiating a language workbench in the embedded software domain. Automated Software Engineering 20(3), 1–52 (2013)

16. Voelter, M.: Preliminary experience of using mbeddr. In: 10th Dagstuhl Workshop on Model-based Development of Embedded Systems, p. 10 (2014)

17. Coplien, J.O.: Multi-paradigm Design for C+. Addison-Wesley (1999)

18. Kats, L.C.L., Visser, E., Wachsmuth, G.: Pure and declarative syntax definition: paradise lost and regained. In: Proceedings of OOPSLA 2010. ACM (2010)

19. Parr, T.J., Quong, R.W.: ANTLR: A Predicated-LL(k) Parser Generator. Software: Practice and Experience 25(7) (1995)

20. Heering, J., Hendriks, P.R.H., Klint, P., Rekers, J.: The syntax definition formalism SDF - reference manual. SIGPLAN 24(11) (1989)

21. Bravenboer, M., Dolstra, E., Visser, E.: Preventing injection attacks with syntax embeddings. In: GPCE 2007, Salzburg, Austria. ACM (2007)

22. Wyk, E.V., Bodin, D., Gao, J., Krishnan, L.: Silver: an Extensible Attribute Grammar System. ENTCS 203(2) (2008)

23. Lämmel, R., Wachsmuth, G.: Transformation of sdf syntax definitions in the asf+sdf meta-environment. Electronic Notes in Theoretical Computer Science 44(2), 9–33 (2001)

24. Anderson, R.: Two-dimensional mathematical notation. In: Fu, K. (ed.) Syntactic Pattern Recognition, Applications. Communication and Cybernetics, vol. 14. Springer (1977)

25. Helm, R., Marriott, K., Odersky, M.: Building visual language parsers. In: Proc. ACM SIGCHI Conf. on Human Factors in Computing Systems, pp. 105–112 (1991)

26. Giammarresi, D., Restivo, A.: Two-dimensional languages. In: Rozenberg, G., Salomaa, A. (eds.) Handbook of Formal Languages. Springer (1997)

27. Pruša, D.: Two-dimensional context-free grammars. In: ITAT 2001, pp. 27–40 (2001)

28. van Rest, O., Wachsmuth, G., Steel, J.R.H., Süß, J.G., Visser, E.: Robust real-time synchronization between textual and graphical editors. In: Duddy, K., Kappel, G. (eds.) ICMB 2013. LNCS, vol. 7909, pp. 92–107. Springer, Heidelberg (2013)

29. Voelter, M.: Integrating prose as first-class citizens with models and code. In: 7th International Workshop on Multi-Paradigm Modeling, MPM 2013, p. 17 (2013)

30. Online Appendix, http://gsd.uwaterloo.ca/projectional-workbenches

31. Likert, R.: A technique for the measurement of attitudes. Archives of Psychology (1932)

32. Nielsen, J.: Usability Engineering. Morgan Kaufmann Publishers (1994)

Bounded Seas
— Island Parsing Without Shipwrecks

Jan Kurš, Mircea Lungu, and Oscar Nierstrasz

Software Composition Group, University of Bern, Switzerland
http://scg.unibe.ch

Abstract. Imprecise manipulation of source code (semi-parsing) is useful for tasks such as robust parsing, error recovery, lexical analysis, and rapid development of parsers for data extraction. An island grammar precisely defines only a subset of a language syntax (islands), while the rest of the syntax (water) is defined imprecisely.

Usually, water is defined as the negation of islands. Albeit simple, such a definition of water is naive and impedes composition of islands. When developing an island grammar, sooner or later a programmer has to create water tailored to each individual island. Such an approach is fragile, however, because water can change with any change of a grammar. It is time-consuming, because water is defined manually by a programmer and not automatically. Finally, an island surrounded by water cannot be reused because water has to be defined for every grammar individually.

In this paper we propose a new technique of island parsing — bounded seas. Bounded seas are composable, robust, reusable and easy to use because island-specific water is created automatically. We integrated bounded seas into a parser combinator framework as a demonstration of their composability and reusability.

1 Introduction

Island grammars [1] offer a way to parse input without complete knowledge of the target grammar. They are especially useful for extracting selected information from source files, for reverse engineering and similar applications. The approach assumes that only a subset of the language syntax is known (the islands), while the rest of the syntax is undefined (the water). During parsing, any unrecognized input (water) is skipped until an island is found.

The common misconception is that water should consume everything until an island is detected. Such a water is easy to define, but it causes composability problems. To be specific, such a water does not allow islands to be embedded into the optional or repetitive rules without giving misleading results. To be correct, water should stop when any of a number of possible islands is encountered. Small changes in the grammar may radically change the nature of the water.

To define an island grammar that will return the unambiguous and correct result we have to define specific water manually for each particular island, contrary to one global water. Yet island-specific water is fragile, hard to define and

B. Combemale et al. (Eds.): SLE 2014, LNCS 8706, pp. 62–81, 2014.
© Springer International Publishing Switzerland 2014

it is not reusable. It is fragile, because it requires reevaluation by a programmer after any change in a grammar. It is hard to define, because it requires the programmer's time for detailed analysis of a grammar. It is not reusable, because island-specific water depends on rules following the island, thus it is tailored to the context in which the island is used — it is not general.

In this paper we suggest a new technique for island parsing: *bounded seas.* Bounded seas are composable, reusable, robust and easy to use. The key idea of bounded seas is that specialized water is defined for each particular island (depending on the context of the island) so that an island can be embedded into optional or repetitive rules. To achieve such composability, an island is never searched behind a boundary defined by the rule following the island. To prevent fragility and to improve reusability, we describe how to compute water automatically, without user interaction. To prove feasibility, we integrated bounded seas into Petit Parser [2], a PEG–based parser combinator framework [3].

The contributions of the paper are: a) a description of bounded seas — a composable, reusable, robust and easy method of island parsing; b) a formalization of the process leading to an island grammar for PEGs; c) and an implementation of bounded seas in a PEG-based parser combinator framework.

Structure. Section 2 motivates this work by presenting the limitations of island grammars with an example. Section 3 presents our solution to overcoming these limitations by introducing bounded seas. Section 4 presents a sea operator for PEGs, which creates bounded sea from an arbitrary PEG expression. Section 5 discusses implementation, applicability of bounded seas in GLL and presents a Java code analysis case study that compares bounded seas with island grammars. Section 6 presents other semi-parsing techniques and highlights similarities and differences between them and bounded seas. Finally, section 7 concludes this paper.

2   Motivating Example

Let us consider the domain specific source code from Listing 1.1. We don't have a grammar specification for the code, because the parser was written using *ad hoc* techniques and the parser code is proprietary. Let us suppose that our task is to extract class and method names.

```
class Shape
    Color color;

    method getColor {
        return color;
    }
    int uid = UIDGenerator.newUID;
endclass
```

Listing 1.1. Source code of the **Shape** class in a proprietary language

2.1   A Naive Island Grammar

To extract the method names, we need a parser. To write a parser, we need a grammar. Because the grammar can easily consist of a hundred rules (*e.g.*, ≈ 80 for Python, ≈ 180 for Java) and since we do not want to spend many hours defining them, we define an island grammar in PEG (see Appendix A) with fewer than ten rules as in Listing 1.2. We initially assume that each class body contains just one method.

The `method` rule is an island. The `methodSea` rule represents a '*method*' island surrounded by water. The `methodSea` rule is defined imprecisely: water skips everything until '*method*' is found. Similarly we define the `methodBody` rule, which consumes an open curly bracket and then skips everything until the closing curly bracket is found.

```
start        ← class
class        ← 'class' id classBody 'endclass'
classBody    ← methodSea

methodSea    ← (!'method' ·)* method (!'endclass'·)*

method       ← 'method' id methodBody
methodBody   ← '{' (!'}' ·)* '}'

id           ← letter (letter / number)*
letter       ← 'a' / 'b' / 'c' ···
number       ← '1' / '2' / '3' ···
```

Listing 1.2. Our first island grammar

Composability Problems. The `methodSea` rule in the grammar in Listing 1.2 uses the naive definition of water. It will work as long as we do not complicate the grammar.

Suppose we now allow multiple classes in a single file (`start  ←  class*`). Parsing the input in Listing 1.3 should fail because `Shape` does not contain a method. However the result, no matter whether we use PEG or CFG, is only one class — `Shape` (instead of `Shape` and `Circle`) — with a method `getDiameter` , which is wrong.

Things do not get better when we allow multiple repetitions of `methodSea` s in a `classBody` (`classBody  ←  methodSea*`). The parser will stay confused and depending on the technology (PEG, CFG), the result will be either incorrect (PEG) or ambiguous (CFG). In case of the ambiguous results, it is nice to know that one of the many results is correct, but how can we know which one?

```
class Shape
    int uid = UIDGenerator.newUID;
endclass

class Circle
    int diameter;

    method getDiameter {
        return diameter;
    }
endclass
```

Listing 1.3. Source code of **Shape** and **Circle** classes

2.2   An Advanced Island Grammar

To make the **methodSea** composable we must make it possible for it to be
embedded into optional (**?**) or repetition (**+** , *****) rules. Thus, we define the
grammar as in Listing 1.4. This new definition can properly parse multiple classes
in a file with an arbitrary number of methods in a class.

```
start       ←  class*
class       ←  'class' id classBody 'endclass'
classBody   ←  (methodSea)*

methodSea   ←  (!'method' !'endclass' .)*
                  method
               (!'method' !'endclass' .)*

method      ←  'method' id methodBody
methodBody  ←  '{'
               (
                 (!'}' !'{' .)*
                   methodBody
                 (!'}' !'{' .)*
               )*
               '}'

id          ←  letter (letter / number)*
letter      ←  'a' / 'b' / 'c' ···
number      ←  '1' / '2' / '3' ···
```

Listing 1.4. Complete and final island grammar

One can see that the syntactic predicates in the **methodSea** are more complicated. They have been inferred from the rest of the grammar by analyzing
what tokens can appear behind the **method** island.

Ease of Use, Robustness, and Reusability Problems. The limitations of defining the `methodSea` by hand are illustrative of the general problems of semi-parsing:

1. Such a definition is time-consuming to produce because it requires programmer's time to analyze the grammar.
2. The definition is fragile, because the predicates need to be re-evaluated after any change in a grammar (*e.g.*, adding inner classes will result in adding `!'class'` into the predicates).
3. Last but not least, the `methodSea` is tailored just for the grammar in Listing 1.4 *e.g.*, it cannot be re-used in a grammar that does not use `'endclass'` as a keyword.

3   Bounded Seas

3.1   The Sea Operator in a Nutshell

We have shown that water must be tailored both to the island within the sea and to the surroundings of the sea (*e.g.*, `methodSea` in Listing 1.4). In this paper, we define a *bounded sea* to be an island surrounded by context-aware water.

To automate the definition of bounded seas we introduce a new operator for building tolerant grammars: *the sea operator*. We use the notation ~island~ to create sea from `island`, which can be a terminal or non-terminal. Instead of having to produce complex definitions of sea, a programmer can use the sea operator which will do the hard work. Listing 1.5 presents how the grammar in Listing 1.4 is defined using the sea operator:

```
class      ← 'class' id classBody 'endclass'
classBody  ← methodSea*

methodSea  ← ~method~
method     ← 'method' id methodBody

methodBody ← '{' ~(methodBody / ε)~* '}'

id         ← letter (letter / number)*
letter     ← 'a' / 'b' / 'c' ···
number     ← '1' / '2' / '3' ···
```

Listing 1.5. Island Grammar from Listing 1.4 rewritten with the sea operator

A rule defined with the sea operator (*e.g.*, ~method~) maintains the composability property of the advanced grammar since by applying the sea operator we search for the island in a restricted scope. Moreover, such a rule is reusable, robust, and uncomplicated to define.

Conceptually two ideas are fundamental for bounded seas.

1. Water is defined for each island so that the search for an island will never cross the boundary defined by the rule that follows the island. For example, `method` islands will be searched only within a class and not in a whole file. The search boundary ensures composability.
2. Water computation in bounded seas is fully automated. The sea is created using the sea operator ~island~ . Once the sea is placed in the grammar, the grammar is analyzed and appropriate water is created without user interaction. This way the sea can be placed in any grammar. In case the grammar is changed, the seas are recomputed automatically. Automatic water computation ensures ease of definition, robustness, and reusability.

Bounded seas can be integrated into a parser combinator framework, a highly modular framework for building a parser from other composable parsers [4]. The fact that a bounded sea can be implemented as a parser combinator demonstrates its composability and flexibility. In fact, the original motivation for this work was the desire to have a reusable approach to semi-parsing that can be integrated with parser combinators.

3.2   The Sea Boundary

A sea boundary limits the scope within which the island can be searched. Water cannot consume anything beyond the boundary. The boundary of the sea consists of the input accepted by any parsing expression that can appear immediately after the island. For example in case of A $\leftarrow$ ~'a'~ (B / C) the boundary of ~'a'~ is any input accepted either by B or by C .

The sea boundary ensures composability. With help of the boundary we can search for methods in a class without the risk that other classes will interfere. This was the issue for the input in Listing 1.3 and the non-bounded grammar from Listing 1.2, which found the **getDiameter** method in the **Shape** class.

The predicates of island-specific water have to be set up so that they stop water in two cases: first, when an island is reached; second, when the boundary is reached. If the boundary is reached before the island is found, water stops and the sea fails. The fact that sea can fail implies that sea can be embedded into optional or repetition expressions. For example, we can define the superclass specification as an optional island.

```
~classDef~ ~superclassSpec~? classBody 'endclass'
```

If **superclassSpec** is not present for the particular class, it will simply fail when reaching **classBody** instead of searching for **superclassSpec** further and further. The same holds for repetitions.

```
classBody ← ~method~*
```

This rule will consume only methods until it reaches '*endclass*' in the input string, since `endclass` forms the boundary of ~method~ , so methods in another class cannot be inadvertently consumed.

We first define bounded seas generally, and later provide a PEG-specific definition.

Definition 1 (Bounded Sea). A *bounded sea* consists of a sequence of three parsing phases:

1. **Before-Water:** Consume the input until an island or the boundary appears. Fail the whole sea if we hit the boundary. Continue if we hit an island.
2. **Island:** Consume an island.
3. **After-Water:** Consume the input until the boundary is reached.

3.3   The Context Sensitivity of Bounded Seas

To make bounded seas useful we decided for a context-sensitive behaviour. A bounded sea recognizes different substrings of an input depending on what surrounds the sea. There are two cases where the context-sensitivity emerges:

1. A bounded sea recognizes different input depending on what immediately follows the sea.
2. A bounded sea recognizes different input depending on what immediately precedes the sea.

Let us demonstrate on rules from Listing 1.6 and two inputs '*..a..b..*' and '*..a..c..*'. On its own, `A` recognizes any input with `'a'` and `B` recognizes any input with `'b'` (see rows 1-4 in Table 1).

```
A   ←  ~'a'~
B   ←  ~'b'~

R1  ←  A              R2  ←  B
R3  ←  A 'b'          R4  ←  A 'c'
R5  ←  A B
```

Listing 1.6. Rules for the context-sensitive behaviour demonstration

However, when the two islands are not alone, their boundary can differ, depending on the context. The boundary of `A` is `'b'` in `R3` and the boundary of `A` is `'c'` in `R4` . Therefore `A` consumes different substrings of input depending whether called from `R3` or `R4` (see rows 5-8 in Table 1).

A more complex case of context-sensitivity, which we call the *overlapping sea problem*, arises when one sea is immediately followed by another. Consider, for example, rule `R5` , where the sea `A` has as its boundary `B` , which is also a sea. Note that the before-water of `B` should consume anything up to its island `'b'` or its own boundary, *including the island of its preceding sea A* . Now,

Table 1. The seas A and B recognize different inputs depending on a context

	Rule	Input	Result
1	R1 ← A	'..a..b..'	A recognizes '..a..b..'
2	R1 ← A	'..a..c..'	A recognizes '..a..c..'
3	R2 ← B	'..a..b..'	B recognizes '..a..b..'
4	R2 ← B	'..a..c..'	B fails
5	R3 ← A 'b'	'..a..b..'	A recognizes '..a..' 'b' recognizes 'b'
6	R3 ← A 'b'	'..a..c..'	A recognizes '..a..b..' 'b' fails
7	R4 ← A 'c'	'..a..b..'	A recognizes '..a..b..' 'c' fails
8	R4 ← A 'c'	'..a..c..'	A recognizes '..a..' 'c' recognizes 'c'
9	R5 ← A B	'..a..b..'	A recognizes '..a..' B recognizes 'b..'
10	R5 ← A B	'..a..c..'	A recognizes '..a..c..' B fails

the before-water of A should consume anything up to either its island 'a' or its boundary B. But the very search for the boundary will now consume the island we are looking for, since B's before-water will consume 'a'! We must therefore take special care to avoid a "shipwreck" in the case of overlapping seas by disabling the before-water of the second sea.

4   Bounded Seas in Parsing Expression Grammars

Starting from the standard definition of PEGs (see Appendix A), we now show how to add the sea operator while avoiding the overlapping sea problem. To define the sea operator, we need the following two abstractions:

1. **The water operator** *consumes uninteresting input* Water ($\approx$) is a new PEG prefix operator that takes as its argument an expression that specifies when the water ends. We discuss this in detail in subsection 4.1.
2. **The NEXT function** *determines the boundary of a sea.* Intuitively, $NEXT(e)$ returns the set of expressions[1] that can appear directly after a particular expression e. The details of the NEXT function are given in subsection 4.2.

Definition 2 (Sea Operator). Given the definitions of $\approx$ and NEXT, we define the sea operator as follows: $\sim$e$\sim$ is a sequence expression

$$\approx(\text{e} \; / \; next_1 \; / \; next_2 \; / \; \cdots \; next_n)$$
$$\text{e}$$
$$\approx(next_1 \; / \; next_2 \; / \; \cdots \; next_n)$$

where $next_i \in NEXT(e)$.

That is, the before-water consumes everything up to the island or the boundary, and the after-water consumes everything up to the boundary.

---

[1] The NEXT function is modelled after FOLLOW sets from parsing theory, except that instead of returning a set of tokens, it returns a set of parsers.

4.1 The *Water* Operator

The purpose of a water expression is to consume uninteresting input. Water consumes input until it encounters the expression specified in its argument (*i.e.,* the *boundary*). We must, however, take care to avoid the overlapping sea problem. If two seas overlap (one sea is followed by another), the second sea bounds the first one. The second sea has to disable its before-water as illustrated in subsection 3.3. We detect overlapping seas as follows: if sea s_1 is invoked from the water of another sea s_2, it means that the water of s_1 is testing for its boundary s_2 and thus s_2 has to disable its before-water. To distinguish between nested seas (*e.g.,* $\sim$'x' $\sim$island$\sim$ 'x'$\sim$) and overlapping seas, we test the position where this sea was invoked. In case of nested seas the positions differ, and in case of overlapping seas they are the same.

Definition 3 (Extended Semantics). In order to detect overlapping seas, we extend the semantics of a PEG $G = \{N, T, R, e_s\}$ with a stack of invoked expressions and their positions. For standard PEG operators there is no change except that an explicit stack S is maintained. We define a relation $\Rightarrow_G$ from tuples of the form (x, S) to the output o, where $x \in T^*$ is an input string to be recognized, $S \notin N$ is a stack consisting of tuples (e, p), where $p \geq 0$ is a position and e is a parsing expression, and $o \in T^* \cup \{f\}$ indicates the result of a recognition attempt. The distinguished symbol $f \notin T$ indicates failure. Function $len(x)$ returns a length of an input x. Function $(e, p) : S$ denotes a stack with tuple (e, p) on the top and stack S below. For $((x, S), o) \in \Rightarrow_G$ we write $(x, S) \Rightarrow o$.

We define $\Rightarrow_G$ inductively as follows (without any semantic changes for standard PEG operators):

$$\textbf{Empty:} \quad \frac{x \in T^*}{(x, (\epsilon, p) : S) \Rightarrow \epsilon}$$

$$\textbf{Terminal (success case):} \quad \frac{a \in T, x \in T^*}{(ax, (a, p) : S) \Rightarrow a}$$

$$\textbf{Terminal (failure case):} \quad \frac{a \neq b \quad (a, \epsilon, S) \Rightarrow f}{(bx, (a, p) : S) \Rightarrow f}$$

$$\textbf{Nonterminal:} \quad \frac{A \leftarrow e \in R \quad (x, (e, p) : S) \Rightarrow o}{(x, (A, p) : S) \Rightarrow o}$$

$$\textbf{Sequence (success case):} \quad \frac{\begin{array}{c}(x_1 x_2 y, (e_1, p) : S) \Rightarrow x_1 \\ (x_2 y, (e_2, p + len(x_1)) : S) \Rightarrow x_2\end{array}}{(x_1 x_2 y, (e_1 e_2, p) : S) \Rightarrow x_1 x_2}$$

$$\textbf{Sequence (failure case):} \quad \frac{(x, (e_1, p) : S) \Rightarrow f}{(x, (e_1 e_2, p) : S) \Rightarrow f}$$

$$\textbf{Sequence (failure case 2):} \quad \frac{\begin{array}{c}(xy, (e_1, p) : S) \Rightarrow x \\ (y, (e_2, p + len(x)) : S) \Rightarrow f\end{array}}{(xy, (e_1 e_2, p) : S) \Rightarrow f}$$

$$\text{Alternation (case 1):} \quad \frac{(xy, (e_1, p) : S) \Rightarrow x}{(x, (e_1/e_2, p) : S) \Rightarrow x}$$

$$\text{Alternation (case 2):} \quad \frac{\begin{array}{c}(x, (e_1, p) : S) \Rightarrow f \\ (x, (e_2, p) : S) \Rightarrow o\end{array}}{(x, (e_1/e_2, p) : S) \Rightarrow o}$$

$$\text{Repetitions (repetition case):} \quad \frac{\begin{array}{c}(x_1 x_2 y, (e, p) : S) \Rightarrow x_1 \\ (x_2, (e*, p + len(x_1)) : S) \Rightarrow x_2\end{array}}{(x_1 x_2 y, (e*, p) : S) \Rightarrow x_1 x_2}$$

$$\text{Repetitions (termination case):} \quad \frac{(x, (e, p) : S) \Rightarrow f}{(x, (e*, p) : S) \Rightarrow \epsilon}$$

$$\text{Not predicate (case 1):} \quad \frac{(xy, (e, p) : S) \Rightarrow x}{(xy, (!e, p) : S) \Rightarrow f}$$

$$\text{Not predicate (case 2):} \quad \frac{(xy, (e, p) : S) \Rightarrow f}{(xy, (!e, p) : S) \Rightarrow \epsilon}$$

Definition 4 (Water Operator). With the extended semantics of PEGs we can define a prefix **water operator** $\approx$. It searches for a boundary and consumes input until it reaches a boundary. If the water starts a boundary of another sea, it stops immediately. Function $seasOverlap(S, p_1)$ returns true if there is a pair ($\approx e, p_2$) on a stack S where $p_1 = p_2$ and e is any parsing expression and returns false otherwise. $x \in T^*$, $y \in T^*$, $z \in T^*$ and function $substring(x)$ returns set of all substrings of x.

$$\text{Overlapping seas case:} \quad \frac{seasOverlap(S, p)}{(x, (\approx e, p) : S) = \epsilon}$$

$$\text{Boundary found case:} \quad \frac{\begin{array}{c}(yz, (e, p) : S) \Rightarrow y \\ (x'', (e, p + len(x')) : S) \Rightarrow f \ \forall x = x'x''x'''\end{array}}{(xyz, (\approx e, p) : S) = x}$$

$$\text{End of input case:} \quad \frac{(yz, (e, pos(x)) : S) \Rightarrow f}{(xyz, (\approx e, p) : S) = xyz}$$

In case of *directly nested seas* (e.g., $\sim\sim$island$\sim\sim$) we obtain the same behaviour as with $\sim$island$\sim$. The function $seasOverlap$ returns true in case a sea is directly invoked from another sea without consuming any input. Applying the rule *Overlapping seas* from Definition 4, water of the inner sea is eliminated and the boundary is the same for the both seas. Therefore $\sim\sim$island$\sim\sim$ is equivalent to $\sim$island$\sim$.

4.2   The NEXT Function

The purpose of the NEXT function is to determine the boundary of a sea. The boundary is an expression that consumes whatever follows the sea. Consider the

```
code         ←  (~class~/~struct~)* mainMethod
class        ←  'class'  ID classBody
stuct        ←  'struct' ID sbody
mainMethod   ←  'public' 'method' 'main' methodBody

classBody    ←  ...
sbody        ←  ...
methodBody   ←  ...
ID           ←  ...
```

Listing 1.7. Definition of code that consists of classes and structures followed by main method

grammar in the example from Listing 1.7. The `code` is defined in a way that it accepts an arbitrary number of class and structure islands in the beginning (classes and structures can be in any order) and there is a main method at the end. Intuitively, another class island, a structure island or a main method can appear after a class island.

The boundary has to be something "solid". An optional expression itself is not a good boundary, because it succeeds for any input. Consider a simple expression ~e~ 'a'? 'b' 'c' . The 'a'? can appear behind the *'island'* but 'b' as well, if 'a' fails. It is certainly not 'c' because it always succeeds 'b' . In this case we have to define a boundary as 'a?' 'b' (not only 'a'?).

Definition 5 (Abstract Simulation). In order to recognize a solid expression we define a relation representing an abstract simulation [5]. We define a relation $\rightharpoonup_G$ consisting of pairs (e, o), where e is an expression and $o \in \{0, 1, f\}$. We will write $e \rightharpoonup o$ for $(e, o) \in \rightharpoonup_G$. If $e \rightharpoonup 0$, then e can succeed on some input while consuming no input. If $e \rightharpoonup 1$, then e can succeed on some input while consuming at least one terminal. If $e \rightharpoonup f$, then e may fail on some input. We will use variable s to represent a $\rightharpoonup_G$ outcome of either 0 or 1. We will define the simulation relation $\rightharpoonup_G$ as follows:

1. $\epsilon \rightharpoonup 0$.
2. $t \rightharpoonup 1, t \in T$.
3. $t \rightharpoonup f, t \in T$.
4. $A \rightharpoonup o$ if $R_G(A) \rightharpoonup o$.
5. $e_1 e_2 \rightharpoonup 0$ if $e_1 \rightharpoonup 0$ and $e_2 \rightharpoonup 0$.
   $e_1 e_2 \rightharpoonup 1$ if $e_1 \rightharpoonup 1$ and $e_2 \rightharpoonup s$.
   $e_1 e_2 \rightharpoonup 1$ if $e_1 \rightharpoonup s$ and $e_2 \rightharpoonup 1$.
6. $e_1 e_2 \rightharpoonup f$ if $e_1 \rightharpoonup f$
7. $e_1 e_2 \rightharpoonup f$ if $e_1 \rightharpoonup s$ and $e_2 \rightharpoonup f$.
8. $e_1/e_2 \rightharpoonup s$ if $e_1 \rightharpoonup s$
9. $e_1/e_2 \rightharpoonup o$ if $e_1 \rightharpoonup f$ and $e_2 \rightharpoonup o$.
10. $e* \rightharpoonup 1$ if $e \rightharpoonup 1$

11. $e* \rightharpoonup 0$ if $e \rightharpoonup f$
12. $!e \rightharpoonup f$ if $e \rightharpoonup s$
13. $!e \rightharpoonup 0$ if $e \rightharpoonup f$

Because this relation does not depend on the input string, and there are a finite number of expressions in a grammar, we can compute this relation over any grammar [5].

Definition 6 (NEXT). If S is a stack of *(expression, position)* pairs representing positions and invoked parsing expressions and if $\overline{\triangle}(S)$ pops an element from the stack S returning a stack S' without the top element and if $s_n, s_{n-1}, ..s_2, s_1$ are expressions on the stack S (top of the stack is to the left, bottom to the right) and if $\square$ is a sequence formed from two sets of parsing expressions such that $S_1 \square S_2 = \{e_i e_j | e_i \in S_1, e_j \in S_2\}$, we define *NEXT(S)* as a set of expressions such that:

- if $s_{n-1} = e_1 e_2$ and $s_n = e_1$ and $e_2 \not\rightharpoonup 0$ then $NEXT(S) = \{e_2\}$
- if $s_{n-1} = e_1 e_2$ and $s_n = e_1$ and $e_2 \rightharpoonup 0$ then $NEXT(S) = \{e_2\} \square NEXT(\overline{\triangle}(S))$
- if $s_{n-1} = e_1 e_2$ and $s_n = e_2$ then $NEXT(S) = NEXT(\overline{\triangle}(S))$
- if $s_{n-1} = e_1/e_2$ and $s_n = e_1$ or $s_n = e_2$ then $NEXT(S) = NEXT(\overline{\triangle}(S))$
- if $s_{n-1} = e*$ and $e = s_n$ then $NEXT(S) = e \cup NEXT(\overline{\triangle}(S))$
- if $s_{n-1} = !e$ and $e = s_n$ then $NEXT(S) = \{\}$

5   Discussion

5.1   Implementation

As a validation of bounded sea composability and reusability we provide an implementation of bounded sea in a PetitParser framework.[2]

5.2   Java Parser Case Study

In the following section we compare four kinds of Java parsers.

1. **PetitJava** is an open source Java parser written using PetitParser [2] by the community around the Moose analysis platform[6]. We used the latest version available online[3].
2. **Naive Island Parser** is an island parser with water defined as a negation of an island. The sea rules in this parser can be reused, because they do not consider their surroundings and they are grammar-independent. The sea rules are defined in a simple form: consume input until an island is found, then consume an island.

---

[2] http://scg.unibe.ch/research/islandparsing/sle2014
[3] http://smalltalkhub.com/#!/~Moose/PetitJava/

3. **Advanced Island Parser** is a more complex version of the naive island parser. The water is more complicated to prevent the most frequent failures of island parser. The sea rules in this parser are hard-wired to the grammar and cannot be reused. The sea rules are customized for a particular islands.
4. **Island Parser with Bounded Seas** is an island parser written using bounded seas. The sea rules were defined using the sea operator.

The PetitJava parser parses Java code[4]. All the island parsers are very similar between themselves, with a similar number of rules. The island parsers were designed to extract only method names in a class. None of the parsers was optimized to provide a better performance.

In this section we compare the three island parsers (almost identical in a structure) written by the first author. Very probably, the advanced island parser can be updated so that it achieves better precision and better performance, but at the cost of considerable engineering work. We want to demonstrate that naive water rules do not work and that the advanced version of water is needed. Moreover, we want to confirm that with bounded seas we can get high precision and performance without the effort required to define an advanced island parser.

Table 2 displays the precision (P) and recall (R) with which the different parsers extract methods from six Java classes. The PetitJava parser had a perfect precision and recall for the cases where it did not fail. The PetitJava failures are due to incomplete and incorrectly specified rules.

Table 2. Precision (P) and recall (R) of the four tested parsers. We indicate with "-" the cases where the PetitJava parser fails with an error

Class Name	PetitJava		Island		Advanced		Bounded		Method Count
	P	R	P	R	P	R	P	R	
java.lang.Class	-	-	0.05	0.05	0.78	0.78	0.91	0.91	108
java.lang.Object	-	-	0.00	0.00	0.91	0.91	0.91	0.91	12
java.lang.Math	1	1	0.02	0.02	0.91	0.93	0.95	1.00	46
java.io.InputStream	1	1	0.00	0.00	0.88	0.88	1.00	1.00	9
java.io.FileInputStream	1	1	0.13	0.13	0.80	0.75	1.00	1.00	16
java.util.ArrayList	-	-	0.07	0.07	0.88	0.82	0.96	0.92	28

Table 3 synthesizes the information in Table 2 and adds information about the effort required to implement the given parser. The best precision and recall are achieved with the PetitJava parser, sacrificing simplicity and robustness. Island parsers provide very good robustness, but the naive island parser does not provide any useful output. The advanced island parser is comparable to the bounded island parser. This is not surprising, considering that bounded seas use the same techniques as the advanced island parser. Support for inner classes means that a parser can be extended to recognize inner classes and methods inside them. The non-bounded island parsers can only search for a flattened list of methods in contrast to bounded seas, which can support nested lists.

---

[4] In this paper, we exclusively consider Java 5 code.

Table 3. Comparison of parsing techniques. The 11 rules of the advanced parser are marked as a medium effort, because the extra rule is not trivial to infer and it is highly interconnected with the rest of the grammar.

	PetitJava	Island	Advanced	Bounded
P & R	very high	very low	high	high
Robustness	low	high	high	high
Supports inner classes	yes	no	no	yes
Effort	≈ 200 rules	10 rules	11 rules	10 rules
	very high	low	medium	low

Table 4 presents a performance comparison of the parsers. The performance of the bounded seas parser is in all the test cases one order of magnitude better than that of the advanced island parser. The performance difference is due to the bounded sea parsers skipping water at the start of boundary of another bounded sea. The Naive and Advanced island parsers are slower than the PetitJava parser.

Table 4. The performance comparison of the four parsers shows that the performance of the bounded seas parser is on par with the one of the PetitJava parser

Class Name	PetitJava [ms]	Island [ms]	Advanced [ms]	Bounded [ms]
java.lang.Class	-	6921	25229	4733
java.lang.Object	-	1058	6000	351
java.lang.Math	941	2077	11000	875
java.io.InputStream	331	638	3135	325
java.io.FileInputStream	338	301	561	301
java.util.ArrayList	-	1025	3831	826

5.3   Generalized LL Parsing

In this paper we have discussed bounded seas for PEGs. However, the essence of bounded seas is not in the grammar formalism used but in the fact that water is specific for each island and it is computed automatically from a stack of invoked expressions. We argue that bounded islands are useful for Context Free Grammars (CFGs) [7] as well.

The key difference between PEGs and CFGs is that CFGs may return ambiguous results whereas PEGs cannot. Implementing an island grammar as a CFG may lead to ambiguous results even though only one of the results is desired. The undesired, remaining results are present only because of vaguely-defined water. This is problematic since it is hard to decide which of the results is the correct one. Bounded seas eliminate ambiguities by adopting a more precise definition of water.

Generalized LL Parsing [8,9] can handle any CFG, allows all the choices of CFGs to be explored in parallel, and, in case of ambiguity returns all the possible results. Bounded seas can be implemented in a GLL parser because their top-down nature allows for a stack of parsing expressions and they support syntactic predicates used in a boundary.

5.4   Terminal Expressions in NEXT

Let us consider the case when NEXT returns a set of terminal expressions. In that case the NEXT function behaves similarly to the FOLLOW function from LL parsing theory [10,11,12]. If $e_i \in NEXT(e)$ is a terminal symbol we avoid the problems with another sea in a boundary of a sea. It simplifies the implementation of bounded seas. On the other hand, the first terminal is only an approximation of the following expression and it does not provide enough precision.

To illustrate, let us return to the grammar from Listing 1.7. Suppose that $NEXT(\text{class})$, instead of returning a set of parsing expressions, returns a set of first terminals { `'class'`, `'struct'`, `'public'` }. If there are other elements in the input that start with `'public'` (e.g., *'public int i = 0.'*), they are indistinguishable from the `mainMethod` from the point of view of the NEXT function.

5.5   Limitations

To compute $NEXT(e_1)$ in a sequence $e_1 e_2$ we need to know the e_2. Yet in some cases, *e.g.*, in monadic parser combinator [3] libraries, the right-hand-side of a sequence is a closure such as:

```
p1 >>= \\result -> p2
```

This means that `e2` is unknown until the result of `e1` is known. In case `e1` is a bounded sea, the result of `e1` cannot be computed before we know `e2`.

Therefore our approach is only applicable if we can compute the e_2 in a sequence $e_1 e_2$ before parsing the e_1. This prevents our solution from being used in some libraries such as the monadic libraries mentioned earlier.

This also limits (but does not forbid) use in context-sensitive grammars, where e_2 depends on a result of e_1. The context sensitive rules such as $e_1 e_2 e_3$ where e_3 depends on a result of e_1 and e_2 is a bounded sea are allowed. Because we use a stack and we compute $NEXT$ during parsing, e_3 can be computed when e_2 starts the parsing.

Bounded seas do not allow for context-sensitive dependencies between an island and its border with one exception. When a sea is bounded by another sea, we disable water if another water is already invoked at the same position.

6 Related Work

Noise Skipping Parsing. GLR* is a noise-skipping parsing algorithm for context-free grammars able to parse any input sentence by ignoring unrecognizable parts of the sentence [13]. The parser nondeterministically skips some words in a sentence and returns the parse with fewest skipped words. The parser is a modification of Generalized LR (Tomita) parsing algorithm [14].

The GLR* application domain is parsing of spontaneous speech. Contrary to the bounded seas presented in this work, GLR* itself decides what is a noise (water in our case) and where it is. In case of bounded seas the positions of a noise (water) are explicitly defined.

Fuzzy Parsing. The term fuzzy parser has been coined by Sniff [15], a commercial C++ IDE, that uses a hand-made top down parser. Sniff can process incomplete programs or programs with errors by focusing on symbol declarations (classes, members, functions, variables) and ignoring function bodies. In linguistics or natural language processing [16], the notion of fuzzy parsing corresponds to an algorithm that recognizes fuzzy languages.

The semi-formal definition of a fuzzy parser was introduced by Koppler [17]. Fuzzy parsers recognize only parts of the language by means of an unstructured set of rules. Compared with whole-language parsers, a fuzzy parser remains idle until its scanner encounters an anchor in the input or reaches the end of the input. Thereupon the parser behaves as a normal parser. Contrary to bounded seas, the fuzzy parsers represent a rather lexical approach, since they do not take a context-free structure into the account.

Island Grammars. Island grammars were suggested by Moonen in 2001 [1] as a method of semi-parsing to deal with irregularities in the artifacts that are typical for the reverse engineering domain. The idea of Moonen is based on a special syntactic rule called *water* that can accept any input. Water is annotated with a special keyword `avoid` that will ensure that water will be accepted only if there is no other rule that can be applied.

Contrary to Moonen, we propose boundaries (based on the NEXT function) that limit the scope in which water can be applied. Because each island has a different boundary, our solution does not use the single water rule; instead our water is tailored to each particular island.

Skeleton Grammars. Skeleton grammars [18] address the issue of false positives and false negatives when performing tolerant parsing by infering a tolerant (skeleton) grammar from a precise baseline grammar.

Our approach tackles the same problem as skeleton grammars: improving the precision of island grammars. They both maintain the composability property and both can be automated. The skeleton grammars use the standard first follow sets known from standard parsing theory [10,11,12] for synchronization (in similar way as we use a boundary). Contrary to skeleton grammars, bounded seas do not require a baseline grammar. Instead, bounded seas have to use a

NEXT set (returning set of expressions instead of set of tokens). Only this way can they achieve the required precision.

7   Conclusion

In this paper we presented bounded seas — composable, reusable, robust and easy to use islands. Contrary to traditional approach of island parsing, bounded seas do compute the scope where water can consume the input. We extended the semantics of PEGs to implement useful and practical bounded seas. The computation of a boundary is done by NEXT function, which inspired by the follow function from a standard parsing theory. The automation of the process that creates the bounded sea ensures that the bounded seas are easy to use and are not error-prone. The bounded seas presented in this work are context-sensitive.

As a validation of bounded seas composability and reusability we provide an implementation of bounded sea as a parser combinator in a PetitParser framework.

Acknowledgments. We gratefully acknowledge the financial support of the Swiss National Science Foundation for the project "Agile Software Assessment" (SNSF project No. 200020-144126/1, Jan 1, 2013 - Dec. 30, 2015).

We also thank CHOOSE, the special interest group for Object-Oriented Systems and Environments of the Swiss Informatics Society, for its financial contribution to the presentation of this paper.

References

1. Moonen, L.: Generating robust parsers using island grammars. In: Burd, E., Aiken, P., Koschke, R. (eds.) Proceedings Eight Working Conference on Reverse Engineering (WCRE 2001), pp. 13–22. IEEE Computer Society (2001), doi:doi:10.1109/WCRE.2001.957806
2. Renggli, L., Ducasse, S., Gîrba, T., Nierstrasz, O.: Practical dynamic grammars for dynamic languages. In: 4th Workshop on Dynamic Languages and Applications (DYLA 2010), Malaga, Spain (2010)
3. Hutton, G., Meijer, E.: Monadic parser combinators, Tech. Rep. NOTTCS-TR-96-4, Department of Computer Science, University of Nottingham (1996)
4. Frost, R., Launchbury, J.: Constructing natural language interpreters in a lazy functional language. Comput. J. 32(2), 108–121 (1989), doi:doi:10.1093/comjnl/32.2.108
5. Ford, B.: Parsing expression grammars: a recognition-based syntactic foundation. In: POPL 2004: Proceedings of the 31st ACM SIGPLAN-SIGACT Symposium on Principles of Programming Languages, pp. 111–122. ACM, New York (2004), doi:doi:10.1145/964001.964011
6. Nierstrasz, O., Ducasse, S., Gîrba, T.: The story of Moose: an agile reengineering environment. In: Proceedings of the European Software Engineering Conference (ESEC/FSE 2005), pp. 1–10. ACM Press, New York (2005), doi:doi:10.1145/1095430.1081707 (invited paper)

7. Chomsky, N.: Three models for the description of language. IRE Transactions on Information Theory 2, 113–124 (1956), http://www.chomsky.info/articles/195609--.pdf
8. Scott, E., Johnstone, A.: Gll parsing. Electron. Notes Theor. Comput. Sci. 253(7), 177–189 (2010), doi:10.1016/j.entcs.2010.08.041
9. Grune, D., Jacobs, C.J.: Generalized LL Parsing. In: Parsing Techniques — A Practical Guide, vol. 1, ch. 11.2, pp. 391–398. Springer (2008)
10. Grune, D., Jacobs, C.J.: Deterministic Top-Down Parsing. In: Parsing Techniques — A Practical Guide, vol. 1, ch. 8, pp. 235–361. Springer (2008)
11. Aho, A.V., Sethi, R., Ullman, J.D.: Compilers: Principles, Techniques and Tools. Addison Wesley, Reading (1986)
12. Aho, A.V., Ullman, J.D.: The Theory of Parsing, Translation and Compiling Volume I: Parsing. Prentice-Hall (1972)
13. Lavie, A., Tomita, M.: Glr* - an efficient noise-skipping parsing algorithm for context free grammars. In: Proceedings of the Third International Workshop on Parsing Technologies, pp. 123–134 (1993)
14. Tomita, M.: Efficient Parsing for Natural Language: A Fast Algorithm for Practical Systems. Kluwer Academic Publishers, Norwell (1985)
15. Bischofberger, W.R.: Sniff: A pragmatic approach to a C++ programming environment. In: C++ Conference, pp. 67–82 (1992)
16. Asveld, P.: A fuzzy approach to erroneous inputs in context-free language recognition. In: Proceedings of the Fourth International Workshop on Parsing Technologies IWPT 1995, pp. 14–25. Institute of Formal and Applied Linguistics, Charles University (1995)
17. Koppler, R.: A systematic approach to fuzzy parsing. Software: Practice and Experience 27(6), 637–649 (1997), doi:10.1002/(SICI)1097-024X(199706)27:6<637:AID-SPE99>3.0.CO;2-3
18. Klusener, S., Lämmel, R.: Deriving tolerant grammars from a base-line grammar. In: Proceedings of the International Conference on Software Maintenance (ICSM 2003), pp. 179–188. IEEE Computer Society (2003), doi:10.1109/ICSM.2003.1235420

A   Parsing Expression Grammars

PEGs were first introduced by Ford [5] and the formalism is closely related to top-down parsing. PEGs are syntactically similar to CFGs [7], but they have different semantics. The main semantic difference is that the choice operator in PEG is ordered — it selects the first successful match — while the choice operator in CFG is ambiguous. PEGs are composed using the operators in Table 5.

PEG Formalization

Definition 7 (PEG Definition). We use the standard definition as suggested by Ford [5]. A *parsing expression grammar* (PEG) is a 4-tuple G = {N, T, R, e_s}, where N is a set of nonterminals, T is a set of terminals, R is a set of rules, e_s is a start expression. $N \cap T = \emptyset$. Each r ∈ R is a pair (A, e), which we write A ← e, where A ∈ N, e is a parsing expression. The parsing expressions are defined inductively, if e, e_1 and e_2 are parsing expressions, then so is:

Table 5. Operators for constructing parsing expressions

Operator	Description
$'\ '$	Literal string
[]	Character class
.	Any character
(e)	Grouping
$e?$	Optional
$e*$	Zero-or-more repetitions of e
$e+$	One-or-more repetitions of e
$\&e$	And-predicate, does not consume input
$!e$	Not-predicate, does not consume input
$e_1\ e_2$	Sequence
$e_1\ /\ e_2$	Prioritized choice

- ϵ, the empty string
- a, any terminal where $a \in T$
- A, any nonterminal where $A \in N$
- e_1e_2, a sequence
- e_1/e_2, a prioritized choice
- $e*$, zero or more repetitions
- $!e$ a not-predicate

The following operators are syntactic sugar:

- **Any Character:** $\cdot$ is character class containing all letters
- **Character class:** $[a_1, a_2, ...a_n]$ character class is $a_1/a_2/../a_n$
- **Optional expression:** $e?$ is e_d/ϵ, where e_d is desugaring of e
- **One-or-more repetitions:** $e+$ is e_de_d*, where e_d is desugaring of e
- **And-predicate:** $\&e$ is $!(!e_d)$, where e_d is desugaring of e

We will use text in quotation marks to refer to terminals *e.g.*, `'a'` , `'b'` , `'class'` . We will use identifiers `A` , `B` , `C` , `class` or `method` to refer to nonterminals. We will use e or indexed e : e_1 , e_2 , ... to refer to parsing expressions.

Definition 8 (PEG Semantics). To formalize the syntactic meaning of a grammar G = $\{N, T, R, e_s\}$, we define a relation $\Rightarrow_G$ from pairs of the form (e, x) to the output o, where e is a parsing expression, $x \in T^*$ is an input string to be recognized and $o \in T^* \cup \{f\}$ indicates the result of a recognition attempt. The distinguished symbol $f \notin T$ indicates failure. For $((e, x), o) \in \Rightarrow_G$ we will write $(e, x) \Rightarrow o$.

$$\textbf{Empty:}\ \frac{x \in T^*}{(\epsilon, x) \Rightarrow \epsilon}$$

$$\textbf{Terminal (success case):}\ \frac{a \in T, x \in T^*}{(a, ax) \Rightarrow a}$$

Terminal (failure case): $\dfrac{a \neq b, \quad (a, \epsilon) \Rightarrow f}{(a, bx) \Rightarrow f}$

Nonterminal: $\dfrac{A \leftarrow e \in R \quad (e, x) \Rightarrow o}{(A, x) \Rightarrow o}$

Sequence (success case): $\dfrac{\begin{array}{c}(e_1, x_1 x_2 y) \Rightarrow x_1 \\ (e_2, x_2 y) \Rightarrow x_2\end{array}}{(e_1 e_2, x_1 x_2 y) \Rightarrow x_1 x_2}$

Sequence (failure case 1): $\dfrac{(e_1, x) \Rightarrow f}{(e_1 e_2, x) \Rightarrow f}$

Sequence (failure case 2): $\dfrac{(e_1, x_1 y) \Rightarrow x_1 \quad (e_2, y) \Rightarrow f}{(e_1 e_2, x_1 y) \Rightarrow f}$

Alternation (case 1): $\dfrac{(e_1, xy) \Rightarrow x}{(e_1/e_2, x) \Rightarrow x}$

Alternation (case 2): $\dfrac{(e_1, x) \Rightarrow f \quad (e_2, x) \Rightarrow o}{(e_1/e_2, x) \Rightarrow o}$

Repetitions (repetition case): $\dfrac{\begin{array}{c}(e, x_1 x_2 y) \Rightarrow x_1 \\ (e*, x_2) \Rightarrow x_2\end{array}}{(e*, x_1 x_2 y) \Rightarrow x_1 x_2}$

Repetitions (termination case): $\dfrac{(e, x) \Rightarrow f}{(e*, x) \Rightarrow \epsilon}$

Not predicate (case 1): $\dfrac{(e, xy) \Rightarrow x}{(!e, xy) \Rightarrow f}$

Not predicate (case 2): $\dfrac{(e, xy) \Rightarrow f}{(!e, xy) \Rightarrow \epsilon}$

Eco: A Language Composition Editor

Lukas Diekmann and Laurence Tratt

Software Development Team, Informatics, King's College London
http://lukasdiekmann.com/, http://tratt.net/laurie/

Abstract. Language composition editors have traditionally fallen into two extremes: traditional parsing, which is inflexible or ambiguous; or syntax directed editing, which programmers dislike. In this paper we extend an incremental parser to create an approach which bridges the two extremes: our prototype editor 'feels' like a normal text editor, but the user always operates on a valid tree as in a syntax directed editor. This allows us to compose arbitrary syntaxes while still enabling IDE-like features such as name binding analysis.

1 Introduction

At its most flexible, language composition gives programmers the ability to use multiple programming languages within a single file (e.g. in this paper we compose HTML, Python, and SQL). Editing composed programs has previously required choosing between two extremes: parsing-based approaches are familiar to programmers, but are either inflexible or prone to ambiguity; whereas SDEs (Syntax Directed Editors) have neither problem, but are insufferably awkward to use [13]. Recent work (e.g. [12,18]) has somewhat ameliorated the limitations of both extremes, but the divide between them, and the inevitable trade-offs, have long been assumed fundamental.

In this paper, we present a fundamentally new approach to editing composed programs which aims for the best of both worlds: it has the 'feel' of parsing-based approaches with the generality of syntax directed editors. The core of our approach is to extend an incremental parser with the new notion of *language boxes*.[1] Incremental parsers parse text as the user types, continuously updating a parse tree. In our approach, when editing a program in language X, one can insert at any place a language box for language Y and edit inside the box (in language Y) or outside the box (in language X). Each box has a separate incremental parser that maintains its own parse tree. Language boxes thus allow arbitrary syntaxes to be composed together without the loss of flexibility or ambiguity problems of traditional text-based approaches. Language boxes may contain any number of language boxes, and can be nested arbitrarily deep. Unlike syntax directed editors, our approach provides a user experience that is virtually identical to a traditional text editor. If only textual languages are used, the only noticeable

---

[1] Our 'language boxes' should not be confused with the modular language definition concept of the same name from [19].

B. Combemale et al. (Eds.): SLE 2014, LNCS 8706, pp. 82–101, 2014.

difference while editing – and a small one at that – is when entering or exiting a language box. The only significant difference from traditional editors is that *Eco* has to save files out as a tree structure rather than as a traditional source file to avoid (re)parsing problems.

Since most programming is currently done in text, our main focus has been on finding a good solution to the long-standing problem of editing textual programs. However, language boxes are not restricted to textual languages: each language box has its own editor which need not be based on parsing – or text – at all.

Our approach is embodied in a prototype language composition editor *Eco*. *Eco* allows users to define composed languages and edit programs against those composed languages. As well as extending an incremental parser with language boxes, we have also added the ability to parse indentation based languages, and to incrementally create ASTs (Abstract Syntax Trees) from parse trees (allowing to easily implement a simple name binding analysis). The version of *Eco* described in this paper can be downloaded from:

http://soft-dev.org/pubs/files/eco/

This paper's contributions are as follows:

1. We extend an incremental parser with language boxes.
2. We show that the resulting editor is useful for textual language composition.
3. We extend the parser to incrementally parse indentation-based languages.
4. We extend the parser to incrementally create ASTs as well as parse trees.
5. We show that language boxes allow the composition of textual and non-textual languages.

An earlier version of this work, with a simple version of language boxes only, was published in workshop form [6]. This paper extends the concept substantially, including new techniques such as incremental parsing of indentation based languages, and incremental ASTs.

This paper is structured as follows. We first introduce the paper's running example (Section 2) before exploring the existing extremes in language composition editing (Section 3). We then introduce Wagner's incremental parser and our implementation of it (Section 5) before introducing language boxes (Section 6). We then extend the incremental parser to parse indentation-based languages (Section 7) and to incrementally create ASTs (Section 8). Finally, we briefly explain how *Eco* supports name binding and non-textual languages (Section 9).

2   Running Example

We use as our running example a composition of HTML, Python, and SQL, leading to the construction of a flexible system equivalent to 'pre-baked languages' like PHP. In essence, we show how a user can take modular languages, compose them, and use the result in *Eco* as shown in Figure 1. We outline how this example composition is defined and used from the perspective of a 'normal' end-user; the rest of the paper is devoted to explaining the techniques which make this use case possible, as well as explaining how important corner cases are dealt with.

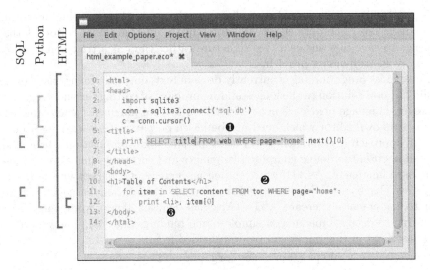

Fig. 1. *Eco* editing a composed program. An outer HTML document contains several Python language boxes. Some of the Python language boxes themselves contain SQL language boxes. Some specific features are as follows. ❶ A highlighted (SQL) language box (highlighted because the cursor is in it). ❷ An unhighlighted (SQL) language box (by default *Eco* only highlights the language box the cursor is in, though users can choose to highlight all boxes). ❸ An (inner) HTML language box nested inside Python.

When an end-user creates a new file in *Eco*, they are asked to specify which language that file will be written in. Let us assume that they choose the composed language named (unimaginatively) HTML+Python+SQL which composes the modular HTML, Python, and SQL languages within *Eco*. Although users can write whatever code they want in *Eco*, this composed language has the following syntactic constraints: the outer language box must be HTML; in the outer HTML language box, Python language boxes can be inserted wherever HTML elements are valid (i.e. not inside HTML tags); SQL language boxes can be inserted anywhere a Python statement is valid; and HTML language boxes can be inserted anywhere a Python statement is valid (but one can not nest Python inside such an inner HTML language box). Each language uses our incremental parser-based editor.

From the user's perspective, their typical workflow for a blank document is to start typing HTML exactly as they would in any other editor: they can add, alter, remove, or copy and paste text without restriction. The HTML is continually parsed by the outer language box's incremental parser and a parse tree constructed and updated appropriately within the language box. Syntax errors are highlighted as the user types with red squiggles. The HTML grammar is a standard BNF grammar which specifies where Python+SQL language boxes are syntactically valid by referencing a separate, modular Python grammar. When the user wishes to insert Python code, they press [Ctrl]+[L], which opens a menu

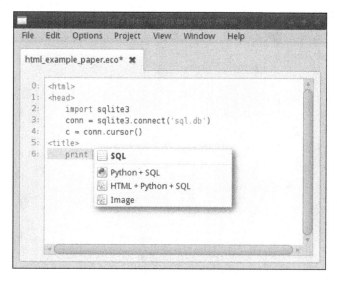

Fig. 2. Inserting a language box opens up a menu of the languages that *Eco* knows about. Languages which *Eco* knows are valid in the current context are highlighted in bold to help guide the user.

of available languages (see Figure 2); they then select Python+SQL from the languages listed and in so doing insert a Python language box into the HTML they had been typing. The Python+SQL language box can appear at any point in the text; however, until it is put into a place consistent with the HTML grammar's reference to the Python+SQL grammar, the language box will be highlighted as a syntax error. Note that this does not affect the user's ability to edit the text inside or outside the box, and the editing experience retains the feel of a normal text editor. As Figure 3 shows, *Eco* happily tolerates syntactic errors – including language boxes in positions which are syntactically invalid – in multiple places.

Typing inside the Python+SQL language box makes it visibly grow on screen to encompass its contents. Language boxes can be thought of as being similar to the quoting mechanism in traditional text-based approaches which use brackets such as ⟦ ⟧; unlike text-based brackets, language boxes can never conflict with the text contained within them. Users can leave a language box by clicking outside it, using the cursor keys, or pressing Ctrl + Shift + L . Within the parse tree, the language box is represented by a token whose type is Python+SQL and whose value is irrelevant to the incremental parser. As this may suggest, conceptually the top-level language of the file (HTML in this case) is a language box itself. Each language box has its own editor, which in this example means each has an incremental parser.

At the end of the editing process, assuming that the user has a file with no syntax errors, they will be left with a parse tree with multiple nested language boxes inside it as in Figure 1. Put another way, the user will have entered a

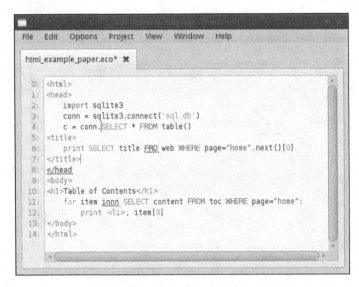

```
 0:  <html>
 1:  <head>
 2:      import sqlite3
 3:      conn = sqlite3.connect('sql.db')
 4:      c = conn.SELECT * FROM table()
 5:  <title>
 6:      print SELECT title FRO web WHERE page="home".next()[0]
 7:  </title>
 8:  </head
 9:  <body>
10:  <h1>Table of Contents</h1>
11:      for item innn SELECT content FROM toc WHERE page="home":
12:          print <li>, item[0]
13:  </body>
14:  </html>
```

Fig. 3. Editing a file with multiple syntax errors. Lines 6, 8 and 11 contain syntax errors in the traditional sense, and are indicated with horizontal red squiggles. A different kind of syntax error has occurred on line 4: the SQL language box is invalid in its current position (indicated by a vertical squiggle).

composed program with no restrictions on where language boxes can be placed; with no requirement to pick a bracketing mechanism which may conflict with nested languages; with no potential for ambiguity; and without sacrificing the ability to edit arbitrary portions of text (even those which happen to span multiple branches of a parse tree, or even those which span different language boxes).

Eco saves files in a custom tree format so that, no matter what program was input by the user, it can be reloaded later. In the case of the HTML+Python+SQL composition, composed programs can be exported to a Python file and then executed. Outer HTML fragments are translated to print statements; SQL language boxes to SQL API calls (with their database connection being to whatever variable a call to `sqlite3.connect` was assigned to); and inner HTML fragments to strings. All of the syntactically correct programs in this paper can thus be run as real programs. For the avoidance of doubt, other syntactic compositions, and other execution models of composed programs are possible (see e.g. [1]) and there is no requirement for *Eco* compositions to be savable as text, nor executed.

3   Parsing and Syntax Directed Editing

In this section we briefly explain the two extremes that bound the overall design space that we work within.

3.1 Parsing-Based Approaches

While there are many possible approaches to parsing text, three approaches can be used as exemplars of the major categories: LR, generalised, and PEG parsing.

Due to Yacc's predominance, LR-compatible grammars are commonly used to represent programming languages. Indeed, many programming language grammars are deliberately designed to fit within LR parsing's restrictions. Unfortunately, composing two LR grammars does not, in general, result in a valid LR grammar [17]. One partial solution to this is embodied in Copper which, by making the lexer lazy and context-sensitive, is able to allow many compositions which would not normally seem possible in an (LA)LR parser [21]. However, this requires nested languages to be delineated by special markers, which is visually obtrusive and prevents many reasonable compositions.

Generalised parsing approaches such as [24] can accept any CFG (Context Free Grammar), including inherently ambiguous grammars. Ambiguity and programming language tools are unhappy bedfellows, since the latter can hardly ask of a user "which parse of many did you intend?" Unfortunately, ambiguity, once allowed through the door, is impossible to eject. Two unambiguous grammars, when composed, may become ambiguous. However, we know that the only way to determine CFG ambiguity is to test every possible input; since most CFGs describe infinite languages, determining ambiguity is undecidable [4]. Although heuristics for detecting ambiguity exist, all existing approaches fail to detect at least some ambiguous grammars [23]. Furthermore, scannerless parsers – those which intertwine tokenization and parsing, and which are the most obviously suited for language composition – introduce an additional form of ambiguity due to the longest match problem [20].

PEGs (Parsing Expression Grammars) are a modern update of a classic parsing approach [8]. PEGs have no relation to CFGs. They are closed under composition (unlike LR grammars) and are inherently unambiguous (unlike generalised parsing approaches). Both properties are the result of the *ordered choice* operator e_1 / e_2 which means "try e_1 first; if it succeeds, the ordered choice immediately succeeds and completes. If and only if e_1 fails should e_2 be tried." However, this operator means that simple compositions such as S ::= a / ab fail to work as expected, because if the LHS matches a, the RHS is never tried, even if it could have matched the full input sequence. To make matters worse, in general such problems can not be determined statically, and only manifest when inputs parse in unexpected ways.

In summary, when it comes to language composition, parsing approaches are either too limited (LR parsing), allow ambiguity (generalised parsing), or are hard to reason about (PEG parsing). While approaches such as Copper [21] and Spoofax [12] have nonetheless been used for some impressive real-world examples, we believe that such issues might limit uptake.

3.2 Syntax Directed Editing

SDE works very differently to traditional parsing approaches, always operating on an AST. AST elements are instantiated as templates with holes, which are then filled in by the user. This means that programs being edited are always syntactically valid and unambiguous (though there may be holes with information yet to be filled in). This side-steps the flaws of parsing-based approaches, but because such tools require constant interaction with the user to instantiate and move between AST elements, the SDE systems of the 70s and 80s (e.g. [22]) were rejected by programmers as restrictive and clumsy [13].

More recently, the MPS editor has relaxed the SDE idiom, making the entering of text somewhat more akin to a normal text editor [18]. In essence, small tree rewritings are continually performed as the user types, so that typing ⎡ 2 ⎤, ⎡Space⎤, ⎡ + ⎤, ⎡Space⎤, ⎡ 3 ⎤ transparently rewrites the 2 node to be the LHS of the + node before placing the cursor in the empty RHS box of the + node where 3 can then be entered in. This lowers, though doesn't remove, one of the barriers which caused earlier SDEs to disappear from view. Language authors have to manually specify all such rewritings, a tedious task. Furthermore, the rewritings only affect the entry of new text. Editing a program still feels very different from a normal text editor. For example deleting nodes requires great care and special actions. Similarly, only whole nodes can be selected from the AST. For example, one can not copy 2 + from the expression 2 + 3 on-screen.

Put another way, MPS is sometimes able to hide that it is a SDE tool, but never for very long. The initial learning curve is therefore relatively steep and unpalatable to many programmers.

4   The Outlines of a New Approach

Our starting hypothesis is that language composition needs an editing approach which can marry SDE's flexible and reliable approach to constructing ASTs with the 'feel' of text editing. In part due to MPS's gradual evolution from a pure SDE to an approach which partially resembles parsing, we decided to start from a parsing perspective and try and move towards SDE. Doing so implicitly rules out any approach which can accept ambiguous grammars. Since the largest class of unambiguous grammars we can precisely define is the $LR(k)$ grammars [14] they were the obvious starting point.[2] In the following sections, we show how one can take an incremental parser which accepts LR grammars and extend it with the notion of language boxes.

5   Incremental Parsing in *Eco*

Traditional parsing is a batch process: an entire file is fed through a parser and a parse tree created. Incremental parsing, in contrast, is an online process: it parses text as the user types and continually updates a parse tree. A number of incremental parsing algorithms were published from the late 70s [9] to the late 90s, gradually improving efficiency and flexibility [16,7]. The last major work in this area was by Wagner [25] who defined a number of incremental

---

[2] Though note there are unambiguous grammars that are not contained within $LR(k)$.

parsing algorithms. We use his LR-based incremental parser which has two major benefits: it handles the full class of LR(k) grammars; and has formal guarantees that the algorithm is optimal. In this section, we give a brief overview of our implementation of Wagner's algorithm.

As with other parsing approaches, our implementation consists of both an incremental lexer and incremental parser. We represent both lexer and grammar with notations that are roughly similar to Yacc. Lexer rules are considered in the order in which they are defined to avoid longest-match ambiguities. Grammars are defined in BNF notation.

Both the lexer and the parser operate on a parse tree. Parse tree nodes are either *non-terminals* (representing production rules in the grammar) or *tokens* (representing terminal symbols). Non-terminals are immutable and have zero or more ordered child nodes. Tokens have an immutable type (e.g. 'int') and a mutable value (e.g. '3'). The minimal parse tree consists of three special nodes: a *Root* non-terminal; and *BOS* (Beginning of Stream) and *EOS* (End of Stream) terminals (both children of *Root*). All nodes created from user input are (directly or indirectly) children of *Root* and are contained between *BOS* and *EOS*.

When the user types, the incremental lexer first either creates, or updates, tokens in the parse tree. The lexer considers where the cursor is in the tree (i.e. where the user is typing) and uses look-ahead knowledge stored in the surrounding tokens to work out the affected area of the change. Newly created tokens are then merged back into the tree. In the simple case where a token's value, but not its type, was changed, no further action is needed. In all other cases, the incremental parser is then run to update the parse tree correctly. All nodes on the path from the changed token to the root of the tree are marked as changed. The incremental parser then starts at the beginning of the tree and tries to reorder the parse tree. Assuming the user's input is syntactically valid, non-terminals are created or removed, as appropriate. The parser tries to reuse non-changed sub-trees as is. Since non-terminals are immutable, sub-trees which can't be reused must be recreated from scratch or cloned from existing nodes.

Syntactically incomplete programs lead to temporarily incorrect parse trees. In such cases, the incremental parser typically attaches tokens to a single parent. When the user eventually creates a syntactically valid program, the tree is rewritten (an example for this can be seen in Figure 4).

5.1   Whitespace

In most programming languages, whitespace (which, from this paper's perspective, also includes comments) is only important inasmuch as it separates other tokens. Traditional lexers therefore consume and discard whitespace. This is unacceptable in our approach, as we need to maintain whitespace in the parse tree to accurately render the user's input (see Section 6.3). We therefore adopt, with small variations, one of Wagner's suggestions for whitespace handling.

When an *Eco* grammar sets the `%implicit_whitespace=true` flag, the grammar is automatically mutated such that references to a production rule `ws` are inserted before the first, and after every, terminal in the grammar. Although the

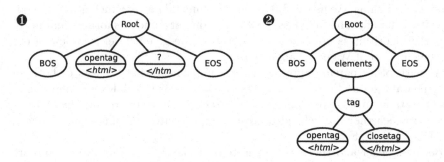

Fig. 4. Parse trees in the process of editing. Non-terminals are represented by ellipses with a name. Tokens are represented by ellipses with a horizontal line; the token's type is above the line; its value below the line. ❶ A parse tree in the process of editing and currently syntactically incorrect. The incremental lexer is able to tell that `</htm` can not be part of the previous token, but is currently unsure what the type of this token should be. The parser is thus not able to order the tokens into a correct tree. ❷ After further editing, the input is syntactically correct. The incremental lexer has been able to determine the type of the `</html>` token and the incremental parser has been able to update the parse tree, inserting appropriate non-terminals as specified by the grammar.

user can define `ws` to whatever they want, a common example of what is added to the grammar and lexer is as follows:

```
ws ::= TABSSPACES
     |

TABSSPACES : [ \t]+
```

Note that the user need not handle newlines as *Eco* handles those separately (see Sections 6.3 and 7).

Although the resulting parse tree records `ws` nodes (which are used for rendering and for ensuring cursor behaviour works as expected), they soon clutter visualizations of parse trees to the point that one can no longer see anything else. In the rest of this paper, we therefore elide `ws` nodes from all parse trees.

6   Language Boxes

Language boxes allow users to embed one language inside another (see Section 2). Language boxes have a type (e.g. HTML), an associated editor (e.g. our extended incremental parser), and a value (e.g. a parse tree). By design, language boxes only consider their own contents ignoring parent and sibling language boxes. We therefore define the notion of the CST (Concrete Syntax Tree), which is a language box agnostic way of viewing the user's input. Different language box editors may have different internal tree formats, but each exposes a consistent interface to the CST. Put another way, the CST is a global tree which integrates together the internal concrete syntax trees of individual language boxes.

In the rest of this section, we examine the characteristics, and consequences, of language boxes.

6.1 Language Modularity

To make language boxes practical, languages need to be defined modularly. *Eco* allows users to define as many languages as they wish. Languages are defined modularly, and may have several sub-components (e.g. grammar, name binding rules, syntax highlighting). For example, a language L which uses the incremental parser editor will contain a BNF grammar which can reference another language M by adding a symbol <M> to a production rule.

In most cases, we believe that users will want to avoid hard-coding references to different languages into 'pure' grammars. We therefore allow grammars to be cloned and (during initialisation only) mutated automatically. The most common mutation is to add a new alternative to a recently loaded grammar. For example, if we have a reference to `python` and `sql` languages, we can create a reference from Python to SQL by executing `python.add_alternative("atom", sql)`.

6.2 Language Boxes and Incremental Parsing

Language boxes fit naturally with the incremental parser because we use a property of CFGs which is rarely of consequence to batch-orientated parsers: parsers only need to know the type of a token and not its value. In our incremental parser approach, nested language boxes are therefore treated as tokens. When the user inserts an SQL language box into Python code, a new node of type `SQL` is inserted into the parse tree and treated as any other token. From the perspective of the incremental parser for the Python code, the language box's value is irrelevant as is the fact that the language box's value is mutable. Language boxes can appear in any part of the text, though, in our example, an SQL language box is only syntactically valid in places where the Python grammar makes a reference to the SQL grammar. Nested language boxes which use the incremental parser have their own complete parse trees, as can be seen in Figure 5.

6.3 Impact on Rendering

While language boxes do not have any impact on the incremental parser, they do have a big effect on other aspects of *Eco*. One obvious change is that they break the traditional notion that tokens are n characters wide and 1 line high. Language boxes can be arbitrarily wide, arbitrarily high, and need not contain text at all. *Eco* cannot simply store text 'flat' in memory and render it using traditional text editing techniques. Instead, it must render the CST onto screen. However, efficiency is a concern. Even a small 19KiB Java file, for example, leads to a parse tree with almost 19,000 nodes. Rendering large numbers of nodes soon becomes unbearably time-consuming.

To avoid this problem, *Eco* only renders the nodes which are currently visible on screen. *Eco* treats newlines in the user's input specially and uses them to

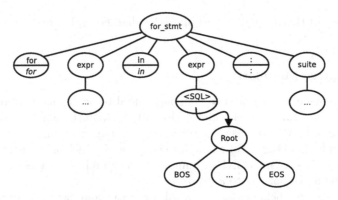

Fig. 5. An elided example of an SQL language box nested within an outer Python language box. From the perspective of the incremental parser, the tree stops at the SQL token. However, we can clearly see in the above figure that the SQL language box has its own parse tree, which thus forms part of the wider CST.

speed up rendering. Similar to Harrison [10], *Eco* maintains a list of all lines in the user's input; whenever the user creates a newline, a new entry is added. Each entry stores a reference to the first CST node in that line and the line's height. Entries are deleted and updated as necessary. Scanning this list allows *Eco* to quickly determine which chunks of the CST need to be rendered, and which do not. Even in our simple implementation, this approach scales to tens of thousands LoC without noticeable lag in rendering.

6.4   Cursor Behaviour

In a normal editor powered by an incremental parser, cursor behaviour can be implemented as in any other editor and stored as a *(line#, column#)* pair. We initially took this approach for *Eco*, but it has an unacceptable corner-case: nested language boxes create 'dead zones' where it is impossible to place the cursor and to enter further text.

Our solution is simple: *Eco*'s cursor is relative to nodes in the CST. In textual languages, the cursor is a pair *(node, offset)* where *node* is a reference to a token and *offset* is a character offset into that token. In normal usage, the arrow keys work as expected. For example, when the cursor is part way through a token, [→] simply increments *offset*; when *offset* reaches the end of a token, [→] sets *node* to the next token in the parse tree and *offset* to 1. [↑]/[↓] is slightly more complex: *Eco* scans from the beginning of the previous / next line, summing up the width of tokens until a match for the current x coordinate is found.

At the end of a nested language box, pressing [→] sets *node* to the next token after the language box while setting *offset* to 1 as described above. This means that if two language boxes end at the same point on screen, *Eco* will seemingly skip over the outer of the two boxes, making it impossible to insert text at that point. If instead the user presses [Ctrl]+[Shift]+[L], the cursor will be set to the

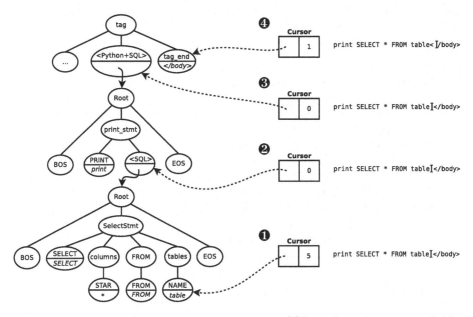

Fig. 6. *Eco*'s cursor behaviour in a program nesting SQL inside Python inside HTML. The cursor is stored as a (node, offset) pair. ❶ In normal program editing, the cursor behaves exactly like any other editor. Typing with the cursor at this position will enter text into the SQL language box right after the `table` token. ❷ After pressing [Ctrl]+[Shift] +[L], the cursor attaches itself to the current node's language box (`<SQL>`). Typing with the cursor at this position will insert text into the Python+SQL language box between the tokens `<SQL>` and `EOS`. ❸ After pressing [Ctrl]+[Shift]+[L] again, typing will insert text into the HTML outer language box (after the Python+SQL language box, and before the `</body>` token). ❹ Assuming the cursor was as in position ❶ and the user pressed [→], the cursor will be moved to this position.

current language box token itself instead of the first token after the language box (since language boxes are tokens themselves, this adds no complexity to *Eco*). When the user starts typing, this naturally creates a token in the outer language box. In this way, *Eco* allows the user to edit text at any point in a program, even in seemingly 'dead' zones (see Figure 6 for a diagrammatic representation).

6.5   Copy and Paste

Eco allows users to select any arbitrary fragment of a program, copy it, and paste it in elsewhere. Unlike an SDE, *Eco* does not force selections to respect the underlying parse tree in any way. Users can also select whole or partial language boxes, and can select across language boxes. *Eco* currently handles all selections by converting them into 'flat' text and reparsing them when they are pasted in. This seems to us a reasonable backup solution since it is hard to imagine what a user might expect to see when a partial language box is pasted in.

However, we suspect that some special-cases would be better handled separately: for example, if a user selects an entire language box, it would be reasonable to copy its underlying tree and paste it in without modification.

7 Indentation-Based Languages

Indentation-based languages such as Python are increasingly common, but require more support than a traditional lexer and parser offer. Augmenting batch-orientated approaches with such support is relatively simple, but, to the best of our knowledge, no-one has successfully augmented an incremental parser before. In this section we therefore describe how we have extended an incremental parser to deal with indentation-based languages.

The basic problem can be seen in this simplified Python grammar fragment:

```
if    ::= IF expr : suite
suite ::= NEWLINE INDENT stmts DEDENT
stmts ::= stmts NEWLINE stmt
        | stmt
```

and an example code fragment using it:

```
if a > 0:
   a = 0
print a
```

We can not simply parse this text and consume all whitespace, as in most languages. Instead, line 2 should generate NEWLINE and INDENT tokens before the a token and a DEDENT token after the 0. The process to create these tokens must be mindful of nesting: if a while statement is nested at the end of an if, two DEDENT tokens must be generated at the same point. Note that indentation related tokens are solely for the parser's benefit and do not affect rendering. Whitespace is recorded as per Section 5.1 and rendered as normal.

7.1 Incrementally Handling Indentation

Eco lexers that set %indentation=true use our approach to incrementally handling indentation. We insert an additional phase between incremental lexing and parsing which looks at changed lines and inserts or removes indentation related tokens as appropriate. To make this possible, we extend the information stored about each line in *Eco* (see Section 6.3) to store the leading whitespace level (i.e. the number of space characters) and the indentation level. These notions are separated, because the same indentation level in two disconnected parts of a file may relate to different leading whitespace levels (e.g. in one if statement, 2 space characters may constitute an indentation level; in another, 4 space characters). For example, the following is valid Python:

```
if x:
  y
if a:
    b
```

```
1    def calc_indentl(l):
2        if prev(l) == None:
3            l.indentl = 0
4        elif prev(l).wsl == l.wsl:
5            l.indentl = prev(l).indentl
6        elif prev(l).wsl < l.wsl:
7            l.indentl = prev(l).indentl + 1
8        else:
9            assert prev(l).wsl > l.wsl
10           prevl = prev(prev(l))
11           while prevl != None:
12               if prevl.wsl == l.wsl:
13                   l.indentl = prevl.indentl
14                   return
15               elif prevl.wsl < l.wsl:
16                   break
17               prevl = prev(prevl)
18           mark_unbalanced(l)
```

Fig. 7. The indentation level calculation algorithm

However, the following fragment is *unbalanced* (i.e. the file's indentation is non-sensical) and should be flagged as a syntax error:

```
if x:
    a
  b
```

For the purposes of this paper, it is sufficient to consider changes to a single line, though *Eco* itself generalises this to simultaneous changes on multiple lines. When a line l is updated, there are two cases. If l's leading whitespace level has not changed, no further recalculations are needed. In all other cases, the indentation level of l, and all lines that depend on it, must be recalculated; indentation related tokens must then be added or removed to each line as needed. Dependent lines are all non-empty lines after l up to, and including, the first line whose leading whitespace level is less than that of l, or to the end of the file, if no such line exists.

We can define a simple algorithm to calculate the indentation level of an individual line l. We first define every line to have attributes `wsl` – its leading whitespace level – and `indentl` – its indentation level. `prev(l)` returns the first non-empty predecessor line of l in the file, returning `None` when no such line exists. The algorithm is shown in Figure 7. There are 4 cases, the first 3 of which are trivial, though the last is more subtle:

1. Lines 2–3: If `prev(l) == None` then l is the first line in the file and its indentation level is set to 0.
2. Lines 4–5: If `prev(l).wsl == l.wsl` then l is part of the same block as the previous line and should have the same indentation level.
3. Lines 6–7: If `prev(l).wsl < l.wsl` then l opens a new block and has an indentation level 1 more than the preceding line.
4. Lines 9–16: If `prev(l).wsl > l.wsl` then either l closes a (possibly multi-level) block or the overall file has become unbalanced. To determine this we have to search backwards to find a line with the same leading whitespace level as l. If we find such a line, we set l's indentation level to that line's level (lines 12–14). If no such line is found (line 11), or if we encounter a line with

a lower leading whitespace level (lines 15–16), then the file is unbalanced and we need to mark the line as such (line 18) to force *Eco* to display an error at that point in the file.

In practise, this algorithm tends to check only a small number of preceding lines (often only 1). The worst cases (e.g. an unbalanced file where the last line is modified and all preceding lines are checked) are $O(n)$ (where n is the number of lines in the file).

Each time a line has been affected by this process, we need to check whether the indentation related tokens in the parse tree match the line's current state. If they do not, the tokens in the parse tree need to be updated appropriately (i.e. the old tokens are removed and replaced). If a line is marked as unbalanced, it requires a single UNBALANCED token; otherwise, we compare a line with its first non-blank predecessor and calculate the correct number of INDENT / DEDENT tokens. Once the parse tree has the correct number of tokens, we rely on the incremental parser to reorder the tree appropriately.

8   Abstracting Syntax Trees

Eco's CST allows it to fully render a program on-screen. Because of this, it contains details that make analysis of the CST painful. For example, we would like to define analyses such as the names in scope in a program (which we can then use to highlight undefined variables, and to code complete names; see Section 9.1) on a tree which abstracts away irrelevant detail. *Eco* therefore maintains an AST which provides a simplified view of the user's data. Different language editors map from the CST to the AST in different ways. Since some editors' data may be non-abstractable, formally the AST contains a non-strict subset of the data in the CST.

In this section, we explain how this relates to the incremental parser. Parse trees in our approach are an extreme example of the pain of a detailed CST: their nesting is partly dictated by the LR parser, and is often very deep; they contain irrelevant tokens, which are necessary only for the parser or to make the language more visually appealing to users; and child nodes are ordered and only accessible via numeric indices. Instead, one would prefer to work with an AST, where the tree has been flattened as much as possible, with irrelevant tokens removed, and with child nodes unordered and addressable by name.

We first describe the simple (relatively standard) rewriting language *Eco* uses to create ASTs from parse trees. We then describe the novel technique we have developed to make AST updates incremental.

8.1   Rewriting Language

The simple rewriting language we use to create ASTs from parse trees is in the vein of similar languages such as TXL [5] and Stratego [3]. In essence, it is a pure functional language which takes parse trees as input and produces ASTs as output. Each production rule in a grammar can optionally define a single rewrite rule. AST nodes have a name, and zero or more unordered, explicitly named, children. The AST is, in effect, dynamically typed and implicitly defined by the rewrite rules.[3]

An elided example from the Python grammar is as follows:

```
1   print_stmt ::= PRINT                {Print(stmts=[])}
2              | PRINT stmt_loop         {Print(stmts=#1)}
3
4   stmt_loop  ::= stmt_loop stmt        {#0 + [#1]}
5              | stmt                     {[#0]}
6
7   stmt       ::= expr                   {#0}
8              | ...
9
10  expr       ::= VAR                    {Var(name=#0)}
11             | ...
```

AST constructors are akin to function calls. Expressions of the form #n take the nth child from the non-terminal that results from a grammar's production rule. Referencing a token uses it as-is in the AST (e.g. line 10); referencing a non-terminal uses the AST sub-tree that the non-terminal points to. For example, Var(name=#0) means "create an AST element named Var with an edge name which points to a VAR token" and Print(stmts=#1) means "create an AST element named Print with an edge stmts which points to the AST constructed from the stmt_loop production rule". A common idiom is to flatten a recursive rule (forced on the grammar author by the very nature of LR grammars) into a list of elements (lines 4 and 5). Note that a rewrite rule can produce more than one AST node (e.g. line 1 produces both a Print node and an empty list node).

8.2   Incremental ASTs

All previous approaches of which we are aware either batch create ASTs from parse trees or use attribute grammars to perform calculations as parsing is performed (e.g. [2]). In this subsection, we explain how Wagner's incremental parser can be easily extended to incrementally create ASTs.

Our mechanism adds a new attribute ast to non-terminals in the parse tree. Every ast attribute references a corresponding AST node. The AST in turn uses direct references to tokens in the parse tree. In other words, the AST is a separate tree from the parse tree, except that it shares tokens directly with the parse tree. Sharing tokens between the parse tree and the AST is the key to our approach since it means that changes to a token's value automatically update the AST without further calculation. Altering the incremental parser to detect changes to tokens would be far more complex.

In all other cases, we rely on a simple modification to the incremental parser. Non-terminals are created by the parser when it reduces one or more elements from its stack. Every altered subtree is guaranteed to be reparsed and, since

---

[3] This is not an important design decision; the AST could be statically typed.

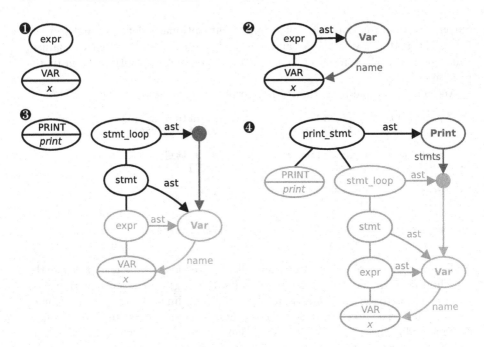

Fig. 8. Incremental AST construction, with the parse tree shown in black and the AST in green. Subtrees that have been reused are in grey / light green. ❶ After typing the input x, the incremental parser creates this parse tree fragment. ❷ After the **expr** non-terminal is created, the rewrite language is run on it creating an **ast** reference to an AST node **Var**. ❸ After changing the input to **print x**, the incremental parser starts to update the parse tree and the associated AST as shown in this in-process fragment. The **stmt** production's rewrite rule simply references whatever AST node its child produces, so **stmt**'s **ast** reference is the existing **Var** node. **stmt_loop** however wraps its contents in a list (the green circle). ❹ The final parse tree and AST. The **print** production rule creates a **Print** AST element with a child **stmts** which is a list containing a **Var** node.

non-terminals are immutable, changed subtrees will lead to fresh non-terminals being created. We therefore add to the parser's reduction step an execution of the corresponding production rule's rewrite rule; the result of that execution then forms the **ast** reference of the newly created non-terminal. We then rely on two properties that hold between the parse tree and AST trees. First, the AST only consists of nodes that were created from the parse tree (i.e. we do not have to worry about disconnected trees within the AST). Second, the rewrite language cannot create references from child to parent nodes in the AST. With these two properties, we can then guarantee that the AST is always correct with respect to the parse tree, since the incremental parser itself updates the AST at the same time as the parse tree. Figure 8 shows this process in action.

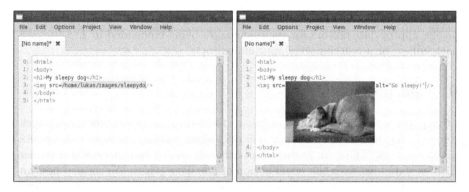

Fig. 9. An example of a non-textual language in *Eco*

This approach is easy to implement and also inherits Wagner's optimality guarantees: it is guaranteed that we update only the minimal number of nodes necessary to ensure the parse tree and AST are in sync.

9   Other Features

9.1   Scoping Rules

Modern IDEs calculate the available variable names in a source file for code completion, and highlight references to undefined names. We have implemented (a subset of) the NBL approach [15] which defines a declarative language for specifying such scoping rules. This runs over the AST created by Section 8. References to undefined variables are highlighted with standard red squiggles. Users can request code completion on partially completed names by pressing `Ctrl` + `Space`. Code completion is semi-intelligent: it uses NBL rules to only show the names visible to a given scope (e.g. variables from different methods do not 'bleed' into each other). We needed to make no changes to the core of *Eco* to make this work. We suspect that other analyses which only require a simple AST will be equally easy to implement.

9.2   Non-textual Languages

Although this paper's main focus has been on textual languages, language boxes liberate us from only considering textual languages. As a simple example of this, the HTML language we defined earlier can use language boxes of type `Image`. Image language boxes reference a file on disk. When an HTML file is saved out, they are serialised as normal text. However, the actual image can be viewed in *Eco* as shown in Figure 9. Users can move between text and image rendering of such language boxes by double-clicking on them. The renderer correctly handles lines of changing heights using the techniques outlined in Section 6.3.

As this simple example may suggest, *Eco* is in some senses closer to a syntactically-aware word processor than it is a normal text editor. Although we have not explored non-textual languages in great detail yet, it is easy to imagine appropriate editors for such languages being embedded in *Eco* (e.g. an image editor; or a mathematical formula editor).

10   Conclusions

In this paper we presented a new approach to editing composed programs, which preserves the 'feel' of normal text editors, while having the power of syntax directed editors. The core of our approach is a traditional incremental parser which we extended with the novel notion of language boxes. We showed how an incremental parser can naturally incrementally create ASTs, allowing us to build on modern IDE features such as name binding analysis. All this is embodied in a prototype editor *Eco*, which readers can download and experiment with.

We divide possible future work into two classes. First are 'engineering issues'. For example, the incremental parser stops rewriting the tree after the first syntactic error, which can make editing awkward. Various solutions (e.g. [25,11]) have been proposed, and we intend evaluating and adjusting these as necessary. Second are 'exploration issues'. For example, we would like to embed very different types of editors (e.g. spreadsheets) and integrate them into the *Eco* philosophy. It is for the most part unclear how this might best be done.

Acknowledgements. This research was funded by Oracle Labs. Edd Barrett, Carl Friedrich Bolz, Darya Kurilova, and Samuele Pedroni gave insightful comments on early drafts. Michael Van De Vanter gave invaluable advice on editor technologies.

References

1. Barrett, E., Bolz, C.F., Tratt, L.: Unipycation: A case study in cross-language tracing. In: VMIL, pp. 31–40 (October 2013)
2. Boshernitsan, M.: Harmonia: A flexible framework for constructing interactive language-based programming tools. Master's thesis, University of California, Berkeley (June 2001)
3. Bravenboer, M., Kalleberg, K.T., Vermaas, R., Visser, E.: Stratego/XT 0.17. A language and toolset for program transformation. Science of Computer Programming 72(1-2), 52–70 (2008)
4. Cantor, D.G.: On the ambiguity problem of backus systems. J. ACM 9(4), 477–479 (1962)
5. Cordy, J.R.: The TXL source transformation language. Science of Computer Programming 61(3), 190–210 (2006)
6. Diekmann, L., Tratt, L.: Parsing composed grammars with language boxes. In: Workshop on Scalable Language Specifications (June 2013)
7. Ferro, M.V., Dion, B.A.: Efficient incremental parsing for context-free languages. In: International Conference on Computer Languages, pp. 241–252 (1994)
8. Ford, B.: Parsing expression grammars: a recognition-based syntactic foundation. In: POPL, pp. 111–122 (January 2004)

9. Ghezzi, C., Mandrioli, D.: Incremental parsing. ACM Transactions on Programming Languages and Systems (TOPLAS) 1(1), 58–70 (1979)
10. Harrison, M.A., Maverick, V.: Presentation by tree transformation. In: Compcon, pp. 68–73 (September 1997)
11. Jalili, F., Gallier, J.H.: Building friendly parsers. In: POPL, pp. 196–206 (January 1982)
12. Kats, L.C.L., Visser, E.: The Spoofax language workbench: Rules for declarative specification of languages and IDEs. In: OOPSLA, pp. 444–463 (October 2010)
13. Khwaja, A.A., Urban, J.E.: Syntax-directed editing environments: Issues and features. In: SAC, pp. 230–237 (February 1993)
14. Knuth, D.: On the translation of languages from left to right. Information and Control 8(6), 607–639 (1965)
15. Konat, G., Kats, L., Wachsmuth, G., Visser, E.: Declarative name binding and scope rules. In: Czarnecki, K., Hedin, G. (eds.) SLE 2012. LNCS, vol. 7745, pp. 311–331. Springer, Heidelberg (2013)
16. Li, W.X.: A new approach to incremental LR parsing. J. Prog. Lang. 5(1), 173–188 (1997)
17. Parikh, R.J.: On context-free languages. J. ACM 13(4), 570–581 (1966)
18. Pech, V., Shatalin, A., Voelter, M.: JetBrains MPS as a tool for extending Java. In: PPPJ, pp. 165–168 (September 2013)
19. Renggli, L., Denker, M., Nierstrasz, O.: Language boxes. In: van den Brand, M., Gašević, D., Gray, J. (eds.) SLE 2009. LNCS, vol. 5969, pp. 274–293. Springer, Heidelberg (2010)
20. Salomon, D.J., Cormack, G.V.: Scannerless NSLR(1) parsing of programming languages. SIGPLAN Not. 24(7), 170–178 (1989)
21. Schwerdfeger, A., Van Wyk, E.: Verifiable composition of deterministic grammars. In: PLDI (June 2009)
22. Teitelbaum, T., Reps, T.: The Cornell program synthesizer: a syntax-directed programming environment. Commun. ACM 24(9), 563–573 (1981)
23. Vasudevan, N., Tratt, L.: Detecting ambiguity in programming language grammars. In: Erwig, M., Paige, R.F., Van Wyk, E. (eds.) SLE 2013. LNCS, vol. 8225, pp. 157–176. Springer, Heidelberg (2013)
24. Visser, E.: Syntax Definition for Language Prototyping. PhD thesis, University of Amsterdam (September 1997)
25. Wagner, T.A.: Practical Algorithms for Incremental Software Development Environments. PhD thesis, University of California, Berkeley (March 1998)

The Moldable Debugger: A Framework for Developing Domain-Specific Debuggers

Andrei Chiş[1], Tudor Gîrba[2], and Oscar Nierstrasz[1]

[1] Software Composition Group, University of Bern, Bern, Switzerland
http://scg.unibe.ch
[2] CompuGroup Medical Schweiz AG, Bern, Switzerland
tudor@tudorgirba.com

Abstract. Debuggers are crucial tools for developing object-oriented software systems as they give developers direct access to the running systems. Nevertheless, traditional debuggers rely on generic mechanisms to explore and exhibit the execution stack and system state, while developers reason about and formulate domain-specific questions using concepts and abstractions from their application domains. This creates an abstraction gap between the debugging needs and the debugging support leading to an inefficient and error-prone debugging effort. To reduce this gap, we propose a framework for developing domain-specific debuggers called the *Moldable Debugger* . The Moldable Debugger is adapted to a domain by creating and combining *domain-specific debugging operations* with *domain-specific debugging views*, and adapts itself to a domain by selecting, at run time, appropriate debugging operations and views. We motivate the need for domain-specific debugging, identify a set of key requirements and show how our approach improves debugging by adapting the debugger to several domains.

1 Introduction

Debugging is a prerequisite for maintaining and evolving object-oriented software systems. Despite its importance it is a complex and time-consuming activity. Together with testing it can take a significant part of the effort required to build a software system [1]. Using inadequate infrastructures for performing these activities can further increase this effort [2].

Debugging is typically performed by using a debugger that allows developers to interact with a running software system and explore its state. This makes the debugger a crucial tool in any programming environment. Nevertheless, there is an abstraction gap between the way in which developers reason about object-oriented applications, and the way in which they debug them.

On the one hand, object-oriented applications use objects to capture and express a model of the application domain. Developers reason about and formulate questions using concepts and abstractions from that domain model. This fosters program comprehension as domain concepts play an important role in software development [3,4]. Furthermore, non-trivial object-oriented applications contain

B. Combemale et al. (Eds.): SLE 2014, LNCS 8706, pp. 102–121, 2014.

rich object models [5]. A common approach to improve the development and evolution of these object models is to take advantage of internal DSLs that, by making use of APIs and of the syntax of the host language, can directly express domain abstractions [6].

On the other hand, classical debuggers focusing on generic stack-based operations, line breakpoints, and generic user interfaces do not allow developers to rely on domain concepts. Approaches that address this problem by offering object-oriented debugging idioms [7] still solve only part of the problem, as they do not capture domain concepts constructed on top of object-oriented programming idioms.

Generic solutions that do not offer a one-to-one mapping between developer questions and debugging support force developers to refine their high-level questions into low-level ones and mentally piece together information from various sources. For example, when developing a parser, we might need to step through the execution until we reach a certain position in the input stream. However, as it has no knowledge of parsing and stream manipulation, a generic debugger requires us to manipulate low-level concepts like sending a message or looking up variables. This abstraction gap leads to an ineffective and error-prone effort [8].

While the debugger of a host language can be used to debug internal DSLs, it still suffers from the aforementioned limitations. When dealing with external DSLs those limitations can be addressed by automatically generating, from the grammar of the DSL, domain-specific debuggers that work at the right level of abstraction [9]. However, this solution does not apply to object-oriented applications if there is no grammar or formal specification capturing the domain model.

There exist two main approaches to address, at the application level, the gap between the debugging needs and debugging support:

- supporting domain-specific debugging operations for stepping through the execution, setting breakpoints, checking invariants [10,11,12] and querying stack-related information [13,14,15].
- providing debuggers with domain-specific user interfaces that do not necessarily have a predefined content or a fixed layout [16].

Each of these directions addresses individual debugging problems, however until now there does not exist one comprehensive approach to tackle the overall debugging puzzle. We propose an approach that incorporates both of these directions in one coherent model. We start from the realization that the most basic feature of a debugger model is to enable the customization of all aspects, and we design a debugging model around this principle. We call our approach the *Moldable Debugger* .

The Moldable Debugger decomposes a domain-specific debugger into a *domain-specific extension* and an *activation predicate*. The domain-specific extension customizes the user interface and the operations of the debugger, while the *activation predicate* captures the state of the running program in which that domain-specific extension is applicable. In a nutshell, the Moldable Debugger model allows developers to *mold* the functionality of the debugger to their own domains by creating domain-specific extensions. Then, at run time, the Moldable Debugger adapts to the current domain by using activation predicates to select appropriate extensions.

A domain-specific extension consists of *(i)* a set of domain-specific *debugging operations* and *(ii)* a domain-specific *debugging view*, both built on top of *(iii)* a *debugging session*. The *debugging session* abstracts the low-level details of a domain. *Domain-specific operations* reify debugging operations as objects that control the execution of a program by creating and combining *debugging events*. We model debugging events as objects that encapsulate *a predicate over the state of the running program* (*e.g.*, method call, attribute mutation) [17]. A *domain-specific debugging view* consists of a set of graphical widgets that offer debugging information. Each widget locates and loads, at run-time, relevant domain-specific operations using an annotation-based approach.

To validate our model, we implemented it in Pharo[1], a modern Smalltalk environment. The Moldable Debugger implementation is written in less than 2000 lines of code. We have instantiated it for several distinct domains and each time the implementation required between 200-600 lines of code. We consider that its small size makes it easy to understand, and makes the adaptation of the debugger to specific domains an affordable activity.

The contributions of this paper are as follows:

- Identifying and discussing four requirements that an infrastructure for developing domain-specific debuggers should support;
- Presenting the Moldable Debugger, a model for creating and working with domain-specific debuggers that integrates domain-specific debugging operations with domain-specific user interfaces;
- Examples illustrating the advantages of the Moldable Debugger model over generic debuggers;
- A prototype implementation of the Moldable Debugger model.

2   Motivation

Debuggers are comprehension tools. They are often used by developers to *understand the run-time behavior of software* and *elicit run-time information* [18,19]. In test-driven development the debugger is used as a development tool given that it provides direct access to the running system [20].

Despite their importance, most debuggers only provide low-level operations that do not capture user intent and standard user interfaces that only display generic information. These issues can be addressed if developers are able to create domain-specific debuggers adapted to their problems and domains. Domain-specific debuggers can provide features at a higher level of abstraction that *(i)* match the domain model of software applications and *(ii)* group contextual information from various sources.

---

[1] http://pharo.org

In this section we establish and motivate four requirements that an infrastructure for developing domain-specific debuggers should support, namely: *domain-specific user interfaces, domain-specific debugging operations, automatic discovery* and *dynamic switching*.

2.1   Domain-Specific User Interfaces

User interfaces of software development tools tend to provide large quantities of information, especially as the size of systems increases. This in turn, increases the navigation effort of identifying the information relevant for a given task. While some of this effort is unavoidable, part of it is simply overhead caused by how information is organized on screen [21].

Consider a unit test with a failing equality assertion. In this case, the only information required by the developer is the difference between the expected and the actual value. However, finding the exact difference in non-trivial values can be daunting and can require multiple interactions such as finding the place in the stack where both variables are accessible, and opening separate inspectors for each values. A better approach is to show a diff view on the two values directly in the debugger when such an assertion exception occurs, without requiring any further action.

This shows that user interfaces that extract and highlight domain-specific information have the power to reduce the overall effort of code understanding [22]. However, today's debuggers tend to provide generic user interfaces that cannot emphasize what is important in application domains. To address this concern an infrastructure for developing domain-specific debuggers should:

- allow domain-specific debuggers to have *domain-specific user interfaces* displaying information relevant for their particular domains;
- support the *fast prototyping* of domain-specific user interfaces for debugging.

While other approaches, like *deet* [23] and *Debugger Canvas* [16], support domain-specific user interfaces for different domains, they do not offer an easy and rapid way to develop such domain-specific user interfaces.

2.2   Domain-Specific Debugging Operations

Debugging is viewed as a laborious activity requiring much manual and repetitive work. On the one hand, debuggers support language-level operations. As a consequence, developers need to mentally construct high-level abstractions on top of them, which can be time-consuming. On the other hand, debuggers rarely provide support for identifying and navigating through those high-level abstractions. This leads to repetitive tasks that increase debugging time.

Consider a framework for synchronous message passing. One common use case in applications using it is the delivery of a message to a list of subscribers. When debugging this use case, a developer might need to *step to when the current message is delivered to the next subscriber*. One solution is to manually step through the execution until the desired code location is reached. Another consists in identifying the code location beforehand, setting a breakpoint there and resuming execution. In both cases developers have to manually perform a series of actions each time they want to execute this high-level operation.

A predefined set of debugging operations cannot anticipate and capture all relevant situations. Furthermore, depending on the domain different debugging operations are of interest. Thus, an infrastructure for developing domain-specific debuggers should:

- *support the creation of domain-specific debugging operations* that allow developers to *express and automate* high-level abstractions from application domains (*e.g.*, creating domain-specific breakpoints, building and checking invariants, altering the state of the running system). Since developers view debugging as an event-oriented process, the underlying mechanism should allow developers to treat the running program as a generator of events, where an event corresponds to the occurrence of a particular action during the program's execution, like: method entry, attribute access, attribute write, memory access, *etc.*
- group together those debugging operations that are relevant for a domain and only make them available to developers when they encounter that domain.

This idea of having *customizable* or *programmable* debugging operations that view debugging as an event-oriented activity has been supported in related works [10,11,12,23]. Mainstream debuggers like GDB have, to some extent, also incorporated it. We also consider that debugging operations should be grouped based on the domain and only usable when working with that domain.

2.3   Automatic Discovery

Based on an observational study of 28 professional developers *Roehm et al.* report that none of them used a dedicated program comprehension tool; some were not aware of standard features provided by their IDE [18]. Another study revealed that despite their usefulness and long lasting presence in IDEs, refactoring tools are heavily underused [24].

In the same way, *developers need help to discover domain-specific debuggers during debugging.* For example, if while stepping through the execution of a program a developer reaches a parser, the developer should be informed that a domain-specific debugger exists that can be used in that context; if later the execution of the parser completes and the program continues with the propagation of an event, the developer should be informed that the current domain-specific debugger is no longer useful and that a better one exists. This way, the burden of finding appropriate domain-specific debuggers and determining when they are applicable does not fall on developers.

Recommender systems typically address the problem of locating useful software tools/commands by recording and mining usage histories of software tools [25] (*i.e.*, what tools developers used as well as how they used them). This requires, at least, some usage history information. To eliminate this need an infrastructure for developing domain-specific debugger should *allow each domain-specific debugger to encapsulate the situations/domains in which it is applicable.*

2.4   Dynamic Switching

Even with just two different types of debuggers, *DeLine et al.* noticed that users needed to switch between them at run time [16]. This happened as users did not know in advance in what situation they would find themselves in during debugging. Thus, they often did not start with the appropriate one.

Furthermore, even if one starts with the right domain-specific debugger, during debugging situations can arise requiring a different one. For example, the following scenario can occur: *(i)* while investigating how an event is propagated through the application *(ii)* a developer discovers that it is used to trigger a script constructing a GUI, and later learns that *(iii)* the script uses a parser to read the content of a file and populate the GUI. At each step a different domain-specific debugger can be used. For this to be feasible, *domain-specific debuggers should be switchable at debug time without having to restart the application.*

2.5   Summary

Generic debuggers focusing on low-level programming constructs, while universally applicable, cannot efficiently answer domain-specific questions, as they make it difficult for developers to take advantage of domain concepts. Domain-specific debuggers aware of the application domain can provide direct answers. We advocate that a debugging infrastructures for developing domain-specific debuggers should support the four aforementioned requirements (*domain-specific user interfaces, domain-specific debugging operations, automatic discovery* and *dynamic switching*).

3   Introducing the "Moldable Debugger" Model

Conventional debuggers force developers to use generic constructs to address domain-specific problems. The Moldable Debugger, on the other hand, explicitly supports domain-specific debuggers that can express and answer questions at the application level. A domain-specific debugger consists of *a domain-specific extension* encapsulating the functionality and *an activation predicate* encapsulating the situations in which the extension is applicable. This model makes it possible for multiple domain-specific debuggers to coexist at the same time.

To exemplify the ideas behind the proposed solution we will instantiate a domain-specific debugger for working with synchronous events[2]. Event-based programming poses debugging challenges as it favors a control flow based on events not supported well by conventional stack-based debuggers.

---

[2] This section briefly describes this debugger. More details are given in Section 4.2.

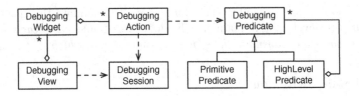

Fig. 1. The structure of a domain-specific extension

3.1   Modeling Domain-Specific Extensions

A domain-specific extension defines the functionality of a domain-specific debugger using multiple *debugging operations* and a *debugging view*. Debugging operations rely on *debugging predicates* to implement high-level abstractions (*e.g.*, domain-specific breakpoints); the debugging view highlights contextual information. To decouple these components from the low-level details of a domain they are built on top of a *debugging session*.

A *debugging session* encapsulates the logic for working with processes and execution contexts (*i.e.*, stack frames). It further implements common stack-based operations like: *step into*, *step over*, *resume/restart process*, *etc.*. Domain-specific debuggers can extend the debugging session to extract and store custom information from the runtime, or provide fine-grained debugging operations. For example, our event-based debugger extends the debugging session to extract and store the current event together with the sender and the receiver of that event.

Debugging predicates detect *run-time events*. Basic run-time events (*e.g.*, method call, attribute access) are detected using a set of *primitive predicates*, detailed in Table 1. More complex run-time events are detected using *high-level predicates* that combine both *primitive predicates* and other *high-level predicates* (Figure 1). Both these types of debugging predicates are encapsulated as objects whose state does not change after creation.

Consider our event-based debugger. This debugger can provide high-level predicates to detect when a sender initiates the delivery of an event, or when the middleware delivers the event to a receiver.

Table 1. Primitive debugging predicates capturing basic events

Attribute read	detects when a field of any object of a certain type is accessed
Attribute write	detects when a field of any object of a certain type is mutated
Method call	detects when a given method is called on any object of a certain type
Message send	detects when a specified method is invoked from a given method
State check	checks a generic condition on the state of the running program (*e.g.*, the identity of an object).

Debugging operations can execute the program until a debugging predicate is matched or can perform an action every time a debugging predicate is matched. They are modeled as objects that can accumulate state. They can implement breakpoints, log data, watch fields, change the program's state, detect violations of invariants, *etc.* In the previous example a debugging operation can be used to stop the execution when an event is delivered to a receiver. Another debugging operation can log all events delivered to a particular receiver without stopping the execution. At each point during the execution of a program only a single debugging operation can be active. Thus, debugging operations have to be run sequentially. This design decision simplifies the implementation of the model, given that two conflicting operations cannot run at the same time.

The Moldable Debugger models a *debugging view* as a collection of graphical widgets (*e.g.*, stack, code editor, object inspector) arranged using a particular layout. At run time, each widget loads a subset of debugging operations. Determining what operations are loaded by which widgets is done at run time via a lookup mechanism of operation declarations (implemented in practice using annotations). This way, widgets do not depend upon debugging operations, and are able to reload debugging operations dynamically during execution.

Our event-based debugger provides dedicated widgets that display an event together with the sender and the receiver of that event. These widgets load and display the debugging operations for working with synchronous events, like logging all events or placing a breakpoint when an event is delivered to a receiver.

Developers can create domain-specific extensions by:

(i) extending the debugging session with additional functionality;
(ii) creating domain-specific debugging predicates and operations;
(iii) specifying a domain-specific debugging view;
(iv) linking debugging operations to graphical widgets;

3.2   Dynamic Integration

The Moldable Debugger model enables each domain-specific debugger to decide if it can handle or not a debugging situation by defining an *activation predicate*. Activation predicates capture the state of the running program in which a domain-specific debugger is applicable. While debugging predicates are applied on an execution context, activation predicates are applied on the entire execution stack. For example, the activation predicate of our event-based debugger will check if the execution stack contains an execution context involving an event.

This way, developers do not have to be aware of applicable debuggers a priori. At each point during debugging they can see what domain-specific debuggers are applicable (*i.e.*, their activation predicate matches the current debugging context) and can switch to any of them.

When a domain-specific debugger is no longer appropriate we do not automatically switch to another one. Instead, all domain-specific widgets and operations are disabled. This avoids confronting users with unexpected changes in the user interface if the new debugging view has a radically different layout/content.

To further improve working with multiple domain-specific debuggers we provide two additional concepts:

(i) A *debugger-oriented breakpoint* is a breakpoint that when reached opens the domain-specific debugger best suited for the current situation. If more than one view is available the developer is asked to choose one.

(ii) *Debugger-oriented steps* are debugging operations that resume execution until a given domain-specific debugger is applicable. They are useful when a developer knows a domain-specific debugger will be used at some point in the future, but is not sure when or where.

4   Addressing Domain-Specific Debugging Problems

To demonstrate that the Moldable Debugger addresses the requirements identified in Section 2 we have instantiated it for four applications belonging to different domains: *testing, synchronous events, parsing* and *internal DSLs*. In this section we detail these instantiations.

4.1   Testing with SUnit

SUnit is a framework for creating unit tests [26]. The framework provides an assertion to check if a computation results in an expected value. If the assertion fails the developer is presented with a debugger that can be used to compare the obtained value with the expected one. If these values are complex, identifying the difference may be time consuming. A solution is needed to *facilitate comparison*.

To address this, we developed a domain-specific debugger having the following components:

Session: extracts the expected and the obtained value from the runtime;
View: displays a diff between the textual representation of the two values. The diff view depends on the domain of the data being compared.
Activation predicate: verifies if the execution stack contains a failing equality assertion.

4.2   An Announcement-Centric Debugger

The *Announcements* framework from Pharo provides a synchronous notification mechanism between objects based on a registration mechanism and first class announcements (*i.e.*, objects storing all information relevant to particular occurrences of events). Since the control flow for announcements is event-based, it does not match well the stack-based paradigm used by conventional debuggers. For example, Section 2.2 describes a high-level action for *delivering an announcement to a list of subscribers*. Furthermore, when debugging announcements it is useful *to see at the same time both the sender and the receiver of an announcement*; most debuggers only show the receiver.

To address these problems we have created a domain-specific debugger, shown in Figure 2. A previous work discusses in more details the need for such a debugger and looks more closely at the runtime support needed to make the debugger possible [27]. This debugger is instantiated as follows:

Session: extracts from the runtime the announcement, the sender, the receiver and all the other subscriptions triggered by the current announcement;

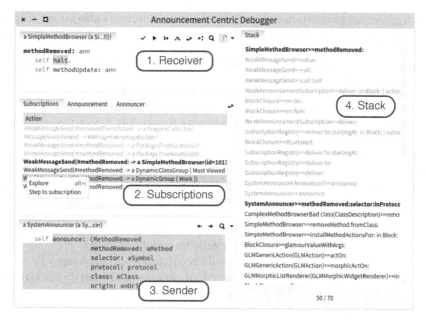

Fig. 2. A domain-specific debugger for announcements: (1)(3) the receiver and the sender of an announcement; (2) subscriptions triggered by the current announcement

Predicates: (i) detect when the framework initiates the delivery of a subscription; (ii) detect when the framework delivers a subscription to an object;

Operations: (i) step to the delivery of the next subscription; (ii) step to the delivery of a selected subscription;

View: shows both the sender and the receiver of an announcement, together with all subscriptions served as a result of that announcement;

Activation predicate: verifies if the execution stack contains an execution context involving an announcement.

4.3   A Debugger for PetitParser

PetitParser is a framework for creating parsers, written in Pharo, that makes it easy to dynamically reuse, compose, transform and extend grammars [28]. A parser is created by specifying a set of grammar productions in one or more dedicated classes. When a parser is instantiated the grammar productions are used to create a tree of primitive parsers (*e.g.*, choice, sequence, negation, *etc.*); this tree is then used to parse the input.

Whereas most parser generators instantiate a parser by generating code, PetitParser generates a dynamic graph of objects. Nevertheless, the same issues arise as with conventional parser generators: generic debuggers do not provide debugging operations at the level of the input (*e.g.*, set a breakpoint when a certain part of the input is parsed) and of the grammar (*e.g.*, set a breakpoint when a grammar production is exercised). Generic debuggers also do not display the source code of grammar productions nor do they provide easy access to the input being parsed.

We have developed a domain-specific debugger for PetitParser by configuring the Moldable Debugger as follows:

Session: extracts from the runtime the parser and the input being parsed;

Predicates: (i) detect the usage of a primitive parser; (ii) detect the usage of a production; (iii) detect when a parser fails to match the input; (iv) detect when the position of the input stream changes to a given value;

Operations: Navigating through the execution at a higher level of abstraction is supported through the following debugging operations:
  - *Next parser*: step until a primitive parser of any type is reached
  - *Next production*: step until a production is reached
  - *Production(aProduction)*: step until the given production is reached
  - *Next failure*: step until a parser fails to match the input
  - *Stream position change*: step until the stream position changes (it either increases, if a character was parsed, or decrease if the parser backtracks)
  - *Stream position(anInteger)*: step until the stream reaches a given position

View: The debugging view of the resulting debugger is shown in Figure 3. We can see that now the input being parsed is incorporated into the user interface; to know how much parsing has advanced, the portion that has already been parsed is highlighted. Tabs are used to group six widgets showing different types of data about the current production, like: source code, structure, position in the whole graph of parsers, an example that can be parsed with the production, *etc.* The execution stack further highlights those execution contexts that represent a grammar production;

Activation predicate: verifies if the execution stack contains an execution context created when using a parser.

4.4   A Debugger for Glamour

Glamour is an engine for scripting browsers based on a components and connectors architecture [29]. New browsers are created by using an internal domain-specific language (DSL) to specify a set of *presentations* (graphical widgets) along with a set of *transmissions* between those presentations, encoding the information flow. Users can attach various conditions to transmissions and alter the information that they propagate. Presentations and transmissions form a model that is then used to generate the actual browser.

The Moldable Debugger relies on Glamour for creating domain-specific views. Thus, during the development of the framework we created a domain-specific debugger to help us understand the creation of a browser:

Session: extracts from the runtime the model of the browser;

Predicates: (i) detect the creation of a presentation; (ii) detect when a transmission alters the value that it propagates; (iii) detect when the condition of a transmission is checked;

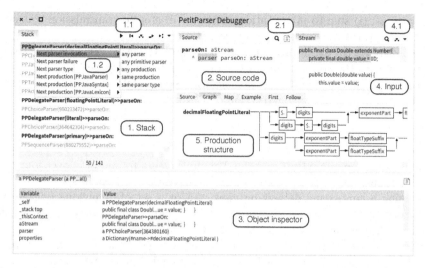

Fig. 3. A domain-specific debugger for PetitParser. The debugging view displays relevant information for debugging parsers ((4) Input, (5) Production structure). Each widget loads relevant debugging operations (1.1, 1.2, 2.1, 4.1).

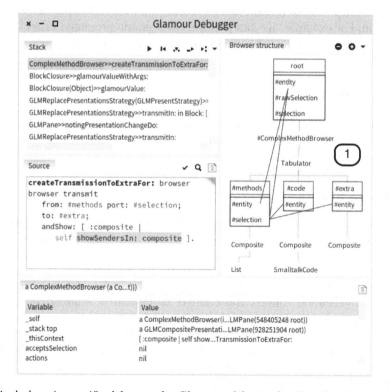

Fig. 4. A domain-specific debugger for Glamour: (1) visualization showing the model of the browser currently constructed

Operations: (i) step to presentation creation; (ii) step to transmission transformation; (iii) step to transmission condition;

View: displays the structure of the model in an interactive visualization that is updated as the construction of the model advances (Figure 4);

Activation predicate: verifies if the execution stack contains an execution context that triggers the construction of a browser.

4.5 Summary

PetitParser, Glamour, SUnit and the Announcements framework cover four distinct domains. For each one we were able to instantiate a domain-specific debugger having a contextual debugging view and/or a set of debugging operations capturing high-level abstractions from that domain. This shows the Moldable Debugger framework addresses the first two requirements.

The two remaining requirements, *automatic discovery* and *dynamic switching*, are also addressed. At each point during debugging developers can obtain a list of all domain-specific debuggers applicable to their current context. This does not require them either to know in advance all available debuggers, or to know when those debuggers are applicable. Once the right debugger was found developers can switch to it and continue debugging without having to restart the application. For example, one can perform the scenario presented in Section 2.4. The cost of creating these debuggers is discussed in Section 6.1.

5   Implementation

The current prototype of the Moldable Debugger[3] is implemented in Pharo, an open-source Smalltalk inspired environment. In this section we discuss several aspects regarding its implementation.

5.1   Controlling the Execution

In the current version the target program is controlled based on debugging predicates that are checked in a *step-by-step* manner after executing each instruction [30,31]. To do this we transform each debugging predicate into a boolean condition that is applied on the execution context. For example, the debugging predicate for detecting if a parser has failed forms a boolean condition that checks if an execution context was created as a result of sending the message initializeMessageAt to an instance of the class PPFailure.

The main advantage of this method is that it is simple to understand and it does not alter the source of the target program. However, it can slow down the target program considerably. To address this concern, debugging operations do not have to be aware that predicates are used to control the target program in

---

[3] More details including demos and installation instructions can be found at:
http://scg.unibe.ch/research/moldabledebugger

a *step-by-step* manner. Thus, a backend based on a different approach, like code instrumentation, could be used. We are currently looking at how to instrument code based on predicates. For example, the previous predicate could be used to instrument the method initializeMessageAt of the class PPFailure.

These two views of either using boolean conditions or code instrumentation to implement debugging operations match the *step* and *break* constructs proposed by *Crawford et al.* [30]. As they discuss, their combination can lead to semantic issues. To avoid those issues only a debugging operation can be active at a time, and debugging operations should not combine instrumentation with step-by-step execution.

5.2   The Moldable Debugger in Other Languages

The current prototype of the Moldable Debugger is implemented in Pharo. It can be ported to other languages as long as they provide a good infrastructure for controlling the execution of a target program and there exists a way to rapidly construct user interfaces for debuggers.

For example, one could implement the framework in Java. Domain-specific debugging operations can be implemented on top of the Java Debugging Interface (JDI) or by using aspects. JDI is a good candidate as it provides explicit control over the execution of a virtual machine and introspective access to its state. Aspect-Oriented Programming [32] can implement debugging actions by instrumenting only the code locations of interest. Dynamic aspects (*e.g.*, AspectWerkz [33]) can further scope code instrumentation at the debugger level. Last but not least, domain-specific views can be obtained by leveraging the functionality of IDEs, like *perspectives* in the Eclipse IDE.

6   Discussion

6.1   The Cost of Creating New Debuggers

The four presented domain-specific debuggers were created starting from a model consisting of 1500 lines of code. Table 2 shows, for each debugger, how many lines of code were needed for the debugging view, the debugging actions, and the debugging session.

Even if, in general, *lines of code* (LOC) must be considered with caution when measuring complexity and development effort, as the metric does not indicate the time needed to write those lines, it gives a good indication of the small size of these domain-specific debuggers. This small size makes the construction cost affordable. Similar conclusions can be derived from the work of *Kosar et al.* that shows that with the right setup its possible to construct a domain-specific debugger for a modelling language with relatively low costs [34].

The availability of such an infrastructure opens new possibilities:

(i) the developers of a library or framework can create and ship a dedicated debugger together with the code, to help users debug that framework or

Table 2. Size of extensions in lines of code (LOC)

	Session	Operations	View	Total
Base model	800	700	-	1500
Default Debugger	-	100	400	500
Announcements	200	50	200	450
Petit Parser	100	300	200	600
Glamour	150	100	50	300
SUnit	100	-	50	150

library. For example, we can envisage the developers of PetitParser and Glamour to have built the custom debuggers themselves and ship them together with the frameworks;

(ii) developers can extend the debugger for their own applications, during the development process, to help them solve bugs or better understand the application.

6.2   IDE Integration

Studies of software developers revealed that they use standalone tools alongside an IDE, even when their IDE has the required features [18]. Furthermore, developers also complain about loose integration of tools that forces them to look for relevant information in multiple places [35]. To avoid these problems the Moldable Debugger framework is integrated into the Pharo IDE and essentially replaces the existing debugger.

The Moldable Debugger along with the domain-specific debuggers presented in Section 4 are also integrated into Moose[4], a platform for data and software analysis [36]. Despite the fact that the performance of the current implementation can be significantly improved, these domain-specific debuggers are usable and reduce debugging time. For example, we are using the domain-specific debugger for PetitParser on a daily basis.

6.3   Open Questions

As software systems evolve domain-specific debuggers written for those systems must also evolve. This raises further research questions like: *"What changes in the application will lead to changes in the debugger?"* or *"How can the debugger be kept in sync with the application?"*. For example, introducing code instrumentation or destructive data reading (as in a stream) can lead to significant changes in an existent debugger.

In this context, a more high-level question is *"What makes an application debuggable?"*. By this we mean what characteristics of an application ease, or

---

[4] http://moosetechnology.org

exacerbate the creation of debuggers or, more generally, what characteristics affect debugging. To draw an analogy, in the field of software testing high coupling makes the creation of unit tests difficult (by increasing the number of dependencies that need to be taken into account) and thus decreases the testability of a software system.

7   Related Work

This work draws its ideas from programmable/scriptable debugging and debugging infrastructures for language workbenches. For clarity we discuss related work with respect to how other approaches support domain-specific debugging operations and user-interfaces for debugging.

7.1   Specifying Domain-Specific Operations

There is a wide body of research on allowing developers to automate debugging tasks by creating high-level abstractions. *MzTake* [11] is a scriptable debugger allowing developers to automate debugging tasks. It treats a running program as a stream of events that can be analyzed using operators, like *map* and *filter*; streams can also be combined to form new streams. The focus in *MzTake* is on automating debugging actions using scripts. It does not provide support for creating domain-specific views for debugging. Developers just have the possibility of visually exploring data by using features from the host IDE, DrScheme.

Dalek [10] is a C debugger employing a dataflow approach for debugging sequential programs: developers create high-level events by combining different types of low-level events. *Coca* [37] is an automated debugger for C using Prolog predicates to search for events of interest over program state. *Acid* [38] makes it possible to write debugging operations, like breakpoints and step instructions, in a language designed for debugging that reifies program state as variables. *Duel* [39] is a high-level language on top of GDB for writing state exploration queries. *Expositor* [12] is a scriptable time-travel debugger that can check temporal properties of an execution: it views program traces as immutable lists of time-annotated program state snapshots and uses an efficient data structure to manage them. These approaches focus on improving debugging by allowing developers to create different types of commands, breakpoints or queries at a higher level of abstraction. However, they have the same drawbacks as *MzTake*: by focusing only on operations they neglect the user interface of debuggers. They also do not provide support for selecting features based on the debugging context.

Object-centric debugging [7] proposes a new way to perform debugging operations by focusing on objects instead of the execution stack. *Reverse watchpoints* use the concept of *position* to automatically find the last time a target variable was written and move control flow to that point [40]. *Whyline* is a debugging tool that allows developer to ask and answer *Why* and *Why Not* questions about program behavior [41]. *Query-based debugging* facilitates the creation of queries over program execution and state using high-level languages [13,14,15]. These approaches are complementary to our approach as they can be used to create other types of debugging operations.

Language workbenches for domain-specific languages (DSL) address debugging by offering debugging abstractions at the level of the DSL [9,42,43]. This solves the debugging problem both at the language and application level only if domain concepts are incorporated directly into the DSL. However, if domain concepts are build on top of a DSL, then DSL debuggers suffer from the same limitations as generic debuggers. Our approach supports, in all cases, debuggers aware of application domains.

7.2   User Interfaces for Debugging

Debugger Canvas [16] proposes a novel type of user interface for debuggers based on the *Code Bubbles* [44] paradigm. Rather then starting from a user interface having a predefined structure, developers start from an empty one on which different bubbles are added, as they step through the execution of the program. Our approach allows developers to create custom user interfaces (views) beforehand and select appropriate interfaces at debug time. *Debugger Canvas* focuses only on the user interface, and does not provide support for adding custom debugging operations. Our approach addresses both aspects.

The Data Display Debugger (DDD) [45] is a graphical user interface for GDB providing a graphical display for representing complex data structures as graphs that can be explored incrementally and interactively. However, if focuses just on providing a default front-end for GDB; it does not offer support for customization, nor other debugging operations then the ones provided by GDB.

jGRASP supports the visualization of various data structure by means of dynamic viewers and a *structure identifier* that automatically select suitable views for data structures [46]. *x*DIVA is a 3-D debugging visualization system where complex visualization metaphors are assembled from individual ones, each of which is independently replaceable [47]. While these approaches allow users to create visualizations specific to their domains they are meant to be embedded within existent debuggers, and thus do not offer debugging operations.

7.3   Unifying Approaches

deet [23] is a debugger for ANSI C that, like our approach, promotes simple debuggers having few lines of code. It further allows developers to extend the user interface and add new commands by writing code in a high-level language. *TIDE* is a debugging framework focusing on the instantiation of debuggers for formal languages (ASF+SDF, in particular) [48]; developers can implement high-level debugging actions like, breakpoints and watchpoints, extend the user interface be modifying the Java implementation of TIDE, and use *debugging rules* to state which debugging actions are available at which logical breakpoints. Unlike these approaches, we propose modeling the customization of debugger through explicit domain-specific extensions and provide support for automatically detecting appropriate extensions at run time.

LISA is a grammar-based compiler generator that can automatically generate debuggers, inspectors and visualizers for DSLs that have a formal language specification [49]. Our approach targets object-oriented systems where such a formal specification is missing.

8 Conclusions

Developers encounter domain-specific questions. Traditional debuggers supporting debugging by means of generic mechanisms, while universally applicable, are less suitable to handle domain-specific questions. The Moldable Debugger addresses this contradiction by allowing developers to created domain-specific debuggers having both custom debugging actions and user interfaces, with a low effort. As a validation, we implemented the Moldable Debugger model and created four different debuggers in less than 600 lines of code each. The Moldable Debugger reduces the abstraction gap between the debugging needs and debugging support leading to a more efficient and less error-prone debugging effort.

Given the large costs associated with debugging activities, improving the workflow and reducing the cognitive load of debugging can have a significant practical impact. With our approach developers can create their own debuggers to address recurring custom problems. This can make considerable economical sense when working on a long lived system. Furthermore, library developers can ship library-specific debuggers together with their product. This can have a practical impact due to the reuse of the library in many applications.

Acknowledgments. We gratefully acknowledge the financial support of the Swiss National Science Foundation for the project "Agile Software Assessment" (SNSF project Nr. 200020-144126/1, Jan 1, 2013 - Dec. 30, 2015). We thank Alexandre Bergel, Jorge Ressia, and the anonymous reviewers for their suggestions in improving this paper. We also thank CHOOSE, the special interest group for Object-Oriented Systems and Environments of the Swiss Informatics Society, for its financial contribution to the presentation of this paper.

References

1. Vessey, I.: Expertise in Debugging Computer Programs: An Analysis of the Content of Verbal Protocols. IEEE Trans. on Systems, Man, and Cybernetics 16(5), 621–637 (1986)
2. Tassey, G.: The economic impacts of inadequate infrastructure for software testing. Technical report, National Institute of Standards and Technology (2002)
3. Littman, D.C., Pinto, J., Letovsky, S., Soloway, E.: Mental models and software maintenance. Journal of Systems and Software 7(4), 341–355 (1987)
4. Rajlich, V., Wilde, N.: The role of concepts in program comprehension. In: Proc. IWPC, pp. 271–278 (2002)

5. Renggli, L., Gîrba, T., Nierstrasz, O.: Embedding languages without breaking tools. In: D'Hondt, T. (ed.) ECOOP 2010. LNCS, vol. 6183, pp. 380–404. Springer, Heidelberg (2010)
6. Fowler, M.: Domain-Specific Languages. Addison-Wesley Professional (2010)
7. Ressia, J., Bergel, A., Nierstrasz, O.: Object-centric debugging. In: Proc. ICSE, pp. 485–495 (2012)
8. Sillito, J., Murphy, G.C., De Volder, K.: Asking and answering questions during a programming change task. IEEE Trans. Softw. Eng. 34, 434–451 (2008)
9. Wu, H., Gray, J., Mernik, M.: Grammar-driven generation of domain-specific language debuggers. Softw. Pract. Exper. 38(10), 1073–1103 (2008)
10. Olsson, R.A., Crawford, R.H., Ho, W.W.: A dataflow approach to event-based debugging. Software - Practice and Experience 21(2), 209–229 (1991)
11. Marceau, G., Cooper, G.H., Spiro, J.P., Krishnamurthi, S., Reiss, S.P.: The design and implementation of a dataflow language for scriptable debugging. Automated Software Engineering 14(1), 59–86 (2007)
12. Khoo, Y.P., Foster, J.S., Hicks, M.: Expositor: scriptable time-travel debugging with first-class traces. In: Proc. ICSE, pp. 352–361 (2013)
13. Lencevicius, R., Hölzle, U., Singh, A.K.: Query-based debugging of object-oriented programs. In: Proc. OOPSLA, pp. 304–317 (1997)
14. Potanin, A., Noble, J., Biddle, R.: Snapshot query-based debugging. In: Proc. ASWEC, p. 251 (2004)
15. Martin, M., Livshits, B., Lam, M.S.: Finding application errors and security flaws using PQL: a program query language. In: Proc. OOPSLA, pp. 363–385. ACM (2005)
16. DeLine, R., Bragdon, A., Rowan, K., Jacobsen, J., Reiss, S.P.: Debugger canvas: industrial experience with the code bubbles paradigm. In: ICSE, pp. 1064–1073 (2012)
17. Auguston, M., Jeffery, C., Underwood, S.: A framework for automatic debugging. In: Proc. ASE 2002, pp. 217–222. IEEE Computer Society (2002)
18. Roehm, T., Tiarks, R., Koschke, R., Maalej, W.: How do professional developers comprehend software? In: Proc. ICSE, pp. 255–265 (2012)
19. Murphy, G.C., Kersten, M., Findlater, L.: How are Java software developers using the Eclipse IDE? IEEE Software (July 2006)
20. Beck, K.: Test Driven Development: By Example. Addison-Wesley Longman (2002)
21. Ko, A., Myers, B., Coblenz, M., Aung, H.: An exploratory study of how developers seek, relate, and collect relevant information during software maintenance tasks. IEEE Trans. Softw. Eng. 32(12), 971–987 (2006)
22. Kersten, M., Murphy, G.C.: Mylar: a degree-of-interest model for IDEs. In: Proc. AOSD, pp. 159–168 (2005)
23. Hanson, D.R., Korn, J.L.: A simple and extensible graphical debugger. In: WINTER 1997 USENIX CONFERENCE, pp. 173–184 (1997)
24. Murphy-Hill, E., Parnin, C., Black, A.P.: How we refactor, and how we know it. In: Proc. ICSE, pp. 287–297 (2009)
25. Murphy-Hill, E., Jiresal, R., Murphy, G.C.: Improving software developers' fluency by recommending development environment commands. In: FSE, pp. 42:1–42:11 (2012)
26. Beck, K.: Kent Beck's Guide to Better Smalltalk. Sigs Books (1999)
27. Chis, A., Nierstrasz, O., Gîrba, T.: Towards a moldable debugger. In: Proc. DYLA, pp. 2:1–2:6 (2013)
28. Renggli, L., Ducasse, S., Gîrba, T., Nierstrasz, O.: Practical dynamic grammars for dynamic languages. In: Proc. DYLA (2010)

29. Bunge, P.: Scripting browsers with Glamour. Master's thesis, University of Bern (2009)

30. Crawford, R.H., Olsson, R.A., Ho, W.W., Wee, C.E.: Semantic issues in the design of languages for debugging. Comput. Lang. 21(1), 17–37 (1995)

31. Lieberman, H., Fry, C.: ZStep 95: A reversible, animated source code stepper. MIT Press (1998)

32. Kiczales, G., Lamping, J., Mendhekar, A., Maeda, C., Lopes, C., Loingtier, J.M., Irwin, J.: Aspect-oriented programming. In: Akşit, M., Matsuoka, S. (eds.) ECOOP 1997. LNCS, vol. 1241, pp. 220–242. Springer, Heidelberg (1997)

33. Bonér, J.: What are the key issues for commercial AOP use: how does AspectWerkz address them? In: Proc. AOSD, pp. 5–6 (2004)

34. Kosar, T., Mernik, M., Gray, J., Kos, T.: Debugging measurement systems using a domain-specific modeling language. Computers in Industry 65(4), 622–635 (2014)

35. Maalej, W.: Task-First or Context-First? Tool Integration Revisited. In: Proc. ASE, pp. 344–355 (2009)

36. Nierstrasz, O., Ducasse, S., Gîrba, T.: The story of Moose: an agile reengineering environment. In: Proc. of ESEC/FSE, pp. 1–10 (2005) (invited paper)

37. Ducassé, M.: Coca: An automated debugger for C. In: International Conference on Software Engineering, pp. 154–168 (1999)

38. Winterbottom, P.: ACID: A debugger built from a language. In: USENIX Technical Conference, pp. 211–222 (1994)

39. Golan, M., Hanson, D.R.: Duel — a very high-level debugging language. In: USENIX Winter, pp. 107–118 (1993)

40. Maruyama, K., Terada, M.: Debugging with reverse watchpoint. In: QSIC (2003)

41. Ko, A.J., Myers, B.A.: Debugging reinvented: Asking and answering why and why not questions about program behavior. In: Proc. of ICSE, pp. 301–310 (2008)

42. Lindeman, R.T., Kats, L.C., Visser, E.: Declaratively defining domain-specific language debuggers. In: Proc. GPCE, pp. 127–136 (2011)

43. Kolomvatsos, K., Valkanas, G., Hadjiefthymiades, S.: Debugging applications created by a domain specific language: The IPAC case. J. Syst. Softw. 85(4), 932–943 (2012)

44. Bragdon, A., Zeleznik, R., Reiss, S.P., Karumuri, S., Cheung, W., Kaplan, J., Coleman, C., Adeputra, F., LaViola Jr., J.J.: Code bubbles: a working set-based interface for code understanding and maintenance. In: CHI, pp. 2503–2512 (2010)

45. Zeller, A., Lütkehaus, D.: DDD — a free graphical front-end for Unix debuggers. SIGPLAN Not. 31(1), 22–27 (1996)

46. Cross II, J.H., Hendrix, T.D., Umphress, D.A., Barowski, L.A., Jain, J., Montgomery, L.N.: Robust generation of dynamic data structure visualizations with multiple interaction approaches. Trans. Comput. Educ. 9(2), 13:1–13:32 (2009)

47. Cheng, Y.P., Chen, J.F., Chiu, M.C., Lai, N.W., Tseng, C.C.: xDIVA: a debugging visualization system with composable visualization metaphors. In: OOPSLA Companion, pp. 807–810 (2008)

48. van den Brand, M.G.J., Cornelissen, B., Olivier, P.A., Vinju, J.J.: TIDE: A generic debugging framework — tool demonstration —. Electron. Notes Theor. Comput. Sci. 141(4), 161–165 (2005)

49. Henriques, P.R., Pereira, M.J.V., Mernik, M., Lenic, M., Gray, J., Wu, H.: Automatic generation of language-based tools using the LISA system. IEE Software Journal 152(2), 54–69 (2005)

Evaluating the Usability of a Visual Feature Modeling Notation

Aleksandar Jakšić[1], Robert B. France[1], Philippe Collet[2], and Sudipto Ghosh[1]

[1] Colorado State University, Computer Science Department, Fort Collins, USA
ajaksic@colostate.edu, {france,ghosh}@cs.colostate.edu
[2] Université Nice Sophia Antipolis / I3S - CNRS UMR 7271, France
philippe.collet@unice.fr

Abstract. Feature modeling is a popular Software Product Line Engineering (SPLE) technique used to describe variability in a product family. A usable feature modeling tool environment should enable SPLE practitioners to produce good quality models, in particular, models that effectively communicate modeled information. FAMILIAR is a text-based environment for manipulating and composing Feature Models (FMs). In this paper we present extensions we made to FAMILIAR to enhance its usability. The extensions include a visualization of FMs, or more precisely, a feature diagram rendering mechanism that supports the use of a combination of text and graphics to describe FMs, their configurations, and the results of FM analyses. We also present the results of a preliminary evaluation of the environment's usability. The evaluation involves comparing the use of the extended environment with the previous text-based console-driven version. The preliminary experiment provides some evidence that use of the new environment results in increased cognitive effectiveness of novice users and improved quality of new FMs.

Keywords: FAMILIAR Tool[1], FAMILIAR, Software Product Lines, Feature Modeling, Software Visualization, Model-Driven Development.

1 Introduction

Feature models (FM) are often used in Software Product Line Engineering (SPLE) to describe variability in a product family. A usable feature modeling tool environment should enable SPLE practitioners to produce good quality models, in particular, models that effectively communicate modeled information.

A number of textual domain-specific modeling languages (DSMLs) for feature modeling [6][7][11][15][21], including FAMILIAR [2–4, 16], have been proposed during the last decade. There are many benefits to using text-based languages to describe the variability [12]. For example, a lightweight textual language can

---

[1] In this work, we refer to the newly developed visual tool as the FAMILIAR Tool. Subsequently, its underlying framework, the DSML language, continues to be referred to as FAMILIAR, as it was the case with the prior work.

B. Combemale et al. (Eds.): SLE 2014, LNCS 8706, pp. 122–140, 2014.
© Springer International Publishing Switzerland 2014

leverage already established tools that are available for editing and manipulating textual language statements. Such support facilitates rapid prototyping of a DSML. Other desirable characteristics that typically come with expressive textual notations with good tool support include interoperability with other textual DSMLs, and scripting support that enables replay of operation sequences, and modular management of scripts [4]. On the other hand, creating and analyzing a large text-based feature model (FM) often requires significant cognitive effort.

Cognitive research is a scientific discipline that attempts to gain insights on how the human mind analyzes information, creates knowledge, and solves problems. There is growing evidence of the cognitive power of visualization [20]. Tool support for visualizing models may help modeling practitioners amplify their cognition [35]. The increase in cognitive effectiveness can lead to improved ability of humans to process information captured in models [28]. There is evidence that visual notations convey information more effectively than text, especially to novices [9]. Our work on extending a textual DSML for FMs and on evaluating the resulting FM development environment is motivated by the following question: *Does the lack of support for visualizing FMs in FM development tools hinder the usability of these tools when managing multiple and large FMs during modeling sessions?*

Our hypothesis is that modeling practitioners, especially novice modelers, would benefit when provided with graphical feature models that use familiar notations (e.g., a FODA-like notation) [26][27]. Allowing modelers to express and visualize feature models in a tree-like top-down hierarchical structure should enhance their ability to develop good quality models that effectively communicate modeled information. Consequently, the tool support for FM visualization should lead to improved user efficiency, effectiveness, and learnability.

In this paper we describe the results of a preliminary experiment conducted to measure and analyze the benefits associated with the use of graphical models when compared to the use of purely textual models. We also describe how we extended the FAMILIAR language and its feature modeling tool environment with support for graphically rendering FMs.

2   Background

Models can help us to break down a complex problem through abstraction. Furthermore, we can also use them to narrow the gap between the problem and solution domains. Attempts to bridge the problem-solution gap with traditional software development approaches are not only labor-intensive but also tedious and error-prone with potential accidental complexities. As a consequence, software development costs as well as time-to-deploy tend to keep increasing [18]. One of the central ideas behind Software Product Line Engineering (SPLE) is to shift away from individually designing software products. Instead, engineers should focus on creating quality models of product families that would, with the help of evolving automation technologies and an emergence of widely supported industry standards, eventually be capable of delivering high quality final products in less time and with no or minimal accidental complexities [31].

SPLE supports explicit modeling of what is common and what differs among software product variants. Under the umbrella of SPLE, several techniques have been proposed including those for automatically generating implementations of family members [13], configuring products [5] and transforming models [25].

2.1   Feature Modeling

When decomposing a family of products in terms of its features, one of the main objectives is to construct a well-structured product line that is typically represented as a feature model. Feature modeling is a popular model-driven approach to describing commonalities and variabilities of a family of (software) products in terms of features. A feature is any distinctive user-visible aspect, or characteristic of a product [17].

The feature model depicted in Figure 1[2] represents a simple laptop family. An FM hierarchically structures features and feature groups, in a tree-like top-down fashion, using parent-child relations. A feature diagram is simply a graphical representation of an FM typically represented as an And-Or tree with nodes as features. An FM can include constraints that further clarify dependencies among features.

An FM can be represented in at least two ways: as a feature diagram, or a textual form. In addition, a SPL tool might internally translate a FM representation to a propositional formula so that it can, for example, verify the validity of a model, and perform various computations on an FM to support, for example, reasoning and composing operations [7, 14, 33]. Transforming an FM from one representation to another should preserve the hierarchy and constraints in their original form. Each product of a SPL corresponds to a valid configuration of an FM. A configuration is obtained by selecting and unselecting features in an FM. A feature model thus defines a set of valid feature configurations. The validity of a configuration is determined by the semantics of a feature model. For example, in Figure 1, screens with sizes 13.3" and 17" are mutually exclusive and cannot be selected at the same time. Similarly, more expensive laptops (i.e., those with 17" screens) must include a warranty meaning that all laptops with 17" screens will also come with the warranty.

As feature models are rapidly emerging as a viable and important systems development tools, they are also becoming increasingly complex. Managing FMs of industrial size is a labor-intensive and error-prone process.

2.2   FAMILIAR

To meet the requirement of handling large and complex FMs in a scalable way, the domain-specific modeling language FAMILIAR was developed [2–4, 16]. FA-MILIAR is an executable scripting language that has the built-in capability

---

[2] For brevity, feature names used in a Laptop FM are abbreviated to combination of letters, underlined in the Feature Diagram example given in Figure 1.

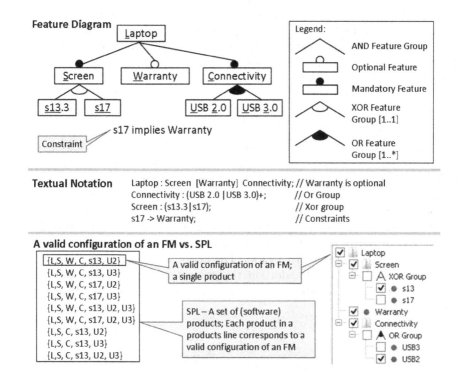

Fig. 1. Example of a Laptop FM with different FM notations

to compose and decompose feature models, and also to manipulate and reason about FMs. FAMILIAR allows stakeholders to describe domain concepts in terms of commonalities and variabilities within a family of software or product systems. Feature models are typically passed in to the FAMILIAR interpreter in a textual notation. In addition, the FAMILIAR language can interpret a script in order to perform a sequence of operations on feature models. Such scripts are reusable.

One of the most powerful characteristics of the FAMILIAR language is its set of composition operators that are designed for supporting the separation of concerns in feature modeling. To the best of our knowledge, FAMILIAR is the only SPL modeling environment capable of working with multiple FMs. As a part of the work presented in this paper, we enhanced FAMILIAR to support FM visualization.

3   Designing the New FAMILIAR Tool

Our goal was to develop an extension of the previous FAMILIAR framework which (1) supports visualization of FMs, (2) provides a configuration editor, (3) enables the persistence of FMs, and (4) embeds the text-based console. The new FAMILIAR Tool [23] would provide an integrated modeling environment within the FAMILIAR framework without requiring the use of any other IDEs (e.g., Eclipse) or plugins. In addition, the tool would still expose all of the original de/composition, reasoning, editing, scripting, interoperability and other facilities of the FAMILIAR language.

3.1 Visualization of Feature Models

Since our development platform was Eclipse with a Java legacy code base, we considered only the visualization kits available on Java platforms such as Zest, JUNG, Prefuse, Protovis, SWT, and GEF. We chose to use Prefuse, a graphical, open source library designed to support the development of interactive visualizations. The architecture of Prefuse utilizes the Visualization Pipeline, which decomposes a design into a piped process of (1) representing abstract data, (2) mapping data into intermediate, visualizable form, and (3) using these visual constructs to provide interactive views. The intent is to improve scalability and representational flexibility. In addition, this separation of concerns supports multiple views, semantic zooming, data and visual transformations, and fine grained customizations [19].

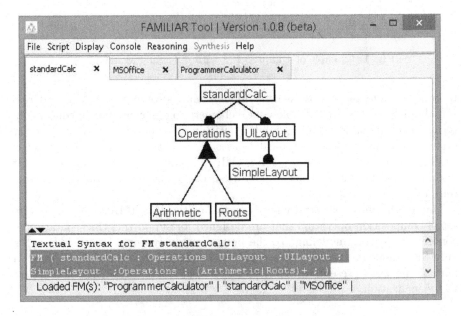

Fig. 2. Example of a visualized FM rendered by the FAMILIAR Tool

The main window of the FAMILIAR Tool (Figure 2) has two components: The visual section (upper frame) and the embedded console section (bottom frame). FMs that are displayed in the visual section are read from and written directly to the FAMILIAR environment. Similarly, textual commands that are issued either interactively through the embedded console or by running a script, are written to the same FAMILIAR environment. Any model update, no matter how it is done (i.e., visually, interactively through command console or through script execution), always keeps the FMs in a fully synchronized and consistent states.

A user can choose to create a new feature model, import a FM from another SPL tool, or load an FM saved in a previous session. A user can create a new FM using (1) interactive pop-up menus, (2) the embedded text console, or (3) a script. An FM is displayed and accessed under a single tab. Executing a script that, among other things, creates several feature models, would create several tabs, each of them containing a pre-loaded feature model. Closing a tab would not remove its associated feature model from the environment, rather, it would unload it.

Integration with the FAMILIAR's interpreter was achieved by forwarding down the system's Java input stream (text-based commands) from the embedded console (GUI control) to the FAMILIAR framework, and by redirecting the system output streams back to the same GUI control. This way, the embedded FAMILIAR console, which is part of tool (bottom part of the main application dialog shown in Figure 2) behaves the same way, syntactically and semantically, as the old standalone text-based tool. Any action that is committed directly through the embedded console control is automatically rendered in loaded graphical FMs. This required maintaining a one-to-one mapping among three internal FM model representations: (1) an FM environment variable with its associated AST model of a feature diagram, (2) a visual FM object with its associated Prefuse interactive view model, and (3) in-memory representation of the serialized FM to XML storage.

We also integrated the existing FeatureIDE FAMILIAR plugin command (i.e. "gdisplay" command) that is used for visualizing feature models within the Eclipse IDE environment. This was achieved through the observer pattern. For example, once the FAMILIAR interpreter detects a "gdisplay" statement, it creates an observer handler as well as an observable event source with the feature model variable name. Then, it subscribes the observer handler event to the event source. Finally, this observable event is handled at the GUI level by loading an appropriate feature model variable that corresponds to the given feature model variable name.

The Configuration Editor is implemented as an interactive Java tree control that represents an FM with its set of selected and/or deselected features. A feature is allowed to be selected or deselected only when the FM's propositional formula is satisfiable.

3.2 FAMILIAR's New Architecture

As depicted in Figure 3, the improved FAMILIAR environment now encompasses three main layers:

Framework: This is the cornerstone of the FAMILIAR language. The framework specifies the language grammar and builds an internal abstract syntax
tree (AST) structure. The interpreter uses 3rd party off-the-shelf solvers
(BDD and SAT) to check satisfiability of an FM's propositional formula. It
also provides rich semantics for FM composition operators (aggregate, merge,
and insert) as well as decomposition operators (slice). Finally, it exposes its
functionality through a non-public Java API interface, which is used by the
UI layer.

UI Layer: This layer exposes the framework to an user. There are three ways
that FAMILIAR can currently be used: (1) As a new FAMILIAR Tool which
integrates the Prefuse visualization framework with FM Editor, Configuration Editor and an embedded console into unique modeling standalone environment, (2) as the legacy text-based console and (3) as an Eclipse Plugin.

Converters/Bridges: This layer integrates several converters and bridges that
allow for integration with other SPL languages and notations.

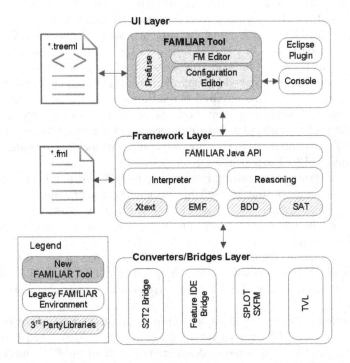

Fig. 3. FAMILIAR environment with the addition of the GUI tool

4   Evaluating the Usability

Usability does not exist in any absolute sense. Rather, it would make sense only
to define it with reference to particular contexts. ISO 9241 [1] defines usability in

terms of the quality of use as the "effectiveness, efficiency and satisfaction with which specified users achieve specified goals in particular environments". Bevan [8] uses this standard to describe a method called MUSiC (Metrics for Usability Standards in Computing) for specifying the context of use when measuring user effectiveness, efficiency, and satisfaction. The context needs to define who the intended users of the system are, the tasks those users will perform with it, and the characteristics of the organizational or social environment in which it will be used. This method seems particularly suitable for our evaluation since (1) it focuses on usability attributes that we are interested in measuring, and (2) it relies on an industrial standard, ISO 9241.

We chose to do a formal experiment since we needed to impose control over the variables that can affect the study outcomes. In addition, we need to be able to achieve replication in an environment where both the difficulty of control and the cost of replication are fairly low.

4.1   Goal, Research Questions, and Context

We formulate the goal of the FAMILIAR Tool evaluation using the Goal-Question Metric (GQM) template [36] as follows:

Goal: Evaluate the FAMILIAR Tool to better understand the impact on usability aspects of implementing feature model visualizations on the FAMILIAR language from the viewpoint of modelers.

Based on this goal, we focus on the following research questions:

RQ1: Does visualization of feature models help modelers to create FMs of better quality?
RQ2: Does visualization of feature models help modelers to manage FMs with better efficiency?
RQ3: Does visualization of feature models help modelers to manage FMs with better effectiveness?

The context selection represented situations where SPL practitioners created new FMs. The controlled experiment was conducted within two groups of graduate Computer Science students with a total of 16 participants from two countries, United States and France. The first group involved 3 graduate Ph.D. students that are under Dr. Robert France's supervision at the Colorado State University (CSU). The second group involved 13 Masters and Ph.D. students that took a graduate SPL course taught by Dr. Philippe Collet, at the University of Nice, Sophia Antipolis (UNS). The UNS participants, a larger sample, formed the treatment group by working only with the new FAMILIAR Tool (Visual). On the other hand, CSU participants formed the control group by working only with the legacy standalone tool (Text-based).

4.2 Hypothesis Formulation

Graphical modeling proponents claim that presenting models in a visualized form helps the user grasp the information landscape more quickly and intuitively. We seek to test this claim in the context of feature modeling.

Hypothesis: Using the FAMILIAR Tool with visualized feature models yields higher FM quality, user effectiveness, and efficiency than using the same tool with text only mode, when creating new FMs.

4.3 Experiment Design

Participants were asked to go through several stages before they ran the main experiment scenario. These stages involved the following: (1) Basic training on SPL, Feature Modeling, and the FAMILIAR language, (2) configuring the FA-MILIAR environment in preparation for the experiment, and (3) the experiment session.

First, we provided minimal overview of SPL, Feature Modeling, and a brief introduction to the FAMILIAR language and its environment. The training provided was at the very basic level, and students did not spend more than one hour before starting the experiment sessions. Second, preparation for the experiment involved getting the FAMILIAR environment properly configured. Finally, the experiment session was no longer than 55 minutes, and it consisted of two sub-tasks (3.1) analyzing the on-line configurator for Audi cars, and then (3.2) modeling it by creating a new FM file for the Audi configurator. Students were asked to work at their own pace, independently of one another. They were also required to record all of their interactions with the tools during the experiment session. By doing this, we could accurately measure the number of modeling tasks that users successfully completed, the accuracy with which users completed tasks (i.e., some quantification of the errors), the duration of tasks, users' learning of the interface, and finally, asses quality of FMs created, and calculate user efficiency and effectiveness.

4.4 Experiment Objects and Variables

There was one independent variable and three target variables as shown in Table 1. The treatment object is the group that used the new FAMILIAR Tool and worked with visualized FMs (V-group). The control object is the group that used a legacy FAMILIAR console and worked with textual FMs (T-group). Since V-group is compared to T-group regarding its FM quality as well as user effectiveness and efficiency, choice of the used tool is the independent variable and FM quality, user effectiveness, and user efficiency are the dependent variables.

Dependent Variable - FM Quality: According to the MUSiC method, quality is a measure of the degree to which the output achieves the task goals. For the purpose of this experiment, quality is expressed in terms of a final FM quality. Table 2 breaks down the criteria that we used to assess the quality of an FM.

Table 1. Experiment variables

Independent Variable	Dependent Variables	Scale of Measurement
Used Tool	FM Quality	Ordinal
	User Effectiveness	Ordinal
	User Efficiency	Ordinal

Table 2. FM quality

Quality	Assigned Weight	Description
Poor	0.2	FM cannot be properly parsed by the tool (i.e., model contains an inconsistent and/or an invalid element(s), or simply it is not syntactically well-formed).
Satisfactory	0.4	FM is properly loaded by the tool but lacks majority of features and/or groups.
Good	0.6	FM is mostly complete (i.e., includes various Audi model lines) and has neither inconsistencies nor invalid elements.
Very good	0.8	FM includes a comprehensive features set but might fail to accurately represent certain group dependencies (e.g., used AND-group when XOR-group would be more appropriate).
Excellent	1.0	FM includes a comprehensive features set, and provides a solid foundation for further breaking down the model as an SPL artifact. Different feature groups, dependencies and constraints were used in terms of both quantity and quality. (i.e., this FM, if offered with an online configurator, has enough details to allow a customer to produce a model of a custom Audi car tailored for her needs).

Dependent Variable - User Effectiveness: To assess user effectiveness, we defined a quantity that is a measure of the amount of a task completed by a user. It is defined as the proportion of the task goals accomplished, as represented in the output of the task. For the purpose of this experiment, the quantity reflects a measure of FM completeness in terms of the number of features, number of constraints, valid configurations and FM depth. Each of those four categories contributes 25% of a total quantity value. Table 3 shows how we calculated quantity as a measure of FM completeness.

The quantity is expressed as a number between 1 and 100 where 1 represents the least complete FM, and 100 represents the most complete FM. Note that the quantity measure does not (and should not) reflect the quality of an FM. Finally, the user effectiveness is given as a percentage, and is calculated using the following formula:

$$UserEffectiveness = (FMQuantity * FMQuality)\%$$

Dependent Variable - User Efficiency: Note that the user effectiveness does not take into account the time required to complete a given task. The user

Table 3. FM completeness

Category	Assigned Weight	Description
# of features	0.25	Up to 29 features
	0.50	30-39 features
	0.75	40-49 features
	1	50 or more
# of constraints	0.25	1 constraint
	0.50	2-3 constraints
	0.75	3-4 constraints
	1	5 or more
Valid configs	0.25	Up to 100 or above 25k
	0.50	Up to 4999 configs
	0.75	Up to 9999 configs
	1	Between 10k and 25k
FM Depth	0.25	Depth of 1
	0.50	Depth of 2
	0.75	Depth of 3
	1	Depth of 4 or more

efficiency calculation does include the time component. The user efficiency is calculated using the following formula:

$$UserEfficiency = \frac{UserEffectiveness}{ScenarioTime}$$

Therefore, the user efficiency measures the user effectiveness in terms of time it takes to complete a task. The higher this number is the more efficient this user is relative to other users.

5   Experimental Results

We used the Small Stata 12.1 package to perform a statistical analysis and chart all of the graphs shown in this section. Table 4 shows the main experiment data.

The last three columns (dependent variables) are determined by the study methodology as described in Section 4.4.

5.1   Observations

Figure 4 shows the box plots for all three dependent variables FM Quality, Effectiveness and Efficiency, grouped by the tool used (T-group and V-group). The box plots show that T-group has no outliers, and the V-group has 2. The medians are indicated by the diamonds. The median values for all dependent variables are higher for V-group than T-group. Each of the box plots illustrates a different skewness pattern. It appears that the Effectiveness in particular exhibits a non-symmetric distribution which might imply non-normal data.

Table 4. Summarized experimental results

Group	Time (min)	# of user errors	# of features created	FM quality	User Effectiveness	User Efficiency
V	24.8	10	38	0.8	55%	0.53
V	11.4	1	23	0.4	23%	0.48
V	18.6	3	44	0.4	18%	0.23
V	16.2	3	37	0.4	13%	0.19
V	45.2	42	48	1.0	75%	0.40
V	25.3	12	39	0.4	18%	0.17
V	20.2	8	26	0.4	15%	0.18
V	29.0	12	71	0.6	38%	0.31
V	12.4	4	37	0.4	23%	0.44
V	19.8	4	54	0.6	34%	0.41
V	13.6	0	46	0.6	30%	0.53
V	6.8	7	27	0.4	10%	0.36
V	5.8	3	27	0.4	18%	0.72
T	30.8	1	51	0.2	15%	0.12
T	9.9	5	17	0.4	15%	0.36
T	16.4	25	10	0.2	13%	0.18

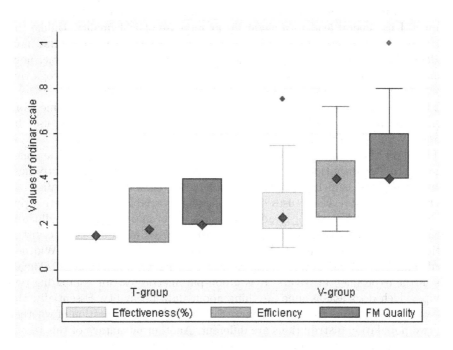

Fig. 4. Box plots of dependent variables, by group

Table 5. Median values of dependent variables, by group

Group	FM Quality	User Effectiveness	User Efficiency
V	0.4	23%	0.40
T	0.2	15%	0.18

In addition to Figure 4, Table 5 shows the calculated median values for all dependent variables by group.

We are not concerned with averages since they do not make sense for ordinal data. Based on our small sample data, there is evidence that participants who used the visualized SPL tool did better than participants who used the text-based tool in terms of all three categories: FM quality, user effectiveness and user efficiency. For example, 2 out of 3 participants from T-group failed to produce a valid FM, whereas all of 13 participants from V-group produced valid FMs that could be independently verified after the experiment was completed. However, we need to determine whether this difference in medians between two groups is statistically significant before we can make stronger experiment conclusions.

Figure 5 shows correlation between a number of features in an FM and its impact on an FM quality. It appears that, for the text-based tool, more features in a model tend to reduce overall quality of an FM. This might make sense since the larger textual models require increased cognitive efforts on the user side. However, the visual tool demonstrates the opposite tendency: More features in an FM in general lead to a slight linear increase of FM quality. Unlike the T-group users, the participants who worked with visualized FMs did not have to deal with the increased cognitive load necessary due to cumbersome, non-human friendly, text models. Rather, they could dedicate more of their cognitive processing power on tasks that would yield higher model quality.

The next question that we need to answer is whether the data come from normal distributions. Unfortunately, our samples are very small. We use the Shapiro-Wilk W test for normal data with a P-value of 0.05 as a cutoff.

The lower the P-value is, the smaller the chance that the sample data comes from a normal distribution. Figure 6 shows that only the P-value of Effectiveness is lower than 0.05, which means that its sample deviates from normality.

Our experimental design uses one independent variable with two levels (independent groups V and T). In addition, the scale of measurement for all three dependent variables is ordinal, and the picture is mixed when it comes to distribution of the data. Because of all of this, we decided to use the Mann-Whitney Rank Sum Test (also known as Wilcoxon Rank Sum Test) for the statistical analysis of the experimental results. It is a non-parametric test for comparing two groups which does not assume anything about data normality. Essentially, the run-sum test attempts to provide a statistical answer to the question of whether the two population distributions are different. Another advantage of this test is that it is not sensitive to outliers. This is an important consideration for the experiment analysis, since it relies on a very small population sample (13 from V-group and 3 from T-group, 16 valid samples in total) with 2 outliers.

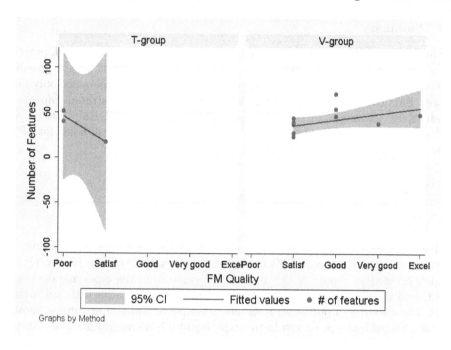

Fig. 5. Scatter plot that correlates a number of features in an FM and its impact on a FM quality

variable	obs	W	V	z	Prob > z
fmquality	16	0.93052	1.408	0.679	0.24841
effectiveness	16	0.77929	4.472	2.975	0.00146
efficiency	16	0.95110	0.991	-0.018	0.50731

Fig. 6. Shapiro-Wilk W test for normal data

The two-sample rank-sum tests the null hypothesis that two independent samples are from populations with the same distribution. With only 16 observations, the departure would have to be substantial to reject the uniform null hypothesis. We used the "porder" option of the rank sum command to calculate this departure, that is, the probability that a random draw from the first sample (T-group) is larger than a random draw from the second sample (V-group). The probabilities for FM Quality, Effectiveness and Efficiency were 10.3%, 16.7% and 17.9% respectively. The finding was that the two-sample rank-sum tests for all three variables rejected the null hypothesis meaning that there is significant statistical difference between the group that used text-based tool and the group that used visual tool.

5.2 Summary

In this experiment, we evaluated the impact of the new tool on novice SPL practitioners when working with relatively small FMs. The experiment results provide some evidence that FM visualizations can be beneficial. The users not only authored FMs of a higher quality but also consistently demonstrated improved productivity expressed in terms of user effectiveness and efficiency. However, further research is required to identify whether this outcome still holds for SPL experts working with FMs on a larger scale.

6   Threats to Validity

6.1   External Validity

Our evaluation is based on the assumption that we were measuring effects of working with representative FMs that model a real-world artifact. However, the models created as a part of this experiment came from the academic environment, and there is no guarantee that they share characteristics with industrial FMs. The majority of published FMs have a couple of hundred features at most. The number of features we saw in the experimental FMs ranged from the 20s to the 70s. One of the largest documented FM is the feature model of a Linux kernel [32] with over 5500 features, and thousands of constraints. An FM of this scale would clearly pose a responsiveness challenge to the FAMILIAR language in its current state; we will continue to work on improving performance of FAMILIAR when applied to very big FMs.

Since this experiment was conducted in two geographic locations, and we had limited resources with time constraints, we could not afford to ask both groups to evaluate both tools. Originally, we wanted to use the blocking technique as a part of our experimental design and rotate the groups, asking each group to replicate the experiment with another tool. However, this turned out to be time consuming and we had to adopt a smaller-scale option. As a consequence, the V-group, which happens to have somewhat better exposure to SPL and Feature Modeling, served as our treatment group working with visualized FMs. This created the specific situation of the experiment that might limit its generalizability. In order to mitigate this risk, we made sure to provide the same introductory training on SPL, Feature Modeling and FAMILIAR to all the participants in each group.

The experiment is conducted exclusively with novice modelers thus limiting its generalizability.

6.2   Internal Validity

A selection bias risk might be introduced when differences between variable groups interact with the independent variables and thus interferes with the observed outcome.

Since we used two tools from the same FAMILIAR environment, we mitigated the tool selection bias risk when evaluating the effect of presenting FMs (e.g., visual vs. textual form). Similarly, all participants were alike (e.g., grad CS students, novice SPL practitioners) with regard to the independent variable.

Repeatedly attempting to perform FM creation during the experiment session, would eventually teach participants to create better FMs in less time. We imposed the restriction of allowing only one session with the tool (with no allowed repetitions), regardless of its outcome.

6.3   Construct Validity

The most significant threat to the construct validity of the experiment is that all of our dependent variables use an ordinal scale. Does the experimental data provide accurate measurements of what it is intended to measure? According to [22], there are several notable threats caused by the ordinal scale measurement. For example, the ordinal labels could be inconsistently interpreted among different users. In addition, the distance between the different labels of an ordinal scale might not present a clear comparison between the significance of various ordinal labels. Taken together, these problems could have impacted the construct validity of the FAMILIAR Tool evaluation.

In order to mitigate this threat we used the statistical techniques that respect the specifics of ordinal data. Our analysis therefore focused on summarizing the central tendencies and statistical significances rather than trying to come up with exact metrics.

7   Related Work

Several previous works consider the importance of software visualization in the context of SPLE, especially for the configuration management phase. Pleuss et al. [29] identify and analyze benefits of the existing software visualization techniques such as feature trees, decision trees, tree maps, and cone trees. Similarly, Cawley et al. [10] combine principles from cognitive theory and visualization techniques. Schneeweiss et al. [30] introduce an interactive technique, the "Feature Flow Maps", which combines tree-oriented feature models and flow map visualizations. Thiel et al. [34] provide summary on techniques, tools and means to support variability through visualization. Janota et al. [24] describe the concept of providing better tool support in an interactive configuration scenarios where users work from one complete configuration to another by adapting only those features that are important to them. The work presented in this paper is complementary with their work since they both aim to reduce the cognitive complexity of large FMs. The difference is that in their work authors investigated interactive forms of visualization whereas we explored the combination of text-based and graphical FM representations to improve usability and model quality.

8   Conclusions and Future Work

In this paper we presented an extension of a textual DSML for feature modeling and an evaluation of the resulting development environment. The evaluation aimed at answering the question: *Does the lack of support for visualizing FMs in FM development tools hinder the usability of these tools when managing multiple and large FMs during modeling sessions?*

We found evidence that using the new FAMILIAR Tool with visualized FMs resulted in an increased cognitive efficiency and effectiveness of novice practitioners which also led to the improved quality of FMs they created. To the best of our knowledge, this is the first work which describes and evaluates combined graphical-textual tooling for feature modeling. Having essentially the same underlying environment for both FAMILIAR tools allowed us to observe the potential benefits of FM visualization, without interfering differences that would likely arise from using different tools. However, an experiment on a larger scale would be required to identify whether this outcome would hold for SPL experts that work with larger and scripted FMs.

A larger scale experiment is thus in our immediate future work plan. The FAMILIAR language has capabilities to manipulate several FMs, to write scripts that inputs and outputs FMs and other relevant types such as configurations. We also want to investigate appropriate visual support when dealing with these operations. To do so, we plan to provide feature diagram visualizations with a more compact form using aggregated values and indicators. In the longer term, we want to tackle issues related to the evolution of feature models, as well as relationships between several FMs, as in multiple software product lines. We expect these advances to provide support and insights for a better and wider usage of feature modeling in software product line engineering.

References

1. ISO 9241-11: Ergonomic requirements for office work with visual display terminals (VDTs) - part 11: Guidance on usability. Tech. rep., International Organization for Standardization, Geneva (1998)
2. Acher, M.: Managing Multiple Feature Models: Foundations, Language and Applications. Ph.D. thesis (2011)
3. Acher, M., Collet, P., Lahire, P., France, R.: FAMILIAR: A Domain-Specific Language for Large Scale Management of Feature Models. Science of Computer Programming (SCP) Special Issue on Programming Languages, 55 (December 2012)
4. Acher, M., Collet, P., Lahire, P., France, R.: Familiar: A domain-specific language for large scale management of feature models. Science of Computer Programming (SCP) Special Issue on Programming Languages 78(6), 657–681 (2013)
5. Asikainen, T., Männistö, T., Soininen, T.: Using a configurator for modelling and configuring software product lines based on feature models. In: Workshop on Software Variability Management for Product Derivation, Software Product Line Conference, SPLC3, pp. 24–35 (2004)
6. Bąk, K., Czarnecki, K., Wąsowski, A.: Feature and meta-models in clafer: Mixed, specialized, and coupled. In: Malloy, B., Staab, S., van den Brand, M. (eds.) SLE 2010. LNCS, vol. 6563, pp. 102–122. Springer, Heidelberg (2011)
7. Batory, D.S.: Feature models, grammars, and propositional formulas. In: Obbink, H., Pohl, K. (eds.) SPLC 2005. LNCS, vol. 3714, pp. 7–20. Springer, Heidelberg (2005)

8. Bevan, N.: Measuring usability as quality of use. Software Quality Journal 4(2), 115–130 (1995)

9. Britton, C., Jones, S.: The untrained eye: how languages for software specification support understanding in untrained users. Human–Computer Interaction 14(1-2), 191–244 (1999)

10. Cawley, C., Healy, P., Botterweck, G.: A discussion of three visualisation approaches to providing cognitive support in variability management (2010)

11. Classen, A., Boucher, Q., Heymans, P.: A text-based approach to feature modelling: Syntax and semantics of TVL. Science of Computer Programming, Special Issue on Software Evolution, Adaptability and Variability 76(12), 1130–1143 (2011)

12. Classen, A., Boucher, Q., Heymans, P.: A text-based approach to feature modelling: Syntax and semantics of {TVL}. Science of Computer Programming 76(12), 1130–1143 (2011),
http://www.sciencedirect.com/science/article/pii/S0167642310001899,
Special Issue on Software Evolution, Adaptability and Variability

13. Czarnecki, K., Eisenecker, U.: Generative Programming: Methods, Tools, and Applications. Addison-Wesley (2000)

14. Czarnecki, K., Wasowski, A.: Feature diagrams and logics: There and back again. In: SPLC 2007, pp. 23–34. IEEE (2007)

15. Deursen, A.V., Klint, P.: Domain-specific language design requires feature descriptions. Journal of Computing and Information Technology 10(1), 1–17 (2002)

16. FAMILIAR: FeAture Model scrIpt Language for manIpulation and Automatic Reasonning, http://familiar-project.github.io/

17. Ferber, S., Haag, J., Savolainen, J.: Feature Interaction and Dependencies: Modeling Features for Reengineering a Legacy Product Line, pp. 37–60 (2002),
http://dx.doi.org/10.1007/3-540-45652-X_15

18. France, R., Rumpe, B.: Model-driven development of complex software: A research roadmap. In: 2007 Future of Software Engineering, FOSE 2007, pp. 37–54. IEEE Computer Society, Washington, DC (2007),
http://dx.doi.org/10.1109/FOSE.2007.14

19. Heer, J., Card, S.K., Landay, J.A.: Prefuse: a toolkit for interactive information visualization. In: Proceedings of the SIGCHI Conference on Human Factors in Computing Systems, pp. 421–430. ACM (2005)

20. Heinz, M., Levin, J.R.: Knowledge acquisition from text and pictures. Elsevier (1989)

21. Hubaux, A., Boucher, Q., Hartmann, H., Michel, R., Heymans, P.: Evaluating a textual feature modelling language: Four industrial case studies. In: Malloy, B., Staab, S., van den Brand, M. (eds.) SLE 2010. LNCS, vol. 6563, pp. 337–356. Springer, Heidelberg (2011)

22. Hubbard, D., Evans, D.: Problems with scoring methods and ordinal scales in risk assessment. IBM Journal of Research and Development 54(3), 2–10 (2010)

23. Jakšić, A.: Familiar tool v1.0.5 (beta) - demo (2014),
http://www.screencast.com/t/BdPgI8yF17Y/

24. Janota, M., Botterweck, G., Marques-Silva, J.: On lazy and eager interactive reconfiguration. In: Proceedings of the Eighth International Workshop on Variability Modelling of Software-Intensive Systems, VaMoS 2014, pp. 8:1–8:8. ACM, New York (2013), http://doi.acm.org/10.1145/2556624.2556644

25. Javier, F., Garcia, P., Laguna, M.A., Gonzalez-carvajal, Y.C., Gonzalez-baixauli, B.: Requirements variability support through mdd and graph transformation

26. Kang, K., Kim, S., Lee, J., Kim, K., Shin, E., Huh, M.: Form: A feature-oriented reuse method with domain-specific reference architectures. Annals of Software Engineering 5(1), 143–168 (1998)
27. Kang, K.C., Cohen, S.G., Hess, J.A., Novak, W.E., Peterson, A.S.: Feature-oriented domain analysis (foda) feasibility study. Tech. rep., DTIC Document (1990)
28. Larkin, J.H., Simon, H.A.: Why a diagram is (sometimes) worth ten thousand words. Cognitive Science 11(1), 65–100 (1987)
29. Pleuss, A., Rabiser, R., Botterweck, G.: Visualization techniques for application in interactive product configuration. In: Proceedings of the 15th International Software Product Line Conferencepp, SPLC 2011, vol. 2, pp. 22:1–22:8. ACM, New York (2011), http://doi.acm.org/10.1145/2019136.2019161
30. Schneeweiss, D., Botterweck, G.: Using flow maps to visualize product attributes during feature configuration. In: SPLC Workshops, pp. 219–228 (2010)
31. Selic, B.: The pragmatics of model-driven development. IEEE Software 20(5), 19–25 (2003), http://dx.doi.org/10.1109/ms.2003.1231146
32. Sincero, J., Schröder-preikschat, W.: The linux kernel configurator as a feature modeling tool (2008)
33. van der Storm, T.: Variability and Component Composition. In: Dannenberg, R.B., Krueger, C. (eds.) ICOIN 2004 and ICSR 2004. LNCS, vol. 3107, pp. 157–166. Springer, Heidelberg (2004), http://www.springerlink.com.gate6.inist.fr/content/k3nlvkm5uqj425x3
34. Thiel, S., Cawley, C., Botterweck, G.: Visualizing software variability. In: Capilla, R., Bosch, J., Kang, K.C. (eds.) Systems and Software Variability Management, pp. 101–118. Springer (2013)
35. Winn, W.: Learning from maps and diagrams. Educational Psychology Review 3(3), 211–247 (1991)
36. Wohlin, C., Runeson, P., Höst, M., Ohlsson, M.C., Regnell, B., Wesslén, A.: Experimentation in software engineering. Springer (2012)

A Metamodel Family for Role-Based Modeling and Programming Languages

Thomas Kühn, Max Leuthäuser, Sebastian Götz,
Christoph Seidl, and Uwe Aßmann

Technische Universität Dresden
Software Technology Group, Dresden, Germany
{thomas.kuehn3,max.leuthaeuser,christoph.seidl,
uwe.assmann}@tu-dresden.de, sebastian.goetz@acm.org

Abstract. Role-based modeling has been proposed almost 40 years ago as a means to model complex and dynamic domains, because roles are able to capture both context-dependent and collaborative behavior of objects. Unfortunately, while several researchers have introduced the notion of roles to modeling and programming languages, only few have captured both the relational and the context-dependent nature of roles. In this work, we classify various proposals since 2000 and show the discontinuity and fragmentation of the whole research field. To overcome discontinuity, we propose a family of metamodels for role-based modeling languages. Each family member corresponds to a design decision captured in a feature model. In this way, it becomes feasible to generate a metamodel for each role-based approach. This allows for the combination and improvement of the different role-based modeling and programming languages and paves the way to reconcile the research field.

1 Introduction

Role-based modeling has been proposed in 1973 by Charles W. Bachman [2] as a means to model complex and dynamic domains, because roles are able to capture both context-dependent and collaborative behavior of objects. Consequently, they were introduced in various fields of research ranging from data modeling [2, 31] via conceptual modeling [56, 26] through to programming languages [3, 35, 8]. Unfortunately, each of these approaches focuses on a specific field without taking results of other fields into account.[1] As a result, the years of research on role-based modeling had almost no influence on software development practice. This is troubling, because current software systems are characterized by increasing complexity and context-dependence. Moreover, they are designed by means of objects and references, introduced in 1967 [45].

Despite the fact that relationships and roles are represented in various domain modeling languages, e.g., the Entity-Relationship Model [13] and the Unified Modeling Language (UML) [52], their implementation is buried in classes

---

[1] Please note that this work considers Role-Based Access Control (RBAC) [17] as a special application for roles with a rather narrow scope.

B. Combemale et al. (Eds.): SLE 2014, LNCS 8706, pp. 141–160, 2014.

containing collections of references making their implementation overly complex and error prone [53, 6]. The situation becomes even worse, if the domain model requires that two unrelated objects take the same place in a relation, because the developer must introduce a counter-intuitive super type for both objects [56]. Unfortunately, while several researchers have introduced the notion of roles to programming languages [10, 8, 11, 37, 51], only few provide an underlying meta-model for their context-dependent or relational roles. To make things worse, only few approaches incorporate both the context-dependent and the relational nature of roles, e.g., [46, 34]. In summary, the various approaches cannot be combined easily because they lack a common metamodel.

This work classifies the various notions proposed since 2000 along 26 features of roles and shows the apparent discontinuity and fragmentation of the whole research field. We attribute this situation to the missing compatibility of the various approaches. To cure this, we propose not only a single metamodel but a family of metamodels for role-based modeling languages (RML). Each member of the family corresponds to the 26 design decisions captured in a feature model. In this way, it becomes feasible to generate a metamodel for two approaches and then combine them by mapping their sibling metamodels to a merged meta-model. This allows for the combination and improvement of the different RMLs and paves the way to reconcile the research field.

This paper is structured as follows. Sect. 2 gives a general introduction to modeling languages, roles, and feature modeling. Afterwards, Sect. 3 introduces the classification scheme used in the next section (Sect. 4) to evaluate the various approaches published since the year 2000. As a result of this evaluation, Sect. 5 introduces a metamodel family for RMLs to overcome the discontinuity and fragmentation in the research field by providing a common source to model and compose existing approaches. The discussion is concluded by highlighting the related work (Sect. 6) and a summary and outlook to further research (Sect. 7).

2   Preliminaries

2.1   Elements of Modeling Languages

A modeling language has syntax (defining the notational aspects) and semantics (defining the meaning) [32]. A metamodel can be seen as an explicit model containing constructs and rules necessary to build more specific models within a domain of interest. Hence, they are models of modeling languages describing their abstract syntax. The *Meta Object Facility* (MOF) [49], for instance, assigns data to the following four meta levels (see Fig. 1a). The instance level (M0) encompasses concrete data. Models are located in the model level (M1). This level covers, e.g., concrete instantiations of UML-models, logical data models or process models that are defining data at M0. Metamodels like mentioned above are contained in the metamodel level (M2). The most abstract level, the meta-metamodel level (M3), is responsible for defining models at M2 and can be bootstrapped by itself to prevent an infinite number of meta-levels.

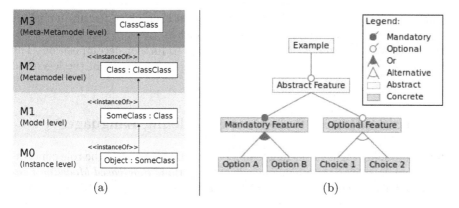

Fig. 1. Visualization of the Meta-Object Facility (a) and feature models (b)

2.2 Ontological Foundations of the Role Concept

To classify the role concept, two meta-predicates are sufficient: rigidity and dependence [24]. *Rigidity*, as explained in [23], distinguishes properties that must
hold for all instances of a concept in every possible world. As an example for
the former, the concept *Human* is rigid, because each instance is necessarily
a human until it ceases to exist. The latter case is further described as *anti-
rigidity* by Guizzardi et al. [29], denoting properties that can cease to hold for
all instances of such a concept. Thus, a *Customer* is *anti-rigid* because every
instance may stop being a customer without ceasing to exist. *Dependence*, as
explained in [24], characterizes properties as being meaningful only in combination with a counter-property. Thus, a dependent property always demands
for another property against which it is semantically founded. For example, the
concept *Customer* is founded against the counter-concept *Seller* in the context
of a *Shop*.

Roles are defined as anti-rigid and dependent concept [24]. The anti-rigidity
characterizes the ability of roles to be played. The dependence characterizes the
need of roles to be defined as part of a context, which includes besides the role
itself at least one corresponding counter-role. In contrast to roles, *naturals* are
defined as rigid and independent concepts. Thus, naturals are not played, but
can serve as players for roles. In addition, naturals do not have to be part of
contexts as they do not require a counter-concept.

2.3 Feature Modeling

Modeling the variability of a certain domain has, among others, been studied in
the context of software product line engineering [14]. Here, an often used technique to capture variability is feature modeling [44]. Therein, a feature model
decomposes a domain's concerns into interconnected features, which form a decision tree. For this purpose, constraints can be defined between the features,
e.g., whether the existence of a feature is mandatory or if a set of features

mutually excludes each other. Fig. 1b depicts an exemplary feature model. It comprises a single top feature (*Example*), which is decomposed into a single optional feature (*AbstractFeature*) being subject to further decomposition. The types of constraints and features used in this paper are shown in the legend of this figure.

3   Classification of Role-Based Modeling Languages

After introducing the basic elements of modeling languages and the role concept, this section presents a thorough analysis of the various *Role-based Modeling Languages* (RML) as well as *Role-based Programming Languages* (RPL) proposed since the year 2000. We choose that year, because Friedrich Steimann published a thorough analysis of RML in that year [56]. Additionally, he identified 15 features of roles useful to classify and compare all subsequent approaches. Since then, many modeling languages utilizing roles have been published. However, only two applied Steimann's classification scheme, namely [11] and [37]. Hence, it is time for another thorough analysis and classification of the various contemporary approaches.

3.1   Steimann's Features

Before we evaluate the literature body, we need to describe our classification scheme. Therefore, we briefly recapitulate *Steimann's classification* and introduce additional features of roles retrieved from the contemporary literature. The latter is crucial, because current approaches have shifted their focus to the context-dependent nature of roles not included in Steimann's classification.

In particular, it contains a list of 15 features attributed to roles by various researchers [56, pp. 86-87]. This list, enumerated in Fig. 2, captures different views on roles. Nevertheless, it has three major drawbacks, if it is used as a classification scheme. First, as Steimann already admitted in [56, pp. 86], some of the listed features are conflicting, e.g., Feature 14 and 15 querying whether a role has a shared or its own identity. Second, there are implicit dependencies among some of the features. Consider, for instance, an approach where roles have no properties and behavior (Feature 1). Such an approach can never satisfy Feature 10, 11 and 13 depending on the structure of roles. Last, several features concern different levels of the model hierarchy. Features 4, 5, 9, 10, 12, 14, and 15 only apply to roles at runtime. Thus, these features cannot be applied to approaches focusing solely on *the model level* (M1). Henceforth, we explicitly associate the features to the levels they affect and, later on, will organize the features in a feature model rather than a plain list. Nevertheless, this initial list of features still proves useful as a classification scheme. However, it does not encompass the view that roles can be used to model context-dependent properties [41] and behavior [37, 50, 43].

1. Roles have properties and behaviors	*(M1, M0)*
2. Roles depend on relationships	*(M1)*
3. Objects may play different roles simultaneously	*(M1, M0)*
4. Objects may play the same role (type) several times	*(M0)*
5. Objects may acquire and abandon roles dynamically	*(M0)*
6. The sequence of role acquisition and removal may be restricted	*(M1, M0)*
7. Unrelated objects can play the same role	*(M1)*
8. Roles can play roles	*(M1, M0)*
9. Roles can be transferred between objects	*(M0)*
10. The state of an object can be role-specific	*(M0)*
11. Features of an object can be role-specific	*(M1)*
12. Roles restrict access	*(M0)*
13. Different roles may share structure and behavior	*(M1)*
14. An object and its roles share identity	*(M0)*
15. An object and its roles have different identities	*(M0)*

Fig. 2. Fiedrich Steimann's 15 classifying features, extracted from [56]

16. Relationships between roles can be constrained	*(M1)*
17. There may be constraints between relationships	*(M1)*
18. Roles can be grouped and constrained together	*(M1)*
19. Roles depend on compartments	*(M1, M0)*
20. Compartments have properties and behaviors	*(M1, M0)*
21. A role can be part of several compartments	*(M1, M0)*
22. Compartments may play roles like objects	*(M1, M0)*
23. Compartments may play roles which are part of themselves	*(M1, M0)*
24. Compartments can contain other compartments	*(M1, M0)*
25. Different compartments may share structure and behavior	*(M1)*
26. Compartments have their own identity	*(M0)*

Fig. 3. Additional classifying features, derived from the literature

3.2 Additional Features

To include the new perspective on roles, this section gives a list of the features attributed to roles that we have identified in the literature.

16. Relationships between roles can be constrained. If roles depend on relationships, then it might be possible to further constrain them by *intra-relationship constraints* [30, 8, 48], i.e., irreflectivity, total order or exclusive parthood.

17. There may be constraints between relationships. In contrast to feature 16, this property suggests the existence of *inter-relationship constraints*, like the subset constraint [31, 30, 10, 48].

18. Roles can be grouped and constrained together. Most approaches suggesting to constrain roles [15, 11, 9] do not permit to group them and apply constraints to a whole group of related roles as suggested in [60, 37].

Together, these three properties specify ways to constrain roles, but do not account for their context-dependence. However, in this case, the use of the term *context* leads to a dichotomy of its meaning. On the one hand, according to Anind

Dey [16], "context [represents] any information that can be used to characterize the situation of an entity". Thus, everything that can be attributed to an object in a situation contributes to its context. On the other hand, within modeling languages, context represents a collaboration or container of a fixed, limited scope [19, 41, 50, 43]. To overcome this dichotomy, researchers avoided the term context by using other terms, i.e., *Environments* [60], *Institutions* [4], *Teams* [36] and *Ensembles* [34]. In turn, we use the term *Compartment* as a generalization of these terms to denote an objectified collaboration with a limited number of participating roles and a fixed scope[2].

19. Roles depend on compartments. Most of the recent approaches agree that roles are dependent on some sort of context. We call them compartments [36, 60, 4, 19, 41, 50, 43, 34]. A typical example of a compartment is a university, which contains the roles *Student* and *Teacher* collaborating in *Courses* [37, 7, 47].

20. Compartments have properties and behaviors like objects [19, 41, 50, 43].

21. A Role can be part of several compartments [4, 60, 19, 46]. This property suggests that a role (type) can be part of more than one compartment. Consider again the role type *Teacher*. It can be used in different compartments, i.e., *School* or *University*, where it might be implemented and constrained differently [4].

22. Compartments may play roles like objects. While most approaches use compartments as a grouping mechanism, compartments can be seen as entities similar to naturals being able to play roles, as well. This view is captured within the metamodel for roles [19] and implemented in ObjectTeams/Java [37].

23. Compartments may play roles which are part of themselves. Continuing the argument of feature 22, compartments might be allowed to play roles belonging to the same compartments, as possible in [19, 37].[3]

24. Compartments can contain other compartments. In addition to the previous properties, three approaches allow compartments to contain other compartments [37, 41, 42]. This *nesting* is proposed to further structure compartments into smaller sub-compartments [37, 42] and, thus, enable the representation of a university containing academic departments which in turn contain faculties.

25. Different compartments may share structure and behavior [40, 41]. This means that definitions of compartments may inherit properties, features, roles, and constraints from each other. However, to fully support inheritance and polymorphism of compartments, the rules of family polymorphism have to be applied [40].

26. Compartments have their own identity. This feature is acknowledged by all approaches who treat compartments as first-class entities of the instance level [60, 37, 46, 50, 42, 34]. Thus, this feature is a prerequisite for the existence of compartments at runtime. However, it is an open question whether this identity is unique or composed from the identities of the participating objects.

From this list, condensed in Fig. 3, it becomes apparent that researchers have successfully applied the concept of roles to the domain of context-dependent (or

---

[2] Note that compartments are defined top-down in the conceptual model whereas contexts are built bottom-up from individual sensor readings.

[3] This feature is described in §2.1.2 (b) of ObjectTeams/Java's language definition [39].

context-aware) systems. This has led to a number of new features attributed to roles affecting both model and instance level. Surprisingly, the definitional dependence of roles [25] is still applicable to compartments representing the definitional boundary and execution scope for their enclosing roles. Hence, the first 18 features highlight the relational nature of roles whereas the last eight emphasize the context-dependent nature of roles. As a result, this list is suitable to further study and classify the various RMLs and RPLs.

4   Survey of Recent Approaches

After devising a proper classification scheme, this section applies it to survey the various contemporary RMLs and RPLs. For that reason, we checked all role-based modeling or programming language (excluding RBAC) published between the year 2000 and 2014 by either *IEEE, ACM, Springer* or *ScienceDirect*. Additionally, only those approaches were selected that provided enough information about their role model to actually apply our classification. In summary, we have selected nine modeling languages ranging from data modeling via conceptual modeling to architecture modeling and seven programming languages with either relational or context-dependent roles. However, due to the fact that some of the identified features of roles only affect the instance level (M0), such features are not applicable to modeling languages defining conceptual models. For programming languages, on the other hand, each feature is applicable because they incorporate both the model and the instance level.

4.1   Modeling Languages

In the following, we investigate the various RMLs proposed for conceptual modeling, data modeling, and generalization of the role concept.

For *conceptual modeling* **Lodwick** [56] is the first formal modeling language for relational roles. Its formal definition includes *natural types* filling *role types*, whereas the latter are placeholders in a binary *relationship*. However, roles are only represented on the conceptual model and do not carry on to instances of that model [56]. **Onto-UML** [28], on the other hand, is an ontologically founded conceptual modeling language developed by Guizzardi et al. [29, 28] to overcome the syntactical and semantical shortcomings of UML. The underlying *Universal Foundational Ontology* (UFO) [27] contains *RoleTypes, RoleMixins*, and *Relators*; and is used to annotate UML classes and relations with stereotypes. Role mixins, however, are only used to model role types playable by unrelated types [29]. In sum, both Lodwick and Onto-UML only deal with the creation of formal conceptual models, but are neither concerned with the representation of roles at runtime nor context-dependent entities. In contrast to them, the **Helena Approach** [34] incorporates both concerns. It was proposed by Hennicker et al. [34] to specify the collaborative behavior of *Ensembles* of distributed *Components* and designed to cope with the high dynamics of collaborative executions. Here, *Ensemble Structures* are reification of collaborations containing *Role*

Types defining the behavior of *Components* playing that role [34]. Additionally, the communication between two roles is restricted by *Role Connectors* [34], i.e. directed channels between two role types, similar to a relationship. Consequently, their model not only captures both natures of roles in a simple model but also the semantics by means of *Labeled Transition Systems*. Nevertheless, they missed to specify the actual interaction between the player and its assuming roles.

In the field of *data modeling*, however, interactions are of no concern. Herein, **Object-Role Modeling (ORM) 2** [30] is the most mature fact-oriented data modeling methodology. Roles, however, are only included as unnamed places in binary relationships. Despite that, ORM provides a large number of available constraints for these relationships including role constraints, inter- and intra-relationship constraints [30]. Nevertheless, it did not embrace the possible flexibility provided by the role concept. This is different for the **Information Networking Model** (INM) [46] designed to overcome the lack of classical RML models to capture context-dependent information. Hence, INM introduces the concept of *Contexts* to group *Roles*. While this approach allows to nest contexts with attributes containing roles, INM cannot constrain the various kinds of relations [46]. In sum, INM would be a good extension to ORM 2, if they were compatible.

In contrast to the previous approaches, the following ones *generalize the role concept*. The **Generic Role Model** [15], for instance, introduces a new inheritance relation, denoted *role relationship*, to permit dynamic changing classes, multiple instantiation of the same class, and context-dependent access [15]. While roles are mingled within the inheritance hierarchy on the model level (M1), they are represented as adjunct objects on the instance level (M0) leading to object schizophrenia [38]. On the down side, it does not account for the relational and context-dependent nature of roles. The **E-CARGO Model** [60], on the other hand, is a role-based model for *computer-supported cooperative work* (CSCW) encompassing *Agents* playing *Roles* collaborating in *Groups* working on *Objects* in defined *Environments* [60]. Groups are used to arrange and manage collaborating agents and their assumed roles [60], whereas environments, such as contexts, specify the workspace of several groups and limit the number of roles played simultaneously [60, Appendix]. Thus, the combination of groups as collaborations and environments as their instantiation resemble compartments. In sum, while the target domain is cooperative work, the underlying model is applicable to role-based software systems as well. Similar to E-CARGO, **Data Context Interaction** (DCI) [50] emphasizes context-dependent roles. Trygve Reenskaug et al. [50] proposed this paradigm to point out that *Data* plays a *Role* in *Interactions* encapsulated in *Contexts* [50]. In particular, objects serve as data containers whose behavior is defined in roles part of a certain context. The context manages the binding of role instances to data objects as well as their interaction [50]. Additionally, several implementations of this paradigm exist, e.g., in Scala [22]. One of the first **Metamodel for Roles** was proposed by Genovese [19] in an attempt to define the most general definition of roles. It incorporates both natures of roles and, thus, introduces *Players*, *Roles* and

Contexts on both the model and instance level together with relations denoting which roles belong to which context and be filled by which player [19]. Furthermore, he introduced *Sessions* to specify the binding of attributes when roles collaborate with one another in a context. Besides that, the only possibility to adjust this general metamodel to a target language is to specify additional constraints to both model and instance level, which is only briefly discussed in [19].

4.2   Programming Languages

After focusing on RMLs, this section investigates contemporary RPLs. Notably, most approaches are extensions to Java, which are either compiled to Java source code [20, 33, 3, 9] or directly to bytecode [36]. Hence, we divide the discussion into RPLs that support *plain roles*, *relational roles*, as well as *contextual roles*.

The first class of RPLs focuses solely on implementing objects playing roles. Hence, **Chameleon** [20] features roles with so called *constituent methods* allowing to overwrite methods of their players, which work like advices in Aspect-oriented Programming (AOP). However, the major drawback of Chameleon is the fact that roles extend their player to gain access to the player, which is both conceptually wrong [56] and limits the flexibility of roles. **Rava** [33] overcomes these issues by employing the *Role-Object-Pattern* [12] extended with the *Mediator-Pattern* [18]. They use special keywords to steer the generation of the necessary management code. Due to the use of the Role-Object Pattern and generation to plain Java, this solution suffers from object schizophrenia [38]. **JavaStage** [9] eludes this problem, by only supporting static roles, i.e., the roles are directly compiled into the possible players as inner classes. To avoid name clashes, it employs a customizable method renaming strategy. Its main advantages is the capability to specify a list of required methods instead of a specific player class. Surprisingly, this approach limits itself to static roles unable to represent their relational and context-dependent nature.

Consequently, we proceed with **Rumer** [8], which contributes relationships as first class citizens and modular verification over shared state. Furthermore, Balzer et al. [8] provide several intra relationship constraints usable to further restrict these relationships. Roles, on the other hand, are the named places of a relationship with attributes and methods but without inheritance. Despite that, roles are only accessible within a relationship and not from their player. Consequently, it is promising to combine this approach with another one with context-dependent roles, described next.

The most sophisticated approach to context-dependent roles so far is **ObjectTeams/Java** (OT/J) [36]. Similar to Chameleon above, OT/J allows to override methods of their player by aspect weaving. Besides that, it introduces *Teams* to represent compartments whose inner classes automatically become roles. Notably, OT/J supports both the inheritance of roles and teams whereas the latter leads to family polymorphism [40]. On the downside, it does neither support multiple unrelated player types for a role type nor first class relationships and only a limited form of constraints. This is similar to **powerJava** [3], which also introduces compartments, denoted *Institutions* [3], whose inner classes represent roles. However, PowerJava features the distinction between role interface and role implementation where the former is callable from outside a specific institution and the latter is the institution-specific implementation of the same interface [1]. Both Rava and powerJava are the only research prototypes providing a working compiler. Nonetheless, the project has been abandoned [59]. A more recent approach towards context oriented programming is **NextEJ** [42] as the successor of EpsilonJ [54]. It provides *Contexts* as first class citizens which do not only group roles but also represent an activation scope at runtime. These *context activation scopes* can be nested and act as a barrier where all roles are instantiated and bound automatically. So far, they only published their type-system of the core calculus [43] and no compiler for NextEJ. Surprisingly, no approach published so far included both relational and context-dependent roles.

4.3   Summary

After describing the various approaches, Table 1 shows the classification of the previous RMLs and RPLs by investigating the number of fulfilled features. The table lists the modeling and programming language approach in chronological order. Each feature can be either fulfilled, not fulfilled, possible to fulfill or not applicable. In detail, we have classified features possible to fulfill if they can be fulfilled by reusing model elements but are not supported by the underlying model, and not applicable if they only affect the instance level not treated by the particular approach. In sum, it depicts the progress in the research field.

At a first glance the surveyed research field seams to advance over the years as each approach increased the number of supported features. However, at a closer look, the table indicates that the research field suffers from fragmentation and discontinuity. The former denotes that each approach focuses solely on a specific goal in a specific domain and do not take results of other related domains into account. To make things worse, our evaluation indicates that more than half of the approaches were unaware of the possible features of roles or other related approaches. Moreover, the features of roles implemented in the various programming languages were not transferred back to modeling languages and vice versa. This might be the result of diversity or negligence in the research community. Discontinuity, on the other hand, highlights the fact that each approach builds its role concept from scratch. None of the investigated approaches reused either formal models or metamodels as their basis for their approach. Moreover, solutions to the representation of roles were not applied to other works but just reinvented. As a result, the various approaches for relational or context-dependent roles cannot be combined easily because they neither share a common underlying model nor a common understanding of roles. Apparently, there is no continuous improvement or combination of previously proposed role-based languages.

In sum, these results are surprising, considering the foundations Steimann [56] provided. The next section proposes a solution to the incompatibility of the various approaches and thus tackles the discontinuity of the research field.

Table 1. Evaluation of role-based modeling and programming languages

Feature	Lodwick 2000 [56]	Generic Role Model 2002 [15]	ORM 2 2005 [30]	E-CARGO Model 2006 [60]	Metamodel for Roles 2007 [19]	INM 2009 [46]	DCI (in Scala) 2009 [50]	Onto-UML 2012 [28]	Helena Approach 2014 [34]	Chameleon 2003 [20]	OT/J 2005 [36]	Rava 2006 [33]	powerJava 2006 [5]	Rumer 2007 [8]	NextEJ 2009 [42]	JavaStage 2012 [9]
1	■	■	□	⊞	■	■	■	■	■	■	■	■	■	■	■	■
2	■	□	■	□	□	⊞	⊞	⊞	⊞	□	⊞	□	⊞	■	⊞	□
3	■	■	■	■	⊞	■	■	⊞	■	■	■	■	■	■	■	■
4	■	■	■	■	■	■	□	∅	■	■	■	□	■	■	■	□
5	■	■	■	■	■	∅	⊞	∅	■	■	■	■	⊞	■	■	□
6	⊞	■	⊞	⊞	∅	□	□	□	□	□	■	□	■	■	□	■
7	■	□	□	⊞	■	□	■	⊞	■	■	□	■	■	⊞	■	■
8	□	■	□	□	■	■	□	■	□	□	■	□	■	□	■	■
9	⊞	□	∅	■	⊞	∅	□	∅	□	■	□	□	■	□	■	□
10	⊞	■	∅	⊞	⊞	■	■	■	■	■	■	■	■	■	■	■
11	⊞	■	□	□	⊞	■	■	■	■	■	■	■	■	■	■	■
12	∅	⊞	∅	■	∅	∅	□	∅	■	■	■	■	■	■	■	■
13	⊞	■	□	□	■	■	□	⊞	□	□	■	■	■	□	□	■
14	■	□	■	⊞	⊞	■	⊞	■	□	⊞	⊞	□	□	■	⊞	□
15	□	■	□	■	⊞	□	⊞	□	■	■	■	■	■	□	■	■
16	■	□	■	□	■	□	□	■	□	□	□	□	□	■	□	□
17	□	□	■	□	■	□	□	■	□	□	□	□	□	□	□	□
18	□	□	□	⊞	□	□	□	□	□	□	■	□	□	⊞	⊞	□
19	⊞	□	⊞	■	■	■	■	⊞	■	□	■	□	⊞	⊞	■	□
20	□	□	□	□	■	■	■	■	■	□	■	□	■	■	■	□
21	⊞	□	□	■	■	⊞	□	■	⊞	□	□	□	■	□	■	□
22	□	□	■	□	■	■	□	□	□	□	■	□	□	■	□	□
23	□	□	□	□	■	□	□	□	□	□	■	□	□	□	□	□
24	□	□	□	□	□	■	□	□	□	□	■	□	⊞	■	■	□
25	□	□	□	□	■	■	□	□	□	□	■	□	□	□	□	□
26	□	□	■	■	⊞	■	■	□	■	□	■	□	⊞	■	■	□
	Modeling Languages									Programming Languages						

■: yes, ⊞: possible, □: no, ∅: not applicable

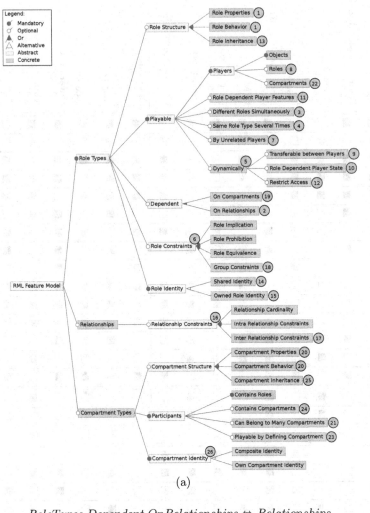

(a)

$$RoleTypes.Dependent.OnRelationships \Leftrightarrow Relationships \tag{1}$$

$$RoleTypes.Dependent.OnCompartments \Leftrightarrow CompartmentTypes \tag{2}$$

$$RoleImplication \Rightarrow RoleEquivalence \tag{3}$$

$$RoleTypes.Playable.Players.Compartments \Rightarrow CompartmentTypes \tag{4}$$

(b)

Fig. 4. Feature model (a) and cross-tree constraints (b) for role-based modeling languages

5 A Metamodel Family for Role-Based Languages

One of the reasons for the discontinuity in the research field is the incompatibility of the various approaches. However, to be able to freely combine the various RMLs and RPLs, they must have compatible metamodels. Unfortunately, only few approaches actually defined and published their underlying metamodel, e.g., [37]. Consequently, it is infeasible to create or combine the metamodels of two approaches. Thus, we propose a method to generate metamodels for RML based on the features of a particular language. Henceforth, we employ feature modeling as the suitable development methodology together with the tool *FeatureIDE* [58] as development environment and *DeltaEcore* [55] to generate the language metamodels in Ecore [57].

5.1 Feature Model for Role-Based Languages

The first step of feature modeling is to generate a feature model as a hierarchical representation of the 26 identified features of roles. In this way, we elucidate the various implicit dependencies of the features presented previously. Fig. 4 (a) depicts the resulting feature model for RML. It encompasses three main feature arcs for *role types*, *relationships*, and *compartment types* to group features dependent on the existence of these entities. Please note that those features are marked mandatory, which is essential for the existence of that entity. Consider for instance that role types must at least be playable by objects. In addition to the dependencies of features evident in the feature model, we had to define four *cross-tree constraints* [58], depicted in Fig. 4 (b). These constraints ensure that a configuration contains all entities on which the *Role Type* depends (Eq. 1 and 2), that *Role Equivalence* is supported, if the *Role Implication* is (Eq. 3), and that compartment types are supported, if compartments can be players (Eq. 4). To further increase the traceability, we annotated each feature with the corresponding number of the feature list (Fig. 2 and 3). Thus, it becomes evident that the resulting feature model captures and elucidates the dependencies of the 26 features of roles. In summary, the feature model can now be used to define a configuration by selecting the various features. For reasons of simplicity, we focus on two particular configurations (of over 7200 possible ones), namely the *feature minimal configuration* and the *feature complete configuration*.

5.2 Feature Minimal Metamodel

In a feature minimal configuration, only mandatory features are selected. Thus, only natural types (with structures and inheritance), which can play role types, exist. Role types, however, are merely annotations, because they only have a name and lack structure, inheritance, and relationships. Fig. 5 shows this minimal configuration of the feature model. This metamodel exhibits, beside the general definition of types with attributes and operations, a specific *Role Model* class. This class represents the default container for all role types (and possibly relationships and *constraints*) generated whenever the configuration does not

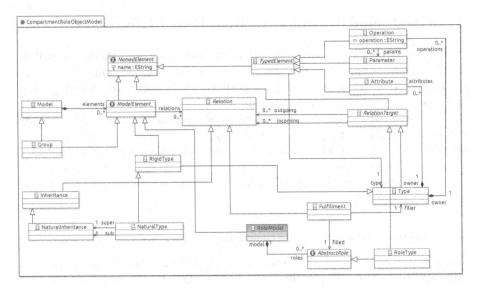

Fig. 5. Ecore metamodel of a feature minimal metamodel

include compartment types. In sum, this model is similar to a standard object-oriented metamodel with the additional ability to mark classes as role types.

5.3   Feature Complete Metamodel

In contrast to the minimal configuration, a feature complete configuration selects as many features as validly possible. However, due to the fact that a metamodel can only reflect features of the model level (M1), we omit all features solely affecting instance level (M0). As a result, the feature complete metamodel incorporates natural types, role types, relationships, and compartment types as classes. Roles can be played by naturals, other roles, and compartments.

Fig. 6 shows the corresponding metamodel highlighting all classes corresponding to the selected features. Thus, it encompasses the various relations between the various types, e.g., the fulfillment relation, the various inheritance relations as well as the different role and relationship constraints. Additionally, it includes a typical list of intra- and inter-relationship constraints, parthood constraints as well as the `RoleGroup` class for constraints on groups of roles. Thus, this metamodel represents the unification of the various features of roles proposed in the literature.

5.4   Mapping Features to Variation Points

After describing both the feature minimal (Fig. 5) and the feature complete metamodel (Fig. 6), this section describes how variants can be derived by adding, modifying and removing classes and references of the feature minimal metamodel.

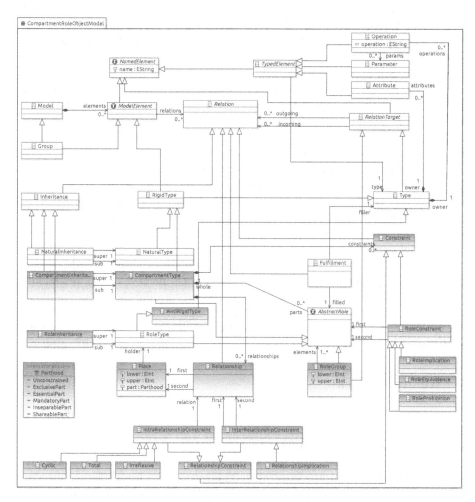

Fig. 6. Ecore metamodel of a feature complete metamodel

Henceforth, we distinguish four kinds of *variation points* of the metamodel family and specify their mapping to the corresponding features. The first kind of variation point directly corresponds to classes (highlighted in Fig. 6), i.e., their existence in the metamodel is directly linked to the selection of a specific feature. More precisely, the following classes directly correspond to features: On Relationships (Feature 2), RoleConstraint (Feature 6), RoleInheritance (Feature 13), IntraRelationshipConstraint (Feature 16), InterRelation-shipConstraint (Feature 17), RoleGroup (Feature 18), and CompartmentInher-itance (Feature 25). Thus, selecting such a feature entails adding the corresponding class together with the respective incoming and outgoing references. The only exception is the CompartmentType class corresponding to Feature 19, which is replaced by a RoleModel class if the feature is deselected. The second kind of variation points correspond to the targets of references in the metamodel. In particular, the *filler* reference of class `Fulfillment` either points to `NaturalType`, `RigidType`, `Type` or to a generic Player interface depending on the combined selection of Features 8 and 22, declaring whether compartments and/or roles can play roles as well. In contrast, the third kind of variation point changes the inheritance relation of specific classes to change their properties or implemented interfaces. Thus, `RoleType` and `CompartmentType` only inherit (indirectly) from *Type*, if Features 1 and 20 are selected, respectively, i.e., they have properties and behavior. Otherwise, they would inherit from `RelationTarget` and in the latter case also from `ModelElement`. A similar example is the inheritance from `AbstractRole`, which is only present if compartments can be nested (Feature 24). The last kind of variation points cannot be captured by standard Ecore models, because they correspond to invariants that must be satisfied by instances of that particular metamodel. This holds for the Features 3, 7, 11, and 23 which broaden the number of valid models. However, we must add one invariant for each of these features if they were not selected. Unfortunately, the specification of these invariants is beyond the scope of this paper. Altogether, these variation points are sufficient to generate each member of the metamodel family for a given configuration by iteratively transforming the feature minimal metamodel. We have developed a generator as a proof of concept[4] by employing the facilities provided by FeatureIDE and the DeltaEcore framework for delta modeling.

6   Related Work

Most of the related work on role-based modeling languages has been discussed previously. Henceforth, we focus on other surveys, metamodels, and feature models for role-based modeling languages.

To our knowledge, only one other *survey* on roles in information systems [61] has been published since the year 2000. This survey has a broader perspective and takes social-roles, modeling-roles, CSCW-roles, RBAC-roles, system-roles as well as agent-roles into account. Additionally, they classify all investigated approaches in their contexts. Nevertheless, our survey is more focused on a rigorous classification of role-based modeling and programming languages.

While several researchers tried to establish a *metamodel* for roles before, none of them was adopted by other approaches. Consider for instance, Lodwick, the formal definition of roles, proposed by Steimann [56] to consolidate the different notions of roles in conceptional modeling. This approach, despite of its generality, suffers from various limitations, e.g., the lack of representation of roles on the instance level (M0) or the consideration of context-dependent roles. Genovese [19] overcomes this by introducing contexts, roles, and players on both the model (M1) and instance level (M0). He tried to establish the most general definition of roles. In fact, his metamodel is too general to be readily applicable to any approach in the literature. This is the case, because one has to specify constraints on each level of the meta level hierarchy. Consequently, the metamodel

---

[4] See `http://st.inf.tu-dresden.de/RML` for the prototypical implementation.

might capture most of the features of roles. However, it is not easily adaptable to the other more limited approaches. The *Generic Role Model* [15], on the other hand, only defines the plays relation on both the model (M1) and the instance level (M0) together with formal semantics. Thus, this metamodel can be viewed as the least common denominator of the various notions of roles. In sum, the proposed metamodel family of RML ranges in between Dahchour's generic role model and Genovese's metamodel.

Last but not least, we are only aware of one other work on the nature of roles [21] providing a *feature model* for roles. This work, however, investigates roles as a language construct and collects and investigates the features of such a construct. Therefore, these features are mostly concerned with the instance level (M0) and are specific to execution environments. This feature model, however, did not consider the context-dependent nature of roles.

7   Conclusion

Roles are both relational and context-dependent by nature. However, most approaches to role-based modeling emphasize only one aspect. Unfortunately, the various approaches cannot be combined easily, due to the lack of compatible metamodels. In this paper, we have approached this problem by first conducting a literature survey and second proposing a family of metamodels for RML. For the former, we added 11 new features emphasizing the context-dependence to the pre-existing features of roles [56]. This feature set has been used to classify the various RML and RPL proposed since 2000. This evaluation has shown that the research field suffers from fragmentation and discontinuity. To overcome the latter issue, we have created a feature model for RML from which a family of metamodels can be generated. In this way, researchers are now able to generate a metamodel for their specific approach and, more importantly, for other approaches they want to reuse or combine. In addition, both the listed features and the feature model can be reused to evaluate or develop subsequent role-based approaches.

Acknowledgements.   This work is funded by the German Research Foundation (DFG) within the Research Training Group "Role-based Software Infrastructures for continuous-context-sensitive Systems" (GRK 1907), in the Collaborative Research Center 912 "Highly Adaptive Energy-Efficient Computing" and the European Social Fund (ESF) and the Federal State of Saxony within project "VICCI" #100098171. Special thanks go to Sebastian Richly, Tobias Jäkel, and Stephan Böhme for their suggestions and to Ulrike Schöbel for improving this paper.

References

[1] Arnaudo, E., Baldoni, M., Boella, G., Genovese, V., Grenna, R.: An implementation of roles as affordances: powerjava (August 31, 2009)
[2] Bachman, C.W.: The programmer as navigator. Commun. ACM 16(11), 635–658 (1973)

[3] Baldoni, M., Boella, G., van der Torre, L.: Powerjava: ontologically founded roles in object oriented programming languages. In: Haddad, H. (ed.) SAC, pp. 1414–1418. ACM (2006)

[4] Baldoni, M., Boella, G., Van Der Torre, L.: Powerjava: ontologically founded roles in object oriented programming languages. In: Proceedings of the 2006 ACM Symposium on Applied Computing, pp. 1414–1418. ACM (2006)

[5] Baldoni, M., Boella, G., van der Torre, L.: Roles as a coordination construct: Introducing powerjava. Electr. Notes Theor. Comput. Sci. 150(1), 9–29 (2006)

[6] Balzer, S., Burns, A., Gross, T.: Objects in context: An empirical study of object relationships. Tech. Rep. 594, ETH Zürich (May 2008)

[7] Balzer, S., Eugster, P., Gross, T.: Relations: Abstracting object collaborations (February 06, 2008)

[8] Balzer, S., Gross, T., Eugster, P.: A relational model of object collaborations and its use in reasoning about relationships. In: Ernst, E. (ed.) ECOOP 2007. LNCS, vol. 4609, pp. 323–346. Springer, Heidelberg (2007)

[9] Barbosa, F.S., Aguiar, A.: Modeling and programming with roles: introducing javastage. Tech. rep., Instituto Politécnico de Castelo Branco (2012)

[10] Bierman, G., Wren, A.: First-class relationships in an object-oriented language. In: Gao, X.-X. (ed.) ECOOP 2005. LNCS, vol. 3586, pp. 262–286. Springer, Heidelberg (2005)

[11] Boella, G., Van Der Torre, L.: The ontological properties of social roles in multi-agent systems: Definitional dependence, powers and roles playing roles. Artificial Intelligence and Law 15(3), 201–221 (2007)

[12] Bäumer, D., Riehle, D., Siberski, W., Wulf, M.: The role object pattern. In: Washington University Dept. of Computer Science (1998)

[13] Chen, P.: The entity-relationship model - toward a unified view of data. ACM Transactions on Database Systems 1(1), 9–36 (1976)

[14] Czarnecki, K., Osterbye, K., Völter, M.: Generative programming. In: Object-Oriented Technology ECOOP 2002 Workshop Reader, pp. 15–29. Springer (2002)

[15] Dahchour, M., Pirotte, A., Zimányi, E.: A generic role model for dynamic objects. In: Pidduck, A.B., Mylopoulos, J., Woo, C.C., Ozsu, M.T. (eds.) CAiSE 2002. LNCS, vol. 2348, pp. 643–658. Springer, Heidelberg (2002)

[16] Dey, A.K.: Understanding and using context. Personal and Ubiquitous Computing 5(1), 4–7 (2001)

[17] Ferraiolo, D., Cugini, J., Kuhn, D.R.: Role-based access control (rbac): Features and motivations. In: Proceedings of 11th Annual Computer Security Application Conference, pp. 241–248 (1995)

[18] Gamma, E., Helm, R., Johnson, R., Vlissides, J.: Design patterns: elements of reusable object-oriented software. Pearson Education (1994)

[19] Genovese, V.: A meta-model for roles: Introducing sessions. In: Roles 2007, p. 27 (2007)

[20] Graversen, K.B., Østerbye, K.: Implementation of a role language for object-specific dynamic separation of concerns. In: AOSD 2003 Workshop on Software-Engineering Properties of Languages for Aspect Technologies (2003)

[21] Graversen, K.B.: The nature of roles. Ph.D. thesis, PhD thesis:/Kasper Bilsted Graversen.–Copenhagen, IT University of Copenhagen Copenhagen (2006)

[22] Grue, M.: ScalaDCI (2014), https://github.com/DCI/scaladci (accessed May 24, 2014)

[23] Guarino, N., Carrara, M., Giaretta, P.: An ontology of meta-level categories. In: KR, pp. 270–280 (1994)

[24] Guarino, N., Welty, C.: A formal ontology of properties. In: Dieng, R., Corby, O. (eds.) EKAW 2000. LNCS (LNAI), vol. 1937, pp. 97–112. Springer, Heidelberg (2000)

[25] Guarino, N., Welty, C.: An overview of ontoclean. In: Handbook on Ontologies, pp. 201–220. Springer (2009)

[26] Guizzardi, G.: Ontological foundations for structure conceptual models. Ph.D. thesis, Centre for Telematics and Information Technology, Enschede, Netherlands (2005)

[27] Guizzardi, G., Wagner, G.: Towards ontological foundations for agent modelling concepts using the unified fundational ontology (UFO). In: Bresciani, P., Giorgini, P., Henderson-Sellers, B., Low, G., Winikoff, M. (eds.) AOIS 2004. LNCS (LNAI), vol. 3508, pp. 110–124. Springer, Heidelberg (2005)

[28] Guizzardi, G., Wagner, G.: Conceptual simulation modeling with onto-uml. In: Proceedings of the Winter Simulation Conference, p. 5. Winter Simulation Conference (2012)

[29] Guizzardi, G., Wagner, G., Guarino, N., van Sinderen, M.: An ontologically well-founded profile for UML conceptual models. In: Persson, A., Stirna, J. (eds.) CAiSE 2004. LNCS, vol. 3084, pp. 112–126. Springer, Heidelberg (2004)

[30] Halpin, T.: ORM 2. In: Meersman, R., Tari, Z. (eds.) OTM-WS 2005. LNCS, vol. 3762, pp. 676–687. Springer, Heidelberg (2005)

[31] Halpin, T.A.: Object-role modeling (ORM/NIAM). In: Handbook on Architectures of Information Systems, pp. 81–102. Springer (1998)

[32] Harel, D., Rumpe, B.: Modeling languages: Syntax, semantics and all that stuff. Tech. rep., Technische Universität Braunschweig (2004)

[33] He, C., Nie, Z., Li, B., Cao, L., He, K.: Rava: Designing a java extension with dynamic object roles. In: 13th Annual IEEE International Symposium and Workshop on Engineering of Computer Based Systems, ECBS 2006, p. 7. IEEE (2006)

[34] Hennicker, R., Klarl, A.: Foundations for ensemble modeling – the HELENA approach. In: Iida, S., Meseguer, J., Ogata, K. (eds.) Specification, Algebra, and Software. LNCS, vol. 8373, pp. 359–381. Springer, Heidelberg (2014)

[35] Herrmann, S.: Object teams: Improving modularity for crosscutting collaborations. In: Akşit, M., Mezini, M. (eds.) Net. Object Days (October 2002)

[36] Herrmann, S.: Programming with roles in ObjectTeams/Java. Tech. rep., AAAI Fall Symposium (2005)

[37] Herrmann, S.: A precise model for contextual roles: The programming language objectteams/java. Applied Ontology 2(2), 181–207 (2007)

[38] Herrmann, S.: Demystifying object schizophrenia. In: Proceedings of the 4th Workshop on MechAnisms for SPEcialization, Generalization and inHerItance, MASPEGHI 2010, pp. 2:1–2:5. ACM, New York (2010)

[39] Herrmann, S., Hundt, C.: Objectteams/java language definition (otjld) version 1.3.1 (May 2013), http://www.objectteams.org/def/1.3.1 (accessed May 28, 2014)

[40] Herrmann, S., Hundt, C., Mehner, K.: Translation polymorphism in object teams. Tech. rep., TU Berlin (2004)

[41] Hu, J., Liu, M.: Modeling context-dependent information. In: Proceedings of the 18th ACM Conference on Information and Knowledge Management, pp. 1669–1672. ACM (2009)

[42] Kamina, T., Tamai, T.: Towards safe and flexible object adaptation. In: International Workshop on Context-Oriented Programming, p. 4. ACM (2009)

[43] Kamina, T., Tamai, T.: A smooth combination of role-based language and context activation. In: FOAL 2010 Proceedings, p. 15 (2010)

[44] Kang, K., Cohen, S., Hess, J., Novak, W., Peterson, A.: Feature-oriented domain analysis (FODA). Tech. rep., Software Engineering Institute, Carnegie Mellon University (1990)

[45] Kay, A.C.: The early history of smalltalk. In: HOPL Preprints, pp. 69–95 (1993)

[46] Liu, M., Hu, J.: Information networking model. In: Laender, A.H.F., Castano, S., Dayal, U., Casati, F., de Oliveira, J.P.M. (eds.) ER 2009. LNCS, vol. 5829, pp. 131–144. Springer, Heidelberg (2009)

[47] Liu, M., Hu, J.: Modeling complex relationships. In: Bhowmick, S.S., Küng, J., Wagner, R. (eds.) DEXA 2009. LNCS, vol. 5690, pp. 719–726. Springer, Heidelberg (2009)

[48] Masolo, C., Guizzardi, G., Vieu, L., Bottazzi, E., Ferrario, R.: Relational roles and qua-individuals. In: AAAI Fall Symposium on Roles, an Interdisciplinary Perspective, pp. 103–112 (2005)

[49] OMG: OMG: Meta Object Facility (MOF) Core Specification. Object Managment Group, 2.4.1 edn. (June 2013), ptc/11-09-13

[50] Reenskaug, T., Coplien, J.O.: The dci architecture: A new vision of object-oriented programming. An article starting a new blog(14pp) (2009), http://www.artima.com/articles/dci_vision.html

[51] Reenskaug, T., Coplien, J.O.: The DCI architecture: A new vision of object-oriented programming. Artima Developer (2011)

[52] Rumbaugh, J., Jacobson, R., Booch, G.: The Unified Modelling Language Reference Manual, 1st edn. Addison-Wesley (January 1999)

[53] Rumbaugh, J.E.: Relations as semantic constructs in an object-oriented language. In: OOPSLA, pp. 466–481 (1987)

[54] Monpratarnchai, S., Tetsuo, T.: The design and implementation of a role model based language, EpsilonJ. In: Proceedings of the 5th International Conference on Electrical Engineering/Electronics, Computer, Telecommunications and Information Technology (ECTI-CON 2008) (2008)

[55] Seidl, C., Schaefer, I., Aßmann, U.: DeltaEcore–a model-based delta language generation framework. In: Modellierung, pp. 81–96 (2014)

[56] Steimann, F.: On the representation of roles in object-oriented and conceptual modelling. Data & Knowledge Engineering 35(1), 83–106 (2000)

[57] Steinberg, D., Budinsky, F., Merks, E., Paternostro, M.: EMF: eclipse modeling framework. Pearson Education (2008)

[58] Thüm, T., Kästner, C., Benduhn, F., Meinicke, J., Saake, G., Leich, T.: Featureide: An extensible framework for feature-oriented software development. Science of Computer Programming 79, 70–85 (2014)

[59] Wielenga, G.: On powerjava: "roles" instead of "objects" (January 2013), https://blogs.oracle.com/geertjan/entry/on_powerjava_roles_instead_of (accessed May 28, 2014)

[60] Zhu, H., Zhou, M.: Role-based collaboration and its kernel mechanisms. IEEE Transactions on Systems, Man, and Cybernetics, Part C: Applications and Reviews 36(4), 578–589 (2006)

[61] Zhu, H., Zhou, M.: Roles in information systems: A survey. IEEE Transactions on Systems, Man, and Cybernetics, Part C: Applications and Reviews 38(3), 377–396 (2008)

AIOCJ: A Choreographic Framework
for Safe Adaptive Distributed Applications

Mila Dalla Preda[1], Saverio Giallorenzo[2],
Ivan Lanese[2], Jacopo Mauro[2], and Maurizio Gabbrielli[2]

[1] Department of Computer Science - Univ. of Verona
[2] Department of Computer Science and Engineering - Univ. of Bologna / INRIA

Abstract. We present AIOCJ, a framework for programming distributed adaptive applications. Applications are programmed using AIOC, a choreographic language suited for expressing patterns of interaction from a global point of view. AIOC allows the programmer to specify which parts of the application can be adapted. Adaptation takes place at runtime by means of rules, which can change during the execution to tackle possibly unforeseen adaptation needs. AIOCJ relies on a solid theory that ensures applications to be deadlock-free by construction also after adaptation. We describe the architecture of AIOCJ, the design of the AIOC language, and an empirical validation of the framework.

1 Introduction

Adaptation is a main feature of current distributed applications, that should live for a long time in a continuously changing environment. Anticipating all the possible adaptation needs when designing an application is very difficult, thus the approaches able to cope with *unforeseen* adaptation needs are the most interesting. Also, for distributed applications like the ones that we consider, it is important to ensure deadlock-freedom (according to [1] about one third of concurrency bugs in real applications are deadlocks). While many techniques ensuring deadlock freedom exist in the literature, e.g., [2–4], to the best of our knowledge, none of them deals with adaptive applications. Indeed, most of the approaches to adaptation offer no guarantee on the behaviour of the application after adaptation [5–7], or they assume to know all the possible adaptations in advance [8], thus failing to cope with unforeseen adaptation needs.

Here we present AIOCJ, a prototype implementation of a framework for programming adaptive distributed applications that guarantees deadlock-freedom by construction (the theoretical foundations ensuring this property are discussed in [9]). AIOCJ is composed of two parts: (*i*) a domain-specific language, called Adaptive Interaction-Oriented Choreographies (*AIOC*) and (*ii*) an *adaptation middleware* that supports adaptation of AIOC programs.

The AIOC language describes applications from a global point of view following the *choreography* paradigm. This paradigm has been applied in different contexts, see, e.g., [2, 10–13], but we are not aware of other tools based on it and targeting adaptive applications. A choreography defines the interactions among the processes of a distributed application. AIOC main innovation consists in two constructs supporting

B. Combemale et al. (Eds.): SLE 2014, LNCS 8706, pp. 161–170, 2014.

adaptation: *scopes* and *adaptation rules*. A scope delimits code that may be adapted in the future. An adaptation rule provides new code to replace the one in a given scope. Interestingly, in **AIOCJ**, adaptation rules can be defined and inserted in the framework while the application is running, to cope with adaptation needs which were not foreseen when the application was designed or even started.

The code below shows a toy AIOC program (left) and an adaptation rule applicable to it (right). On the left, Lines 2-4 define a scope in which the local variable msg of process user is set to "Hello World". The keyword prop defines properties of the scope (prefixed by N). In this case, the name property is set to "hello_world". At Line 5 user sends the content of msg to a second process (display), that stores it in its local variable msg. On the right, Lines 2-3 define the *applicability condition* of the rule, i.e., the name property of the scope should be set to "hello_world", and the environmental property E.lang should be equal to "it". Line 4 shows the code that will replace the one of the scope, i.e., variable msg of user will be set to "Ciao Mondo" (Italian for "Hello World").

```
1   aioc {                                    1   rule {
2     scope @user{                            2     on { N.name == "hello_world"
3       msg@user = "Hello World"              3       and E.lang == "it" }
4     } prop { N.name = "hello_world"};       4     do { msg@user = "Ciao Mondo" }
5     send: user( msg ) -> display( msg ) }   5   }
```

An AIOC program describes a full distributed application. **AIOCJ** generates, for each distributed process, a service written in Jolie [14, 15], a Service-Oriented orchestration language.

The adaptation middleware consists of a set of adaptation rules stored in multiple, possibly distributed, *adaptation servers*, and of an *adaptation manager* that mediates the interactions between the adaptive application and the various adaptation servers.

Structure of the paper. Section 2 presents an overview of the **AIOCJ** framework, while Section 3 describes its implementation. Section 4 shows a preliminary validation of the framework, with tests on the performances of **AIOCJ**. In Section 5 we discuss related work and future directions of research. A short demo of the use of the framework is available in the companion technical report [16].

2   Overview: The AIOCJ Framework

This section first defines the architectural model that supports adaptation of **AIOCJ** applications and then it introduces the syntax of the AIOC language via an example (for a formal presentation of AIOC syntax and semantics see [9]).

The AIOCJ Middleware. We consider applications composed of processes deployed as services on different localities, including local state and computational resources. Each process has a specific duty in the choreography and follows a given protocol. Processes interact via synchronous message passing over channels, also called *operations*. Adaptation is performed by an adaptation middleware including an adaptation manager and some, possibly distributed, adaptation servers. The latter are services that act as repositories of adaptation rules and may be (manually) added or removed at runtime. Running adaptation servers register themselves on the adaptation manager. The running application may interact with the adaptation manager to look for applicable adaptation rules. The effect of an adaptation rule is to replace a scope with new code that answers a given adaptation need. The adaptation manager checks the rules according to the registration order of the adaptation servers, returning the first applicable rule, if any.

The AIOC Language. The language relies on a set of roles that identify the processes in the choreography. Let us introduce the syntax of the language using an example where Bob invites Alice to see a film.

```
1   include isFreeDay from "calendar.org:80" with http
2   include getTicket from "cinema.org:8000" with soap
3   preamble {
4     starter: bob
5     location@bob = "socket://localhost:8000"
6     location@alice = "socket://alice.com:8000"
7     location@cinema = "socket://cinema.org:8001" }
8   aioc{
9     end@bob = false;
10    while( ! end )@bob{
11      scope @bob {
12        free_day@bob = getInput( "Insert your free day" );
13        proposal: bob( free_day ) -> alice( bob_free_day );
14        is_free@alice = isFreeDay( bob_free_day );
15      } prop { N.scope_name = "matching day" };
16      if( is_free )@alice {
17        scope @bob {
18          proposal: bob( "cinema" ) -> alice( event );
19          agreement@alice = getInput( "Bob proposes " + event +
20            ", do you agree?[y/n]");
21          if( agreement == "y" )@alice{
22            end@bob = true;
23            book: bob( bob_free_day ) -> cinema( book_day );
24            ticket@cinema = getTicket( book_day );
25            { notify: cinema( ticket ) -> bob( ticket )
26            | notify: cinema( ticket ) -> alice( ticket ) }}
27        } prop { N.scope_name = "event selection" } };
28      if( !end )@bob {
29        _r@bob = getInput( "Alice refused. Try another date?[y/n]" );
30        if( _r != "y" )@bob{ end@bob = true }}}
```

Listing 1.1. Appointment program

The code starts with some deployment information (Lines 1-7), discussed later on. The behaviour starts at Line 9. The program is made by a cycle where Bob first checks when Alice is available and then invites her to the cinema. Before starting the cycle, Bob initialises the variable end, used in the guard of the cycle, to the boolean value false (Line 9). Note the annotation @bob meaning that end is local to Bob. The first instructions of the while are enclosed in a scope (Lines 11-15), meaning that they may be adapted in the future. The first operation within the scope is the call to the primitive function getInput that asks to Bob a day where he is free and stores this date into the local variable free_day. At Line 13 the content of free_day is sent to Alice via operation proposal. Alice stores it in its local variable bob_free_day. Then, at Line 14, Alice calls the external function isFreeDay that checks whether she is available on bob_free_day. If she is available (Line 16) then Bob sends to her the invitation to go to the cinema via the operation proposal (Line 18). Alice, reading from the input, accepts or refuses the invitation (Line 19). If Alice accepts then Bob first sets the variable end to true to end the cycle. Then, he sends to the cinema the booking request via operation book. The cinema generates the tickets using the external function getTicket and sends them to Alice and Bob via operation notify. The two notifications are done in parallel using the parallel operator | (until now we composed statements using the sequential operator ;). Lines 18-26 are enclosed in a second scope with property N.scope_name = "event selection". If the agreement is not reached, Bob decides, reading from the input, if he wants to stop inviting Alice. If so, the program exits.

We remark the different meanings of the annotations @bob and @alice. When prefixed by a variable, they identify the owner of the variable. Prefixed by the boolean guard of conditionals and cycles, they identify the role that evaluates the guard. Prefixed by the keyword scope, they identify the process coordinating the adaptation of that scope. A scope, besides the code, may also include some properties describing the current implementation. These can be specified using the keyword prop and are prefixed by N. For instance, each scope of the example includes the property scope_name, that can be used to distinguish its functionality.

AIOCJ can interact with external services, seen as functions. This allows both to interact with real services and to have easy access to libraries from other languages. To do that, one must specify the address and protocol used to interact with them. For instance, the external function isFreeDay used in Line 14 is associated to the service deployed at the domain "calendar.org", reachable though port 80, and that uses http as serialisation protocol (Line 1). External functions are declared with the keyword include. To preserve deadlock freedom, external services must be non-blocking. After function declaration, in a preamble section, it is possible to declare the locations where processes are deployed. The keyword starter is mandatory and defines which process must be started first. The starter makes sure all other processes are ready before the execution of the choreography begins.

Now suppose that Bob, during summer, prefers to invite Alice to a picnic more than to the cinema, provided that the weather forecasts are good. This can be obtained by adding the following adaptation rule to one of the adaptation servers. This may even be done while the application is running, e.g., while Bob is sending an invitation. In this case, if the first try of Bob is unsuccessful, in the second try he will propose a picnic.

```
1   rule {
2     include getWeather from "socket://localhost:8002"
3     on { N.scope_name == "event selection" and E.month > 5 and E.month < 10 }
4     do { forecasts@bob = getWeather( free_day );
5       if( forecasts == "Clear" )@bob{
6         eventProposal : bob( "picnic" ) -> alice( event )
7       } else { eventProposal : bob( "cinema" ) -> alice( event ) };
8       agreement@alice = getInput( "Bob proposes "  + event +
9         ", do you agree?[y/n]");
10      if( agreement == "y" )@alice {
11        end@bob = true |
12        if( event == "cinema" )@alice {
13          //cinema tickets purchase procedure
14  }}}}
```

Listing 1.2. Event selection adaptation rule

A rule specifies its applicability condition and the new code to execute. In general, the applicability condition may depend only on properties of the scope, environment variables, and variables belonging to the coordinator of the scope. In this case, the condition, introduced by the keyword on (Line 3), makes the rule applicable to scopes having the property scope_name equal to the string "event selection" and only during summer. This last check relies on an environment variable month that contains the current month. Environment variables are prefixed by E.

When the rule applies, the new code to execute is defined using the keyword do (Line 4). In this case, the forecasts can be retrieved calling an external function getWeather (Line 4) that queries a weather forecasts service. This function is declared in Line 2. If the weather is clear, Bob proposes to Alice a picnic, the cinema otherwise. Booking (as in Listing 1.1, Lines 23-26) is needed only if Alice accepts the cinema proposal.

As detailed in [9], to obtain a deadlock-free application, we require the code of choreographies and rules to satisfy a well-formedness syntactic condition called *connectedness*. Intuitively, connectedness ensures that sequences of actions are executed in the correct order and avoids interference between parallel interactions. Requiring this condition does not hamper programmability, since it naturally holds in most of the cases, and it can always be enforced automatically via small patches to the choreography which preserve the behaviour of the program, as discussed in [17]. Also, checking connectedness is efficient, i.e., polynomial w.r.t. the size of the code [9].

3   Implementation

Our prototype implementation of AIOCJ is composed of two elements: the AIOCJ Integrated Development Environment (IDE), named AIOCJ-ecl, and the adaptation middleware that enables AIOC programs to adapt, called AIOCJ-mid.

AIOCJ-ecl is a plug-in for Eclipse [18] based on Xtext [19]. Xtext provides features such as syntax highlighting, syntax checking, and code completion, which help developers in writing choreographies and adaptation rules. Also, starting from a grammar, Xtext generates the parser for programs written in the AIOC language. Result of the parsing is an abstract syntax tree (AST) we use to implement (*i*) the checker for connectedness for choreographies and rules and (*ii*) the generation of Jolie code for each role. The connectedness check has polynomial computational complexity [9] thus making it efficient enough to be performed on-the-fly while editing the code.

The target language of code generation is Jolie [14]. Jolie supports architectural primitives such as dynamic embedding, aggregation, and redirection that we exploit to implement the adaptation mechanisms. Moreover, Jolie supports a wide range of communication technologies (TCP/IP sockets, local memory, Bluetooth) and of data formats (e.g., HTTP, SOAP, JSON). AIOCJ inherits this ability. The compilation generates a Jolie service for each role. The execution of scopes is delegated to sub-services accessed using Jolie redirection facility. Adaptation is enacted by disabling the current sub-service and replacing it with a new one, obtained from the adaptation server. To grant to all the sub-services access to variables, the state is stored by a dedicated sub-service local to the role. Auxiliary messages are exchanged to ensure that both the adaptation and the choices taken by the if and while constructs are done in a coordinated way. In particular, the scope execution not only requires interaction with the adaptation manager, but also communications among the different roles, ensuring that they all agree on whether adaptation is needed or not, and, in case, on which rule to apply. Indeed, the decision is taken by the role coordinating the adaptation and then communicated to other roles. Note that the different roles cannot autonomously take the decision, since if they take it at different times, changes in the environment or in the sets of available rules may lead to inconsistent decisions.

Synchronous message exchange is implemented on top of an asynchronous communication middleware by a sub-service that works as a *message handler*. The message handler of the starter role also ensures that, before the actual communication in the choreography starts, all the roles are ready.

AIOCJ-mid is implemented in Jolie and it includes:

- many, possibly distributed, *adaptation servers* where rules are published. Adaptation servers can be deployed and switched on and off at runtime;
- an *adaptation manager* that acts as a registry for adaptation servers and clients;
- an *environment* service that stores and makes available environment information. Environment information can change at any moment.

When an AIOCJ program reaches a scope, it queries the adaptation manager for a rule matching that scope. The adaptation manager queries each adaptation server sequentially, based on their order of registration. Each server checks the applicability condition of each of its rules. The first rule whose applicability condition holds is applied. In particular, the code of the rule is sent to the role coordinating the adaptation (via the adaptation manager) which distributes it to the involved roles. In each role, the new code replaces the old one. The study of more refined policies for rule selection, e.g., based on priorities, is a topic for future work.

4 Validation

In this section, we give a preliminary empirical validation of our implementation. The main aim is to test how our mechanisms for adaptation impact on performances.

In the literature, to the best of our knowledge, there is no approach to adaptation based on choreography programming. Thus, it is difficult to directly compare our results with other existing approaches. Moreover, we are not aware of any established benchmark to evaluate adaptive applications. For this reason, we tested AIOCJ performances by applying it to two typical programming patterns: *pipes* and *fork-joins*. Since we are interested in studying the cost of adaptation, our scenarios contain minimal computation and are particularly affected by the overhead of the adaptation process. Clearly, the percentage of the overhead due to adaptation will be far lower in real scenarios, which are usually more computationally intensive. In the first scenario, we program a pipe executing n tasks (in a pipe, the output of task t_i is given as input to task t_{i+1}, for $i \in \{1, \ldots, n-1\}$). To keep computation to a minimum, each task simply computes the increment function. In the fork-join scenario, n tasks are computed in parallel. Each task processes one character of a message of length n, shifting it by one position. The message is stored in an external service.[1]

To enable adaptation, each task is enclosed in a scope. We test both scenarios with an increasing number of tasks $n \in \{10, 20, \ldots, 100\}$ to study how performances scale as the number of adaptation scopes increases. We evaluate performances in different contexts, thus allowing us to understand the impact of different adaptation features, such as scopes, adaptation servers, and adaptation rules.

---

[1] The code of both scenarios is in the companion technical report [16].

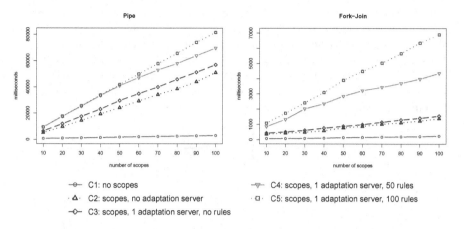

Fig. 1. Times of execution of the pipe (left) and the fork-join (right) scenarios

Context 1: no scopes, no adaptation servers, no rules;

Context 2: each task is enclosed in a scope, no adaptation servers, no rules;

Context 3: each task is enclosed in a scope, one adaptation server, no rules;

Context 4: as Context 3, but now the adaptation server contains 50 rules. Each rule is applicable to a unique scope i, and no rule is applicable to scopes with $i > 50$. The rules are stored in random order.

Context 5: as Context 4, but with 100 rules, one for each scope.

Each rule in Contexts 4 and 5 is applicable to one specific scope only (through a unique property of the scope), hence when testing for 50 rules, only the first 50 scopes adapt.

We repeated every test 5 times. We performed our tests on a machine equipped with a 2.6GHz quad-core Intel Core i7 processor and 16GB RAM. The machine runs Mavericks 10.9.3, Java 1.7.55, and Jolie r.2728. Figure 1 shows the tests for the pipe (left) and the fork-join (right). Both charts display on the x-axis the number of tasks/scopes and on the y-axis the execution time in milliseconds.

As expected, in both scenarios there is a significant gap between Contexts 1 and 2. In words, the introduction of scopes has a strong effect on performances. The ratio is 1:13 for the pipe scenario and 1:5.5 for the fork-join scenario. This is due to the auxiliary communications needed to correctly execute a scope. The observed overhead is higher in the pipe scenario, since different scopes check for adaptation in sequence, while this is done in parallel for the fork-join scenario.

Adding an adaptation server (from Context 2 to Context 3) has little impact on performances: 19% of decay for pipe, and 17% for fork-join. The figures are reasonable, considered that Context 3 adds only one communication w.r.t. Context 2.

On the contrary, there is a notable difference when adding rules to the adaptation server (Context 4 is 1.4 times slower than Context 3 for the pipe scenario, 2.9 for the fork-join scenario). In Contexts 4 and 5, performances are really close up to 50 scopes (in the pipe scenario they almost overlap) although Context 5 has twice the rules of Context 4. This illustrates that the time to test for applicability of rules is negligible. Hence, the highest toll on performances is related to actual adaptation, since it requires to transfer and embed the new code. This is particularly evident in the fork-join scenario where multiple adaptations are executed in parallel and the adaptation server becomes a bottleneck. This problem can be mitigated using multiple distributed adaptation servers.

The fact that the most expensive operations are scope execution and actual adaptation is highlighted also by the results below. The table shows the cost of different primitives, including scopes in different contexts. Times are referred to 5 executions of the sample code in the companion technical report [16].

Test	Time (ms)	Test	Time (ms)
assignment	2.2	scope, 1 adaptation server, 1 matching rule	280.6
interaction	4.2	scope, 1 adaptation server, 50 rules, none matching	254.2
if statement	16.6	scope, 1 adaptation server, 50 rules, 1 matching	338.6
scope, no adaptation server	129.4	scope, 1 adaptation server, 100 rules, none matching	310.2
scope, 1 adaptation server, no rule	203.8	scope, 1 adaptation server, 100 rules, 1 matching	385

As future work we will exploit these results to increase the performances of our framework, concentrating on the bottlenecks highlighted above. For instance, scope execution (as well as conditionals and cycles) currently requires many auxiliary communications ensuring that all the processes agree on the chosen path. In many cases, some of these communications are not needed, since a process will eventually discover the chosen path from the protocol communications. Static analysis can discover redundant communications and remove them. Another improvement is letting the adaptation server send the new code directly to the involved roles, skipping the current forward chain.

5   Related Work and Conclusion

This paper presented a framework for programming rule-based adaptation of distributed applications. Its distinctive trait is that, being based on a choreographic approach, it guarantees deadlock-freedom by construction for the running distributed application, even in presence of adaptation rules which were unknown when the application was started, and for any environment condition.

Adaptation is a hot topic, and indeed there is a plethora of approaches in the literature, see, e.g., the surveys [20, 21]. However, approaches based on formal methods are only emerging recently and few of them have been implemented in a working tool. In particular, the use of choreographies to capture and define adaptive applications is a novel idea. For a discussion of works on adaptation with formal bases, but which have not been implemented, we refer to [9]. Here, we just recall [22], which exploits a choreographic approach for self-adaptive monitoring of distributed applications.

Among the implemented approaches, the most related to ours is JoRBA [5]. JoRBA features scopes and adaptation rules similar to ours. However, JoRBA applications are not distributed and JoRBA does not guarantee any property of the adapted application.

In [23] choreographies are used to propagate protocol changes to the other peers, while [24] presents a test to check whether a set of peers obtained from a choreography can be reconfigured to match a second one. Differently from ours, these works only provide change recommendations for adding and removing message sequences.

Various tools [25–27] exploit automatic planning techniques in order to elaborate, at runtime, the best sequence of activities to achieve a given goal. These techniques are more declarative than ours, but, to the best of our knowledge, they are not guaranteed to always find a plan to adapt the application.

Among the non-adaptive languages, Chor [2] is the closest to ours. Indeed, like ours, Chor is a choreographic language that compiles to Jolie. Actually, AIOCJ shares part of the Chor code base. However, due to the different semantics of the sequential operator and the lack of the parallel composition in Chor, a faithful encoding of the scenarios in Section 4 is not possible, especially for the fork-join scenario. On an almost equivalent implementation of the pipe scenario, Chor proves to be more efficient than AIOCJ.

In the future, we would like to test the expressive power of our language, trying to encode patterns of adaptation from existing approaches. An obvious benefit of such an encoding is that it will capture patterns of adaptation used in real-case scenarios, guaranteeing also deadlock freedom, which is not provided by other approaches. This task is cumbersome, due to the huge number and heterogeneity of those approaches. Nevertheless, we already started it. In particular, in the website [28], we show how to encode examples coming from distributed [29] and dynamic [30] Aspect-Oriented Programming (AOP) and from Context-Oriented Programming (COP) [31]. In general, we can deal with cross-cutting concerns like logging and authentication, typical of AOP, viewing point-cuts as empty scopes and advices as adaptation rules. Layers, typical of COP, can instead be defined by adaptation rules which can fire according to contextual conditions captured by the environment. Possible extensions of our framework include the use of asynchronous communications in the AIOC language and the introduction of mechanisms to deal with exceptions and failures. Finally, we would like to pursue a systematic analysis of the workflow change patterns like the ones presented in [32, 33], showing how these patterns are captured by AIOCJ.

References

1. Lu, S., Park, S., Seo, E., Zhou, Y.: Learning from mistakes: a comprehensive study on real world concurrency bug characteristics. In: ASPLOS, pp. 329–339. ACM (2008)
2. Carbone, M., Montesi, F.: Deadlock-Freedom-by-Design: Multiparty Asynchronous Global Programming. In: POPL, pp. 263–274. ACM (2013)
3. Gößler, G., Sifakis, J.: Component-Based Construction of Deadlock-Free Systems. In: Pandya, P.K., Radhakrishnan, J. (eds.) FSTTCS 2003. LNCS, vol. 2914, pp. 420–433. Springer, Heidelberg (2003)
4. Naik, M., Park, C.-S., Sen, K., Gay, D.: Effective static deadlock detection. In: ICSE, pp. 386–396. IEEE (2009)
5. Lanese, I., Bucchiarone, A., Montesi, F.: A Framework for Rule-Based Dynamic Adaptation. In: Wirsing, M., Hofmann, M., Rauschmayer, A. (eds.) TGC 2010, LNCS, vol. 6084, pp. 284–300. Springer, Heidelberg (2010)
6. Bucchiarone, A., Marconi, A., Pistore, M., Raik, H.: Dynamic Adaptation of Fragment-Based and Context-Aware Business Processes. In: ICWS, pp. 33–41. IEEE Press (2012)
7. Chen, W.-K., Hiltunen, M.A., Schlichting, R.D.: Constructing Adaptive Software in Distributed Systems. In: ICDCS. LNCS, vol. 6084, pp. 635–643. Springer (2001)
8. Zhang, J., Goldsby, H., Cheng, B.H.C.: Modular Verification of Dynamically Adaptive Systems. In: AOSD, pp. 161–172. ACM (2009)

9. Dalla Preda, M., Gabbrielli, M., Giallorenzo, S., Lanese, I., Mauro, J.: Deadlock Freedom by Construction for Distributed Adaptive Applications. Technical Report, http://arxiv.org/pdf/1407.0970v1.pdf
10. Carbone, M., Honda, K., Yoshida, N.: Structured communication-centered programming for web services. ACM Trans. Program. Lang. Syst. 34(2), 8 (2012)
11. Scribble website, http://www.jboss.org/scribble
12. Lanese, I., Guidi, C., Montesi, F., Zavattaro, G.: Bridging the Gap between Interaction- and Process-Oriented Choreographies. In: SEFM, pp. 323–332. IEEE Press (2008)
13. World Wide Web Consortium, Web Services Choreography Description Language Version 1.0 (2005), http://www.w3.org/TR/ws-cdl-10/
14. Jolie website, http://www.jolie-lang.org/
15. Montesi, F., Guidi, C., Zavattaro, G.: Composing services with JOLIE. In: Proc. of ECOWS 2007, pp. 13–22. IEEE Press (2007)
16. Dalla Preda, M., Giallorenzo, S., Lanese, I., Mauro, J., Gabbrielli, M.: AIOCJ: A Choreographic Framework for Safe Adaptive Distributed Applications. Technical Report, http://arxiv.org/pdf/1407.0975.pdf
17. Lanese, I., Montesi, F., Zavattaro, G.: Amending choreographies. In: WWV, vol. 123, pp. 34–48. EPTCS (2013)
18. Eclipse website, http://www.eclipse.org/
19. Xtext website, http://www.eclipse.org/Xtext/
20. Ghezzi, C., Pradella, M., Salvaneschi, G.: An evaluation of the adaptation capabilities in programming languages. In: SEAMS, pp. 50–59. ACM (2011)
21. Leite, L.A.F., et al.: A systematic literature review of service choreography adaptation. Service Oriented Computing and Applications 7(3), 199–216 (2013)
22. Coppo, M., Dezani-Ciancaglini, M., Venneri, B.: Self-adaptive monitors for multiparty sessions. In: PDP, pp. 688–696. IEEE (2014)
23. Rinderle, S., Wombacher, A., Reichert, M.: Evolution of Process Choreographies in DY-CHOR. In: Meersman, R., Tari, Z. (eds.) OTM 2006. LNCS, vol. 4275, pp. 273–290. Springer, Heidelberg (2006)
24. Wombacher, A.: Alignment of choreography changes in BPEL processes. In: IEEE SCC, pp. 1–8. IEEE Press (2009)
25. Cugola, G., Ghezzi, C., Pinto, L.S.: DSOL: a declarative approach to self-adaptive service orchestrations. Computing 94(7), 579–617 (2012)
26. Baresi, L., Marconi, A., Pistore, M., Sirbu, A.: Corrective Evolution of Adaptable Process Models. In: Nurcan, S., Proper, H.A., Soffer, P., Krogstie, J., Schmidt, R., Halpin, T., Bider, I. (eds.) RIMS 1982. LNBIP, vol. 147, pp. 214–229. Springer, Heidelberg (2013)
27. Bucchiarone, A., Marconi, A., Mezzina, C.A., Pistore, M., Raik, H.: On-the-Fly Adaptation of Dynamic Service-Based Systems: Incrementality, Reduction and Reuse. In: Basu, S., Pautasso, C., Zhang, L., Fu, X. (eds.) ICSOC 2013. LNCS, vol. 8274, pp. 146–161. Springer, Heidelberg (2013)
28. AIOCJ website, http://www.cs.unibo.it/projects/jolie/aiocj.html
29. Pawlak, R., et al.: JAC: an aspect-based distributed dynamic framework. SPE 34(12), 1119–1148 (2004)
30. Yang, Z., Cheng, B.H.C., Stirewalt, R.E.K., Sowell, J., Sadjadi, S.M., McKinley, P.K.: An aspect-oriented approach to dynamic adaptation. In: WOSS, pp. 85–92. ACM (2002)
31. Hirschfeld, R., Costanza, P., Nierstrasz, O.: Context-oriented Programming. Journal of Object Technology 7(3), 125–151 (2008)
32. Weber, B., Rinderle, S., Reichert, M.: Change Patterns and Change Support Features in Process-Aware Information Systems. In: Krogstie, J., Opdahl, A.L., Sindre, G. (eds.) CAiSE 2007 and WES 2007. LNCS, vol. 4495, pp. 574–588. Springer, Heidelberg (2007)
33. Casati, F., Ceri, S., Pernici, B., Pozzi, G.: Workflow Evolution. Data Knowl. Eng. 24(3), 211–238 (1998)

fUML as an Assembly Language for Model Transformation[*]

Massimo Tisi[1], Frédéric Jouault[2], Jérôme Delatour[2]
Zied Saidi[1], and Hassene Choura[1]

[1] AtlanMod team (Inria, Mines Nantes, LINA), Nantes, France
firstname.lastname@inria.fr
[2] TRAME team (ESEO), Angers, France
firstname.lastname@eseo.fr

Abstract. Within a given modeling platform, modeling tools, such as model editors and transformation engines, interoperate efficiently. They are generally written in the same general-purpose language, and use a single modeling framework (i.e., an API to access models). However, interoperability between tools from different modeling platforms is much more problematic.

In this paper, we propose to leverage fUML in order to address this issue by providing a common execution language. Modeling frameworks can then be abstracted into generic actions that perform elementary operations on models. Not only can user models benefit from a unified execution semantics, but modeling tools can too.

We support this proposal by showing how it can apply to a model transformation engine. To this end, a prototype compiler from ATL to fUML has been built, and is described. Finally, we conclude that fUML has some useful properties as candidate common execution language for MDE, but lacks some features.

1 Introduction

A modeling platform (e.g., Eclipse Modeling [2]) consists of a set of modeling tools (e.g., constraint checkers, comparators, transformation engines) that can be used together. Interoperability between tools of a given platform is typically achieved by two means: 1) a common programming language (e.g., Java), and 2) a common modeling framework (e.g., EMF: Eclipse Modeling Framework [1]).

Interoperability across modeling platforms generally relies on a common interchange format (e.g., a given version of XMI [3]) to exchange models. However, modeling tools cannot be exchanged (i.e., ported) so easily between platforms that rely on different programming languages or modeling frameworks. Therefore, some tools are either not available on some platforms, or have multiple implementations that are possibly inconsistent.

Moreover, some tools are actually execution engines for modeling languages. Such tools implement the semantics of modeling languages. For instance, an

---

[*] This work is partially supported by the MONDO (EU ICT-611125) project.

B. Combemale et al. (Eds.): SLE 2014, LNCS 8706, pp. 171–190, 2014.
© Springer International Publishing Switzerland 2014

OCL [4] constraint evaluator implements the semantics of OCL. Therefore, exchanging semantics implemented in tools is as problematic as exchanging tools.

We argue that a common modeling Virtual Machine (VM) may be used to implement a variety of modeling tools. We call *modeling VM* a virtual machine that abstracts the specifics of modeling platforms: programming language, and modeling framework. Tools built on top of this VM, or compiled to this VM, become portable across all modeling platforms providing an implementation of the VM.

We then consider the requirements for such a VM in the context of Model-Driven Engineering (MDE) and we show that fUML [5] could be used as a modeling VM for MDE. This application of fUML is different from its typical usage scenario. Instead of only using fUML to specify the behavior of models created by users of a modeling platform, we propose to also use it to provide execution for modeling tools. We are thus considering the use of models, expressed in fUML, at the runtime of modeling tools. When used in this way, fUML shares some characteristics with assembly languages: it is only **rarely used directly**, and complex fUML models are only **rarely displayed in a readable way**. The fUML specification recognizes these points, and defines a textual language to represent fUML activities.

This paper extends our previous paper [6] and improves over our preliminary analysis by showing how this applies to the specific case of model transformation. To this end, we provide a proof-of-concept compiler from ATL to fUML, whose source code is freely available at the paper's website[1]. We leverage this prototype in order to assess the suitability of fUML as an assembly language for model transformation. We also show that, however, making fUML actually usable in this way requires modifying it. Some modifications, like adding support for UML interruptions and exceptions, can also benefit users who model systems in fUML. Others are specifically intended for its use as a modeling VM assembly language. Therefore, the purpose of this paper is not to impose fUML in this role, but simply to position it as a possible assembly language for MDE, and to express our interest in exploring this idea further.

The analogy between fUML and assembly language is similar (and inspired by) the well-known analogy "Javascript is assembly language for the Web" [7,8]. Obviously, this is only an analogy that has its limits. For instance, fUML (like Javascript) is at a higher level of abstraction than assembly languages typically are. However, we strongly believe that this analogy may be as beneficial to MDE as the analogy about Javascript is to the Web.

The paper is organized as follows: Section 2 motivates the need for a modeling VM and introduces our illustrative example. Section 3 presents the requirements for such a VM in the MDE context, and discusses how fUML may fulfill them. Section 4 shows the practical applicability of our proposal by putting it into practice on the ATL model transformation language. Finally, we discuss related works in Section 5, and conclude in Section 6.

---

[1] http://www.emn.fr/z-info/atlanmod/index.php/ATL2fUML

2 Motivation

2.1 The Need for a Modeling VM

In this section, we motivate the need for a modeling VM that may be used as an execution platform for modeling tools. In the remainder of the paper, we refer to the language that this VM executes as its *VM language*. For instance, Java bytecodes form the VM language of the Java virtual machine.

A classical VM such as the Java VM provides abstractions for: 1) actual hardware (e.g., processor, memory, peripherals), and 2) operating system (e.g., Windows, Linux). This makes tools running on top of a classical VM independent of hardware and operating system. A modeling VM additionally provides abstractions for: 3) modeling framework (e.g., EMF), 4) general-purpose language used to implement the modeling platform (e.g., Java, C#, C++), and 5) version of the implementation language. Therefore, tools running on top of a modeling VM are also independent of the modeling platform, and of how it is implemented.

With a modeling VM, it becomes possible to develop modeling tools that can run on any modeling platform that supports it. Moreover, certain kinds of optimizations may be performed on modeling VMs independently of tools.

A modeling VM may be used to provide execution to a wide variety of modeling tools such as: simulator, animator, debugger, comparator (diff, merge), version control, importer, exporter, constraint checker, or formal checker. Some modeling tools are actually execution engines for modeling languages used to specify: transformations (model to model, model to text, or text to model), constraints, etc. There are two main approaches to implement an execution engine: translation of programs to the VM language (i.e., compilation), or interpretation of programs by an interpreter expressed in the VM language.

Another significant application for a modeling VM is the implementation of standards. For instance, the MDA standards from the OMG[2] may be implemented on top of a modeling VM:

- **Execution engines for languages:** Object Constraint Language (OCL), fUML , MOF Model to Text Transformation Language (MOFM2T) [9], and Query / View / Transformation (QVT) [10].
- **Importer and exporter** for XML Metadata Interchange (XMI), Action Language for Foundational UML (Alf) [11], and Human-Usable Textual Notation (HUTN) [12].

Furthermore, if a modeling VM is standardized, it may make sense to provide reference implementations for other standards on top of it.

2.2 Motivating Example: ATL

To show the practical applicability of fUML as virtual machine for existing MDE tools, we focus on model-transformation tools, which we believe to be reasonably

---

[2] As listed at: http://www.omg.org/spec/

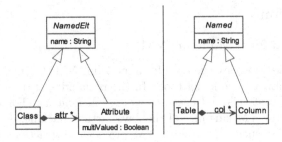

Fig. 1. Metamodels: ClassDiagram and Relational

representative of modeling tools. In particular, we choose to provide a proof-of-concept implementation of the well-known ATL transformation language on top of fUML.

We illustrate the ATL language with a simplified version of a classical model transformation example: *ClassDiagram2Relational*, from a *ClassDiagram* model to a *Relational* model. The source metamodel is a very simplified version of UML class diagram, and is shown in the left-hand side of Fig. 1. This *ClassDiagram* metamodel includes *Class* and *Attribute* that inherit a name property from the abstract meta-class *NamedElt*. Furthermore, the meta-class *Class* can contain attributes (reference *attr*) that can be multi-valued (property *multiValued*). The *Relational* metamodel, which is the target of our transformation, is shown in the right-hand side of Fig. 1. This metamodel defines the *Table*, and *Column* concepts, which inherit a name attribute from the abstract meta-class *Named*. Each *Table* can contain (reference *col*) any number of *Columns*.

The goal of this transformation is:

- To create for every *Class* exactly one *Table* with the same name.
- To create for every single-valued *Attribute* exactly one *Column* with the same name.
- Each *Table* must have exactly one *Column* per single-valued *Attribute* of the corresponding *Class*, with the same names.

The ATL implementation code for *ClassDiagram2Relational* consists of two simple rules, which are shown in Listing 1.1.

Listing 1.1. ATL ClassDiagram2Relational transformation

```
1 module ClassDiagram2Relational;
2 create OUT : Relational from IN : ClassDiagram;
3
4 rule Class2Table {
5     from
6         c : ClassDiagram!Class
7     to
8         out : Relational!Table (
9             name <- c.name,
10            col <- c.attr
11        )
12 }
13
14 rule Attribute2Column {
15     from
```

```
16            a : ClassDiagram!Attribute (
17                not a.multiValued
18            )
19     to
20            out : Relational!Column (
21                name <- a.name
22            )
23  }
```

Rules in ATL describe the transformation from a source model to a target model by relating metamodels. They have a source pattern (*from part* or *input pattern*), and a target pattern (*to part* or *output pattern*). The source pattern consists of an input variable declaration, and optionally a guard (or filter), which is used to impose conditions on the source elements. In the target pattern, rules declare which elements of the target model the source pattern has to be transformed to. The target pattern consists of a set of elements, and a sequence of bindings for each element. Each binding initializes one property of a target element.

This ATL listing starts with the module name (line 1), followed by its signature (line 2) that declares the source and target models with their respective metamodels. The first rule *Class2Table* (lines 4 to 12) has one source pattern element (lines 5 to 6) of type *Class* from the source metamodel *ClassDiagram*, and one target pattern element (lines 7 to 11) of type *Attribute* from the target metamodel *Relational*, intended to create a *Table* target element for each *Class* source element. This rule also contains two bindings. The first binding (line 9) is used to initialize the name of target *Table* as the same name as source *Class*. According to the second binding (line 10) the *col* reference has to contain all columns that have been created from the attributes of associated *Class*. The second rule *Attribute2Column* (lines 14 to 23) aims at creating an homonym (according to the binding at line 21) *Column* target element (lines 19 to 22) for each single-valued *Attribute* source element (lines 15 to 18). This rule contains a guard (line 17) that selects only the single-valued *Attributes*.

3   The Modeling VM

3.1   Requirements

Among the plethora of languages that have been defined or simply used by the MDE community, several may be considered as candidates for the role of assembly language. At the time of writing this paper, the Java+EMF combination is widely used by MDE tools, and can very well be considered as an MDE VM.

In this section we enumerate a set of requirements for an MDE assembly language, that despite not being mandatory, would increase the value of the VM language:

– **Computational completeness.** Using the VM language it must be possible to specify any possible model operation, i.e., any computable function on models.

- **Model handling.** Models and model elements should be manipulated as first-class entities by the language, without the need to encode them into other data structures.
- **No over-specification.** When translating other languages to it, the VM language should not require the specification of irrelevant information. For instance, the VM language should allow programs to specify sequencing between instructions only if necessary, allowing for implicit parallelism (this property is especially significant now that virtually every computer is multicore). Analogously the VM language should not impose an order for side-effect free evaluations, thus allowing for eager or lazy evaluation of a given program when needed.
- **Exception handling.** Language constructs for exception handling at the VM level are not mandatory, but would simplify the use of the VM language.
- **Introspection and Reflection.** When a model-driven tool uses introspection and reflection, its implementation over the VM is made easier if this support is embedded in the VM language. For instance, reflective access to model elements is a commonly used feature in MDE tools implementation. Moreover, some tools also provide reflective model access to the user.
- **Modularity/Composability.** It should be possible to compile parts of tools into separate modules to be composed in the VM language.
- **VM code as a model.** For uniformity with the development platform, VM code should be represented in the form of a model. Model interchange mechanisms (e.g., XMI) can then be leveraged for VM code as well. This would also allow the manipulation of VM code using VM language. This is similar to the higher-order transformation concept [13], and may be leveraged to use model transformation to specify compilers that target the VM language.
- **High-performance implementation.** It should be possible to build a high-performance implementation of the language, thus reducing the performance penalty of using a VM.
- **Wide availability.** The language and its implementation should be publicly available, and widely used in the community.
- **Standard.** The VM language should be recognized as a standard (e.g., an OMG standard), and its formal semantics should be publicly available.

At this stage, it should be noted that conflicts between requirements cannot be completely resolved. For instance, **high-performance implementation** may rely on static computation of a control flow, which may be seen as contradicting **no over-specification**. An answer to these requirements will be a trade-off. Finally, there are properties that are typically valuable for a language in MDE, but that have no primary importance for a VM language, such as: human-readability, conciseness, and maintainability[3].

We compare fUML to other candidate modeling VMs in order to see which aspects of fUML are adequate, and which may need to be improved. Table 1

---

[3] For instance, Java bytecode is barely readable (especially in binary format), not especially concise, and generally not maintained directly.

gives an overview with the set of requirements presented above as rows, and languages under consideration as columns.

Because fUML is the only OMG standard at the right level of abstraction to play the role of VM language, we have no other points of comparison from OMG. The set of languages we take into consideration is: 1) the Java VM language, a general-purpose VM language currently targeted by several MDE tools, especially in the Eclipse modeling platform, 2) the ATL VM language[4], a high-level VM for model manipulation, 3) the fUML language version 1.1 [5]. This set is not meant to be exhaustive, as several other languages could be included in this comparison, such as: QVT, Kermeta [15], or Epsilon [5]. However, these other languages are at higher abstraction levels than the three considered languages, and than typical assembly languages. The considered languages are representative of classical (JVM), and model-oriented (ATL VM and fUML) VMs.

3.2 fUML as Assembly

In this section we argue that fUML is an interesting candidate to be an assembly language for MDE: it satisfies many of the identified requirements, and is expected to satisfy most of the others.

As shown in Table 1, the computational completeness requirement is satisfied by all three languages under consideration. However, only one of the three VMs, namely the ATL VM, natively handles model elements as first-class entities. This requirement is in general satisfied by VMs that, like the ATL VM, are designed for MDE. General purpose VMs like the Java VM can still provide a uniform model access by using common modeling frameworks like EMF. fUML is designed to exclusively handle instances of UML classifiers. However, it can be generalized to handle any model element by lifting its semantics to MOF, similarly to what has been done in xMOF [16]. Another possibility would be to implement a modeling framework in fUML, but this would not provide direct access to the modeling framework used by the host platform.

There are three rows of Table 1 that illustrate which control is provided by the VM language over code execution. In particular we focus on the possibility of specifying that 1) some operations may be executed sequentially or in parallel, 2) evaluations may be performed in a lazy or eager way, 3) operations may be executed without a specific execution order. The Java VM imposes a sequential order between its instructions, but allows for explicitly defined coarse-grained parallel operations (as Threads) or lazy evaluations by relying on programming libraries written in VM bytecode. We call this approach *in-language* in Table 1. Similarly, the ATL VM bytecode is based on fixed sequences of imperative instructions, and its current implementation does not allow to specify parallelism or laziness. However, two experimental versions have notably been created to support: a) coarse-grained parallelism with interesting results in terms of speedup [17], and

---

[4] We refer to the most recent version of the ATL VM, named EMFTVM [14], unless specified otherwise in a cell of Table 1.

[5] http://www.eclipse.org/epsilon/

Table 1. Languages and requirements

	Java VM bytecode	ATL VM bytecode	fUML
Computational completeness	yes	yes	yes
Model handling	only by using modeling framework	yes	only UML Instance-Specifications (but has been lifted to MOF [16])
High-performance implementation	yes	yes	no (but expected)
Wide availability	++	+	- (++ expected)
Parallel operations	in-language	no (but linguistic in ParallelVM [17])	linguistic
Eager/Lazy evaluation	in-language	no (but linguistic in LazyVM [18])	in-language (but linguistic may be added, as in UML activities)
No execution order over-specification	fixed execution order	fixed execution order	execution order not imposed
Exception handling	yes	no	no (but it may be added, as in UML activities)
Introspection and Reflection	yes	only reflective model access	no
Modularity/ Composability	yes	yes	yes
VM code as a model	no	yes	yes
MDA Standard	no	no	yes

b) lazy evaluation of transformation rules [18]. Finally, in fUML, parallelism is a *linguistic* feature of the language, that allows the definition of fine-grained regions of parallel execution. fUML does not require to impose an execution order between instructions, as it provides a specific dataflow semantics for edges. Explicit control flow is nonetheless supported. Lazy evaluation is not explicitly supported by fUML linguistic features but can be still implemented by specific modeling patterns. Moreover, UML activity diagrams have a linguistic support for lazy evaluation (with *ValueInputPin* and *ActionPin*) and an extension of fUML in this sense would be possible.

Among the three VMs, the more mature Java and ATL VMs provide high-performance implementations, but a similarly efficient machine is expected also for fUML. Actually, fUML is in theory in a better position to have especially efficient implementations on future many-cores computing platforms, because it can be used to express significantly more of (if not all) the fine-grained parallelism in a problem [19]. Finally, while fUML is today the least popular VM among the three choices, we expect it to become widely available once the standard is mature. fUML availability may first be driven by users'need to execute their own models. This will incidentally enable execution of MDE tools built on top of it.

Advanced features like exception handling and reflection are only supported by the Java VM. All VM languages implement at least a modularity/composability mechanism. With respect to the other two VMs, the fUML option has the important benefits of representing VM code as a model and of being an OMG standard. Moreover, UML supports interruptible regions and exceptions, which could therefore be supported by future fUML versions.

4   fUML as Assembly for ATL

As an example of a roadmap that MDE tools may follow to comply to a common modeling VM, we discuss the case of the ATL transformation language. A possible roadmap may involve replacing the current version of the ATL compiler (that compiles towards the ATL VM) with a new compiler towards fUML, encoding transformation rules as flows of fUML activities. fUML activities, lifted to the MOF level, would directly modify the models under transformation. An immediate benefit of this new compiler w.r.t. the old one would be the possibility of leveraging the innate parallelism of fUML by exploiting fUML parallel execution regions in the generation. When semantically equivalent implementations of fUML in different modeling platforms are available, the same ATL transformation will be executable on any of these platforms.

In this section we present a proof-of-concept compiler that translates a subset of the ATL language to fUML. To illustrate how this translation is performed we reuse the example of Section 2 by describing an implementation of *Class-Diagram2Relational* as an fUML model. This implementation uses the xMOF (eXecutable MOF) framework [16], which is a metamodeling language integrating fUML with MOF. xMOF has been originally built to enable users to specify the behavioral semantics of their domain-specific modeling languages. We simply leverage it to provide MDE tool execution as discussed in previous sections.

4.1   ClassDiagram2Relational in fUML

Fig. 2 depicts the metamodel of the *ClassDiagram2Relational* execution, which consist of the syntax metamodel in the upper part and the runtime configuration metamodel in the lower part.

Syntax Metamodel. The elements of the syntax metamodel can be divided into three groups. The first group consists of the meta-class *Transformation*, the abstract meta-class *Trace*, and its sub-classes. For each matched rule one sub-class of *Trace* is created (e.g., *TraceC2T* for rule *Class2Table* and *TraceA2C* for rule *Attribute2Column*). Trace classes have references pointing to the meta-classes of the source and target pattern of the corresponding rules. For example the meta-class *TraceC2T* has two references, *sourceTraceC2T* pointing to *Class* and *targetTraceC2T* pointing to *Table*. The other two groups of meta-classes are copies of the transformation source and target metamodels, with the addition, for each meta-class, of references toward the related transformation traces.

Runtime Configuration Metamodel. The runtime configuration metamodel (lower part of Fig. 2) defines the operational semantics of the transformation. It contains configuration meta-classes providing a runtime representation of the

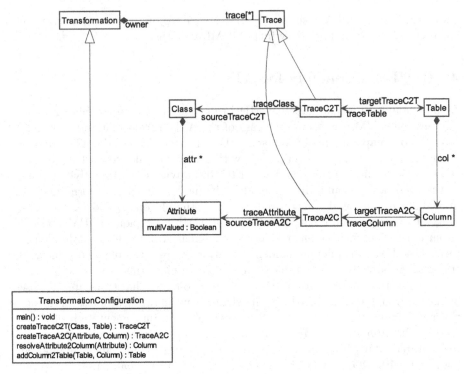

Fig. 2. Excerpt of *ClassDiagram2Relational* execution metamodel

syntax metamodel. Semantics is defined by defining operations in these meta-classes, and associating them to fUML activities.

The runtime configuration metamodel in Fig. 2 contains the class *Transforma-tionConfiguration*, which includes the operations *main*, *createTraceC2T*, *create-TraceA2C*, *resolveAttribute2Column* and *addColumnToTable*. The metamodel also contains a configuration class for each meta-class defined in the syntax metamodel, with no operation (these classes are omitted in Fig. 2 for the sake of simplicity).

Main Activity. In our *ClassDiagram2Relational* xMOF example, for each oper-ation one activity having the same name is created to specify its behavior. Fig. 3 represents the *main* activity, that initiates and controls the global execution.

The *main* activity is divided into two parts (left and right hand sides of Fig. 3) that run sequentially, since they are linked by the only control flow of the diagram. The left-hand side represents the *matching* phase of the transformation rules, while the right-hand side is the *apply* phase, responsible for computing and setting all target properties.

The goal of the matching phase is to create, for each match of a transformation rule, an empty element in the target model as well as a trace link. In our example, this phase creates one instance each of *Table* and of *TraceC2T* for each *Class* (like the *Class2Table* ATL rule), and one instance each of *Column* and of *TraceA2C*

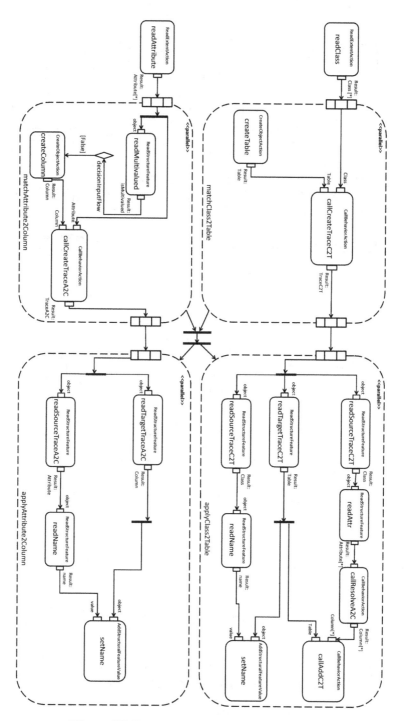

Fig. 3. fUML activity: Transformation::main()

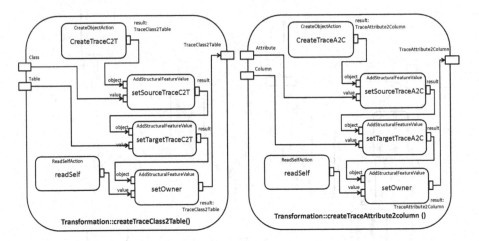

Fig. 4. fUML activites: Traces activities

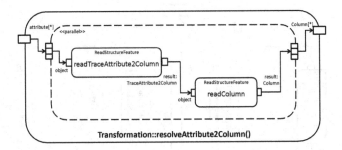

Fig. 5. fUML activity: Transformation::resolve()

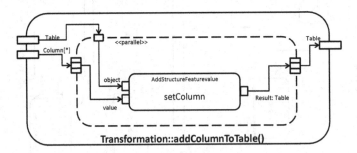

Fig. 6. fUML activity:Transformation::addColumnToTable()

for each single-valued *Attribute* (like the *Attribute2Column* ATL rule). We will discuss the two matching rules separately.

For *Class2Table*, the flow starts by reading all instances of *Class* from the input model, using the Read Extent Action *readClass*. The content of the *match-Class2Table* expansion region is executed in parallel for all the *Classes*. Since *Class2Table* matches every *Class* without further constraints, *matchClass2Table* simply contains two actions: a Create Object Action to create a *Table*, and a Call Behavior Action that launches a trace creation activity. The output of this expansion region is a list of *TraceC2T*s.

The lower expansion region represents the matching phase of the *Attribute2-Column* rule. The region processes in parallel all the *Attributes* of the source model. The *Attribute2Column* rule has a guard, which checks if the attribute is single-valued. This guard is represented by a Read Structural Feature Action which reads the value of attribute *isMultivalued* and a decision node that passes the control if the attribute is false. In this case the next actions create a *Column* and a *TraceA2C*, analogously to the previous rule.

The *apply* part is represented in the right-hand side of Fig.3, by expansion regions *applyClass2Table* and *applyAttribute2Column*, which are executed in parallel.

ApplyAttribute2Column aims to set the name of the *Columns* created in the matching phase with the name of the corresponding *Attributes*. It takes as input the list of *TraceA2C* elements from the previous phase. For each element of this list it 1) finds the target Column to initialize (*readTargetTraceA2C*), 2) reads the name of the corresponding attribute (*readSourceTraceA2C* and *readName*), and 3) sets the value of the name in the target *Column* (*setName*).

The *applyClass2Table* region aims to set the name of the generated *Tables* by a chain of actions that is analogous to the previous rule (*readTargetTraceC2T*, *readSourceTraceC2T*, *readName*, and *setName*). *ApplyClass2Table* also contains a second (upper) flow, that adds to the *Table* the *Columns* generated by the other rule. This flow uses the *resolveAttribe2Column* activity to find the *Columns* generated from *Attributes* of the corresponding *Class*. Finally, the *addColumns2Table* activity is called to put the collection of *Columns* into the *Table*.

Trace Creation Activities. The fUML implementation of *ClassDiagram2Relational* contains a trace creation activity for each transformation rule. These activities are called by the main activity when a new trace link needs to be created.

Fig.4 shows the trace creation activities for the *Class2Table* and *Column2-Attribute* rules. The *createTraceClass2Table* activity aims at creating and returning an instance of *TraceC2T* which has three references: 1) *sourceTraceC2T* pointing to the input *Class*, 2) *targetTraceC2T* pointing to the input *Table*, and 3) *owner* pointing to the *Transformation*. These references are set by a sequence of AddStructuralFeature actions *setSourceTraceC2T*, *setTargetTraceC2T* and *setOwner*. Finally, the newly created trace is returned. Trace creation for *Column2Attribute* is analogous.

Trace Resolution Activities. Fig. 5 shows the *resolveAttribute2Column* activity. This activity *resolves* the *TraceA2C* link, meaning that, given an *Attribute* element it returns the correspondent *Column* element. Resolution is performed by navigating from the source element to the trace link, and then from the trace link to the target element. Navigations are performed by ReadStructuralFeature actions that are inserted into an expansion region, so as to be able to resolve elements sets as well as single elements.

Auxiliary Activities. Auxiliary activities like *addColumnsToTable* in Fig. 6 are added to facilitate the assignment of a collection to a reference. In this case the activity takes as inputs a list of *Columns* and a *Table*, and returns this *Table* after cycling on the collection and adding its elements to the reference *col*.

4.2   Mapping ATL to fUML

In the previous section, while describing the fUML representation of the small *ClassDiagram2Relational* transformation, we introduced the main concepts of the compilation of ATL towards fUML. Around these concepts we built a prototype ATL-to-fUML compiler that is able to translate simple declarative transformations. In particular, the compiler is capable to translate Listing 1.1 into the implementation of Figures 2 to 6.

While the generation of trace-creation, trace-resolution, and auxiliary activities can be trivially induced from the example, we use Figures 7 and 8 to illustrate the general schema for generating the main activity.

For the matching phase (Fig. 7), the type of the source elements to match is translated into an fUML ReadExtentAction for that type. Each element of the matched type is analyzed in parallel thanks to an expansion region. The OCL expression used as the rule guard is translated into an fUML flow calculating a boolean. A decision node triggers the creation of the corresponding target elements and trace link only when the guard is satisfied. Finally, trace links are produced by a call to the generated trace creation activity, and the set of trace links is collected as the output of the expansion region.

The set of trace links is taken in input by the rule application phase (Fig. 8), which assigns a value to the properties of target elements created in the previous phase. The expansion region starts a parallel flow for each trace link, i.e. for each rule application. The value of the target properties are computed thanks to a value expression, that is the translation in fUML of the OCL expressions in the ATL code. The computed value is used to assign an attribute or a reference in the target model. The assignment is done by an AddStructuralFeatureValueAction in case of single-valued properties or by a call to an auxiliary activity in case of multi-valued properties.

While Figures 7 and 8 illustrate the compilation of the ATL main structures in fUML, translating OCL expressions into the "guard expression" or "value expression" placeholders is not a trivial problem. Our current proof-of-concept compiler is able to translate OCL boolean operators, property navigation and equalities, but work has yet to be done for full OCL support.

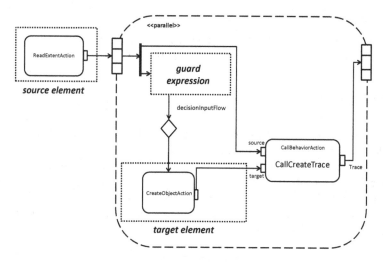

Fig. 7. Translation of the rule matching part

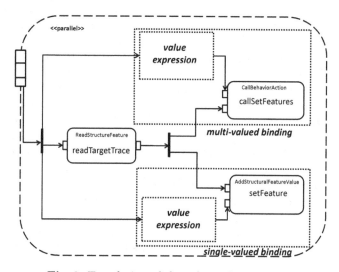

Fig. 8. Translation of the rule application part

The compiler is itself written in ATL (i.e., it is a higher-order transformation [13]). The compiler is completely written in declarative style by solely relying on ATL matched rules, providing a clear correspondence between ATL and fUML metamodels. While the full code of the transformation rules is available at the paper website[6], Table 2 summarizes the correspondence between the ATL syntax and the fUML/xMOF syntax.

---

[6] http://www.emn.fr/z-info/atlanmod/index.php/ATL2fUML

It is mostly because of our limited support for OCL that our compiler at the current stage can not be itself compiled into fUML. Our next step will be to extend the compiler to fully bootstrap our approach.

4.3 Discussion

Although readability of an assembly language is not necessary, the fUML model generated from the *ClassDiagram2Relational* ATL transformation is relatively readable. One reason is that modularity has been achieved by separating different parts into different behaviors. Of course, readability of generated fUML models will most probably not scale to larger, more complex transformations. However, it may be leveraged to teach and explain the semantics of a modeling tool (such as the ATL engine) by generating fUML models corresponding to simple examples. This generation can use the same compiler as the one used for complex cases. Continuing on readability, we observed that the compiler itself is relatively readable as an ATL-to-fUML declarative transformation when compared to the legacy ATL-to-bytecode compiler.

Before switching to xMOF, we attempted to create a standard fUML version, using Papyrus as execution engine. However, that version could not directly use model elements, but only UML classifier instances. xMOF solved that issue, but then again xMOF is still a non-standard version of fUML lifted to MOF. Considering that OCL also started as a UML-only constraint and query language before being lifted to MOF, there is hope that fUML may follow the same path.

In Section 2, we mentioned the possibility of optimizing a common VM for performance independently of the tools built on top of it. Although we have not tested this with the fUML common VM approach, this has already been experimented for ATL. The original "Regular ATL VM" (released in 2004) was not very efficient. Therefore, in 2007, we decided to implement a new EMFVM from scratch. This new VM supports the exact same bytecode, but has a better architecture, and is better optimized. The ATL compiler was not impacted at all. We believe that a similar path could be followed by fUML-based VMs.

With respect to the use of a modeling VM to implement standards, it should be noted that the fUML standard already comes with a reference implementation of fUML specified in fUML. Although this may not seem useful in concrete cases, we can imagine scenarios in which it actually is. For instance, a modeling platform may have an efficient fUML VM that is good at providing execution for tools, but may lack a good fUML simulator or animator, which users need for their own models. An implementation of fUML tailored for emulation and simulation may then run on top of the more efficient fUML VM tailored for tool execution. The way current fUML implementations based on the reference implementation work is arguably close to this situation. Indeed, the reference implementation is in part a serialization of the text-based fUML definition of fUML in fUML from the specification.

Finally, we listed in Section 3.1 a requirement (named no over-specification) that VM code should not be sequential when this is not imposed by the semantics of the tool. Regarding this requirement, we can note that in our example we

Table 2. Mapping ATL metamodel - fUML metamodel

Source element	Generated elements (symbolic name)
Module	BehavioredEClass ('TransformationConfiguration') BehavioredEClass ('TraceConfiguration') BehavioredEOperation ('main') JoinNode ForkNode Activity ('main') EPackage ('ATL2fUMLConfiguration')
MatchedRule	BehavioredEClass ('Trace Configuration') BehavioredEClass ('InPattern Configuration') BehavioredEClass ('OutPattern Configuration') BehavioredEOperation ('createTrace') Activity ('createTrace') CreateObjectAction ('create Trace') AddStructuralFeatureValueAction ('setSource') AddStructuralFeatureValueAction ('setTarget') AddStructuralFeatureValueAction ('setOwner') ReadSelfAction ('Read Self') ExpansionNode ('inputApply') ExpansionRegion ('Apply') ForkNode
MatchedRule (s.isMultivalReference())	BehavioredEOperation ('resolve') Activity ('resolve') ExpansionRegion ('Resolve Expansion Region') ExpansionNode ('input Element expansion Region') ExpansionNode ('output Element expansion Region') ReadStructuralFeatureAction ('read Trace') ReadStructuralFeatureAction ('read OutPattern') BehavioredEOperation ('add OutPattern') Activity ('add OutPattern') ExpansionRegion ('Set References Expansion Region') ExpansionNode ('input Expansion Node') ExpansionNode ('input Expansion Node') ExpansionNode ('output Expansion Node') AddStructuralFeatureValueAction ('set OutPattern')
SimpleOutPatternElement	ReadStructuralFeatureAction ('read Target') ForkNode
Binding	ReadStructuralFeatureAction ('read') ReadStructuralFeatureAction ('read Source inPattern') CallBehaviorAction 'callActivity resolve'
Binding (s.isAttribute() <> OclUndefined)	AddStructuralFeatureValueAction ('set property Name')
Binding (s.isAttribute() = OclUndefined)	CallBehaviorAction ('callActivity resolve') CallBehaviorAction ('Call Behavior Action')
NavigationOrAttributeCallExp (s.getRootFilter().oclType().name= 'InPattern')	ReadStructuralFeatureAction ('read')
OperatorCallExp	LiteralBoolean
SimpleInPatternElement	ReadExtentAction ('read') ExpansionNode ('input Match') ExpansionNode ('output Match') CreateObjectAction ('createOutPattern') CallBehaviorAction ('callCreateTrace')
SimpleInPatternElement (s.refImmediateComposite().filter <> OclUndefined)	ForkNode DecisionNode ExpansionRegion ('match')
SimpleInPatternElement (s.refImmediateComposite().filter = OclUndefined)	ExpansionRegion ('match')

managed to have only one control-flow synchronization point. It is used to make sure that trace links are not accessed before they are all created. Therefore, we find it especially interesting that the fine-grained parallelism of ATL semantics can be modeled so elegantly.

5   Related Work

Efforts to provide a common modeling platform and repository date from the beginning of MDE. While EMF is today the *de facto* standard, other well-known proposals exist, like NetBeans Metadata Repository [20] and Univers@lis [21]. Modeling tools developed over one of these platform are generally tied to the chosen framework. Several works investigated interoperability of modeling tools among different platforms. For instance [22] investigates interoperability issues among different metamodeling platforms. [23] focuses on the interoperability of modeling tools through the use of a bus that provides several predefined data interchange and conversion services.

Some works specifically address interoperability of model-transformation engines. The Integrated Transformation Environment (ITE) [24] allows users to use many transformation engines in the same environment. [14] proposes a common virtual machine to have different model-transformation languages interoperate on EMF. A general schema for the migration of a model transformation engine to a different platform has been investigated in [25], together with a practical experimentation migrating ATL from EMF to Microsoft DSL Tools.

We are not aware of any related work that proposes a single "assembly language" for all kinds of modeling tools. However, our proposed approach may be used in complement to other approches such as the ones mentioned in this section. For instance, a common VM approach, for instance based on fUML, may be used to exchange tools (e.g., as fUML models) over a model bus, which may also be useful to synchronize multiple modeling frameworks. This synchronization may for instance be useful because not all tools may be exchangeable as fUML models.

6 Conclusion

In this work, we explained that interoperability between modeling tools across modeling platforms may be simplified by the use of a common modeling Virtual Machine (VM). This VM provides execution to modeling tools written in (or compiled to) its language. We showed the applicability of this approach by providing a proof-of-concept implementation of ATL over the fUML VM. There are two notable possible ways to extend this work: 1) improving ATL coverage in order to show that it scales to more complex tools, and 2) applying it to more modeling tools (possibly beyond model transformation tools).

Although fUML is not fully ready to be the language for such a modeling VM, it is one of the best candidates. Once the problems mentioned in Section 3.2 are addressed, it does not lack many features to be usable for many kinds of tools. However, we have not considered tools that have a stronger dependency to a given platform. For instance, graphical model editors generally have a strong dependency to a windowing toolkit, which is complex to abstract in a VM.

Execution performance of fUML may be limited on full-fledged fUML engines, which provide complete simulation of the flow of tokens. These tools (e.g., [26]) are extremely useful when fUML is used to specify behavior of user models. However, when fUML is used as a VM, techniques similar to those used for asm.js [27] may be used to increase performance: definition of a simpler subset of fUML, and ahead-of-time compilation to machine code. Therefore, performance should not, in the long run, be an issue that prevents using fUML as proposed in this paper.

References

1. Steinberg, D., Budinsky, F., Merks, E., Paternostro, M.: EMF: Eclipse Modeling Framework. Pearson Education (2008)
2. Gronback, R.C.: Eclipse Modeling Project: A Domain-Specific Language (DSL) Toolkit. Eclipse Series. Pearson Education (2009)
3. Object Management Group (OMG): XML Metadata Interchange (XMI), v2.4.2 (April 2014), http://www.omg.org/spec/XMI/2.4.2/
4. Object Management Group (OMG): Object Constraint Language (OCL), v2.4 (February 2014), http://www.omg.org/spec/OCL/2.4/
5. Object Management Group (OMG): Semantics of a Foundational Subset for Executable UML Models (fUML), v1.1 (August 2013), http://www.omg.org/spec/FUML/1.1/
6. Jouault, F., Tisi, M., Delatour, J.: fUML as an Assembly Language for MDA. In: Modeling in Software Engineering Workshop at ICSE 2014 (2014)
7. Kappe, D.: Is Javascript the Assembly Language of Web 2.0?, http://pathfindersoftware.com/2007/03/is_javascript_t/ (accessed July 22, 2013) (archived by WebCite® at http://www.webcitation.org/6IIxYG22S) (March 2007)
8. Hanselman, S., Meijer, E.: JavaScript is Assembly Language for the Web: Semantic Markup is Dead! Clean vs. Machine-coded HTML, http://www.hanselminutes.com/274/javascript-is-assembly-language-for-the-web-semantic-markup-is-dead-clean-vs-machine-coded (accessed July 22, 2013) (archived by WebCite® at http://www.webcitation.org/6IIz8ZvNt) (July 2011)
9. Object Management Group (OMG): MOF Model To Text Transformation Language (MOFM2T), 1.0 (January 2008), http://www.omg.org/spec/MOFM2T/1.0/
10. Object Management Group (OMG): Meta Object Facility (MOF) 2.0 Query/View/Transformation, V1.2 (Beta), http://www.omg.org/spec/QVT/1.2/ (May 2014)
11. Object Management Group (OMG): Concrete Syntax For A UML Action Language: Action Language For Foundational UML (ALF), v1.0.1, http://www.omg.org/spec/ALF/1.0.1/ (October 2013)
12. Object Management Group (OMG): UML Human-Usable Textual Notation (HUTN), v1.0 (August 2004), http://www.omg.org/spec/HUTN/1.0/
13. Tisi, M., Jouault, F., Fraternali, P., Ceri, S., Bézivin, J.: On the use of higher-order model transformations. In: Paige, R.F., Hartman, A., Rensink, A. (eds.) ECMDA-FA 2009. LNCS, vol. 5562, pp. 18–33. Springer, Heidelberg (2009)
14. Wagelaar, D., Tisi, M., Cabot, J., Jouault, F.: Towards a general composition semantics for rule-based model transformation. In: Whittle, J., Clark, T., Kühne, T. (eds.) MODELS 2011. LNCS, vol. 6981, pp. 623–637. Springer, Heidelberg (2011)
15. Muller, P.-A., Fleurey, F., Jézéquel, J.-M.: Weaving Executability into Object-Oriented Meta-languages. In: Briand, L.C., Williams, C. (eds.) MoDELS 2005. LNCS, vol. 3713, pp. 264–278. Springer, Heidelberg (2005)
16. Mayerhofer, T., Langer, P., Wimmer, M.: Towards xMOF: executable DSMLs based on fUML. In: Proceedings of the 2012 Workshop on Domain-Specific Modeling, DSM 2012, pp. 1–6. ACM, New York (2012)
17. Tisi, M., Martínez, S., Choura, H.: Parallel Execution of ATL Transformation Rules. In: Moreira, A., Schätz, B., Gray, J., Vallecillo, A., Clarke, P. (eds.) MODELS 2013. LNCS, vol. 8107, pp. 656–672. Springer, Heidelberg (2013)

18. Tisi, M., Martínez, S., Jouault, F., Cabot, J.: Lazy execution of model-to-model transformations. In: Whittle, J., Clark, T., Kühne, T. (eds.) MODELS 2011. LNCS, vol. 6981, pp. 32–46. Springer, Heidelberg (2011)
19. Vishkin, U.: Is Multicore Hardware for General-purpose Parallel Processing Broken? Commun. ACM 57(4), 35–39 (2014)
20. NetBeans Metadata Repository, http://mdr.netbeans.org
21. Belaunde, M.: A pragmatic approach for building a user-friendly and flexible uml model repository. In: France, R.B. (ed.) UML 1999. LNCS, vol. 1723, pp. 188–203. Springer, Heidelberg (1999)
22. Kühn, H., Murzek, M.: Interoperability issues in metamodelling platforms. In: Konstantas, D., Bourrières, J.P., Léonard, M., Boudjlida, N. (eds.) Interoperability of Enterprise Software and Applications, pp. 215–226. Springer London (2006)
23. Blanc, X., Gervais, M.-P., Sriplakich, P.: Model bus: Towards the interoperability of modelling tools. In: Aßmann, U., Akşit, M., Rensink, A. (eds.) MDAFA 2003. LNCS, vol. 3599, pp. 17–32. Springer, Heidelberg (2005)
24. Blanc, X., Gervais, M.P., Lamari, M., Sriplakich, P.: Towards an Integrated Transformation Environment (ITE) for Model Driven Development (MDD), Invited Session "Model Driven Development". In: 8th World Multi-Conference on Systemics, Cybernetics and Informatics (SCI 2004). LNCS (2004), Model Driven Architecture: Foundations and Applications, International Institute of Informatics and Systemics (IIIS) (2004) INT LIP6 MoVe
25. Brunelière, H., Cabot, J., Clasen, C., Jouault, F., Bézivin, J.: Towards model driven tool interoperability: Bridging eclipse and microsoft modeling tools. In: Kühne, T., Selic, B., Gervais, M.-P., Terrier, F. (eds.) ECMFA 2010. LNCS, vol. 6138, pp. 32–47. Springer, Heidelberg (2010)
26. Mayerhofer, T., Langer, P., Kappel, G.: A runtime model for fUML. In: Proceedings of the 7th Workshop on Models@run.time, MRT 2012, pp. 53–58. ACM, New York (2012)
27. Herman, D., Wagner, L., Zakai, A.: asm.js (December 2013), http://asmjs.org/spec/latest/

Respect Your Parents: How Attribution and Rewriting Can Get Along

Anthony M. Sloane, Matthew Roberts, and Leonard G.C. Hamey

Department of Computing, Macquarie University, Sydney, Australia

Abstract. Attribute grammars describe how to decorate static trees. Rewriting systems describe how to transform trees into new trees. Attribution is undermined by rewriting because a node may appear in both the source and product of a transformation. If an attribute of that node depends on the node's context, then a previously computed value may not be valid. We explore this problem and formalise it as a question of ancestry: the context of a node is given by the tree's parent relationships and we must use the appropriate parents to calculate attributes that depend on the context. We show how respecting parents naturally leads to a view of context-dependent attributes as tree-indexed attribute families. Viewed in this way, attribution co-exists easily with rewriting transformations. We demonstrate the practicality of our approach by describing our implementation in the Kiama language processing library.

1   Introduction

Tree attribution and tree rewriting are two fundamental paradigms of software language engineering. On the one hand, attribution focuses on calculating properties of a given program represented as a syntax tree. Attribute grammars are a standard way to declaratively specify the way in which trees should be attributed. On the other hand, rewriting concentrates on transforming a program represented by a syntax tree into a program or other artefact represented by another tree.

Attribution and rewriting are more usefully deployed together to solve a language engineering task. For example, in a compiler we might obtain an initial tree from a syntax analyser and perform some attribution on it to check some basic static properties. We might transform the initial tree into another one, perhaps to desugar complex constructs into simpler ones. Following this transformation, we might calculate attributes of the desugared tree to determine information that is needed for a further transformation process that produces the output we desire such as compiled code.

The ease with which such a process can be described is deceptive, since the detail of combining attribution and rewriting contains a subtle trap. It is common for rewriting implementations to use immutable data representations and deploy structure sharing since duplication of nodes can lead to significant extra memory use [1]. For example, a desugaring transformation might retain some parts of the input tree if those parts do not contain any complex constructs.

B. Combemale et al. (Eds.): SLE 2014, LNCS 8706, pp. 191–210, 2014.

If nodes are shared between trees, how do we think of their attributes? These nodes are unchanged by the rewriting process and are shared by the before and after trees for efficiency reasons. A shared node may have different ancestors in the two trees and attributes that depend on these ancestors may well have different values depending on which set of ancestors we use. For example, the type of an expression may be different after rewriting if the type of a variable it uses has been changed. The type of the variable is given by the context of the expression in a particular tree, not as a property of the expression node itself. The core problem is to identify which attributes are valid after rewriting and which are not so that we do not need to recompute valid ones and we can avoid using invalid ones.

In this paper we describe how we addressed this problem in the context of our Kiama Scala-based language processing library [2], its implementation of attribute grammars [3] and its use of strategic term rewriting for transformation. Since it is based on Scala, Kiama uses object representations for trees and reference equality to implement node identity. Our aim was to develop a disciplined way to structure Kiama-based attribution under these conditions so that we could perform arbitrary rewriting of trees without invalidating previously calculated attribute values or obscuring the identity of the trees in which attribute values were valid.

The essence of our approach is that attribution should be performed with respect to the whole tree, not just with respect to a node in the tree (Section 2). Context-dependent attributes rely on the parent relationships to explore the context and its properties. It is the tree that defines the parent relationships between nodes, not the nodes themselves. If we base context-dependent attribution solely on the identity of a node then we are asking for trouble since that node may have more than one context if it is shared.

Our technical solution is to define context-dependent attributes as tree-indexed attribute families, not as single attributes (Section 3). To use one of these attribute families we must supply a tree to get an attribute that is valid for computations within that tree. At that point, regular attribute evaluation takes over without change. With attribute families, it becomes impossible to use a context-dependent attribute without thinking about the tree in which it is computed. Moreover, this tree-based focus is completely independent of the mechanism by which the tree was obtained. We can use any rewriting process we like without affecting the attribution.

We have implemented this approach in Kiama (Section 4). We previously relied on a mutable parent field in each tree node which was updated after a rewriting step. Because the parent had potentially changed it was necessary to erase all attribute values in case they were now invalid in the rewritten tree. Our changes mean that the mutable parent field has been removed, but no other changes were necessary to the core of the attribution and rewriting components. All of the existing Kiama test specifications were easily moved to the new scheme. We can now interleave attribution and rewriting of trees that share nodes without any danger.

We compare our approach to those of related attribute grammar-based systems that feature some element of rewriting or tree transformation (Section 5). We believe our approach is the first time that a general scheme for attribution has been given that can interoperate safely with arbitrary rewriting without the implementations of attribution or rewriting being dependent on each other.

2   Background

We begin by discussing examples of attribution and rewriting of simple tree structures to illustrate where problems can occur. This discussion motivates our solution which we describe informally here and more formally in the next section.

Our examples are based on simple arithmetic expressions that conform to the following context-free syntax rules:

$$\textbf{Top : Root ::= Node}$$
$$\textbf{Num : Node ::= Int}$$
$$\textbf{Plus : Node ::= Node Node}$$

Thus, the tree

$$\textbf{Top(Plus(Plus(Num(1), Num(2)), Plus(Num(3), Num(4))))}$$

represents the expression $(1 + 2) + (3 + 4)$ and is depicted in Figure 1.

2.1   Attribution

Suppose that we are interested in the *height* of nodes as measured by their maximum distance from a leaf. The following attribute grammar equations suffice to specify this attribute.[1]

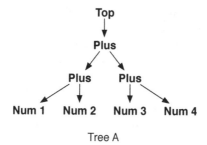

Tree A

Fig. 1. Tree A represents the arithmetic expression $(1 + 2) + (3 + 4)$.

---

[1] Throughout the paper we use a generic attribute grammar notation that can easily be translated into the notations of particular tools. Context-free grammar rules are augmented by equations that specify how to calculate attributes of tree nodes using constants, pre-defined operations and the values of attributes at other nodes.

Num : Node ::= Int
Node.height $= 0$

Plus : Node$_1$ ::= Node$_2$ Node$_3$
Node$_1$.height $= 1 + \mathbf{max}(\mathbf{Node_2.height, Node_3.height})$

The height of a **Num** is always zero since it is a leaf. The height of a **Plus** node is one more than the maximum of the heights of its children. Subscripts are used in the equations to distinguish between multiple occurrences of the **Node** symbol in **Plus** rule. Applying these equations in Tree A tells us that the height of node 1 is two and the height of node 4 is zero.

In effect, the height attribute equations define a pattern of computation that proceeds upward in the tree from the leaves to the node of interest. Traditionally, this kind of attribute is called a *synthesized attribute*.

In contrast, some attributes naturally depend on the context of the node at which they are computed and the information flows downward in the tree. For example, consider calculating the *depth* of a node in a tree which is its distance from the root. In traditional terminology, depth is an *inherited attribute* whose definition is given by equations that are associated with every rule that specifies context for the **Node** symbol.

Top : Root ::= Node
Node.depth $= 0$

Plus : Node$_1$ ::= Node$_2$ Node$_3$
Node$_2$.depth $=$ **Node$_1$.depth** $+ 1$
Node$_3$.depth $=$ **Node$_1$.depth** $+ 1$

These equations explain why the **Top** production is needed. Without it, there would be no context for the topmost **Node**. The **Top** context defines a depth of zero for its constituent **Node**, whereas a **Plus** context increments the depth by one. Applying these equations in Tree A tells us that the depth of node 1 is zero and the depth of node 4 is two.

The height and depth attributes are simple but attributes like them are the basis of any attribute grammar. Information is propagated up or down the tree from the place where it is available to where it is needed. A typical synthesized attribute is the value of a constant expression in a programming language. Name analysis can be performed using attributes that propagate information about declarations up to nodes that define scopes and then down to nodes that represent uses.

Modern attribute grammar systems build more advanced concepts on top of synthesized and inherited attributes, such as short-hand notations to make it easier to transport information up and down the tree, and attributes defined by fixed point computation. Extensions such as reference attributes and circular attributes are also supported by Kiama and similar systems. In this paper we focus on simple attributes in our examples, but the technique extends to more complex ones, since it does not affect the attribute evaluation mechanisms.

2.2   Rewriting

With the height and depth attributes in place, we now consider a rewriting transformation. The left-hand side of Figure 2 shows Tree A, repeated from Figure 1 with node numbers added for identification. The right-hand side of Figure 2 shows Tree B, a possible result of rewriting Tree A. In Tree B a new Plus node with a zero left child has been added at the top, and the right-most leaf has been incremented. These changes are typical of the effects of rewriting: embedding an existing tree in a new context, and changing a deeply-nested sub-tree.

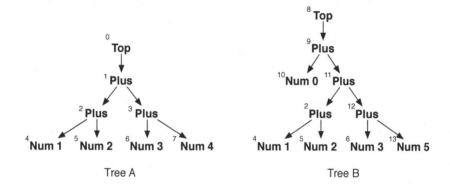

Fig. 2. Trees A and B represent arithmetic expressions $(1+2)+(3+4)$ and $0+((1+2)+ (3+5))$, respectively. The superscripts number the individual nodes for identification in the text.

If we assume that sharing is allowed, that Tree B was produced from Tree A, and that trees are immutable, Tree B can share nodes 2, 4, 5 and 6 with Tree A. Nodes 9 and 10 in Tree B have no counterpart in Tree A. Node 13 results from rewriting node 7. Whenever a node is rewritten, all its ancestor nodes must also be replaced because they have at least one new child, even though they have not been explicitly transformed. This is the reason for replacing nodes 1, 3 and 7 by nodes 8, 11 and 12.

2.3   The Problem and Solutions

The central problem that we aim to address is how to compute the attributes of nodes that are shared between two trees. In some cases, the way that the attribute is computed means that its value cannot be affected by the sharing. Specifically, computation at a shared node n of an attribute that is only dependent on information from the sub-tree rooted at n cannot be influenced by rewriting since that sub-tree has not changed. For example, the height attribute is such an attribute and it is easy to see that the heights of nodes 2, 4 and 5 are the same in both Tree A and Tree B. In other cases, the nature of the attribute is to depend on the context of the node at which it is evaluated. A shared node might have different contexts in the two trees and hence different values for the attribute in those trees. For example, the depth of node 2 in Tree A is one, but in Tree B it is two since an extra node has been added above it.

The simplest approach to combining attribution and rewriting in the presence of sharing is to just calculate all of the attributes during a traversal of the tree from the root. It does not matter if a node is shared if we reach it via a path from the root in the relevant tree since that path gives us the context in that tree. Modern attribute grammar systems tend to prefer a more dynamic approach where attribute occurrences are only evaluated when needed [4,5,3]. Conceptually we ask a node for the value of one of its attributes which might trigger evaluation of attributes of other nodes. A primary motivation for this form of evaluation is interactive applications where we want to respond as quickly as possible with just what is needed. For example, in a development environment if we want to display a tool-tip for the code under the mouse pointer, we don't want to wait for a traversal to calculate every attribute if we can get the appropriate tool-tip with a much smaller set.

Assuming that we don't want to re-evaluate all of the attributes, we need a way to evaluate an attribute in a rewritten tree without having the context be an implicit piece of information in the evaluator. Our key observation is that attributes like depth depend on the parent relationships of the tree in which it is used. We must *respect the parents* in order to get a sensible result. Accordingly, our general solution is to regard context-dependent attributes as being parameterised by the tree in which they are being evaluated. In other words, instead of being attributes, they are tree-indexed attribute families. We must first supply the relevant tree and then we get an attribute that can be used safely for computations in that tree.

This approach has three main advantages. First, attribute families that are tree-indexed cannot be used without explicitly supplying the appropriate tree. This requirement removes the possibility of confusion that is present if the context is a property of tree nodes independent of the trees in which they occur. Second, because the tree has a separate identity to the nodes within it, a node can participate in more than one tree without problem. Significantly, attribution and rewriting do not need to be aware of each other, yet can operate together. Third, not having to erase attributes after rewriting should lead to efficiency gains since attributes that are still valid do not have to be re-calculated.

2.4   Kiama

Our main practical motivation for this work was to improve the implementation of attribute grammars in the upcoming 2.0 release of our Kiama language processing library [2,3]. Kiama combines attribute grammars with strategic term rewriting in the style of Stratego [6]. We aimed to make context-dependent attributes safer when used in concert with rewriting based on generic tree traversals.

Kiama departs somewhat from the traditional view of attribute grammars used above to define the height and depth attributes. Instead of being defined by associating equations with grammar productions, Kiama attributes are defined by pattern matching against the tree structure at the node of interest. When a pattern matches a node, then the corresponding expression is used to calculate the value of the attribute at the node. In effect, a pattern and corresponding expression together define an equation for the attribute. Section 3 formalises the relevant aspects of this way of writing attribute grammars and gives examples.

Kiama's focus on pattern matching to decide which equation to apply means there is no clear distinction between synthesized and inherited attributes. In fact, one equation for an attribute can use the context to define the attribute value (inherited aspect) while another equation for the same attribute can use just child nodes (synthesized aspect). In a traditional setting the synthesized and inherited aspects would need to be split into separate attributes since one would need to be defined in the context of the relevant node. A consequence of Kiama's approach is that it is not necessary to introduce extra context productions in order to specify inherited attributes of the root of the tree. For example, we can define the expression example from the previous sections without needing the extra **Top** production to add context at the root of the expression tree. Section 3 shows how this can be done.

The attribution libraries in Kiama 1.x assume that the tree nodes contain a mutable parent field [3]. After a rewriting step, the parent fields must be updated to reflect the participation of shared nodes in the new tree, since those fields represent the parent relationships of the old tree. Updates to the parent fields potentially invalidate previously computed attribute values. To be safe, we must currently erase all of those values. There is no static check that this operation is performed and subtle bugs can be created if it is omitted. Even if the erasure is performed, we waste effort if erased values would have still been valid in the new tree. Moreover, after rewriting we cannot compute context-dependent attributes in the old tree at all since its parent information in shared nodes has been overwritten.

The approach developed in this paper removes these drawbacks. Kiama no longer assumes the existence of mutable parent fields. It is not possible to access a context-dependent attribute without specifying which tree is relevant. Computed attribute values remain valid after rewriting since the parent relationships from the old tree are still valid. We can calculate attributes on the old tree after rewriting just by using the old tree's parents. Attribution and rewriting don't have to know details of each other's implementation. In summary, our new approach means that attribution and rewriting can be freely mixed and that the possibility of bugs due to subtleties of their interaction is greatly diminished.

3   How to Respect Your Parents

In this section we make these ideas concrete by formalising Kiama-style attribute grammars that respect their parents. We are only concerned with the dynamic evaluation behaviour of our attribute grammars. Therefore, we simplify the presentation by assuming that they do not contain any static errors that in Kiama would be ruled out by the Scala compiler. For example, we assume that the patterns in attribute definitions are non-linear and that the right-hand side of a case does not refer to unbound variables. We assume that constructors are always applied to the correct number of arguments in tree construction and in patterns. We do not consider aspects such as which attributes are defined for which node types since these aspects are orthogonal to our main topic.

3.1   A Core Attribute Grammar Language

Figure 3 summarises the abstract syntax of programs in a core attribute grammar language that is consistent with Kiama. The core language omits more complex Kiama attributes such as reference, higher-order and circular attributes. Each of these kinds of attribute can be incorporated into our scheme with no extra mechanisms and we have done so in our implementation.

A program consists of one or more definitions of trees and attributes, followed by one or more expressions that calculate values using those definitions. Definitions can bind variables to tree values. We assume that x ranges over the names of global variables and over the names of variables bound by pattern matching. Trees are defined over constructors C_n of arity $n >= 0$ that we assume are pre-defined and fixed. A tree is created by an application $C_n(t_1, \ldots, t_n)$ of a constructor C_n to sub-trees $t_1, \ldots, t_n$.

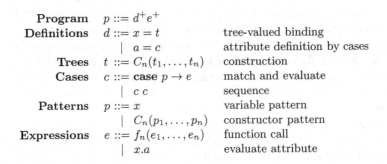

Fig. 3. Abstract syntax of the core attribute grammar language

Definitions can also bind attribute names to equations given by one or more pattern matching cases. The meta-variable a ranges over the names of attributes. Each case of an attribute definition specifies a match of a pattern against the node at which the attribute is being evaluated. If the pattern matches, the corresponding expression is evaluated to determine the value of the attribute at that node. Cases are applied in program order. Patterns are either variable patterns x which match any tree, or constructor patterns $C_n(p_1, \ldots, p_n)$ which match only trees whose root is formed by the constructor C_n and whose children match the patterns $p_1, \ldots, p_n$.

We assume f_n ranges over the names of globally available functions with arity $n >= 0$. An expression $f_n(e_1, \ldots, e_n)$ applies function f_n to the expressions $e_1, \ldots, e_n$. To simplify the presentation we assume that we can use standard mathematical functions using infix notation. We also assume the existence of a function for conditional expression evaluation written e ? e : e which only evaluates one of its second and third arguments.

An expression $x.a$ evaluates the attribute a at node x. Evaluation of this form of expression involves applying the definition of attribute a to the node bound to variable x.

We can write the height attribute from Section 2 using the core language as follows.

> **height** $=$
>   **case Num**$(i) \rightarrow 0$
>   **case Plus**$(l, r) \rightarrow 1 + \mathbf{max}(l.\mathbf{height}, r.\mathbf{height})$

3.2 Parents as Node Properties

One way to incorporate access to parents in this Kiama view of attribute grammars is to regard them as being properties of the tree nodes. Formally, we can assume that there is a global function **parent**(x) that returns the parent of a node x. We assume an auxiliary function **isRoot**(x) that returns true if and only if **parent** is not defined at x.

We can write the **depth** attribute from Section 2 as follows using the **parent** and **isRoot** functions.

> **depth** $=$
>   **case** $n \rightarrow \mathbf{isRoot}(n)$? 0 : **parent**$(n).\mathbf{depth} + 1$

As discussed in Section 2, the problem with this approach is that a given node x may participate in more than one tree. Which parent do we get when we call **parent**(x)? Which root returns true from **isRoot**? If the parent property cannot change, then presumably we get the parent of the first tree in which x participates. We will not be able to correctly compute attributes for later trees. If the parent property is mutable, then we have to be careful to compute only attributes on the old tree before the property changes and only attributes of the new tree after the change. This dependence on mutability makes attribute computations fragile.

3.3 Parents as Tree Properties

Our solution is to focus on the parent relationships of a tree, rather than on the parents of nodes. The parent relationships of a tree can be calculated by traversing from the root, if they are not otherwise available. Thus, **parent** is now a function from the relevant tree to the parent partial function for that tree. We now write **parent**$(x_1)(x_2)$ to get the parent of node x_2 in the tree that is rooted at the node bound to x_1. **isRoot**(x_2) becomes **isRoot**$(x_1)(x_2)$ where

x_1 is the root of the relevant tree; this operation can be implemented by a simple reference equality test.

In this new scheme, the definition of **depth** must be modified to have access to the current tree that is being attributed since it needs to use that tree's parent relationships. A simple way to think of this modification is that the depth attribute becomes an attribute family indexed by the tree. In other words, we don't just have one depth attribute, we have one for each possible tree.

We formalise attribute families by extending the core language to include a new definition form.

$$\textbf{Definitions} \quad d ::= \ldots \qquad \text{previous forms}$$
$$| \quad a(x) = c \quad \text{attribute family}$$

In the attribute family form, the variable x refers to the tree rooted at the node bound to variable x. We also need a new expression form to pass the tree rooted at x_1 to a family a to get an instance that can be evaluated at the node bound to x_2.

$$\textbf{Expressions} \quad e ::= \ldots \qquad \text{previous forms}$$
$$| \quad x_2.a(x_1) \quad \text{instantiate attribute family and evaluate}$$

With these extensions, the definition of the depth attribute becomes

$$\textbf{depth}(x_1) =$$
$$\textbf{case } x_2 \rightarrow \textbf{isRoot}(x_1)(x_2) \; ? \; 0 \; : \; \textbf{parent}(x_1)(x_2).\textbf{depth}(x_1) + 1$$

Thus, the attribute is now insulated against tree changes since it is statically impossible to use **depth** without specifying the relevant tree.

3.4   Discussion

The key benefit of the attribute family approach is that by construction we rule out accessing the parent of the wrong tree, rather than allowing access to the parents at any time and relying on discipline to access them only at an appropriate time.

If we are defining an attribute that does not use the context, it can be defined by a regular definition since it does not need the tree. If we need the context, then we must use an attribute family and give a name to the context in the family definition. The dependence on the tree is now explicit and the user of an attribute family is required to provide the appropriate tree.

What about an attribute a_1 that does not require the context directly but whose definition uses an attribute a_2 that does require the context? We can choose from a couple of options depending on the situation. The first option should be used when it is meaningful for a_1 to be defined with respect to a specific context, not for all trees. We would define a_1 using a normal definition and pass that specific context when invoking a_2. For example, this case occurs when code has been transformed in a way that changes types but error messages should refer to user-specified types as defined by the original tree. The second option should be used when a_1 must be defined for all contexts and, if being applied in tree t, calls to a_2 should use t too. In this case we would define both a_1 and a_2 as families.

Another issue in the definition of an attribute like **depth** above is what happens if the node x_2 is not actually in the tree rooted at x_1? In this case x_2 is not the root and the **parent**(x_1) relation is not defined at x_2. Since our setting is a pure embedding of attribute grammars in another language, there is no easy way to statically prevent this situation. Nodes can be created at any time and the host language provides no connection between a node and the tree(s) that it is in. We currently ensure that **parent** and similar functions cause a run-time error if passed a node that is not in the tree which they are using. We are investigating ways to use Scala's type system to check for this situation statically. A similar approach based on a separately-defined attribute grammar language could build more safe-guards into the specification language.

4 Kiama Implementation

We now describe how we implemented the approach from the previous section. Kiama is a library for the Scala programming language [7] so we are able to use Scala's general-purpose facilities to implement attribute families. Kiama's existing attribute implementation was minimally affected by the changes. We just removed the implementation of the mutable parent field and information derived from it. Kiama's rewriting library was unaffected by the changes.

4.1 Relations

The base of our implementation is a new generic `Relation[T,U]` type defined over two types `T` and `U` (Figure 4). A relation is created from a sequence of tuples that define its graph. The operations are derived from the graph and are standard. For example, `compose` allows a relation to be composed with another that has a compatible type.

Because Kiama is based on Scala it is easy to provide relations with pattern matching support. Scala supports user-defined pattern matching via extractors [8]. We use extractors to allow any relation to be used in a pattern. For example, if R is a relation, then the pattern $R(p)$ will succeed if and only if R contains only a single tuple where the first component matches the node to which the pattern is applied and the second component matches p. The pattern $R.pair$ allows matching patterns against both the first and second components; $R.pair(p_1, p_2)$ will succeed if and only if R contains only a single tuple where the first component matches pattern p_1 and the second component matches p_2. We show concrete examples of using this sort of pattern matching in Section 4.3.

4.2 Trees

The `Tree` class uses the general relation type to provide access to trees and their node relationships. Figure 5 shows representative parts of the `Tree` interface. A

```
class Relation[T,U] (val graph : Seq[(T,U)]) {

    // Composition
    def compose[S] (st : Relation[S,T]) : Relation[S,U]

    // Domain
    def domain : Seq[T]
    def containsInDomain (t : T) : Boolean

    // Range
    def range : Seq[U]
    def containsInRange (u : U) : Boolean

    // Image and pre-image
    def image (t : T) : Seq[U]
    def preimage (u : U) : Seq[T]

    // Invert
    def invert : Relation[U,T]

    // Union
    def union (r : Relation[T,U]) : Relation[T,U]

}
```

Fig. 4. Part of Kiama's `Relation` interface. A relation is defined over the generic types T and U.

`Tree[T,U]` is created by providing the root value of some type U. The base type of all tree nodes is some other type T and we require that U is a sub-type of T (i.e., U <: T).

The base node type T is required to be a sub-type of Scala's `Product` type which enables us to determine the tree structure generically. Product values have generic access to their component fields. The `child` relation is computed by traversing throughout the tree from the root collecting pairs of nodes where one is a direct descendant of the other. We compute this value lazily since there is no need to perform that traversal if we don't use the child relation.

The `Tree` class also provides a suite of other relations which are derived from `child`. The `parent` relation is just the inverse of `child`. `siblings` is calculated by composing the `parent` relation with `child`. For example, if a is a child of b and b is a parent of c then a is a sibling of c. Other similar derived relations not shown in the figure give access to previous and next node, and so on. All of these relations are computed lazily since they might not be needed.

Some node properties are not dependent on the tree since they only depend on components of the node or its children. (Recall that nodes are immutable so these factors cannot change if a node is shared among trees.) For example, whether or not a node is a leaf cannot change if that node appears in more than

```
class Tree[T <: Product,U <: T] (val root : U) {
    // Base child relation
    lazy val child : Relation[T,T]

    // Derived relations
    lazy val parent : Relation[T,T]
    lazy val siblings : Relation[T,T]

    // Properties
    def index (t : T) : Int
    def isFirst (t : T) : Boolean
    def isLast (t : T) : Boolean
    def isRoot (t : T) : Boolean
}

object Tree {
    def isLeaf[T <: Product] (t : T) : Boolean
}
```

Fig. 5. Part of Kiama's `Tree` interface. Generic type `T` is the base type of tree nodes and type `U` is the type of the root node. The `Tree` object provides operations that do not depend on a specific tree.

one tree. Tree-independent operations such as `isLeaf` are static methods that accompany the `Tree` class.

4.3   Examples

In the Kiama setting, a tree-indexed attribute is just a class or a method that takes a `Tree`-value argument. For example, we can define the height and depth attributes from earlier sections as shown in Figure 6.

`height` is a regular attribute defined as it would be with Kiama 1.x. `attr` is the Kiama attribute creation method which takes a single argument that is a collection of cases to specify the attribute equations. `attr` implements attribute caching and dynamic circularity testing on top of the equation definitions. We made no changes to `attr` for this present work.

In contrast to `height`, `depth` requires access to the context. In Figure 6, `depth` is defined in a class whose constructor takes the tree as an argument.[2] In effect, the class defines a reusable module of attribution. A client of this module would have to first instantiate the class with the desired tree. The definition of `depth` uses the tree to access the parent relationship. In the first equation the pattern `tree.parent (p)` will succeed only if the matched node has a single parent in that tree and it will bind that parent node to the variable `p`. The variable is used in the right-hand side of the equation `depth (p) + 1` to recursively get

---

[2] The constructor arguments of a Scala class are given in the class heading and the body of the class definition is the constructor implementation. Constructor arguments are in scope throughout the class definition.

```
val height : Node => Int =
    attr {
        case Num (_)     => 0
        case Plus (l, r) => 1 + height (l).max (height (r))
    }

class DepthModule (tree : Tree[Node,Node]) {

    def depth : Node => Int =
        attr {
            case tree.parent (p) => depth (p) + 1
            case _               => 0
        }

}
```

Fig. 6. Kiama version of the height and depth attributes

the depth of the parent. The second equation will only be reached if the node has no parent, which means it must the root of the tree.

Instead of defining a module of related attributes using a class, we could define a family for a single attribute by using a method that takes the tree as an argument. In our experience this approach is less useful than using a class, since it is common for many related attributes to need access to the tree. It is easier to group these attributes in a module and then pass the tree once when the module instance is created than it is to pass the tree explicitly to many separate attribute definitions.

Cooperation between different attribute families is achieved in different ways that depend on how the families are defined. If they are defined in the same module, then the context is implicitly available to both families, so it need not be passed. If the families are defined in different modules, then a calling attribute will need to be given a reference to the module instance that defines the called attribute. Similarly, a family defined by a method can call a family defined in a module if it has a reference to the relevant module instance. Finally, if two families are defined by parameterised methods, then the context will need to be passed explicitly between them. Which of these situations applies will depend on the overall structure of an application, so it is hard to be definitive about the implication of use families. To give some expectations, we report in the next section on our experiences of converting Kiama's test suite to use the new approach.

4.4   Experience

We have converted our extensive Kiama test suite across to the new style of context-dependent attributes. The suite includes implementations of various languages including lambda calculus, Prolog and various cut-down versions of Java.

In all cases we have defined attribution modules that collect many related attributes, following the module pattern of Figure 6. Most of the code has not increased in size at all since we just converted singleton implementations of attribution modules into classes and now access the context in attribute equations via the tree's parent relation instead of via the tree node fields. A small code size increase is incurred where modules are instantiated since we must create an instance of the module instead of just accessing a singleton.

The biggest Kiama test is an Oberon-0 compiler that was previously built for the 2011 LDTA Tool Challenge. This compiler is built from more than twenty separate traits comprising around 2000 lines of Scala code. The traits are mixed together to form the artefacts required by the challenge. In the previous version, the attribution components relied on the **parent** field of nodes. In the new version the components are passed the relevant trees and, if they are transformation components, return new trees. For example, one component performs desugaring of FOR and CASE statements into WHILE and IF statements, respectively. The desugarer is given the input tree so it can use attributes that depend on it such as those supplied by name and type analysis. After the tree has been rewritten it is returned as a new tree that is then consumed safely by the next transformation or code generator. Previously, we needed to be careful to erase attributes of the old tree before the new tree was returned in case some of them were no longer valid.

Throughout our examples we now make extensive use of relational pattern matching where we need to check if a nearby node is there, optionally pattern match on it, and bind it. These patterns replace direct access to the parent via a tree node. The tree relations are the basis of properties such as `isRoot` which is true if the node is the root of the tree. The tree module also supplies operations that do not depend on the specific tree, but just on the node, such as `isLeaf`, `firstChild` and `lastChild`.

Nested patterns are particularly useful. For example, the pattern

```
u @ IdnUse (i1)
```

succeeds in the Oberon-0 compiler if matched against an identifier use node. It binds that node to the variable u and the identifier string to i1. The pattern

```
ProcDecl (IdnDef (i2), _, _, _)
```

matches procedure declaration nodes and binds the variable i2 to the procedure identifier. We can nest these two patterns inside a parent pair pattern to help implement a check that the identifier used at the end of an Oberon-0 procedure declaration (i1) is the same as the one used in the procedure's heading (i2).[3]

```
case tree.parent.pair (u @ IdnUse (i1),
                  ProcDecl (IdnDef (i2), _, _, _)) =>
    message (u, s"end procedure name $i1 should be $i2",
             i1 != i2)
```

---

[3] The relatively verbose form `tree.parent.pair` can be abbreviated by imports and aliases, but we choose to show the full form to keep the explanation simple.

Kiama's message facility is used here to generate a message if i1 and i2 are not the same and place the message at the location of the identifier use (node u).

As another example, the following pattern was used in a dataflow example to see if the current node has both a next sibling (n) and a Block parent.

```
tree.parent.pair (tree.next (n), _ : Block)
```

In both of these examples, the explicit use of tree ensures that these context-dependent matches are performed with respect to the tree that was provided when these modules were created. We have thereby reduced the risk that we will accidentally check in the wrong tree.

A secondary benefit of having the tree available in an attribute definition is that we can directly refer to the root node. A direct reference can be used to short-cut the usual pattern of attribution where an attribute computed at the root node has to be transported one step at a time down to where it is needed.

5   Related Work

We focus our discussion on related work that substantially involves attribute grammars and that incorporates some aspect of tree transformation or rewriting in combination with attribution.

Incremental Attribute Evaluation. One approach to dealing with changes in attributed trees is to recompute attributes where necessary to take changes into account. A notable early example of incremental attribute evaluation is Reps' work to generate language-based editors that were specified using attribute grammars [9], but there are many later incremental approaches. Recent examples include work by Saraiva and Swierstra [10] and Bransen et al. [11]. Incremental evaluation requires some knowledge of attribute dependencies and the detail of tree changes in order to recalculate only when necessary. Bürger's RACR library for Scheme [12] is of particular interest since it incorporates arbitrary tree rewriting. RACR builds a dynamic attribute dependency graph during evaluation so it knows which attributes are influenced by rewrites. In contrast, our approach might cause some unnecessary recalculation of context-dependent attributes in a rewritten tree, but we do not need to keep track of attribute dependencies or have any dependence between attribution and rewriting. It is future work to investigate how our approach can be adapted to share computed values between different instances of the same attribute family where it is safe to do so.

Object-Based Attribute Grammar Systems. Some attribute grammar systems generate evaluators for object-oriented languages and hence directly share some of the concerns of Kiama for mutability and shared tree nodes.

JastAdd has pioneered many recent extensions of the basic paradigm including reference and circular attributes [4,13]. It generates evaluators in Java, including tree node classes that implement the attribute as methods. Each of these classes contains a mutable parent field, so tree nodes cannot participate in more than one tree. In addition to its main attribute grammar specification notations, JastAdd incorporates a form of rewrite rule [14]. It arranges to invoke these rules as part of the attribute evaluation process. Unfortunately, attributes of trees that are being rewritten may be recalculated as rewriting proceeds, only to be finalised when later rewriting cannot affect their values. We believe that this approach blurs the distinction between an attribute representing a property of a node and a mutable variable that may change as execution proceeds. In our scheme attributes will only ever have one value within a particular tree. Also, in JastAdd the rewriting approach is intricately embedded in the attribute evaluation process, whereas attribution and rewriting are independent in our approach.

Silver is another prominent Java-based attribute grammar system [5]. Silver distinguishes between trees that have no attribute values and ones that do (so-called "decorated trees"). Attributes are evaluated by passing them a reference to the tree context. Thus, in theory it is possible to decorate a node with respect to more than one tree by passing in a different context. However, as far as we can tell, Silver does not explicitly deal with node instances that are shared by two trees. Since attributes are computed lazily and their values stored, it would appear to be necessary to clear those values if we wanted to evaluate those attributes in another tree that shared some nodes, as in older versions of Kiama. Silver supports language extension via a form of higher-order attribute grammar called forwarding [15]. New tree fragments can be computed as attribute values that are associated with existing tree nodes and forward some attribution requests to those nodes. Forwarding, in essence, is a specialised form of tree transformation by augmentation and is supported directly by the Silver evaluation approach. In contrast, our approach can support arbitrary tree transformations that are independent of attribute evaluation.

Functional Attribute Grammar Systems. There is a long tradition of attribute grammar systems based on or in functional programming languages [16]. By and large, these systems do not encounter the same issues with sharing since in pure value-based functional languages sharing is not observable. Hence, there is no option to associate attribute information with a node instance since there is no way to tell that instance apart from another that has the same fields.

We briefly note two functional attribution approaches that have some characteristics in common with our approach. Zippers can be used in functional languages to keep track of the current location during a generic tree traversal [17]. Martins *et al.* use generic zippers to embed attribute grammars in a pure functional language [18]. During evaluation the zipper encodes the path taken from the root to the node of interest in a similar way to a traditional tree-walking attribute evaluator. It is non-trivial to start a zipper-based evaluator at a particular node as we do in our approach, since the context would have to be manually created. Accordingly zipper-based approaches assume a traversal from the root.

An alternative to zipper-based approaches for context tracking in functional languages was developed by Gaillourdet *et al.* [19]. A cyclic position structure is created to mirror the structure of the tree upon which attribution is to be performed. Nodes in the position structure have parent links to give access to the context of a node. This approach is similar to Kiama's previous approach in that it equips each node with a component that gives access to its parent in a particular tree structure. The functional setting means that quite a bit of work has to be done to define the form of a position structure based on the tree syntax and construct one for a particular tree. In contrast, our reference equality-based setting allows us to use the relationships between the nodes themselves and a separate mirroring structure is not needed.

Rewriting-Based Attribution Systems. Kats *et al.* incorporated attribute grammar features into ASTER which is an extension of the Stratego strategic programming language [6,20]. This combination of attribution on a rewriting base contrasts with Kiama's approach where attribution and rewriting can cooperate but are implemented separately. ASTER uses the generic traversal operators of Stratego to implement *decorators* that abstract patterns of attribute computation away from a specific tree structure. ASTER's focus on traversal from a node of interest is similar to Kiama's focus on the relationships between nodes. Reflection on the tree structure is used in ASTER to obtain access to a node's context via its parent. This reliance on a single parent reference means that ASTER cannot express attribution of shared nodes.

Relational Representations of Programs. Finally, we note that the use of relations to represent relationships between program components is a well-used idea. A non-trivial early example is Linton's OMEGA system which uses a relational database to store program information [21]. Since the aim of this kind of work is different from ours we do not consider it further, except to mention the Rascal language which incorporates high-level support for relations to support meta-programming [22]. It is possible that Kiama's new support for relations can be generalised beyond trees to support this kind of processing.

6   Conclusion and Future Work

We described how attribution and rewriting of trees can get along in an object-based implementation with reference equality. The key is to design context-dependent attribution to be parameterised by the tree in which that attribution is to be performed, thereby defining attribute families. This approach solves the problem of deciding what attributes mean when nodes are shared between trees as a result of rewriting.

We have implemented the approach in the Kiama language processing library and its test suite. Context-dependent attribute definitions were adjusted to depend on the tree, but no changes were needed in the attribute evaluation implementation so the approach works for all existing kinds of attributes including reference and circular attributes. The definition and evaluation of attributes is completely independent of how rewriting is achieved and requires no knowledge of which rewrites have occurred.

The main area for future work is to further improve reuse of attribute values in rewritten trees. At the moment we reuse all attributes that do not depend on the context. However, some context-dependent attribute occurrences will be valid in a rewritten tree if they do not use the part of the context that has changed. We are developing techniques to take advantage of this situation without requiring detailed cooperation between attribution and rewriting. Part of this work will be a detailed profiling exercise to understand how the evaluation of attributes is affected by the shift to attribute families.

Acknowledgements. Development of the approach described in this paper benefited greatly from discussions with our colleague Dominic Verity. We also thank the anonymous reviewers for their helpful suggestions.

References

1. van den Brand, M.G.J., Klint, P.: ATerms for manipulation and exchange of structured data: It's all about sharing. Information and Software Technology 49(1), 55–64 (2007)
2. Sloane, A.M.: Lightweight language processing in kiama. In: Fernandes, J.M., Lämmel, R., Visser, J., Saraiva, J. (eds.) Generative and Transformational Techniques in Software Engineering III. LNCS, vol. 6491, pp. 408–425. Springer, Heidelberg (2011)
3. Sloane, A.M., Kats, L.C.L., Visser, E.: A pure embedding of attribute grammars. Science of Computer Programming 78, 1752–1769 (2013)
4. Hedin, G., Magnusson, E.: JastAdd: an aspect-oriented compiler construction system. Science of Computer Programming 47(1), 37–58 (2003)
5. Van Wyk, E., Bodin, D., Gao, J., Krishnan, L.: Silver: An extensible attribute grammar system. Science of Computer Programming 75, 39–54 (2010)
6. Bravenboer, M., Kalleberg, K.T., Vermaas, R., Visser, E.: Stratego/XT 0.16: components for transformation systems. In: Proceedings of the 2006 ACM SIGPLAN Symposium on Partial Evaluation and Semantics-Based Program Manipulation, pp. 95–99. ACM (2006)
7. Odersky, M., Spoon, L., Venners, B.: Programming in Scala, 2nd edn. Artima Press (2010)
8. Emir, B., Odersky, M., Williams, J.: Matching objects with patterns. In: Ernst, E. (ed.) ECOOP 2007. LNCS, vol. 4609, pp. 273–298. Springer, Heidelberg (2007)
9. Reps, T.W.: Generating Language-based Environments. Massachusetts Institute of Technology, Cambridge (1984)
10. Saraiva, J., Swierstra, S.D., Kuiper, M.: Functional incremental attribute evaluation. In: Watt, D.A. (ed.) CC 2000. LNCS, vol. 1781, pp. 279–294. Springer, Heidelberg (2000)
11. Bransen, J., Dijkstra, A., Swierstra, S.D.: Lazy stateless incremental evaluation machinery for attribute grammars. In: Proceedings of the Workshop on Partial Evaluation and Program Manipulation, pp. 145–156. ACM (2014)
12. Bürger, C.: RACR: A Scheme Library for Reference Attribute Grammar Controlled Rewriting. Dresden University of Technology (2014),
   http://racr.googlecode.com

13. Magnusson, E., Hedin, G.: Circular reference attributed grammars–their evaluation and applications. Science of Computer Programming 68(1), 21–37 (2007)
14. Ekman, T., Hedin, G.: Rewritable reference attributed grammars. In: Odersky, M. (ed.) ECOOP 2004. LNCS, vol. 3086, pp. 147–171. Springer, Heidelberg (2004)
15. Van Wyk, E., de Moor, O., Backhouse, K., Kwiatkowski, P.: Forwarding in attribute grammars for modular language design. In: Nigel Horspool, R. (ed.) CC 2002. LNCS, vol. 2304, pp. 128–142. Springer, Heidelberg (2002)
16. Johnsson, T.: Attribute grammars as a functional programming paradigm. In: Kahn, G. (ed.) FPCA 1987. LNCS, vol. 274, pp. 154–173. Springer, Heidelberg (1987)
17. Adams, M.D.: Scrap your zippers: a generic zipper for heterogeneous types. In: Proceedings of the ACM SIGPLAN Workshop on Generic Programming, pp. 13–24. ACM (2010)
18. Martins, P., Fernandes, J.P., Saraiva, J.: Zipper-based attribute grammars and their extensions. In: Du Bois, A.R., Trinder, P. (eds.) SBLP 2013. LNCS, vol. 8129, pp. 135–149. Springer, Heidelberg (2013)
19. Gaillourdet, J.-M., Michel, P., Poetzsch-Heffter, A., Rauch, N.: A generic functional representation of sorted trees supporting attribution. In: Voronkov, A., Weidenbach, C. (eds.) Programming Logics. LNCS, vol. 7797, pp. 72–89. Springer, Heidelberg (2013), http://dx.doi.org/10.1007/978-3-642-37651-1_4
20. Kats, L., Sloane, A.M., Visser, E.: Decorated attribute grammars: Attribute evaluation meets strategic programming. In: de Moor, O., Schwartzbach, M.I. (eds.) CC 2009. LNCS, vol. 5501, pp. 142–157. Springer, Heidelberg (2009)
21. Linton, M.A.: Implementing relational views of programs. In: Proceedings of the Symposium on Practical Software Development Environments, pp. 132–140. ACM (1984)
22. Klint, P., van der Storm, T., Vinju, J.: EASY meta-programming with rascal. In: Fernandes, J.M., Lämmel, R., Visser, J., Saraiva, J. (eds.) Generative and Transformational Techniques in Software Engineering III. LNCS, vol. 6491, pp. 222–289. Springer, Heidelberg (2011)

Monto: A Disintegrated Development Environment

Anthony M. Sloane, Matthew Roberts, Scott Buckley, and Shaun Muscat

Department of Computing, Macquarie University, Sydney, Australia

Abstract. Integrated development environments play a central role in the life of many software developers. Integrating new functionality into these environments is non-trivial and forms a significant barrier to entry. We describe our Monto architecture which aims to address this problem. Monto components communicate via text messages across an off-the-shelf messaging layer. The architecture imposes limited constraints which enables easy combination of components to form an environment. A prototype implementation shows that this approach is practical and shows promise for full-featured development environments.

1 Introduction

Integrated development environments (IDEs) are an important part of the toolkit of many software developers. They provide facilities for editing, interrogating, transforming, running and debugging source code. Their integrated nature means that developers can perform all of these tasks without leaving the IDE.

In recent years, impressive progress has made it easier for software language engineers to extend IDEs. The IDEs themselves provide extension frameworks that allow new plugins to be combined with existing facilities. Language engineers have integrated their tools into these frameworks to achieve high-level specification of IDE components.

Despite this progress in bringing language engineering tooling closer to language designers and developers, tying that tooling to a particular IDE framework is a serious limitation. For example, the considerable effort used to develop an Eclipse plug-in for a new language probably doesn't provide any support for other environments. This tie-in also makes it harder for researchers to make new research results from language engineering accessible to practitioners. For example, having great tooling in Eclipse is of no help to developers who write their code in IntelliJ IDEA, Netbeans or a text editor. Requiring developers to move to a particular IDE platform is often not practical. Even if researchers can settle on an IDE they then have to make their tool infrastructure work with that IDE which may require language changes or other compromises.

An alternative to a highly coupled framework for IDE extension is one that aims to limit coupling to a bare minimum while still allowing feature integration. We call this sort of framework a *disintegrated development environment (DDE)* to indicate that it comprises parts that are as separate as possible but maintains the overall goals of IDEs. This paper describes our prototype *Monto DDE*, its

B. Combemale et al. (Eds.): SLE 2014, LNCS 8706, pp. 211–220, 2014.

architecture and our preliminary experiences using it to build IDE-like facilities. Our goal with the Monto project is to explore a minimalist approach, its design and practicality; this paper reports our first steps.

We motivate Monto by discussing problems met by tool builders and developers that arise from a highly integrated approach (§2). We also discuss related work that environment builders have proposed to solve similar problems and upon which we build. These considerations led us to a view that a broadcast architecture should be used to reduce coupling between components. Communication should be as simple as possible to minimise overhead and enable components to be written quickly in any language.

The Monto architecture distinguishes between *sources* that publish notifications when changes to user-edited text occur, *servers* that provide functionality, and *sinks* that consume products from servers (§3). A *broker* mediates between sources, servers and sinks. All communication between Monto components is text encoded in JSON messages (§4). The ZeroMQ library [1] is used for fast communication between components. Using off-the-shelf technology for communication means that Monto components can be written in a wide variety of languages.

We discuss our experience with a prototype implementation of the Monto architecture (§5). We have implemented sources and sinks as plug-ins for the Sublime Text editor [2]. Our experiments show that components can be integrated with little effort using the Monto approach. Use of simple messages and a fast messaging layer means that interactive performance is good enough for live update even though many messages and processes are involved.

Our contribution is to show that this approach to building environments is practical and suffices to implement basic features of more integrated approaches. Future experiments are needed to explore more advanced functionality.

2   Motivation and Related Work

Integrated development environments such as Eclipse, IntelliJ IDEA and NetBeans provide powerful facilities for program development. However, it is widely agreed that developing plug-ins for non-trivial new languages in these environments is not for the faint-hearted. Success stories such as the Java Development Tools in Eclipse are the product of many years of development by many developers. Effort on this scale is beyond all but the most well-resourced organisations.

Many researchers have attempted to address the difficulty of adding support for new languages to IDEs or similar systems. Most notably, the IDE Metatooling Platform (IMP) for Eclipse [3,4] abstracts the Eclipse framework to make it easier to build language-specific services. The Spoofax/IMP project integrates the Stratego term rewriting language and related domain-specific languages into Eclipse [5,6]. Language designers can easily use Spoofax to develop custom support for new languages, including syntax highlighting, code folding and name definition-use navigation. All of these facilities integrate well with the rest of Eclipse. As the name suggests, Spoofax/IMP is based on an evolution of IMP rather than on the core Eclipse frameworks. Spoofax is a form of language workbench which is a category of environment specifically designed to make it easy to build new language support [7]. There are many other workbenches that implement different approaches to language specification. For example, the Meta Programming System (MPS) provides a general editing framework in which new languages can be specified by defining abstract syntax, projections from that syntax to text, analyses, code generation, and so on [8].

Text editors are the other main kind of front-end used for software development. Similar to IDEs, editors often provide plug-in architectures, but usually operate at a lower level. For example, most editor extension mechanisms rely on text-based processing such as regular expression matching to perform syntax highlighting, in contrast with IDE plug-ins that usually integrate full parsers. The tendency in editor plug-in frameworks is to make it easy to add extensions, usually at the cost of having to operate in a reasonably primitive environment. Some editors support sophisticated extensions that reuse existing infrastructure. For example, the ENhanced Scala Interaction Mode for Emacs (ENSIME) project reuses the Scala compiler to provide support for IDE-like features in a Scala programming mode for Emacs [9].

Much of this work on providing language-support in IDEs, workbenches and text editors is impressive, but it is based on a fundamental assumption. Developers of new language tooling are expected to use a specific platform, such as Eclipse plus Stratego, MPS or Emacs. This assumption means that it is non-trivial to use this tooling in other settings. For example, there is no easy way for a developer who prefers the IntelliJ IDEA environment to use Spoofax.

The difficulty of using tooling in different integrated contexts leads to general component architectures for software tooling. The idea is to develop a framework in which a variety of tools can cooperate, yet remain somewhat separate. Communication between tools allows them to exchange information. A primary motivation for our work is the TOOLBUS coordination architecture which is based on message passing [10]. TOOLBUS has been used to develop coordinated tooling in the language engineering space [11]. Another related approach is embodied in the Linda coordination language which bases communication between parallel processes around a shared store of general data tuples [12].

Architectural approaches such as TOOLBUS and Linda are a step in the right direction since they allow individual separated components to provide functionality while the framework handles the communication between components. However, they still impose non-trivial integration requirements. For example, TOOLBUS uses a process algebra-based scripting language to describe how tools interact. While such a description undoubtedly provides benefits, it does impose a barrier to entry. Linda requires custom support to access the tuple store.

These considerations led us to wonder whether we could reduce coupling between components even further while still employing a largely decoupled approach in the style of TOOLBUS and Linda. The novel aspect of our solution is to disintegrate as much as possible and remove the need for a coordination language by simplifying the interaction between components. In the Monto architecture components play simple defined roles and are unaware of the existence of other components. No overall coordination specification is required. In architectures like TOOLBUS many different kinds of messages are sent between components. We reduce the number of message types to two. Moreover, we follow the lead of Unix and Web technology by only sending text messages with a simple structure to keep coupling low.

3   Monto Architecture

Monto contains *sources, servers* and *sinks* (Figure 1). The components run independently either as separate processes or as threads in one or more processes, all of which may be running on a single machine or on multiple machines. Most likely a single process will interact with the user by operating as both a source and multiple sinks, while many servers run as separate local or remote processes. A source reacts when text is changed by a user (step 1). The source publishes

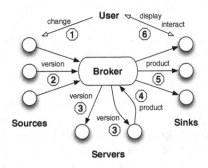

Fig. 1. Monto architecture overview

a complete version of the changed text (step 2) which is passed to servers by a broker (step 3).

In this paper we assume that versions are sent in a fine-grained manner so that each change results in a separate message. A typical source might be a plug-in for a text editor that is triggered each time the user makes a modification to a file buffer. To keep things simple in our prototype, the broker passes on every version to every server. A registration scheme could easily be added to reduce message traffic but we haven't found it to be necessary.

Servers react to versions by sending responses that contain products which are derived from the version text (step 4). A single server may respond to every version or just to certain ones. For example, a server that knows how to perform semantic analysis checks for a particular language will only respond versions written in that language, whereas one that provides information about version control status will respond to every version that involves a tracked file.

The broker passes the products to the sinks (step 5). Usually a sink will display some part of the product to the user, possibly inducing some further user interaction (step 6). As for servers, sinks are often designed to only react to certain kinds of product. A typical sink might react to a product containing an outline by showing the outline in a text editor buffer or IDE view. A sink that knows how to handle text completion might display options from a completion product so that the user can select one.

The Monto architecture is specifically designed to minimise coupling between the components. The broker exists so that sources do not need to be aware of the identity or location of the servers and sinks. Similarly, servers can work without having to be aware of the sinks that consume their products. Sinks do not need to know anything about the servers that produce the products they receive.

4   Communication

The choice of communication technology directly affects which languages can be used to implement Monto components and hence indirectly influences which other technologies can participate. For example, choosing a Java-specific communication mechanism would mean that JVM-based languages could easily be used but others would be ruled out. Basing things on Java would mean that Eclipse and other Java-based IDEs would be able to participate as sources or sinks, but text editors that are implemented in C could not be easily incorporated.

We use the ZeroMQ messaging technology [1] to implement communication in Monto. ZeroMQ is a convenient layer on top of basic socket-level communication, but otherwise does not impose any constraints on the information that can be communicated. ZeroMQ-compatible libraries exist for most mainstream languages, so it is easy for components to interoperate without sharing an implementation language. ZeroMQ is also very fast since it imposes minimal overhead above the basic communication layer. Speed is important since messages from sources to servers to sinks are being used to provide interactive functionality.

Monto sends messages over ZeroMQ sockets as text and the ZeroMQ layer takes care of issues such breaking large messages into smaller pieces and re-assembling them at the other end. ZeroMQ also takes care of queueing messages. Sending a message using ZeroMQ is typically a couple of lines of code. Servers and sinks use a blocking operation to wait for an incoming message to arrive.

Message Formats. The choice of message format strongly affects the simplicity and power of the framework. Using message formats that make few assumptions about the information that is being communicated means that the framework will not impose too much on the way that it can be used. For example, if changes were notified by sending an abstract syntax tree of the version according to some grammar, we would make it inconvenient to write servers that wish to process the version as lines of text, perhaps to perform a spell check.

The simplest message format we can use is uninterpreted plain text. However, it is useful to have slightly more structure so that servers and sinks have something by which to discriminate between messages. We use the JSON structured text format. As for ZeroMQ, an advantage of JSON is that encoders and decoders are available for many languages.

Version Messages. Messages that describe a version contain:

– source: a unique string that identifies the source of the version,
– language: the name of the language in which the source is written,
– contents: the complete text of the version, and
– selections: objects that describe the current selected regions in the source.

The source string is usually the name of a file that is backing the content that is being edited. The contents of a version message do not necessarily correspond to the current contents of the file since the user may not have saved it.

The language field is used so that servers can react only to text that is written in a language that they understand. The language "text" is used if no other language is suitable. Using a string to encode the language is the simplest method, but introduces some imperfections. For example, who determines which language names are acceptable in a version message? We could specify the legal names up-front using some form of enumeration type, but we stick with a string so that the framework is as flexible as possible. Coordination of language names must be done by convention outside the framework.

The contents field contains the complete text of the version. One obvious possibility for modification of this design is to send just the nature of the change itself. Our view is that this kind of extension would complicate the messaging too much and would tie the framework too closely to particular kinds of changes. The price we pay is that servers may be recalculating information that could have otherwise been determined in a more incremental fashion, or they must become somewhat stateful. So far we have not found this to be a limitation.

Most sources have some notion of the *current selection* which describes the editing position in the text and what, if any, of the text has been highlighted by the user. The selection field of a version message supports servers that take the user's current focus of attention into account. For example, a server that determines completion possibilities needs to know where the cursor is.

Product Messages. Messages that communicate a product contain:

- source: the unique identifier of the source to which this product relates,
- product: the type of the product,
- language: the language in which the product text is written, and
- contents: the content of the product as text.

The source field is used to associate the product with the source of the version that triggered it. Sinks can react to products that pertain to a source in which they are interested. For example, a sink that is waiting for a code completion product would react to products that apply to the initiating source.

The product field identifies its type and is used by sinks to react only to products that they can handle. For example, a sink that wants to display an outline view for any source would ignore the source field but check that the product field indicates an outline. Monto enforces no discipline on product names, so like language name they must be agreed by convention outside the framework.

The language and contents fields are used similarly to their role in version messages. Sometimes a server will produce text in a particular language. For example, if the server is formatting the version text then the product language will be the same as that of the corresponding source message. If the server is compiling Java code then the product language might be "JVM byte code".

Version and product messages can contain extra fields to communicate information above the basic level mandated by the framework. For example, a particular source might include information about the change that created a version, in case that information is of use to a server but would be hard for the server to calculate itself. Similarly, a server can provide extra information in a product message for use by sinks. This sort of extra information would be provided and used by convention between developers of Monto components.

Running Monto. Monto consists of a loose collection of components that run autonomously. A script simplifies starting and stopping the broker and any servers that the user desires to use. The script is driven by a simple configuration file that specifies paths, command-line arguments, etc.

To avoid overwhelming the servers with many small changes to the same source in a small period of time, the broker collects only the most recent version message for each source and periodically sends it to the servers. The timing has been adjusted to balance between sending too many messages to the servers and not reacting quickly enough for good interactive use. The broker can be implemented in any language that can communicate using JSON messages over ZeroMQ. In our prototype it is implemented by about 40 lines of Python but can easily be implemented in a compiled language if speed becomes a problem.

Other than the broker and servers, the user must also run sources and sinks. Normally these components will be implemented by plug-ins in an editing environment of the user's choice so they will be automatically started up when that environment starts or as the result of user commands.

5   Experience

We have been experimenting with the Monto prototype framework to build various sources, servers and sinks. Our aim so far has been to explore to see if our simple approach is sufficient to encompass typical IDE-like functionality. We particularly wanted to see whether an approach that requires sending messages between components performs well enough to make a usable environment.

Sublime Text. Our current experiments use the Sublime Text 3 editor [2]. We have built a Monto plug-in for Sublime Text in 250 lines of Python. The plug-in relies on 100 further lines that are independent of Sublime Text and can be used by any Python-based Monto component. When the plug-in is loaded, Sublime Text acts as a source for any buffer that the user is editing. A version is published each time a buffer is created, modified and when a selection is moved.

The plug-in provides a command by which the user can create new views that display Monto products, which we call *Monto views*. A Monto view can optionally display products that relate to all sources or just those for the source that held the focus when the command was run. Similarly, new arrivals of a product can be appended to the existing text in a Monto view or replace it.

Figure 2 shows a Sublime Text window editing a factorial program written in the Java-subset language MiniJava (top left). The user has three Monto views to display products: the abstract syntax tree of the program (a form of outline, top right), the abstract syntax tree pretty-printed as MiniJava code (bottom left), and a translation of into Java Virtual Machine bytecode (bottom right).

The Monto views in Figure 2 are updated continuously as the developer edits the program. Adding a new local variable declaration in the `ComputeFac` method will cause a new node representing that declaration to appear in the tree view, a pretty-printed version of that declaration to appear in the pretty-print view, and the bytecode to be updated to reflect that a new local variable slot is needed.

Fig. 2. Sublime Text: MiniJava factorial program and three Monto views

All of these updates happen nearly instantaneously so the overhead of interpreting messages and reacting to them appears to be low. This observation confirms that at least for basic functionality the performance of a Monto-based environment is sufficient for interactive use. We have not conducted a comprehensive benchmark against other alternatives and we make no claim about how more advanced features will perform since those features are part of future work.

The plug-in provides other ways in which Monto products can be used. For example, a product containing formatted source code might replace the current selection. A product can also be used by a code completion command as suggestions in a pop-up menu. In fact, since a product is just text, the only limitation on the way it can be used is the capability of the editor.

Any other extensible text editor or IDE could play the role that Sublime Text does in our experiments. All that is required is a way to detect when the user has made changes to the text that they are editing, a way to send a ZeroMQ message containing that version, and a way to react to products coming in from servers. If an editor can be extended in Python it can reuse the Monto library used by the Sublime Text plug-in. Otherwise, similar functionality would need to be implemented in that editor's extension language.

There is no requirement that a single program act as both the source and sink as Sublime Text does. For example, products that result from changes happening in one editor can be displayed in another one. A fan-out structure could be used to send products to more than one viewer, so that multiple developers can observe editing as it happens during a pair coding session. A server that simply reflects versions back out as products would enable live observation of editing, but observing developers could also create other views as needed. For example, a server that automatically runs tests on changed code could report to developers who are running a test result display sink.

MiniJava Compiler Server. One typical use of a DDE is to interface with existing compiler code. Rather than duplicate the compiler code within the environment, we wish to reuse it. In fact, the products shown in Figure 2 were produced using a server that is a small extension of existing Scala code for a MiniJava compiler. The compiler is written using our Kiama language processing library [13,14]. 90 lines of Scala wraps any Kiama compiler so that it acts as a Monto server; no modifications must be made to the compiler code. The wrapping code uses off-the-shelf Java libraries for JSON encoding and ZeroMQ.

If a syntax error is introduced in the MiniJava source then the products shown in Figure 2 will be empty since those products are not defined when the version text doesn't parse. The MiniJava compiler also has an error product that reports any syntax or semantic errors from the compilation process. Thus, if desired, a developer can augment the shown views with one that continuously updates with the current compiler error messages.

Wrapping Text-Based Tools. Many command-line tools exist that would be of use in a development environment but were developed independently with their own user interface. For example, there are many lint tools that produce a textual report of code quality problems beyond those diagnosed by compilers. We have built a wrapper script to enable these sorts of tools to be used with other Monto components. The script runs as a server that executes a shell command each time a version is received, captures the output of the command, and sends it back as a product. It is easy to use this wrapper to incorporate the output of those tools in a Monto view so that, for example, lint reports can be viewed in the editor and are updated automatically as code changes.

6   Conclusion and Future Work

Our initial experiments have shown that a minimalist disintegrated development environment approach has some promise. With a relatively small amount of effort we were able to build a simple framework that provides an editing experience with quick feedback to source code changes. By factoring the framework into independent components that communicate via simple messages, we do not require component developers to buy into a complex framework. Having said that, we do not claim on this evidence that a Monto-based environment can rival well-established IDEs with complex plug-ins.

Current work is investigating more advanced facilities, how they fit into a disintegrated world and whether our simple framework is sufficient to support them with acceptable performance. Of particular interest is the ability of Monto to incorporate servers that reside across the network, perhaps to provide access to functionality that is impossible or hard to install on a local machine. Some other areas of current investigation are: source mapping to relate product text to version text; incorporation of a project view so that servers can work at the project level not just at the file level; products that are HTML or SVG and sinks that are web browsers; sinks that display graphical output; build feedback; execution-based products for live coding, debugging and testing; wrapping version control tools; and read-eval-print-loop-based servers.

Acknowledgements. Štěpán Šindelář provided useful feedback on the paper. We also thank the anonymous reviewers for their helpful suggestions.

References

1. Hintjens, P.: ZeroMQ: Messaging for Many Applications. O'Reilly (2013)
2. Skinner, J.: Sublime Text 3, http://www.sublimetext.com/3
3. Charles, P., Fuhrer, R.M., M., S.,J. S.: IMP: A meta-tooling platform for creating language-specific IDEs in Eclipse. In: Proceedings of Conference on Automated Software Engineering, pp. 485–488. ACM (2007)
4. Charles, P., Fuhrer, R.M., M., S.,J. S., Evelyn, D., Jurgen, V.: Accelerating the creation of customized, language-specific IDEs in Eclipse. In: Proceedings of Conference on Object Oriented Programming Systems Languages and Applications, pp. 191–206. ACM (2009)
5. Kats, L.C.L., Kalleberg, K.T., Visser, E.: Domain-specific languages for composable editor plugins. In: Proceedings of the Workshop on Language Descriptions, Tools, and Applications. Electronic Notes in Theoretical Computer Science, vol. 253, pp. 149–163. Elsevier (2009)
6. Kats, L.C.L., Visser, E.: The Spoofax language workbench: rules for declarative specification of languages and IDEs. In: Proceedings of Conference on Object Oriented Programming Systems Languages and Applications, pp. 444–463. ACM (2010)
7. Erdweg, S., et al.: The state of the art in language workbenches. In: Erwig, M., Paige, R.F., Van Wyk, E. (eds.) SLE 2013. LNCS, vol. 8225, pp. 197–217. Springer, Heidelberg (2013)
8. Voelter, M.: Embedded software development with projectional language workbenches. In: Petriu, D.C., Rouquette, N., Haugen, Ø. (eds.) MODELS 2010, Part II. LNCS, vol. 6395, pp. 32–46. Springer, Heidelberg (2010)
9. Cannon, A.: Enhanced Scala Interaction Mode for Emacs (ENSIME), https://github.com/ensime/ensime-src
10. Bergstra, J.A., Klint, P.: The discrete time ToolBus—a software coordination architecture. Science of Computer Programming 31, 205–229 (1998)
11. den van Brand, M.G.J., et al.: The ASF+SDF meta-environment: A component-based language development environment. In: Wilhelm, R. (ed.) CC 2001. LNCS, vol. 2027, pp. 365–370. Springer, Heidelberg (2001)
12. Ahuja, S., Carrier, N., Gelernter, D.: Linda and friends. Computer 19(8), 26–34 (1986)
13. Sloane, A.M.: Lightweight language processing in kiama. In: Fernandes, J.M., Lämmel, R., Visser, J., Saraiva, J. (eds.) Generative and Transformational Techniques in Software Engineering III. LNCS, vol. 6491, pp. 408–425. Springer, Heidelberg (2011)
14. Programming Languages Research Group. Macquarie University, The Kiama language processing library, http://kiama.googlecode.com

Model Checking of CTL-Extended OCL Specifications[*]

Robert Bill[1], Sebastian Gabmeyer[1], Petra Kaufmann[1], and Martina Seidl[2]

[1] Business Informatics Group, TU Wien, Austria
{bill,gabmeyer,kaufmann}@big.tuwien.ac.at
[2] Institute for Formal Models and Verification, JKU Linz, Austria
martina.seidl@jku.at

Abstract. In software modeling, the Object Constraint Language (OCL) is an important language to specify properties that a model has to satisfy. The design of OCL reflects the structure of MOF-based modeling languages like UML and its tight integration results in an intuitive usability. But OCL allows to express properties only in the context of a single instance model and not with respect to a sequence of instance models that capture the execution of the system.

In this paper, we show how OCL can be extended with CTL-based temporal operators to express properties over the lifetime of an instance model. We formally introduce syntax and semantics of our OCL extension cOCL. The properties specified with our OCL extension can be verified with our explicit state space model checking framework, called MocOCL. In a case study, we illustrate the expressiveness and usability of our approach and evaluate the performance of our implementation.

1 Introduction

In software and hardware verification [9,14,18], *model checking* is currently one of the most widely used verification techniques to show that a system satisfies its specification.[1] Model checking requires a formal representation of the system and a specification that often consists of a set of temporal logic formulas formulated in, e.g., the branching-time logic CTL [6].

In the context of model-based engineering (MBE), software models[2] are the core artifacts to specify and develop a system. In contrast to traditional software engineering, where models mainly serve as design artifacts during the early project phases, an MBE project uses models at every stage of the development process and finally generates executable code and other deliverables therefrom.

---

[*] This work is supported by the Vienna Science and Technology Fund (WWTF) under grant ICT10-018.

[1] Usually, a specification consists of a set of properties that the system should satisfy. We will, however, often use the terms *specification* and *property* interchangeably.

[2] The term *model* is heavily overloaded in computer science. We encounter logical models in the context of model checking and software models in the context of MBE. In case of ambiguities we use the term *software model* when referring to the latter.

B. Combemale et al. (Eds.): SLE 2014, LNCS 8706, pp. 221–240, 2014.
© Springer International Publishing Switzerland 2014

Hence, the correctness of the models is a prerequisite for the correctness of the system that is presented to the end-user [25]. Consequently, formal verification techniques find their way into the MBE processes to help detect and avoid errors in the models. A popular choice for this task is model checking. Recent works and tools like HUGO/RT [19], GROOVE [17], and PROCO [15], to name but a few, show that software models can be verified with model checking. In general, the verification of software models by model checking abides the following scheme. Throughout its lifetime a system, which is described by the software model, passes through many states; each such state is represented by a distinct instance model. A sequence of states, called a *trace*, describes the execution of the system from an initial to some intermediate or final state. The system's specification describes the set of allowed, i.e., *valid*, traces. A model checker then verifies whether the execution traces of the system starting from a given initial state are a subset of the valid traces described by the specification. If the model checker determines a violating trace, it reports the found *counterexample trace* to the user.

Currently, many approaches use an off-the-shelf model checker and require the modeler to express the specification in the language of this model checker. Therefore, the modeler is required to study and understand the translation of the system's software model to the model checker's input format. Moreover, the specification is often expressed in a language that is different from the languages available in the modeling environment. To overcome this drawback, we present a CTL-based temporal extension for the Object Constraint Language (OCL), called cOCL. While OCL can only express constraints on a single instance model, cOCL can formulate constraints over sequences of instance models representing execution traces of the system. For verifying properties expressed in cOCL, we realized the model checker MocOCL.

The structure of this paper is as follows. We introduce a motivating example in Section 2 and explain the core ideas behind our approach. In Section 3, we present the syntax and semantics of our CTL-based OCL extension and introduce our model checking framework in Section 4 together with numerous examples in the concrete syntax of our model checker. We then discuss the model checking algorithm as well as some realization details of our tool. In Section 5, we present a first evaluation of our approach regarding its usability and performance. Finally, we review related approaches in Section 6 and conclude with an outlook to future work. This paper is a substantial revision of the extended abstract [3] presented at the OCL 2013 workshop. An unabridged version that includes the questionnaire of the case study (Sec. 5) is also available [4].

2   Motivating Example

To motivate the work presented in this paper we use a variation of the well-known Pacman game,[3] which we use due to its intuitiveness and its easy adaptability

---

[3] http://en.wikipedia.org/wiki/Pac-Man

to larger game instances, i.e., increasing board size and number of ghosts, to test the scalability of our model checking algorithm.

Structure and Game Play. The game is played on a board consisting of square fields, each of which has at most four neighboring fields. Each field has a unique ID and some fields contain a treasure, indicated by a Boolean flag. Pacman plays against one or more ghosts. Each player, Pacman or the ghosts, is placed on one field of the board. The static structure of the game's implementation is shown in Figure 2a. Figure 1 uses the graphical syntax and shows a Pacman game instance with four fields, a treasure on field 4, Pacman on field 1, and a ghost on field 3. The game is played as follows. The players move turn-wise in no fixed order. Pacman has to find one of the treasures, which are placed somewhere on the board. If he finds one, he wins the game. If, however, Pacman moves onto a field with a ghost or if a ghost moves onto Pacman's field, Pacman looses the game.

Fig. 1. Pacman's World

Implementation. We use graph transformation rules to implement the behavior of the game. The first rule, *Move Pacman*, is depicted in Figure 2(a) and describes one move of Pacman. The second rule, *Move Ghost* (Figure 2(b)), describes one move of a ghost. Pacman and the ghosts are only allowed to move if the game is not over yet, that is, no one moves if Pacman is on a treasure field or if Pacman and a ghost meet on the same field. Note, however, that the first restriction is not enforced by the *Move Ghost* rule; hence, ghosts may still move if Pacman already found the treasure. In Section 4.2, we show how to detect this violation of the rules. Figure 3 exemplarily illustrates two applications of the *Move Pacman* graph transformation and the subsequent changes to the current state. First, Pacman moves from field 1 to field 2 and in the next round Pacman moves from field 2 to field 4, which contains the treasure. In this scenario, Pacman wins.

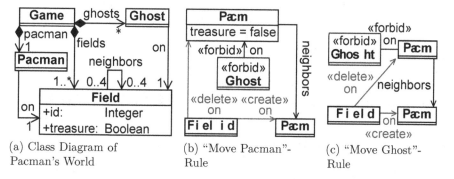

(a) Class Diagram of Pacman's World

(b) "Move Pacman"-Rule

(c) "Move Ghost"-Rule

Fig. 2. Implementation of the Pacman game with graph transformations

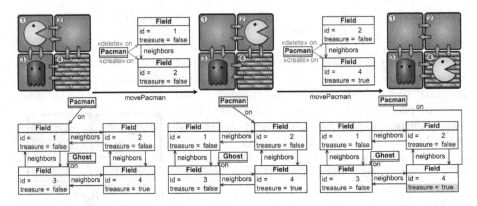

Fig. 3. Example for Transformations

Verification Tasks. In the example above, we have seen one specific trace showing a winning strategy for Pacman. Yet, if we want to verify that the game always terminates when Pacman found a treasure, it is not enough to consider only some specific traces but all possible traces have to be explored.

For expressing and solving these verification tasks, temporal aspects of the system behavior have to be considered. Such verification questions are difficult to express in OCL because it neither provides operators to express constraints that must hold, e.g., *always* or *eventually*, nor the semantic notions to describe execution traces. To this end, we propose to use our OCL extension cOCL.

MocOCL at a Glance. Our tool MocOCL realizes an explicit state model checking approach. We construct the state space of the Pacman game iteratively. In our implementation, we use the graph transformation tool HENSHIN [1] that explores the state space by recursively applying all matching graph transformation rules to the user-provided initial model. The full state space resulting from recursively applying the rules *Move Pacman* and *Move Ghost* to the initial model (Fig. 1) is depicted in Figure 4. The *initial state* in the bottom-left corner of the figure is highlighted in green with a bold border and the end states are marked red with a dashed border. The transitions between the states show possible moves of Pacman and the ghost. Overall there are $4*4 = 16$ different states (the ghost has to be placed on each field and Pacman has to be placed on each field). After each exploration step MocOCL evaluates the cOCL expression and, if enough states have been explored to conclude that the expressions either holds or fails, the verification stops. Finally, MocOCL returns a report that explains the result of the verification.

3   A Temporal Extension of OCL

In this section, we formally introduce syntax and semantics of cOCL, which extends OCL with CTL operators. We assume familiarity with model checking

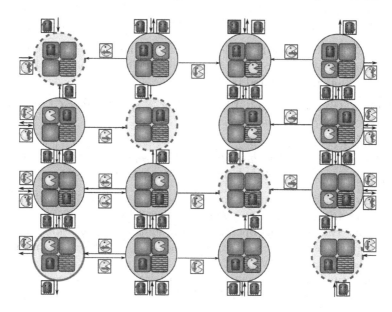

Fig. 4. State Space of the Pacman Game

and CTL [2,7]. We integrate cOCL into the formal semantics of OCL and kindly refer to the work of Richters and Gogolla [24] for the details on the syntax and semantics of OCL. Due to space constraints and for ease of presentation, we reproduce only those definitions that are essential to the understanding of the subsequent explanations.

OCL expressions are always defined w.r.t. a model M consisting of classes which are described by their attributes and operations as well as associations between classes characterized by multiplicities and roles. Such a model provides the basis for defining OCL expressions in form of a signature $\Sigma_M = (\mathcal{T}_M, \Omega_M, \mathcal{V})$ where $\mathcal{T}_M$ is a set of types, Ω_M is a set of operations, and $\mathcal{V}$ is additionally a set of variables. By $V_t \subseteq \mathcal{V}$ we denote the set of variables of type $t \in \mathcal{T}_M$. The instantiation of such a model is given by objects, links, and attribute values and is also called *snapshot*. In the following, we denote a specific snapshot of a model M by $\sigma(M)$. Due to space restrictions, we abstain from a complete formal introduction of the notion of model.

Definition 1 (Syntax of OCL). *Let $\Sigma_M = (\mathcal{T}_M, \Omega_M, \mathcal{V})$ be the signature of model M as described above. Then Expr_t is the set of expressions of type t defined as follows.*

i. If $v \in \mathrm{Var}_t$ then $v \in \mathrm{Expr}_t$.
ii. If $v \in \mathrm{Var}_{t_1}, e_1 \in \mathrm{Expr}_{t_1}, e \in \mathrm{Expr}_t$ then $(\mathsf{let}\ \ v = e_1\ \mathsf{in}\ e) \in \mathrm{Expr}_t$.
iii. If $\omega : t_1 \times \ldots \times t_n \to t \in \Omega_M$ and $e_i \in \mathrm{Expr}_{t_i}$ then $\omega(e_1, \ldots, e_n) \in \mathrm{Expr}_t$.
iv. If $e_1 \in \mathrm{Expr}_{Bool}$ and $e_2, e_3 \in \mathrm{Expr}_t$ then $\mathsf{if}\ e_1\ \mathsf{then}\ e_2\ \mathsf{else}\ e_3\ \mathsf{endif} \in \mathrm{Expr}_t$.
v. If $e_1 \in \mathrm{Expr}_{Collection(t_1)}, v_1 \in \mathrm{Var}_{t_1}, v_2 \in \mathrm{Var}_t$, and $e_2, e_3 \in \mathrm{Expr}_t$ then e_1
$\to \mathsf{iterate}(v_1; v_2 = e_2 \mid e_3) \in \mathrm{Expr}_t$.

The set of OCL expressions over Σ denoted by OCL_M is given by $\bigcup_t \mathrm{Expr}_t$.

Due to space restrictions, Definition 1 does not contain the definitions related to type hierarchies and inheritance. Adding these definitions neither changes nor impacts our approach presented below.

Definition 2 (Syntax of cOCL). *Let M be a model with OCL expressions OCL_M. Then cOCL is defined as follows.*

i. If $e \in \mathrm{OCL}_M$, then $e \in cOCL$.
ii. Let $\mathrm{Expr}_{Bool} \subseteq cOCL$ be the set of boolean expressions in cOCL. If $e_1, e_2 \in \mathrm{Expr}_{Bool}$ then $\mathsf{AX}e_1$, $\mathsf{EX}e_1$, $\mathsf{A}e_1\mathsf{W}e_2$, $\mathsf{E}e_1\mathsf{W}e_2$, $\mathsf{A}e_1\mathsf{U}e_2$, $\mathsf{E}e_1\mathsf{U}e_2 \in \mathrm{Expr}_{Bool}$.

Our extension introduces three temporal operators, *next* (X), *weak until* (W), and *(strong) until* (U), which are quantified either existentially (E) or universally (A). We define two additional operators, *eventually* (F) and *globally* (G), by the following equivalences: $\mathsf{EF}\varphi \equiv \mathsf{E}\,true\,\mathsf{U}\,\varphi$ and $\mathsf{AF}\varphi \equiv \mathsf{A}\,true\,\mathsf{U}\,\varphi$, and $\mathsf{EG}\varphi \equiv \mathsf{E}\,\varphi\,\mathsf{W}\,false$ and $\mathsf{AG}\varphi \equiv \mathsf{A}\,\varphi\,\mathsf{W}\,false$. Note that *next*, *eventually*, and *globally* have a single subformula as argument, whereas the *weak until* and *until* operators have two subformulas. Before we define the semantics of the temporal operators, we formally introduce the term *transition system* which describes all possible executions of a system.

Definition 3 (Transition System). *The transition system $\mathcal{TS}_M$ associated with a model M is a hextuple $(\mathcal{S}, \iota, T, \mathcal{A}, \mathcal{B}, \mathcal{E})$ consisting of a set $\mathcal{S}$ of states, an initial state $\iota \in \mathcal{E}$, a transition relation $T \subseteq \mathcal{S} \times \mathcal{A} \times \mathcal{S}$, a set $\mathcal{A}$ of actions, a set $\mathcal{B}$ of variable assignments, and the environment relation $\mathcal{E} \subseteq \mathcal{S} \times \mathcal{B}$. An environment $\tau \in \mathcal{E}$ is a pair (σ, β) with $\sigma \in \mathcal{S}$ and $\beta \in \mathcal{B}$.*

For each state $\sigma \in \mathcal{S}$ the set of possible objects is given by σ_{class}, the set of possible associations by σ_{assoc}, and the set of possible attributes by σ_{attrs}. A variable assignment is a function $\beta : Var_t \to Val_t$ that, given a variable name, returns the current value of the associated variable of type t. An action is a partial function $\alpha : \sigma_{class} \to \sigma_{class} \cup \{\bot\}$ mapping objects from one state to corresponding objects of another state or to $\bot$ if no such object exists.

The concept of an *environment* $\tau = (\sigma, \beta)$ has been introduced in [24]. For specific execution traces, we define the term *path* as follows.

Definition 4 (Path). *Let $\mathcal{TS}_M = (\mathcal{S}, \iota, T, \mathcal{A}, \mathcal{B}, \mathcal{E})$ be the transition system associated with a model M. A path π is a finite or infinite sequence of environments $(\tau_0\tau_1\tau_2\ldots)$ with $\tau_i \in \mathcal{E}$ and $(\tau_i, \tau_{i+1}) \in \{((\sigma_i, \beta_i), (\sigma_{i+1}, \beta_{i+1})) \mid \beta_{i+1} = \mathrm{mapvar}(\beta_i, \alpha), (\sigma_i, \alpha, \sigma_{i+1}) \in T\}$ for all $0 \leq i$. For a path $\pi = (\tau_0\tau_1\tau_2\ldots)$, we define the projection function $\pi(i) = \tau_i$. The length of a path $|\pi| = n$ for finite paths $\pi = (\tau_0 \ldots \tau_n)$, and $|\pi| = \infty$ for infinite paths $\pi = (\tau_0\tau_1\tau_2\ldots)$. By $\mathrm{pth}(\mathcal{TS}_M)$ we denote the set of all possible paths of $\mathcal{TS}_M$.*

The function **mapvar** : $\mathcal{B} \times \mathcal{A} \to \mathcal{B}$ takes a variable assignment β_s of source state σ_s and an action $\alpha \in \mathcal{A}$ and updates β_s with respect to α resulting in a variable assignment β_t for the successor state σ_t. We are now able to define the semantics of cOCL as follows.

Definition 5 (Semantics). *Let* $\mathcal{TS}_M = (\mathcal{S}, \iota, T, \mathcal{A}, \mathcal{B}, \mathcal{E})$ *be the transition system associated with model M as defined above. The semantics of a cOCL expression w.r.t. a context $\tau \in \mathcal{B}$ with $\tau = (\sigma, \beta)$ is defined by the rules i.–vi. originating from Definition 2 of [24] and the additional rules vii.–xi. for the temporal extension.*

i. $I[\![v]\!](\tau) := \beta(v)$

ii. $I[\![\text{let } v = e_1 \text{ in } e_2]\!](\tau) := I[\![e_2]\!]((\sigma, \beta[v/I[\![e_1]\!](\tau)]))$

iii. $I[\![\omega(e_1, \ldots, e_n)]\!](\tau) := I(\omega)(\tau)(I[\![e_1]\!](\tau), \ldots, I[\![e_n]\!](\tau))$

iv. $I[\![\text{ if } e_1 \text{ then } e_2 \text{ else } e_3 \text{ endif}]\!](\tau) = \begin{cases} I[\![e_2]\!](\tau) & \text{if } I[\![e_1]\!](\tau) := true \\ I[\![e_3]\!](\tau) & \text{if } I[\![e_1]\!](\tau) := false \\ \bot & \text{otherwise} \end{cases}$

v. $I[\![e_1 \rightarrow \text{iterate}(v_1; v_2 = e_2 | e_3)]\!](\tau) := I[\![e_1 \rightarrow \text{iterate}'(v_1 | e_3)]\!](\tau')$ *where* $\tau' = (\sigma, \beta')$ *and* $\tau'' = (\sigma, \beta'')$ *are environments with modified variable assignments:* $\beta' := \beta[v_2/I[\![e_2]\!](\tau)]$, $\beta'' := \beta'[v_2/I[\![e_3]\!](\sigma, \beta'[v_1/x_1])]$

vi. $I[\![\mathsf{A}\, e_1 \,\mathsf{U}\, e_2]\!](\tau) := \{\pi \mid \pi \in \text{pth}(\mathcal{TS}_M), \pi(0) = \tau, \not\exists n \in \mathbb{N}, n \leq |\pi| : (I[\![e_2]\!](\pi(n)) = \text{true} \wedge \forall 0 \leq i < n : I[\![e_1]\!](\pi(i)) = \text{true})\} = \emptyset$

vii. $I[\![\mathsf{E}\, e_1 \,\mathsf{U}\, e_2]\!](\tau) := \{\pi \mid \pi \in \text{pth}(\mathcal{TS}_M), \pi(0) = \tau, \exists n \in \mathbb{N}, n \leq |\pi| : (I[\![e_2]\!](\pi(n)) = \text{true} \wedge \forall 0 \leq i < n : I[\![e_1]\!](\pi(i)) = \text{true})\} \neq \emptyset$

viii. $I[\![\mathsf{A}\, e_1 \,\mathsf{W}\, e_2]\!](\tau) := \{\pi \mid \pi \in \text{pth}(\mathcal{TS}_M), \pi(0) = \tau, \not\forall n \in \mathbb{N}, n \leq |\pi| : (I[\![e_1]\!](\pi(n)) = \text{false} \rightarrow \exists i \in \mathbb{N}, i \leq n : I[\![e_2]\!](\pi(i)) = \text{true})\} = \emptyset$

ix. $I[\![\mathsf{E}\, \phi \,\mathsf{W}\, \psi]\!](\tau) := \{\pi \mid \pi \in \text{pth}(\mathcal{TS}_M), \pi(0) = \tau, \exists n \in \mathbb{N}, n \leq |\pi| : (I[\![e_1]\!](\pi(n)) = \text{false} \rightarrow \exists i \in \mathbb{N}, i \leq n : I[\![e_2]\!](\pi(i)) = \text{true})\} \neq \emptyset$

x. $I[\![\mathsf{E}\,\mathsf{X}\, e]\!](\tau) := \{\pi \mid \pi \in \text{pth}(\mathcal{TS}_M), \pi(0) = \tau \wedge |\pi| \geq 1 \wedge I[\![e]\!](\pi(1)) = \text{true}\} \neq \emptyset$

xi. $I[\![\mathsf{A}\,\mathsf{X}\, e]\!](\tau) := \{\pi \mid \pi \in \text{pth}(\mathcal{TS}_M), \pi(0) = \tau \wedge |\pi| \geq 1 \wedge I[\![e]\!](\pi(1)) \neq \text{true}\} = \emptyset$

The semantics of the *eventually* and *globally* operators follow directly from the above definitions. The only free variable allowed in cOCL expressions is `self`, corresponding to the root object of the state, called $root(\sigma)$ in the following, the cOCL expression is evaluated in. We define *satisfiability* of cOCL expressions as follows.

Definition 6 (Satisfiability). *A cOCL expression ϕ is* satisfiable *w.r.t. a transition system $\mathcal{TS}_M$ with initial state ι iff $I[\![\phi]\!](\iota) = \text{true}$.*

In the remainder of this paper, we discuss how the model checker MocOCL verifies cOCL specifications, discuss its implementation, and evaluate its performance and usability. In Table 1 we list examples of cOCL expressions, which illustrate typical application scenarios of cOCL in the context of the `Game` class (Fig. 2a) of the previously introduced Pacman game. The cOCL expressions are phrased in the concrete syntax of MocOCL that we introduce in the next section.

Table 1. Examples of cOCL expressions in the concrete syntax of MocOCL.

natural language	cOCL expression
Initially, there is a field containing a treasure.	`self.fields->exists(field | field.treasure)`
The game is over/not over.	`Always Next false/Exists Next true`
The game will surely be over sometimes.	`Always Eventually (Always Next false)`
Pacman will find the treasure in all cases.	`Always Eventually self.pacman.on.treasure`

If the treasure is next to Pacman, he can always find it in the next turn.	`Always Globally`
	`    self.pacman.on.neighbor->exists(field.treasure)`
	`    implies (Exists Next self.pacman.on.treasure)`

As long as not all fields next to Pacman are occupied by ghosts, there is a possibility that the game is not over after the next turn.	`Always Globally`
	`    self.pacman.on.neighbor->exists(field |`
	`    self.ghosts->forAll(g | field <> g.on) implies`
	`    (Exists Next (Exists Next true)))`

As long as the game is not over, every ghost may move to at least two different positions.	`Always self.ghosts->`
	`    forAll(g | g.on.neighbor->select(field |`
	`    Exists Next g.on = field)->size() >= 2)`
	`Unless (Always Next false)`

4 The Model Checker MocOCL

The implementation of MocOCL consists of two parts, a backend that realizes an explicit state model checker and a graphical user interface.

4.1 Backend

The backend consists of a parser for the textual concrete syntax of cOCL and the model checker MocOCL that verifies cOCL specifications.

The *concrete syntax* enhances the readability of cOCL expressions. It allows us to write the temporal operators in their familiar long forms, i.e., $X\varphi$, $F\varphi$, $G\varphi$, $\varphi W \psi$, and $\varphi U \psi$ become **Next** φ, **Eventually** φ, **Globally** φ, φ **Unless** ψ, and φ **Until** ψ. The universal and existential path quantifiers preceding the temporal operators become **Always** and **Exists** or, alternatively, **Sometimes**. Table 1 shows examples of MocOCL expressions in the concrete syntax. In our implementation, we extended the concrete syntax of OCL given by an Xtext grammar[4] resulting in an editor with syntax highlighting for cOCL expressions and a Java API.

The prototypical, EMF-based[5] implementation of the MocOCL model checker performs the actual verification task as follows. Given an Ecore-conformant model, an instance model that represents the system's initial state, a set of model transformations, and a cOCL specification, MocOCL generates the state space iteratively and, at every step, it verifies the cOCL specification on-the-fly. Finally, it reports to the modeler information on the reason of the verification result.

In MocOCL, the state space consists of a set of graphs. Each graph corresponds to an instance of the system and thus represents a system's state at a discrete point in time. Given a graph transformation system $\mathcal{G} = (\mathcal{R}, \iota)$ with graph rewrite rules $\mathcal{R}$ and an initial state ι, the function $\textbf{step}_\mathcal{R} \colon \mathcal{S} \to P(\mathcal{S} \times \mathcal{M})^6$ handles the step-wise exploration of the state space where $\mathcal{S}$ denotes the set of all states and $\mathcal{M}$ the set of all partial mappings between states $\sigma_1, \sigma_2 \in \mathcal{S}$. It expects as input a state σ_s and returns a set of pairs (σ_t, m) where σ_t denotes the successor state of σ_s and $m \in \mathcal{M}$ defines a morphism $m : \sigma_{Class} \to \sigma_{Class} \cup \{\bot\}$ that maps objects in σ_s to corresponding objects in σ_t or to $\bot$ if no such object exists. The successor state σ_t is obtained from σ_s by applying a rewrite rule $r \in \mathcal{R}$ to the graph represented by σ_s. We write $\sigma_s \overset{r,m}{\Rightarrow} \sigma_t$ to denote that σ_s is rewritten to σ_t by rule $r \in \mathcal{R}$ at match m [11]. The state space exploration function is then defined as $\textbf{step}_\mathcal{R}(\sigma_s) = \bigcup_{r \in \mathcal{R}}\{(\sigma_t, m) | \sigma_s \overset{r,m}{\Rightarrow} \sigma_t\}$. The helper function $\textbf{succ} \colon \mathcal{E} \to P(\mathcal{E})$ returns all environments reachable by a transition from the source environment $\tau_s = (\sigma_s, \beta_s)$ and is defined by $\textbf{succ}((\sigma_s, \beta_s)) := \{(\sigma_t, \beta_t) | (\sigma_t, m) \in \textbf{step}_\mathcal{R}(\sigma_s), \beta_t = \text{mapvar}(\beta_s, m)\}$ with mapvar as defined in the previous section.

This implementation gives us a transition system $\mathcal{TS}_M = (\mathcal{S}, \iota, T, \mathcal{A}, \mathcal{B}, \mathcal{E})$ with initial state $\iota \in \{(\sigma, \beta_\iota[\texttt{self}/\text{root}(\sigma)]) | \sigma \in \mathcal{G}\}, \beta_\iota = \emptyset, T = \{(\sigma_s, m, \sigma_t) | \sigma_s \overset{r,m}{\Rightarrow} \sigma_t, r \in \mathcal{R}, \sigma_s, \sigma_t \in \mathcal{S}\}$, $\mathcal{A}$ being the set $\mathcal{M}$ of partial state mappings, $\mathcal{E}$ being the transitive closure of the $\textbf{succ}$ function applied to the initial environment ι, and $\mathcal{S}$ and $\mathcal{B}$ being all states and variable assignments occurring in an environment.

The algorithm for *evaluating* cOCL expressions of the form $(\mathsf{A}|\mathsf{E})\,\phi\,(\mathsf{U}|\mathsf{W})\,\psi$ is shown in Figure 5. To ease the presentation we drop intermediate checks allowing the algorithm to abort early in some cases, i.e. if a cycle was found during the evaluation or an element is added to a set required to be empty if the property holds. The algorithm proceeds as follows. First, it constructs the sets Φ and Ψ that contain all states where φ or ψ hold, respectively, and a third set η that contains all states reachable from a φ-state but where neither φ nor ψ hold. The worklist ω contains all nodes that need to be processed. The algorithm sets the worklist to the initial environment τ_ι and uses the $\textbf{succ}$ function to iteratively expand the set of reachable environments. It evaluates φ

---

[4] http://www.eclipse.org/Xtext/
[5] http://www.eclipse.org/modeling/emf/
[6] $P(X)$ is the set of all finite subsets of X.

```
/*Evaluates the given cOCL expression.
τ₁: start environment; POp: Path operator, Always or Exists;
TOp: Temporal operator, Until or Unless; returns: true iff the expression holds*/
function evaluate(τ₁, (POp φ TOp ψ)) : Bool
```

1 $\omega := \{\tau_\iota\};$ /*worklist */	20 $\Delta_l := \emptyset;$
2 $\Phi := \emptyset;$ /*fulfilling ϕ, but not ψ */	21 **repeat**
3 $\Psi := \emptyset;$ /*fulfilling ψ */	22 $\Delta_l := \Delta;$
4 $\eta := \emptyset;$ /*fulfilling neither ϕ nor ψ */	23 $\Delta := \{\tau \in \Phi \mid succ(\tau) \cap (\Phi \setminus \Delta_l) = \emptyset\};$
5 **while** $\omega \neq \emptyset$	24 **until** $\Delta = \Delta_l$
6 **pick** $\tau = (\sigma, \beta) \in \omega;$	25 $Z := \{\tau \in \Phi \mid succ(\tau) = \emptyset\};$
7 $\omega := \omega \setminus \{\tau\};$	26
8 **if** $I[\![\phi]\!](\tau)$ **or** $I[\![\psi]\!](\tau)$ **then**	27 **switch** (POp, TOp)
9 **if** $I[\![\psi]\!](\tau)$ **then**	28 **case** (Always, Until):
10 $\Psi := \Psi \cup \{\tau\};$	29 **return** $\Phi = \Delta$ **and** $Z = \emptyset$ **and**
11 **else**	$\eta = \emptyset;$
12 $\Phi := \Phi \cup \{\tau\};$	30 **case** (Always, Unless):
13 $\omega := \omega \cup succ(\tau) \setminus (\Phi \cup \Psi \cup \eta);$	31 **return** $\eta = \emptyset$
14 **end if**	32 **case** (Exists, Until):
15 **else**	33 **return** $\Phi \neq \emptyset;$
16 $\eta := \eta \cup \{\tau\}$	34 **case** (Exists, Unless):
17 **end if**	35 **return** $\Phi \neq \emptyset$ **or** $Z \neq \emptyset$ **or** $\Phi \neq \Delta;$
18 **end while**	36 **end switch**
19 $\Delta := \emptyset;$	

Fig. 5. Until/Unless Algorithm Pseudo Code

and ψ in each environment τ and assigns τ to the corresponding sets Φ and Ψ, or to η if neither φ or ψ hold. Once every reachable environment is assigned to either Φ, Ψ, or η, the algorithm constructs the set Δ, which contains all environments from Φ that do not lie on an infinite path that does not leave Φ. That is, all environments in Φ that are part of a circular path are not in Δ. Finally, the algorithm builds the set Z that contains all deadlocked environment in Φ, i.e., environments that have no successor. Then, $I[\![A \phi \mathsf{U} \psi]\!](\tau)$ holds if η is empty, and Φ contains neither cycle nor deadlock; $I[\![E \phi \mathsf{U} \psi]\!](\tau)$ holds if Ψ is not empty; $I[\![A \phi \mathsf{W} \psi]\!](\tau)$ holds if η is empty; and $I[\![E \phi \mathsf{W} \psi]\!](\tau)$ holds if Ψ is not empty or Φ contains a cycle. Expressions $(\mathsf{A}|\mathsf{E})\mathsf{X}\phi$ are implemented as $I[\![(\mathsf{A}|\mathsf{E})\mathsf{X}\phi]\!]((\sigma, \beta)) := (\forall|\exists)n \in succ(\sigma, \beta) : I[\![\phi]\!](n) = \text{true}$, where we check if all (at least one) successor of the current state satisfies φ.

The evaluation of a cOCL expression yields a *report* that, besides returning the result of the evaluation, contains a *cause* or explanation for the result. A cause is associated with a cOCL expression. It stores the result of the evaluation of the associated expression and, for each relevant sub-expression, a sub-cause. A sub-expression is *relevant* if it influences the result of its super-expression. For example, if the sub-expression φ in φ **or** ψ evaluates to **true** then no sub-cause is generated for ψ as the evaluation of φ uniquely determines the result of φ **or** ψ. If, however, both φ and ψ evaluate to **false**, then a sub-cause for each of the

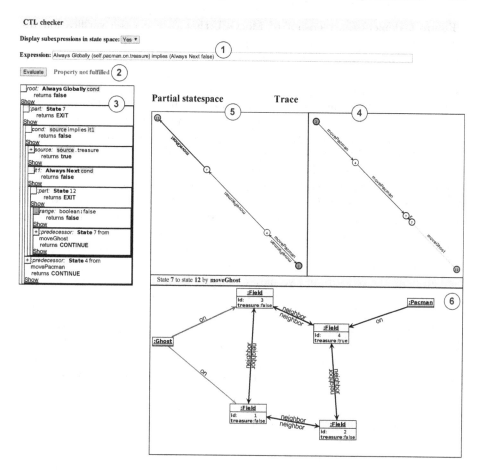

Fig. 6. Visualization of a cause in the MocOCL tool

two sub-expressions is generated and stored in the cause of $\varphi\, \textbf{or}\, \psi$. Note that the cause generation is not necessarily deterministic, as is the case, for example, if both φ and ψ evaluate to **true** in $\varphi\, \textbf{or}\, \psi$.

4.2 Frontend

The MocOCL implementation, which is based on the Eclipse OCL project,[7] works in two phases, (i) step-wise exploration of the state space and evaluation of the provided cOCL expression on the thus far generated state space and (ii) visualization and report generation that provide useful information for the modeler on the reason of a specific result. The realization of the first phase is discussed above; in the following, we present the user interface and the report generation of our tool.

---

[7] http://www.eclipse.org/projects/project_summary.php?projectid=
modeling.mdt.ocl

Figure 6 depicts a screenshot of MocOCL that displays the verification result for the initial 2×2 board (Fig. 1), the graph transformation rules *Move Pacman* and *Move Ghost* (Fig. 2), and the cOCL expression `Always Globally (self.pacman.on.treasure) implies (Always Next false)`. This cOCL expression states that whenever Pacman finds the treasure, no further states can be reached, i.e., the game ends. The MocOCL user interface consists of the following parts: (1) an input field for the cOCL specification, (2) the result of the verification, i.e., whether the cOCL specification is satisfied or not, (3) the cause that textually describes (4) the trace of the evaluation, which is embedded in (5) the partial state space. Further, upon clicking on a state or transition from (3) the cause, (4) the trace, or (5) the partial state space, the selected state or transition is visualized in (6) the object diagram pane. The changes caused by a transition are highlighted in red and green indicating the deletion and creation of an association, respectively.

In the example displayed in Figure 6, the specification is not satisfied, i.e., the game does not end if Pacman finds a treasure. The cause shows a scenario where Pacman finds the treasure in two moves starting from the initial state (state 2) and moving first to state 4 and then to state 7. However, there is a transition moveGhost leading from state 7 to state 12. This transition is selected in (4) the trace and is highlighted in blue. The changes associated with the transition are displayed in (6) the object diagram pane. The deletion and creation of the on relation between the ghost and two adjacent fields describes the ghost's move. Consequently, the ghost may perform moves after Pacman already resides on the treasure field. Thus, the implementation does not satisfy the specification of the game and needs to be fixed by introducing an additional *Negative Application Condition* for the *Move Ghost* rule such that a ghost may no longer move once Pacman found the treasure.

A demo version of MocOCL is available as a browser version at

http://www.modelevolution.org/mococl/

and can be used without any installation efforts. In the demo version the initial model is fixed to the 2×2 board shown in Fig. 1 due to memory limitations on the server. A browser-based version for custom installations, which is not restricted to the Pacman model, is available for download at

http://www.modelevolution.org/prototypes/mococl.

5   A First Experimental Case Study

We performed an evaluation of cOCL's and MocOCL's *usability* and *performance*. In both cases we used the Pacman game described above because (i) its game play is simple and (ii) its complexity can be increased easily by raising the number of fields on the game board or the number of ghosts.

Table 2. Evaluation results based on self–estimated proficiency

Prior Knowledge	Exercises			Subjective Evaluation		
	Low	Medium	High	Low	Medium	High
Structural Models	12	8	10.5	8	7.5	7
Behavioral Models	8	10.1	11	7	7.7	6
OCL	12	9.6	11.5	8	6.9	8
Graph transform.	10	9.4	11.7	7.3	6.8	7.7
Standard Logics	9.5	10.3	10.4	5	7.4	8
Temporal Logics	10.4	9.9	–	6.8	8.3	–
Model checkers	10	–	10.4	6.5	–	8.0

5.1   Usability

Experimental Setup. Concerning the evaluation of the usability of our verification framework, we are interested in(i) the intuitiveness of the cOCL language, i.e., the combination of OCL expressions and temporal operators, and (ii) the usability of MocOCL's user interface, most notably the presentation of the cause. Thus, we conducted a series of qualitative, semi-structured interviews with 11 researchers with expertise in MBE or in formal verification, and some in both. Each test person was interviewed separately for one to two hours. The interviews were structured as follows.

The interview started with an introduction to model checking in the context of MBE. The Pacman game discussed in Section 2 served as the running example. Depending on the expertise of the test persons, background on either structural and behavioral modeling or model checking was given to ensure a common level of understanding. Next, the cOCL language was presented with several examples similar to those in Table 1. Then, the test persons had to solve exercises and were encouraged to use MocOCL's web interface to find the solutions. These exercises were grouped into three blocks, each block raising the level of difficulty gently. First, the test persons were required to match a set of cOCL expressions to their corresponding natural language explanations. Next, the test persons were asked to explain the meaning of several cOCL expressions in natural language. Finally, the test persons had to formulate cOCL expressions on their own. The last question of the exercises the test person to assert required whether the game is over after Pacman finds the treasure. The task setup was identical to the scenario depicted in Figure 6. In the final part of the interview the test persons were asked to provide feedback on whether it was "Easy", "Medium", "Hard", or "Infeasible" to (i) read cOCL expressions, (ii) write cOCL expressions, and (iii) use MocOCL's interface.

The questionnaire used during the interview, including the exercises and the subjective evaluation, is shown in the extended technical report.

Results. All participants successfully revealed the defect in the graph transformation rule *Move Ghost* (Fig. 2) with the help of MocOCL. Even in this small example, however, only few of the test persons were able to detect the defect without the tool. Thus, we may conclude that MocOCL is supportive when model checking is performed in the context of MBE. The interviews also showed that some background on CTL is indispensable to apply the temporal operators and path quantifiers correctly. While most participants reported that reading the cOCL expressions is intuitive, test persons without any prior exposition to formal verification and model checking in particular expressed difficulties phrasing such expressions on their own. In particular, the existential path quantifier which wo originally called "sometimes" caused confusion among the test persons and many suggested to use the more intuitive term "exists". To avoid the name clash and ambiguities with OCL's exists operator we revised cOCL's concrete syntax such that (i) all cOCL keywords are capitalized and (ii) the keyword Exists was introduced as an additional existential path quantifier. Further feedback resulted in slight visualization improvements; in particular, we now color start and end nodes of the evaluation trace.

Table 2 summarizes the overall evaluation results. Initially each participant was asked to provide a self-assessment of his/her expertise in various domains that we considered relevant for using MocOCL. Each participant was then assigned to his/her matching expertise group ("Low", "Medium" or "High") in each domain.

The table contains the average number of points given by persons of a specific expertise group in a certain domain. In total, a person could score a maximum number of twelve points in the exercise part and award up to nine points during the subjective evaluation. Each task was awarded either zero points for a wrong or missing answer, one point for a partially correct answer, i.e. the use of $\rightarrow$ instead of the OCL implies, and two points for a completely correct answer. The first block, was considered an single task while the three cOCL expressions which had to be interpreted and the two cOCL expressions which had to be written were considered as individual tasks each. A test person that solves the matching task and provide the correct meaning of two cOCL expressions and only a single, partially correct, solution for writing a cOCL expression scores seven points.

For the subjective evaluation, each person had to decide how hard "Reading cOCL", "Writing cOCL" and "Tool use" were. The answer "Easy" yielded three points, "Medium" two points, "Hard" one point and "Infeasible" zero points. The total value is the sum of values for answers for the individual domains. A test person that experienced *reading cOCL* was easy, *writing cOCL* was hard, and *using the tool* was medium awards six out of nine points.

Discussion. The evaluation provided valuable insights on the usability of our tool. However, to obtain statistically relevant results we have to increase the number and the diversification of our test persons. We plan to contribute such an extensive user study in the course of our Model Engineering class, a master course offered during the winter term providing a test-bed of up to 100 students.

Overall, we could observe a trend that the knowledge of behavioral models and logics increases the odds of successfully applying MocOCL to verification tasks, while expertise in graph transformations, OCL, and standard modeling does not.

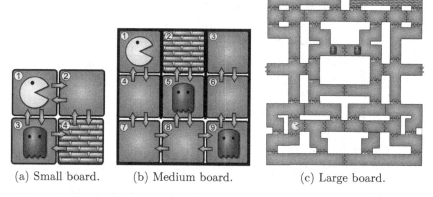

| (a) Small board. | (b) Medium board. | (c) Large board. |

Fig. 7. Different configurations of the Pacman game used for the evaluation

In contrast, persons knowing model checking and logics, but not knowing graph transformations gave lower ratings in the subjective evaluation.

We concluded that MocOCL should provide other facilities to specify dynamic behavior, for example, state machines or a subset of the Java programming language. In future evaluations, we will also have to consider direct comparisons to other tools like GROOVE.

Additional feedback that we received is hard to capture by facts in tables. This includes the way some people were interested in using the tool by playing around with various features. This encouraging observation seems to confirm the chosen approach of how to realize MocOCL. In contrast, the language itself seems to be too hard for immediate use since no one tried out custom expressions beyond those required for the tasks. Finally, even though the interviews were scheduled for a duration of up to two hours, we felt that the time required for an in–depth evaluation with a single person should be even higher. As this seems to expect too much from a volunteering test person we plan to restructure the exercise part such that the tasks can be solved before the actual interview.

5.2 Performance

Experimental Setup. In order to asses the performance of our implementation, we measured runtimes required for different board sizes and different numbers of ghosts. Along these parameters we are able to scale the size of the state space and observe the behavior of our tool with increasing state space sizes. An upper bound for the state space size is $n^{(g+1)}$ with n being the number of fields and g being the number of ghosts. The initial configurations of the used boards are shown in Fig. 7. We ran our performance tests with three different configurations, (i) a 2×2 board with one ghost (Fig. 7(a)), (ii) a 3×3 board with two ghosts (Fig. 7(b)), and (iii) a maze of 34 fields with zero, one, and two ghosts (Fig. 7(c)).

On each game configuration, we evaluated the following three queries:

- `Always Globally true`
- `Exists Eventually pacman.on.treasure`

Table 3. Runtimes of MocOCL (times are given in ms)

	Field	Gh.	St.	gentime		evaltime		total	
				avg	std	avg	std	avg	std
State space generation	small	1	16	25	6.1	20	5.9	46	7
	medium	2	405	1051	623.3	114	42.6	1165	657.6
	large	0	34	128	63.8	20	5.1	148	68.9
	large	1	1156	7712	381.4	258	68.6	7970	437.4
	large	2	20230	213k	16.3k	5164	432.6	218k	16.4k
Pacman on treasure	small	1	10	19	21.3	29	2.4	48	22.4
	medium	2	120	124	18.3	63	19.9	188	36.2
	large	0	34	85	9.9	28	0.4	113	10
	large	1	631	1932	57.8	114	28.9	2046	38.9
	large	2	6920	30685	167.9	1819	34.5	32504	187.3
Pacman wins	small	1	10	15	19.7	65	9.7	80	19
	medium	2	176	128	115.4	266	94.8	393	128.3
	large	0	34	88	18.1	45	7.4	133	18.9
	large	1	631	2095	223.5	316	66.3	2411	224.6
	large	2	6920	22878	557.8	10772	16.2	33650	566.1

– Exists Eventually pacman.on.treasure and
  ghosts->forAll(g | g.on <> pacman.on)

Although the first expression is trivially true, MocOCL traverses the entire state space to assert its correctness because it does not implement any simplification rules for the input query yet. Thus, we use this first expression to analyze MocOCL's runtime behavior when traversing state spaces of different sizes. The second expression queries whether Pacman eventually finds a treasure. The last query contains a more complicated OCL sub-expression in order to validate if Pacman can always win the game. The experiments were performed on an Intel i5-2410M Machine with 2.30 GHz and 8 GB RAM.

Results. The runtimes of our experiments are summarized in Table 3. The first query is called *state space generation*, the second query is called *Pacman on treasure*, and the third query is called *Pacman wins*. The column *Gh.* contains the number of ghosts and the column *St.* contains the number of generated states. Further, the table shows the overall runtime of our tool (column *total*), which we split into the time necessary to generate the state space (column *gentime*) and the time required to evaluate the cOCL expressions (column *evaltime*) by caching the state space. We repeated each run five times and report the average runtime as well as the standard deviation. Overall all queries could be answered within less than five minutes. But if we add a third ghost to the large field, the 8 GB of memory are insufficient to answer the given queries.

Discussion. In its current state, we observe that our tool is not competitive in terms of performance, even without a direct comparison to other tools. For the moment, however, we clearly focus on the tight integration of OCL and model checking-based verification, not so much on the performance. This is directly reflected in the performance results of the current implementation shown in Table 3, which we discuss in the following. We observe a high standard deviation for all expressions when run on the more complicated 3×3–field. We suspect this to be due to the various online JVM optimizations. These optimizations are also likely the cause for the generation time of the "Pacman wins"–expression being significantly lower then the generation time of the "Pacman on treasure"–expression even though the same number of states are generated. The excessive increase in evaluation time for the "Pacman wins"–expression for more ghosts originates from the forAll–expression covering a different number of ghosts. In the case of no ghosts, the expression just needs to ensure that there are no ghosts in each state which is fast. In the case of one or more ghosts, the expression has to check that the position of each ghost is different to the position of Pacman.

Our approach scales approximately as well as comparable solutions like GROOVE. Our benchmarks show that our implementation spends significant amounts of time on both the state space generation and the evaluation of the cOCL expression; thus, it is sensible to look into improvements in both areas. A more efficient cOCL evaluation might also reduce the state space generation time if fewer states need to be generated.

6   Related Work

We discuss related works focusing on temporal extensions for OCL first, followed by reviews of model checkers that verify whether a system, whose structure and behavior is described by (graphical) models, satisfies its specification. For an in-depth discussion on verification approaches in the context of MBE we refer the interested reader to [13].

Temporal Extensions. Distefano et al. [8] propose a CTL-based logic, called BOTL, to specify static and dynamic properties of object-oriented systems. But instead of extending OCL, they map OCL onto BOTL; hence, they provide formal semantics for a large part of OCL based on BOTL. Ziemann et al. [29] suggest an extension based on linear time logic, which is similar in nature to our CTL-based solution. Soden and Eichler [26] also present a linear time-based extension for OCL and define the operational semantics of MOF-conforming models with the Model Execution Framework for Eclipse (MXF) [27]. This allows them to describe a finite execution trace through a sequence of changes. Flake and Mueller [12] use state charts to describe the behavior of associated class diagrams and time-based traces to capture the execution of the system. They propose a UML Profile to specify state-oriented, real-time invariants, whose semantics are defined by a mapping to clocked CTL formulas. Bradfield et al. [5] embed OCL into the observational μ-calculus. They suggest the use of predefined templates with intuitive semantics, from which the underlying μ-calculus formula is automatically generated. Likwise, Kanso and Taha [16] introduce a temporal extension based on Dwyer *et al.*'s patterns for the specification of properties for finite state systems [10]. They define a scenario-based semantics for their extension, where each scenario is a finite sequence of events.

Verification Engines. Mullins and Oarga [22] present EOCL, an extension inspired by BOTL, that augments OCL with CTL operators. The operational semantics of EOCL are defined over object-oriented transition systems. They announce and describe SOCLe, a tool that translates class, state chart, and object diagrams into an abstract state machine and checks on-the-fly if the system satisfies a given EOCL specification.The GROOVE framework [17] verifies object-oriented systems modeled as attributed, type graphs with inheritance relations. It is similar to MocOCL in that it represents system states as graphs and the system's behavior by graph transformations. But, in contrast, it uses standard CTL and LTL to formulate the system's specification. Recently, abstraction techniques have been implemented to handle infinite state spaces by over-approximating system behaviors [23]. Al-Lail *et al.* [20] describe systems with class diagrams and the operations' contracts, given by OCL pre- and postconditions, capture the behavior of the system. They use TOCL [29] to specify reachability and safety properties. Their model checker builds a *Snapshot Transition Model* that consists of snapshots, which represent a state of the system, and transitions, which run from source states that satisfy an operation's precondition to target states that satisfy the postcondition. With the USE Model Validator [28] they perform a depth-bounded search for sequences of snapshots that violate the specification and, if one is found, visualizes the violating sequence as a UML sequence diagram. Dingel et al. [21,30] verify UML–RT state machines symbolically using a CTL–extension without transforming to another model checker, but representing their models as Functional Finite State Machines. In contrast to MocOCL, OCL is not part of their language.

To the best of our knowledge, MocOCL is currently the only framework that (i) integrates its CTL-extension seamlessly into the formal semantics of OCL, (ii) implements the evaluation of CTL operators directly within the OCL evaluation engine, and thus (iii) performs the verification and result reporting directly at the modeling layer.

7   Conclusion and Future Work

In this paper, we present syntax and semantics of cOCL, our OCL extension with CTL-based temporal operators. Further, we describe the implementation and technical feasibility of our MocOCL model checker that verifies cOCL specifications of software systems, whose static structure is described by Ecore-conformant models and whose behavior is defined by a set of graph transformations. We conducted a first user study, where we invited colleagues to solve a set of verification tasks with our tool. The results of this user study are already incorporated into MocOCL and they improved, among others, the concrete syntax of cOCL.

A performance evaluation shows that our approach is able to verify models of various sizes. With increasing state space sizes, memory consumption becomes a major issue. This is, however, an inherent problem of model checking in general, which suffers from the state explosion problem and, for practical application, several tuning techniques can be applied. In our current prototype, we do not use such techniques yet. Thus, in future work, we plan to employ symbolic model checking and abstraction techniques to improve runtimes and memory consumption.

Besides technical issues we are also interested in improving the usability of our tool. The aim is (i) to further explore the intuitiveness of the combination of temporal operators and OCL expressions and (ii) the presentation of the evaluation result, in particular, with respect to the reconstructability of the cause. A larger user study is planned to improve future versions of the tool.

References

1. Arendt, T., Biermann, E., Jurack, S., Krause, C., Taentzer, G.: Henshin: Advanced Concepts and Tools for In-Place EMF Model Transformations. In: Petriu, D.C., Rouquette, N., Haugen, Ø. (eds.) MODELS 2010, Part I. LNCS, vol. 6394, pp. 121–135. Springer, Heidelberg (2010)
2. Baier, C., Katoen, J.P.: Principles of model checking. MIT Press (2008)
3. Bill, R., Gabmeyer, S., Kaufmann, P., Seidl, M.: OCL meets CTL: Towards CTL-Extended OCL Model Checking. In: Kleine Büning, H. (ed.) CSL 1995. LNCS, vol. 1092, pp. 13–22. Springer, Heidelberg (1996)
4. Bill, R., Gabmeyer, S., Kaufmann, P., Seidl, M.: Model Checking of CTL-Extended OCL Specifications. Tech. Rep. BIG-TR-2014-2, E188 - Institut für Softwaretechnik und Interaktive Systeme; Technische Universität Wien (2014)
5. Bradfield, J.C., Küster Filipe, J., Stevens, P.: Enriching OCL Using Observational Mu-Calculus. In: Kutsche, R.-D., Weber, H. (eds.) FASE 2002. LNCS, vol. 2306, pp. 203–217. Springer, Heidelberg (2002)
6. Clarke, E.M., Emerson, E.A.: Design and Synthesis of Synchronization Skeletons Using Branching-Time Temporal Logic. In: Kozen, D. (ed.) Logic of Programs 1981. LNCS, vol. 131, pp. 52–71. Springer, Heidelberg (1982)
7. Clarke, E.M., Grumberg, O., Peled, D.: Model checking. MIT Press (1999)
8. Distefano, D., Katoen, J.-P., Rensink, A.: On a Temporal Logic for Object-Based Systems. In: Formal Methods for Open Object-Based Distributed Systems IV. IFIP AICT, vol. 49, pp. 305–325. Springer, Heidelberg (2000)
9. D'Silva, V., Kroening, D., Weissenbacher, G.: A Survey of Automated Techniques for Formal Software Verification. IEEE Transactions on Computer-Aided Design of Integrated Circuits and Systems 27(7), 1165–1178 (2008)
10. Dwyer, M.B., Avrunin, G.S., Corbett, J.C.: Patterns in Property Specifications for Finite-State Verification. In: Proceedings of the 21st International Conference on Software Engineering, pp. 411–420. ACM (1999)
11. Ehrig, H., Ehrig, K., Prange, U., Taentzer, G.: Fundamentals of Algebraic Graph Transformation. Springer (2006)
12. Flake, S., Müller, W.: Formal semantics of static and temporal state-oriented OCL constraints. Software and System Modeling 2(3), 164–186 (2003)

13. Gabmeyer, S., Kaufmann, P., Seidl, M.: A feature-based classification of formal verification techniques for software models. Tech. Rep. BIG-TR-2014-1, Institut für Softwaretechnik und Interaktive Systeme; Technische Universität Wien (2014)
14. Jhala, R., Majumdar, R.: Software model checking. ACM Comput. Surv. 41(4) (2009)
15. Jussila, T., Dubrovin, J., Junttila, T., Latvala, T.L., Porres, I.: Model Checking Dynamic and Hierarchical UML State Machines. In: Models in Software Engineering. LNCS, vol. 4364, p. 15. Springer (2006)
16. Kanso, B., Taha, S.: Temporal Constraint Support for OCL. In: Czarnecki, K., Hedin, G. (eds.) SLE 2012. LNCS, vol. 7745, pp. 83–103. Springer, Heidelberg (2013)
17. Kastenberg, H., Rensink, A.: Model Checking Dynamic States in GROOVE. In: Valmari, A. (ed.) SPIN 2006. LNCS, vol. 3925, pp. 299–305. Springer, Heidelberg (2006)
18. Kern, C., Greenstreet, M.R.: Formal Verification in Hardware Design: A Survey. ACM Transactions on Design Automation of Electronic Systems (TODAES) 4(2), 123–193 (1999)
19. Knapp, A., Wuttke, J.: Model Checking of UML 2.0 Interactions. In: Kühne, T. (ed.) MoDELS 2006. LNCS, vol. 4364, pp. 42–51. Springer, Heidelberg (2007)
20. Lail, M.A., Abdunabi, R., France, R., Ray, I.: An Approach to Analyzing Temporal Properties in UML Class Models. In: Proceedings of the 10th International Workshop on Model Driven Engineering, Verification and Validation (MoDeVVa 2013). CEUR Workshop Proceedings, vol. 1069, pp. 77–86. CEUR-WS.org (2013)
21. Moffett, Y., Dingel, J., Beaulieu, A.: Verifying Protocol Conformance Using Software Model Checking for the Model-Driven Development of Embedded Systems. IEEE Software Engineering 39(9), 1307–13256 (2013)
22. Mullins, J., Oarga, R.: Model Checking of Extended OCL Constraints on UML Models in SOCLe. In: Bonsangue, M.M., Johnsen, E.B. (eds.) FMOODS 2007. LNCS, vol. 4468, pp. 59–75. Springer, Heidelberg (2007)
23. Rensink, A., Zambon, E.: Neighbourhood Abstraction in GROOVE. ECEASST 32, 44–56
24. Richters, M., Gogolla, M.: OCL: Syntax, Semantics, and Tools. In: Clark, A., Warmer, J. (eds.) Object Modeling with the OCL. LNCS, vol. 2263, pp. 42–68. Springer, Heidelberg (2002)
25. Selic, B.: What will it take? A view on adoption of model-based methods in practice. Software and Systems Modeling 11, 513–526 (2012)
26. Soden, M., Eichler, H.: Temporal Extensions of OCL Revisited. In: Paige, R.F., Hartman, A., Rensink, A. (eds.) ECMDA-FA 2009. LNCS, vol. 5562, pp. 190–205. Springer, Heidelberg (2009)
27. Soden, M., Eichler, H.: Towards a model execution framework for Eclipse. In: Proceedings of the 1st Workshop on Behaviour Modelling in Model-Driven Architecture, Enschede, the Netherlands, pp. 1–4. ACM Press, New York (2009)
28. Soeken, M., Wille, R., Kuhlmann, M., Gogolla, M., Drechsler, R.: Verifying UML/OCL models using Boolean satisfiability. In: Design, Automation and Test in Europe, pp. 1341–1344. IEEE (2010)
29. Ziemann, P., Gogolla, M.: OCL Extended with Temporal Logic. In: Broy, M., Zamulin, A.V. (eds.) PSI 2003. LNCS, vol. 2890, pp. 351–357. Springer, Heidelberg (2004)
30. Zurowska, K., Dingel, J.: Model Checking of UML-RT Models Using Lazy Composition. In: Moreira, A., Schätz, B., Gray, J., Vallecillo, A., Clarke, P. (eds.) MODELS 2013. LNCS, vol. 8107, pp. 304–319. Springer, Heidelberg (2013)

Unifying and Generalizing Relations
in Role-Based Data Modeling and Navigation

Daco Harkes and Eelco Visser

Delft University of Technology, The Netherlands
d.c.harkes@student.tudelft.nl, visser@acm.org

Abstract. Object-oriented programming languages support concise navigation of relations represented by references. However, relations are not first-class citizens and bidirectional navigation is not supported. The relational paradigm provides first-class relations, but with bidirectional navigation through verbose queries. We present a systematic analysis of approaches to modeling and navigating relations. By unifying and generalizing the features of these approaches, we developed the design of a data modeling language that features first-class relations, n-ary relations, native multiplicities, bidirectional relations and concise navigation.

1 Introduction

Object-oriented programming languages model data with object graphs. Navigation through object graphs is simple; following references leads to related objects. But references in object graphs are one-directional and cannot be navigated backwards. Bidirectional navigation can be obtained by storing references on both sides of relations between objects. But keeping such redundant references consistent requires bookkeeping code. By contrast, relational databases support bidirectional navigation. Foreign keys can be used in queries to navigate both ways. There is no need for redundant references. Queries are however not as concise as navigation through references.

Proposals for object-oriented languages with first-class relations provide bidirectional navigation [3]. These languages remove the need for manually keeping references consistent but navigation is done through querying, which is still verbose. There are modeling techniques that are yet different from object-oriented and relational modeling: Object-Role modeling [7], Entity-Relationship modeling [6], UML [10] and undirected graphs.

In this paper, we present a systematic analysis of the design space of relations in data modeling and present a new data modeling language that unifies and generalizes relations. In particular, our contributions are:

- We extrapolate Steimann's approach [19] to model multiplicities using annotations in Java to *native multiplicities* that are integrated into the type system (Section 2).
- A systematic analysis of approaches to modeling relations (Section 3).

B. Combemale et al. (Eds.): SLE 2014, LNCS 8706, pp. 241–260, 2014.
© Springer International Publishing Switzerland 2014

```
class Student { }

class Course {
  @any(ArrayList.class) Student student;

  void addStudent(@any(ArrayList.class) Student s){
    this.student += s;
  }
}
```

Fig. 1. Multiplicity annotations in Java

- A new relational data modeling language featuring native multiplicities, bidirectional navigation, n-ary relations, first-class relations, and concise navigation expressions based on the analysis (Section 4).
- A formal definition of the type system (Section 5) and operational semantics (Section 6) of this language.

2   Native Multiplicities

The first thing we need to fix to get relations right is the treatment of their cardinality or *multiplicity*. Encoding of *to-many* relations as associations to collections results in a discontinuity in programming style [19]:

- Navigating *one-to-one* and *many-to-one* relations produces singleton values, while navigating through *one-to-many* and *many-to-many* relations produces collections of values. Thus, the caller has to unwrap the result before using it; for example by using an iterator.
- The caller has to deal with different sub-type substitution conditions. Suppose **Student** extends **Person**. Assigning an **Student** to a **Person** is fine (*to-one*), but trying to assign Set<Student> to Set<Person> will trigger a type error (*to-many*).
- The call semantics is call-by-value for *to-one* and call-by-reference for *to-many*. Collection objects are passed by reference, so that they can be modified the callee. Call-by-value semantics for collections requires immutable collections.

Multiplicity Annotations. To address these issues, Steimann proposes an extension of regular object-oriented programming with multiplicities [19]. He presents an extension of Java with multiplicity. Expressions of a singleton value type can return an arbitrary number of objects of this type. Figure 1 illustrates the approach with a small example in which a **Course** has an association to **Student**. Through the @any annotation the association is declared to be to-many instead of using a collection type.

```
class Student {
  String! name;
  Course* courses;
  int! numCourses(){ return count(this.courses); }
}
class Course {
  Student* students;
  void addStudent(Student+ s){ this.students += s; }
  int? avgNumCourses(){ return avg(this.students.numCourses()); }
}
```

Fig. 2. Native multiplicities in Java

Native Multiplicities. We have extrapolated Steimann's annotations based approach and integrated multiplicities into the type system to arrive at *native* multiplicities. Type expressions use one of the following four multiplicity operators (similar to regular expressions) to denote the possible range of values:

- t? is $[0, 1]$ an optional value of type t
- t! is $[1, 1]$ a required value of type t
- t* is $[0, n)$ zero or more values of type t
- t+ is $[1, n)$ one or more values of type t

The ! can be omitted as $[1, 1]$ is the default multiplicity.

As a sketch, Figure 2 illustrates native multiplicities in an extension of Java. We have not formalized an extension of Java, but rather integrated native multiplicities in our relational data modeling language. In Section 5 we formalize a type system for that language including multiplicities. The type system ensures that the actual number of values at run-time is always inside the specified range. For example, assigning an optional string (a value of type String?) to a student.name will trigger a type error: *multiplicity error:* $[1, 1]$ *expected,* $[0, 1]$ *given.* Our language also supports expected multiplicities for function arguments. The built-in function count handles any multiplicity and any type and it returns exactly one integer with the number of values passed. The built-in function avg also handles $[0, n)$ values and the argument type must be numeric. The return multiplicity of avg depends on its input multiplicity. If a programmer supplies $[0, n)$ as input the return multiplicity will be $[0, 1]$. The average of no values does not exist, so no value will be returned in that case. If the programmer supplies $[1, n)$ as input the return multiplicity is $[1, 1]$. With at least one value there is always an average computable. We use this model of multiplicities, reasoning over ranges, in the type system of our language.

3   Design Space for Role-Based Relations

There are several proposals in the literature for extending data modeling to better support data modeling with relations. This section presents a systematic analysis of the design space of relations in data modeling taking in into account these proposals. Figures 3 and 4 summarize the complete design space in tabular form emphasizing its regularities. From this analysis a new data modeling language emerges which unifies and generalizes the various approaches to modeling relations.

In all our examples we assume the language to have native multiplicities instead of using collections that would be needed in a plain OO approach. The running example data model defines `Students` who are enrolled in `Courses`, sometimes via a first-class `Enrollment` relation. For the sake of the example, students can be enrolled in zero or more courses (`*` multiplicity), and courses should have at least one student (`+` multiplicity). In the example expressions we use `Student` 'bob' and `Course` 'math'. For each point in the design space we give a type graph diagram describing the data model, a textual specification of the data model, and expressions for querying the model. For the expressions we use `=>` to express the result of evaluation.

3.1 Overview

Before discussing each point in the design space (Figures 3 and 4) individually, we first introduce the categories represented by the columns and rows.

Columns: Four Modeling Paradigms. The four columns in the design space represent four modeling paradigms.

Object-Oriented. Relations between objects are defined through reference valued attributes, which can be navigated in one direction only. The name of the relation is the name of the attribute in the source class. The relation is unknown to the target class. A relation can also be modeled by, redundantly, maintaining a reference attribute on the other side of the relation, as well, allowing bidirectional navigation. However, this requires code for keeping the two sides of the relation consistent. We do not cover models with redundant information in our design-space analysis, as this is an undesirable property.

Relational. In a relational database schema references are expressed as foreign keys; an identifier corresponds to a memory address and a foreign key to a reference into memory. An important difference is that these references can be navigated in two directions through queries in a query language (SQL). ER and UML diagrams are also located in this column, but they only provide schema definitions, not queries. Because queries are verbose we introduce our own notation for forward and backward navigation through references. For forward navigation we use the the normal field access notation. For backward navigation from an object o we need to find all the objects of type T that refer to o through references r, which is expressed by `o<-(T.r)`. For example, to find the students enrolled in a course c we use the navigation expression `c<-(Student.courses)`.

Object-Role Modeling. A distinguishing feature of ORM [7] is that associations between objects have a different name on both sides. This conceptually solves the problem of not being able to refer to a reference backwards. Similarly, inverse properties in WebDSL [20] tie two fields in different classes together as inverses.

Graph databases. In contrast to the directed edges in the previous three paradigms, graph databases feature undirected edges. In this model the edge names are defined in both source and target namespaces. As with the ORM paradigm there is always a name available in the namespace of participating objects, but in this case this name is identical for both sides. There is one disadvantage of this model: modeling asymmetric same type relations is nontrivial. Consider a `TreeNode` with a parent and children. If a node p has a parent edge to another node q, then q also has a parent edge to p. This can be solved through indirection (J and K), but that is not particularly elegant.

Rows: Three Relation Models. The three rows in the design space correspond to three ways of modeling a relation.

Edge. The simplest way of representing a relation is through an edge between two nodes (either directed or undirected). This is a concise way of specifying a relation but it has the disadvantage that the relation is not a first-class citizen (see below). Also it is not possible to declare ternary, or higher arity, relations with edges.

Tuple (Ordered Roles). By lifting relations to objects they become *first-class citizens*, i.e. relations can have attributes, and relations can be the subject in other relations. A relation object modeled as a tuple has ordered roles. The absence of role names requires the order (or position) of the roles to be used for navigation. For binary relations this entails four predefined navigation operators (see E). But for higher arity relations 2^n operators are required, which does not scale.

Object (Named Roles). Giving the roles in a relation names makes navigation understandable and makes modeling n-ary relations feasible.

3.2   Detailed Description of Points in Design Space

We discuss each of the points A to K in the design space (Figures 3 and 4).

Object-Oriented (A, B and C). There are multiple patterns for modeling relations in objected-oriented languages [16]. As mentioned before, we replace collections by multiplicities and do not consider patterns with redundant references for bidirectional navigation. Three basic patterns remain: reference (A), relation tuple (B), and relation class (C), which we assume to be familiar to the reader. It is noteworthy that a language extension is not required for the representation

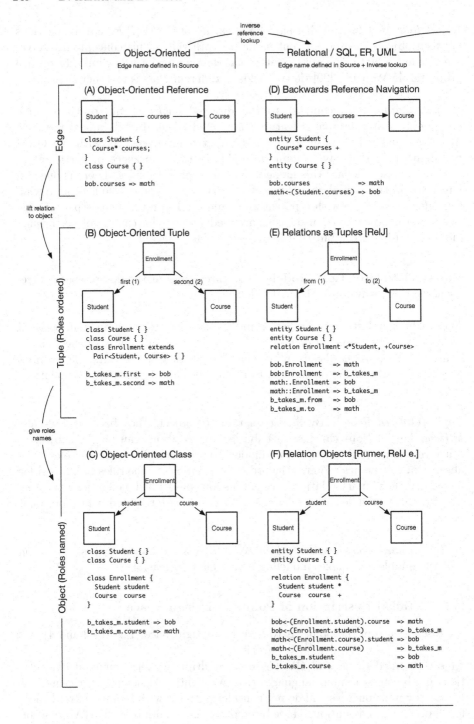

Fig. 3. Design space of relations in data modeling and navigation (part 1)

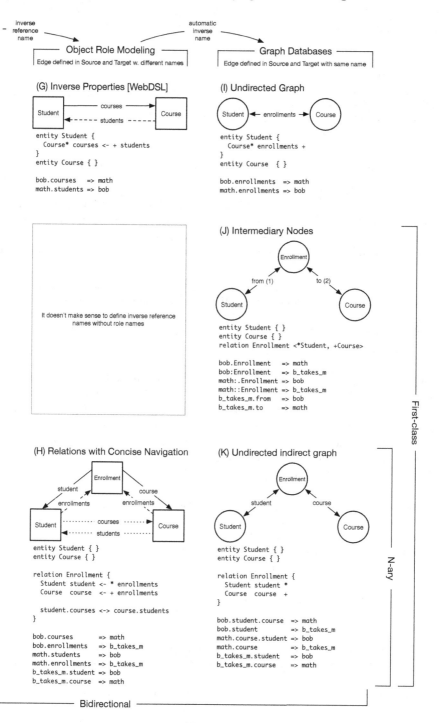

Fig. 4. Design space of relations in data modeling and navigation (part 2)

```
class Student { }
class Course { }
relationship Enrollment (Student, Course) { int grade; }

bob.Enrollment          // bob's courses
bob:Enrollment          // Enrollment-type relation objects
bob:Enrollment.grade
b_takes_m.from          // bob
b_takes_m.to            // math
```

Fig. 5. First-class citizen tuple based relations in RelJ [4]

of first-class relations. The term first-class is sometimes used for having a dedicated language construct, but a dedicated language construct is not required for adding attributes to relations or letting relations participate in other relations. First-class relations based on tuples (B) have been implemented as a Java library [15].

Backwards reference navigation (D). If we extend an object-oriented language with facilities for backwards reference lookup (`o<-(T.r)`) we can use a single reference for bidirectional navigation. Note that in this case the object graph is identical to the single reference pattern (A).

Relation as Tuples (E). The RelJ Java extension lifts relations to tuple objects [4]. In RelJ different operators are used to disambiguate between different navigation operations (Figure 5). RelJ provides no facilities for bidirectional navigation. However, that is not a conceptual limitation. Adding two operators (`:.` and `::`) would allow backward navigation, as suggested in (E). While this is theoretically extensible to relations with more than two participants, it requires adding new operators for each participant.

Relation Objects (F). Naming roles allows usable extension to n-ary relations. This is the model used by Rumer [2,3] as illustrated in Figure 6. While Rumer's implementation does not support n-ary relations, it provides the ingredients needed for n-ary relations: role names and first-class citizenship. A proposed extension for RelJ [22] adds names to roles, as illustrated in Figure 7, and is essentially equivalent to Rumer's syntax. As an alternative query syntax, we propose `math<-(Enrollment.course).student`, which is closer to the usual navigation syntax: from an object (`math`) find all relations with that object in one of its roles (`Enrollment.course`), and produce objects in the other role (`student`). All these notations are rather verbose, even if more concise than full blown SQL queries. We would prefer a more concise notation for navigating n-ary relations.

Inverse Properties (G) WebDSL [20] supports bidirectional navigation without a verbose syntax for inverse lookups by means of *inverse properties* [9] as illustrated in Figure 8. Explicit names on both sides of an association simplifies navigation to just following named references. However, these names have to be

```
class Student { }
class Course { }
relationship Enrollment participants (Student student, Course course) {
  int grade;
}
Enrollment.select(s_c: s_c.course == math).student; // math students
```

Fig. 6. First-class relations with named roles in Rumer [2,3]

```
class Student { }
class Course { }
relationship Enrollment
    extends Relation (Student student, Course course, Student tutor) {
  int grade;
}
Enrollment[course == math].student; // math students
```

Fig. 7. Ternary relation extension proposal for RelJ [22]

defined in both the source and target class. In (G) we have normalized this to a single property definition with two names; the second name is used for the backwards reference from target to source.

Concise Relations (H). Combining the advantages of (F) and (G), we arrive at our proposal for a unified and generalized approach to modeling relations (H). Relations are first-class citizens: (1) relations can have attributes and (2) relations can be the subject in other relations. In addition, relations can have any number of roles (n-ary relations). By explicitly providing a name for the navigation between each pair of participants in the relation we get concise navigation expressions: (1) from relation to participant and back (b_takes_m.student and bob.enrollments), and (2) from participant to other participant (bob.courses) and back (math.students). Instead of defining these names in the source and target classes, as in (G), all names are introduced in the relation. The declaration of a role T r <- m i introduces a role r of type T with inverse i with multiplicity m. This provides navigation from relation to participant through r and navigation from participant to relation through i. A declaration r1.n1 <-> r2.n2 introduces names for navigation between participants: r1.n1 leads to r2 and r2.n2 leads to r1. In contrast to (G), these declarations do not introduce attributes in the participant classes, but rather shortcuts. For example, bob.courses is a shortcut for bob.enrollments.course. This approach naturally extends to n-ary relations, as illustrated in Figure 9.

```
entity Student { courses : Set<Course> }
entity Course { students : Set<Student> (inverse=Student.courses) }
math.students  // math students
bob.courses    // bobs courses
```

Fig. 8. Inverse properties in WebDSL

```
entity Student { }
entity Course { }
relation Enrollment {
  Student student <- * enrollments
  Course  course  <- + enrollments
  Student tutor   <- * tutoring

  student.courses <-> course.students
  student.tutors  <-> tutor.students
  course.tutors   <-> tutor.courses
}
```

Fig. 9. Ternary relation with concise navigation (H) (this paper)

Undirected Graphs (I, J, K). Graph databases also feature three relation patterns. The simple edge (I), adding an intermediary node without role names (J), and an intermediary node with role names (K). Since without edge names, edge directionality does not matter (J) is equivalent to (E). So we will only cover (I) and (K).

The simple edge (I) cannot be used to model asymmetric same type relations. Asymmetric relations of the different types can be disambiguated by the type one starts navigating from, but if both participants have the same type their role is ambiguous. Disambiguation can be done through indirection (I or K). With indirection (K) navigation from participant to participant is navigating two edges. With undirected edges role names cannot be reused with different relations concerning the same entity. Consider adding another relation where Course also participates as course. math. course now becomes ambiguous. The language could then be extended with the type of the node navigating to, but this is equivalent to the backwards reference navigation: naming the edge and the type on the other side. So that would bring us back at (F).

It seems there is a fundamental trade-off between undirected and directed graphs when considering reference names. The directed graph (column two) requires an extra identifier (the target type) to navigate edges backwards. To get rid of this extra identifier we can automatically define the edge name on both sides. This is gets us to the undirected graph (column four). In undirected graphs we have ambiguities. Adding an extra identifier (the target type) to disambiguate brings us back at the directed graphs.

4   A Relational Data Modeling Language

We have designed a language for data modeling featuring native multiplicities, bidirectional navigation, n-ary relations, first-class relations, and concise navigation expressions based on point (H) in the design space. In this section we discuss two extensions of the basic idea of (H) and the grammar of the language. In the next sections we give a formal definition of the type system and operational semantics.

```
relation Enrollment { Student* Course+ }
```

expands to (lower case participant type, lower case relation type, add s for * and +)

```
relation Enrollment {
  Student student <- * enrollments
  Course  course  <- + enrollments
}
```

expands to (use role name, add s for * and +)

```
relation Enrollment {
  Student student <- * enrollments
  Course  course  <- + enrollments
  student.courses <-> course.students
}
```

Fig. 10. Expansion of concise relation definition

```
entity Student {
  Int? avgGrade = avg( this.enrollments.grade )
}
```

Fig. 11. Relations language with derivation

Concise Definition of Relations. While navigation according to (H) is very concise, the definition of a relation is somewhat verbose due to the introduction of names for each of the arrows in the diagram. In many cases we can derive these names from the types of the roles. Figure 10 illustrates how a definition with implicit names is expanded to a definition with explicit names. This automatic expansion can of course lead to name collisions, for example if the participant classes have an attribute with a name introduced by a relation. In this case the programmer has to (partially) specify names explicitly.

Derived Attributes. To express business logic in data models, we extend entities and relations with *derived attributes*. The value of a derived attribute is described in terms of the values of other attributes and relations as illustrated in Figure 11. Thus, if one of the underlying values changes, the derived attribute is updated.

Grammar. The grammar of the relations language is given in Figure 12. a, i, r and t are respectively attribute, inverse, role and entity-type names. The roles, r, are the solid arrows in the design space diagram and the inverses/shortcuts, i, are the dashed and dotted arrows. a', i', r', r'', and t' refer to these names. The lookup expression (t [a == e]) is only intended to look up objects of a certain type with a certain attribute value in the heap. It is not our intention to provide a full-fledged query language; our focus is on navigation expressions.

Prototype. We have implemented this language on the language designers workbench Spoofax [11]. The prototype is publicly available.[1] The type system and semantics described in the next sections matches those of the prototype.

---

[1] https://github.com/metaborg/relationstagv0.2.0

$$Program ::= \text{model } Entity^* \text{ execute } e$$
$$Entity ::= \text{entity } t \; \{ \; Attribute^* \; \}$$
$$\qquad | \text{ relation } t \; \{ \; Attribute^* \; Role^* \; Shortcut^* \; \}$$
$$Attribute ::= p \; m \; a$$
$$\qquad | \; p \; m \; a = e$$
$$Role ::= t' \; r \; <- \; m \; i$$
$$Shortcut ::= r' \; . \; i \; <-> \; r'' \; . \; i$$
$$p \in PrimitiveType ::= \text{Boolean} \mid \text{Int} \mid \text{String}$$
$$m \in Multiplicity ::= \; ? \mid \; ! \mid \; * \mid \; +$$
$$e \in Expr ::= f \; (\; e \;) \quad | \quad e_1 \oplus e_2 \quad | \quad ! \, e \quad | \quad e_1 \, ? \, e_2 : e_3$$
$$\qquad | \; e \; . \; a' \quad | \quad e \; . \; i' \quad | \quad e \; . \; r'$$
$$\qquad | \text{ true } | \text{ false } | \; literalInt \mid literalString$$
$$\qquad | \text{ this } | \; t \; [\; a == e \;]$$
$$f \in AggrOp ::= \text{min} \mid \text{max} \mid \text{avg} \mid \text{sum} \mid \text{concat} \mid \text{count} \mid \text{conj} \mid \text{disj}$$

$$\oplus \in \{+, -, *, /, \%, \&\&, ||, >, >=, <, <=, ==, !=, <+, ++\}$$

Fig. 12. The grammar of the relations language

5   Type System

Our language features static typing. Everything in the language has both a *type* and a *multiplicity*. These are defined orthogonally.

Meta variables. In the the static and dynamic semantic rules we use a meta variables for looking up definitions on usage sites.

$$\mathcal{P} \in Program : EntityMap \times Expr$$
$$\mathcal{E} \in EntityMap : EntityName \to AttributeMap \times InverseMap \times RoleMap$$
$$\mathcal{A} \in AttributeMap : AttrName \to PrimitiveType \times Multiplicity \times Expr$$
$$\mathcal{I} \in InverseMap : InverseName \to EntityName \times RoleName \times RoleName$$
$$\mathcal{R} \in RoleMap : RoleName \to EntityName \times Multiplicity$$

A program $\mathcal{P}$ is a tuple, $(\mathcal{E}, e)$, where $\mathcal{E}$ is a map from entity (and relation) names to entity definitions and e is the main expression.

Entity definitions are triples $(\mathcal{A}, \mathcal{I}, \mathcal{R})$, where $\mathcal{A}$ is a map from attribute names to attribute definitions, $\mathcal{I}$ is a map of inverse names to their origin and $\mathcal{R}$ is a map from role names to role definitions. Both entities and relations define entities. We refer to an entity t's attribute, inverse and role map as $\mathcal{A}_t$, $\mathcal{I}_t$ and $\mathcal{R}_t$ respectively.

Attribute definitions are triples (p, m, e), where p is the primitive type, m is the multiplicity and e is the optional derivation expression. If e has no derivation expression it is equal to nil. Role definitions are tuples (t, m), where t is an entity name and m is a multiplicity. Inverse (and shortcut) definitions are triples (t, r_1, r_2) where r_1 and r_2 are roles in entity t. The inverse map definition is best explained by example:

```
entity Enrollment {
  Student student <— * enrollment
  Course  course  <— + enrollment
  student.courses <—> course.students
}
```

$$\mathcal{I}_{Student} : \text{'enrollment'} \rightarrow \text{'Enrollment'} \times \text{'student'} \times nil$$
$$\text{'courses'} \quad \rightarrow \text{'Enrollment'} \times \text{'student'} \times \text{'course'}$$
$$\mathcal{I}_{Course} : \text{'enrollment'} \rightarrow \text{'Enrollment'} \times \text{'course'} \quad \times nil$$
$$\text{'students'} \quad \rightarrow \text{'Enrollment'} \times \text{'course'} \quad \times \text{'students'}$$

The inverses of roles are mapped back to the role in the relation they are the inverse of. In this case r_2 is **nil**. The shortcut is translated to two records, one for both participant types. The inverse maps are used as the backwards reference navigation mechanism.

Lastly, to simplify static and dynamic semantics we transform the shortcut expressions to an inverse and a role expression by the transformation rule:

$$\frac{e : t_1 \quad \mathcal{I}_{t1}(i_1) = (t_2, r_1, r_2) \quad \mathcal{I}_{t1}(i_2) = (t_2, r_1, \text{nil})}{e \, . \, i_1 \; \rightarrow \; e \, . \, i_2 \, . \, r_2}$$

Types. There are two type sorts: p (*primitive types*) and t (*entity types*). All attributes are primitive types. Entities and relations define entity types. Roles, inverses and shortcuts in a relation are entity types.

Most typing rules are straightforward, so we only cover the rules that are non-standard. The aggregation rule (AGGR) is interesting. Since multiplicities are encoded orthogonally the aggregation functions are of type int $\rightarrow$ int. The multiplicity operators choice and concatenate work with any type. They only check whether both operands have the same type and propagate the type (MULT).

With roles and inverses one can conceptually navigate over the type graph defined by the entities and relations. The type of a navigation expression is naturally the place where one ends up in the model after navigating. When navigating from a relation to a participant the type is the participant's type (ROLENAV). When navigating from a participant to a relation, by an inverse, we find the type of the relation by looking up the inverse definition (INVNAV).

Multiplicities. For multiplicities there are two notational conventions: single characters from the concrete syntax and ranges. We use the ranges notation in the multiplicity rules as it gives us access to the upper and lower bounds directly.

Binary operators mimic maybe-Monad behaviour for zero or one values: a maybe value as input for the computation returns a maybe value as output. Taking the Cartesian product between the bags of values and applying the operation to each pair provides this behaviour. The multiplicity range is expressed as taking the minimum of both lower bounds and the maximum of the upper bounds (BINOP). The division and modulo operators exhibit slightly different behaviour (DIVOP). Since dividing by zero has no result, at least one value in

$$\frac{c \in \{true, false\}}{c : boolean} \quad \text{[Bool]}$$

$$\frac{}{literalInt : int} \quad \text{[Int]}$$

$$\frac{}{literalString : string} \quad \text{[Str]}$$

$$\frac{}{\theta \vdash this : \theta} \quad \text{[This]}$$

$$\frac{\oplus \in \{+, -, *, /, \%\} \quad e_1 : int \quad e_2 : int}{e_1 \oplus e_2 : int} \quad \text{[Math]}$$

$$\frac{e_1 : string \quad e_2 : string}{e_1 + e_2 : string} \quad \text{[Conc]}$$

$$\frac{\oplus \in \{\&\&, ||\} \quad e_1 : boolean \quad e_2 : boolean}{e_1 \oplus e_2 : boolean} \quad \text{[AndOr]}$$

$$\frac{e : boolean}{! e : boolean} \quad \text{[Not]}$$

$$\frac{\oplus \in \{>, >=, <, <=\} \quad e_1 : t \quad e_2 : t \quad t \in \{int, string\}}{e_1 \oplus e_2 : boolean} \quad \text{[Cmp]}$$

$$\frac{e_1 : t \quad e_2 : t \quad \oplus \in \{==, !=\}}{e_1 \oplus e_2 : boolean} \quad \text{[Eq]}$$

$$\frac{e_1 : boolean \quad e_2 : t \quad e_3 : t}{e_1 ? e_2 ":" e_3 : t} \quad \text{[Cond]}$$

$$\frac{e : int \quad f \in \{avg, min, max, sum\}}{f(e) : int} \quad \text{[Aggr]}$$

$$\frac{e : boolean \quad f \in \{conj, disj\}}{f(e) : boolean} \quad \text{[Logic]}$$

$$\frac{e : \_}{count(e) : int} \quad \text{[Count]}$$

$$\frac{e_1 : t \quad e_2 : t \quad \oplus \in \{<+, ++\}}{e_1 \oplus e_2 : t} \quad \text{[Mult]}$$

$$\frac{e : t \quad \mathcal{A}_t(a) = (p, \_ \cdot \_)}{e . a : p} \quad \text{[Attr]}$$

$$\frac{e : t_a \quad \mathcal{A}_t(a) = (t_a, \_)}{t [a == e] : t} \quad \text{[Lookup]}$$

$$\frac{e : t \quad \mathcal{R}_t(r) = (t_r, \_)}{e . r : t_r} \quad \text{[RoleNav]}$$

$$\frac{e_1 : t_1 \quad \mathcal{I}_{t1}(i) = (t_2, \_, nil)}{e . i : t_2} \quad \text{[InvNav]}$$

Fig. 13. Type rules

$$\frac{c \in \{true, false, false, Int, String\}}{c \sim [1,1]} \quad \text{[Const]}$$

$$\frac{\oplus \in \{+, -, *, \&\&, ||, >, \quad >=, <, <=, ==, !=\} \quad e_1 \sim [l_1, u_1] \quad e_2 \sim [l_2, u_2]}{e_1 \oplus e_2 \sim [min(l_1, l_2), max(u_1, u_2)]} \quad \text{[BinOp]}$$

$$\frac{\oplus \in \{/, \%\} \quad e_1 \sim [\_, u_1] \quad e_2 \sim [\_, u_2]}{e_1 \oplus e_2 \sim [0, max(u_1, u_2)]} \quad \text{[DivOp]}$$

$$\frac{e_1 \sim [l_1, 1] \quad e_2 \sim [l_2, u_2] \quad e_3 \sim [l_3, u_3] \quad m = [min(l_1, l_2, l_3), max(u_2, u_3)]}{e_1 ? e_2 ":" e_3 \sim m} \quad \text{[Cond]}$$

$$\frac{e \sim m}{! e \sim m} \quad \text{[Not]}$$

$$\frac{f \in \{avg, min, max, conj, disj\} \quad e \sim [l, n)}{f(e) \sim [l, 1]} \quad \text{[Aggr]}$$

$$\frac{f \in \{sum, count\}}{f(e) \sim [1,1]} \quad \text{[Aggr2]}$$

$$\frac{e_1 \sim [0, u_1] \quad e_2 \sim [l_2, u_2]}{e_1 <+ e_2 \sim [l_2, max(u_1, u_2)]} \quad \text{[Choice]}$$

$$\frac{e_1 \sim [1, u_1]}{e_1 <+ e_2 \sim [1, u_1]} \quad \text{[Choice2]}$$

$$\frac{e_1 \sim [l_1, \_] \quad e_2 \sim [l_2, \_]}{e_1 ++ e_2 \sim [max(l_1, l_2), n)} \quad \text{[Concat]}$$

$$\frac{e \sim [l_1, u_1] \quad \mathcal{A}_{t_e}(a) = (\_, [l_2, 1], \_)}{e . a \sim [min(l_1, l_2), u_1]} \quad \text{[Attr]}$$

$$\frac{}{t [a == e] \sim [0, n)} \quad \text{[Lookup]}$$

$$\frac{e : t \quad e \sim m \quad \mathcal{R}_t(r) = (\_, \_)}{e . r \sim m} \quad \text{[RoleNav]}$$

$$\frac{e_1 : t_1 \quad \mathcal{I}_{t1}(i) = (t_2, r, nil) \quad \mathcal{R}_{t2}(r) = (\_, [l_2, u_2])}{e . i \sim [min(l_1, l_2), max(u_1, u_2)]} \quad \text{[InvNav]}$$

Fig. 14. Multiplicity rules

$$\frac{a = (\_, [\_, 1], \text{nil})}{\vdash a} \qquad \text{[AttrDec]}$$

$$\frac{a = (p, [l_1, 1], e) \qquad e : p \qquad e \sim [l_2, 1] \qquad l_1 \leq l_2}{\vdash a} \qquad \text{[AttrDec2]}$$

$$\frac{r = (t, m) \qquad \mathcal{E}(t) = (\_, \_)}{\vdash r} \qquad \text{[RoleDec]}$$

$$\frac{i = (t, r_1, \text{nil}) \qquad \mathcal{R}_t(r_1) = (\_, \_)}{\vdash i} \qquad \text{[InvDec]}$$

$$\frac{i = (t, r_1, r_2) \qquad \mathcal{R}_t(r_1) = (\_, \_) \qquad \mathcal{R}_t(r_2) = (\_, \_)}{\vdash i} \qquad \text{[ShortcutDec]}$$

$$\frac{\theta' = t \qquad \forall a \in dom(\mathcal{A}_t) : \theta' \vdash a \qquad \forall r \in dom(\mathcal{R}_t) : \theta' \vdash r \qquad \forall i \in dom(\mathcal{I}_t) : \theta' \vdash i}{\vdash t} \qquad \text{[EntityDec]}$$

$$\frac{\theta' = \bot \qquad \forall t \in dom(\mathcal{E}) : \theta' \vdash t \qquad \theta' \vdash e : \_ \qquad \theta' \vdash e \sim \_}{\vdash (\mathcal{E}, e)} \qquad \text{[ProgramDec]}$$

Fig. 15. Attribute, role, inverse, shortcut, entity and program well-formedness

both operands might still result in no answer. Instead of throwing a division by zero exception zero answers are given for any denominator equal to zero.

The CHOICE operator chooses at runtime the left expression if it has a result, and otherwise the right expression. The multiplicity is defined as the maximum of both upper and lower bound, except if the left lower bound is one. Then we know that the left expression will always be chosen. Note that it does not make sense to use the choice operator in that case, because the right expression will be dead code. The CONCAT operator combines the results of both expressions. This means that we might always have more than one value at runtime; thus the upper bound is n. The lower bound is the maximum of both.

Attributes are allowed to be either [0,1] or [1,1]. In the first case attribute access decreases the lower bound to zero, as the attribute might not be set (ATTR). A role always has exactly one value, so role navigation leaves multiplicity intact (ROLENAV). Navigation to relations entities participate in behaves like a SQL join between the input expression entities and the relation. Like binary operators this means taking the lowest lower bound and the highest upper bound.

Well-formedness. Programs are well-formed if they satisfy the rules in Figure 15. Attributes are only allowed to have a multiplicity of at most one, their type has to be primitive (which is enforced by the syntax definition already) and if a derivation is specified, it should be of the correct type and its multiplicity should fit inside the target range. Role declarations are well-formed if the entity playing the role exists in the entity map. Inversions are well-formed if the role exists in the entity of which they are the inverse and shortcuts are well-formed if both roles exist in the entity. Entity definitions are well-formed if all their attributes, inverses and roles are well-formed and a program is well-formed if all its entities and the main expression are well-formed. We only consider well-formed programs.

6   Dynamic Semantics

We specify evaluation rules for a big-step semantics. We use the I-MSOS notational style, which implicitly propagates stores if they are not mentioned [14].

Stores. In order to evaluate a program an entity store Σ and relation store Δ must be passed; our language is a data modeling and navigation language and does not provide facilities to add, edit or remove data. Expression in addition get passed a this-reference θ.

$$\Sigma, \Delta \vdash p \Downarrow v \qquad \text{(Evaluation of program)}$$
$$\Sigma, \Delta, \theta \vdash e \Downarrow v \qquad \text{(Evaluation of expressions)}$$

The entity store corresponds to the usual heap: a map from object references to a map from attribute names to their values. The relation store is used for storing all relations between entities. It is a map from relation name, relation object reference and role name to the reference of the object playing this role. The this-reference is a single reference to an object.

$$\Sigma \in EntityStore : Reference \rightarrow AttributeStore$$
$$AttributeStore : AttrName \rightarrow Value$$
$$\Delta \in RelationStore : EntityName \times Reference \times RoleName \rightarrow Reference$$
$$\theta \in ThisReference : Reference$$

Store well-formedness. Figure 16 describes what it means means for these stores to be well-formed. The entity store is well-formed if all the entities in it are well-formed. An entity is well-formed if (1) all records in its attribute store are well-formed, (2) all its required, non-derived attributes have been set (3) all its roles have a value and (4) the number of relation records, that point to it for a certain role that he plays, is within the multiplicity range specified for that role.

An attribute record is well-formed if it has a value of the correct type. The relation store is well-formed if all its records are well-formed. A relation record is well-formed if its references point to entities. Finally the this-reference is well-formed if it points to an entity. We assume a well-formed entity and relation stores for evaluation.

Evaluation rules All the evaluation rules have a specific form: they operate on bags. Expressions can return any number of values, modeling this with bags is a natural choice. A nice example of this is the rule for binary operations (BINOP). The left and right expressions evaluate to a bag of values, the Cartesian product of these bags is taken and on each pair of values the operator is applied. For single values a normal computation is performed, for maybe values a maybe computation and for many values a Cartesian product computation. Most evaluation rules follow this pattern.

Aggregation operations are defined for at least a single value (AGGR) and for empty lists there is predefined behaviour (AGGR2 and SUM). CHOICE returns

$$\frac{\forall (ref \to astore) \in \Sigma : \vdash (ref \to astore)}{\vdash \Sigma} \qquad \text{[EntityStore]}$$

$$\frac{\begin{array}{l} ref : t \\ \forall (a \to v) \in astore : \ ref \vdash (a \to v) \\ \forall (a \to p, [1,1], \_) \in \mathcal{A}_t : \ astore(a) = \_ \\ \forall (r \to \_, \_) \in \mathcal{R}_t : \Delta(t, ref, r) = \_ \\ \forall (i \to t_2, r_2, nil) \in \mathcal{I}_r : \\ \quad (|\{v \mid \Delta(t_2, \_, r_2) = v\}| = m \quad \mathcal{R}_{t2}(r_2) = (\_, [l,u]) \quad l \le m \le u) \end{array}}{\vdash (ref \to astore)} \qquad \text{[EntityRecord]}$$

$$\frac{e : t \qquad \mathcal{A}_t(a) = (t_a, \_, \_) \qquad v : t_a}{e \vdash a \to v} \qquad \text{[AttrRecord]}$$

$$\frac{\forall (t \ v_1 \ r \to v_2) \in \Delta : \vdash (t \ v_1 \ r \to v_2)}{\vdash \Delta} \qquad \text{[RelationStore]}$$

$$\frac{v_1 : t \quad \Sigma(v_1) = \_ \quad \mathcal{R}_t(r) = (t_2, \_) \quad v_2 : t_2 \quad \Sigma(v_2) = \_}{\vdash t \ v_1 \ r \to v_2} \qquad \text{[RelationRecord]}$$

$$\frac{\Sigma(\theta) = \_}{\vdash \theta} \qquad \text{[ThisReference]}$$

Fig. 16. Store well-formedness

$$\frac{c \text{ is constant}}{c \Downarrow \{\mid c \mid\}} \qquad \text{[Const]}$$

$$\frac{}{\theta \vdash \text{this} \Downarrow \{\mid \theta \mid\}} \qquad \text{[This]}$$

$$\frac{\begin{array}{l} \oplus \in \{+, -, *, \&\&, ||, >, \\ \quad >=, <, <=, ==, !=\} \\ e_1 \Downarrow V_1 \qquad e_2 \Downarrow V_2 \end{array}}{e_1 \oplus e_2 \Downarrow \{\mid v_1 \oplus v_2 \mid v_1 \in V_1, \ v_2 \in V_2 \mid\}} \qquad \text{[BinOp]}$$

$$\frac{e_1 \Downarrow V_1 \qquad e_2 \Downarrow V_2 \qquad \oplus \in \{/, \%\}}{e_1 \oplus e_2 \Downarrow \{\mid v_1 \oplus v_2 \mid v_2 \ != 0, \ v_1 \in V_1, \ v_2 \in V_2 \mid\}} \qquad \text{[Div]}$$

$$\frac{e \Downarrow V}{! \ e \Downarrow \{\mid \neg v \mid v \in V \mid\}} \qquad \text{[Not]}$$

$$\frac{e_1 \Downarrow V_1 \qquad e_2 \Downarrow V_2 \qquad e_3 \Downarrow V_3}{e_1 \ ? \ e_2 : e_3 \Downarrow \{\mid v_1 \ ? \ v_2 : v_3 \mid v_1 \in V_1, \ v_2 \in V_2, \ v_3 \in V_3 \mid\}} \qquad \text{[Cond]}$$

$$\frac{\begin{array}{l} f \in \{\text{avg}, \min, \max, \text{conj}, \text{disj}, \text{sum}\} \\ e \Downarrow V \qquad |V| \ge 1 \end{array}}{f(e) \Downarrow \{\mid f(V) \mid\}} \qquad \text{[Aggr]}$$

$$\frac{\begin{array}{l} f \in \{\text{avg}, \min, \max, \text{conj}, \text{disj}\} \\ e \Downarrow \emptyset \end{array}}{f(e) \Downarrow \emptyset} \qquad \text{[Aggr2]}$$

$$\frac{e \Downarrow \emptyset}{\text{sum}(e) \Downarrow \{\mid 0 \mid\}} \qquad \text{[Sum]}$$

$$\frac{e \Downarrow V}{\text{count}(e) \Downarrow \{\mid |V| \mid\}} \qquad \text{[Count]}$$

$$\frac{e_1 \Downarrow V_1 \qquad e_2 \Downarrow V_2}{e_1 <+ e_2 \Downarrow (V_1 \ != \emptyset) \ ? \ V_1 : V_2} \qquad \text{[Choice]}$$

$$\frac{e_1 \Downarrow V_1 \qquad e_2 \Downarrow V_2}{e_1 ++ e_2 \Downarrow V_1 \cup V_2} \qquad \text{[Concat]}$$

$$\frac{e \Downarrow V \qquad e : t \qquad \mathcal{A}_t(a) = (\_, \_, nil)}{\Sigma \vdash e \ . \ a \Downarrow \{\mid \Sigma(v)(a) \mid v \in V \mid\}} \qquad \text{[Attr]}$$

$$\frac{\begin{array}{l} e \Downarrow V \qquad e : t \qquad \mathcal{A}_t(a) = (\_, \_, e_2) \\ V_2 = \{\mid v_2 \mid (\theta' \vdash e_2 \Downarrow \{v_2\}), \ \theta' \in V \mid\} \end{array}}{e \ . \ a \Downarrow V_2} \qquad \text{[At2]}$$

$$\frac{e \Downarrow V \qquad e : t}{\Delta \vdash e \ . \ r \Downarrow \{\mid \Delta(t, v, r) \mid v \in V \mid\}} \qquad \text{[RoleNav]}$$

$$\frac{\begin{array}{l} e \Downarrow V \qquad e : t \qquad \mathcal{I}_t(i) = (t, r, nil) \\ V_2 = \{\mid v_2 \mid \Delta(t, v_2, r) = v, \ v \in V \mid\} \end{array}}{\Delta \vdash e \ . \ i \Downarrow V_2} \qquad \text{[InvNav]}$$

$$\frac{\begin{array}{l} p = (\mathcal{E}, x) \qquad \theta' = \bot \\ \Sigma, \Delta, \theta' \vdash x \Downarrow v \end{array}}{\Sigma, \Delta \vdash p \Downarrow v} \qquad \text{[Program]}$$

Fig. 17. Evaluation rules (Big Step SOS). "$\{\mid \ \mid\}$" is bag notation [5]

the value of the left expression, if it has at least one value, otherwise the value of the right expression. CONCAT combines all values, regardless of how many there are. Attributes can either be normal or have a derivation expression. For normal attributes a lookup is done in the attribute map of each entity passed into the expression (ATTR). The lookup of unset attributes fails, but these are filtered out. Derivations behave like a method call without arguments (AT2). Navigation works differently for navigating through a role or through an inverse. Navigating by role does a simple map lookup for each value (ROLENAV). Navigating by inverse does a reverse map lookup on the role it is the inverse of (INVNAV). Finally the program executes the main expression with the stores.

7   Related Work

Our work builds on research in different fields: language constructs for relations, navigating and querying relations and multiplicities. Specific differences with our work are highlighted per article.

Languages with first-class relations. The Rumer language by Balzer has first-class relations [2,3]. It features first-class relations with named roles and queries. Rumer provides reactive queries as well as imperative code. It has cardinalities specified in constraints and implements binary relationships. Our approach differs in the fact that our modeling language does not support imperative code, multiplicities are part of the type system and we implement relations of all degrees.

Classages is a language that also features relations [12]. Classages is targeted at modelling the interactions and interaction life span between objects. It features static and dynamic relations, bidirectional relations and multiplicities. Our approach has in common that it has bidirectional relations but we are focused on modeling data instead of interactions.

Pearce and Noble extended Java with first-class relationships using aspects [17]. Relations are modeled as external tuples and objects are agnostic to relations they are in. Their approach to behavioural changes of objects based on their relations should be implemented by aspects, externally. Our approach is the opposite, entities know what relations they participate in. This allows specifying relation dependent behaviour in derivations.

RelJ is first-class relationship extension to Java by Biermann and Wren [4,22]. In their approach they support relationships as first-class citizens. The relations are also modeled as tuples, where the roles have a position in the tuple but no name. In our approach the roles are named and unordered; allowing navigation based on roles. Their relations are binary and one-directional. In the technical report they also sketch an extension with named roles [4]. In this sketched extension relations can have any arity and support bidirectional navigation.

Nelson implemented first-class relationships in Java [15]. This is a library and not a language extension. Mutable sets of tuples are used as first-class constructs to model relations. Without specific language constructs this approach does not supply additional semantics for relations and thus cannot provide additional static type checking.

Languages with non first-class relations. In 1987 Rumbaugh was the first to add relations to a language [18]. His approach is pre-processor based and dynamic. It does not have relations as first-class citizens.

In 1991 a relationship mechanism for a Strongly Typed Object-Oriented Database Programming language introduced statically typed relations as part of a language [1]. The paper explains the data model definition and transactions. It does however not explain in detail how querying or navigation is done.

WebDSL introduced inverse properties which inspired the inverses [20]. Refer to Section 3 for details.

Queries of relations in object-oriented languages. The Java Query Language (JQL) adds queries to Java [21]. There is no additional support for relations, so navigation uses value-based joins like in SQL. LINQ also uses value-based joins [13]. These approaches are in the left column of the design space (Section 3). In contrast, our navigation is based on the role names of relations.

Multiplicities in programming languages. In Content over Container: Object-Oriented Programming with multiplcities Steimann adds multiplicity annotations to Java in order to remove the Collection containers [19]. Refer to Section 2 for details.

Finally the ideas for this paper were presented in the ACM Student Research Competition [8]. The design space analysis and formal semantics of the language are new to this paper. Also the syntax changed as a result of the design-space analysis.

8   Conclusion

Unification and generalization of relations led to a new data modeling and navigation language. This goes hand in hand with native multiplicities. Both the relations aspect and the native multiplicities aspect lead to more a more concise definition and navigation of relationships; removing maintenance of reference consistency, removing collection classes and providing single identifier navigation by inverses and shortcuts.

Future work. We would like to add more aspects orthogonally to the type system. Our first candidates are ordered/unordered and unique/duplicates. It is worth exploring how well different aspects can be modelled orthogonally in a type system.

Also we would like to extend our language to provide type-and-multiplicity-safe operations on data. Adding or removing entities and relations might invalidate the multiplicity constraints on relations. We would like to catch these potential errors by static analysis and indicate to the programmer that he should catch that situation. The goal is to make sure that multiplicity-safe operations will never trigger runtime errors because a multiplicity constraint for a relation is violated. We would like to explore if we can ensure correct multiplicities at runtime statically.

References

1. Albano, A., Ghelli, G., Orsini, R.: A relationship mechanism for a strongly typed object-oriented database programming language. In: VLDB, pp. 565–575 (1991)
2. Balzer, S.: Rumer: a Programming Language and Modular Verification Technique Based on Relationships. Ph.D. thesis, ETH, Zürich (2011)
3. Balzer, S., Gross, T.R., Eugster, P.T.: A relational model of object collaborations and its use in reasoning about relationships. In: Ernst, E. (ed.) ECOOP 2007. LNCS, vol. 4609, pp. 323–346. Springer, Heidelberg (2007)
4. Bierman, G., Wren, A.: First-class relationships in an object-oriented language. In: Gao, X.-X. (ed.) ECOOP 2005. LNCS, vol. 3586, pp. 262–286. Springer, Heidelberg (2005)
5. Buneman, P., Libkin, L., Suciu, D., Tannen, V., Wong, L.: Comprehension syntax. SIGMOD 23(1), 87–96 (1994)
6. Chen, P.P.: The entity-relationship model - toward a unified view of data. Tods 1(1), 9–36 (1976)
7. Halpin, T.: Object-role modeling (orm/niam). In: Handbook on architectures of information systems, pp. 81–103. Springer (2006)
8. Harkes, D.: Relations: a first class relationship and first class derivations programming language. In: AOSD, pp. 9–10 (2014)
9. Hemel, Z., Groenewegen, D.M., Kats, L.C.L., Visser, E.: Static consistency checking of web applications with WebDSL. JSC 46(2), 150–182 (2011)
10. Jacobson, I., Booch, G., Rumbaugh, J.E.: The unified software development process - the complete guide to the unified process from the original designers. Addison-Wesley object technology series. Addison-Wesley (1999)
11. Kats, L.C.L., Visser, E.: The Spoofax language workbench: rules for declarative specification of languages and IDEs. In: OOPSLA, pp. 444–463 (2010)
12. Liu, Y.D., Smith, S.F.: Interaction-based programming with classages. In: OOPSLA. pp. 191–209 (2005)
13. Meijer, E., Beckman, B., Bierman, G.M.: Linq: reconciling object, relations and xml in the .net framework. In: Sigmod, p. 706 (2006)
14. Mosses, P.D., New, M.J.: Implicit propagation in structural operational semantics. ENTCS 229(4), 49–66 (2009)
15. Stephen, Nelson, J.N., Pearce, D.J.: Implementing first-class relationships in java. Proceedings of RAOOL 8 (2008)
16. Noble, J.: Basic relationship patterns. Pattern Languages of Program Design 4 (1997)
17. Pearce, D.J., Noble, J.: Relationship aspects. In: AOSD, pp. 75–86 (2006)
18. Rumbaugh, J.E.: Relations as semantic constructs in an object-oriented language. In: OOPSLA, pp. 466–481 (1987)
19. Steimann, F.: Content over container: object-oriented programming with multiplicities. In: OOPSLA, pp. 173–186 (2013)
20. Visser, E.: WebDSL: A case study in domain-specific language engineering. In: GTTSE, pp. 291–373 (2007)
21. Willis, D., Pearce, D.J., Boyland, J.: Efficient object querying for java. In: Thomas, D. (ed.) ECOOP 2006. LNCS, vol. 4067, pp. 28–49. Springer, Heidelberg (2006)
22. Wren, A.: Relationships for object-oriented programming languages. University of Cambridge, Computer Laboratory, Technical Report 702(UCAM-CL-TR-702) (November 2007)

Simple, Efficient, Sound and Complete Combinator Parsing for All Context-Free Grammars, Using an Oracle

Tom Ridge

University of Leicester, Leicester, UK

Abstract. Parsers for context-free grammars can be implemented directly and naturally in a functional style known as "combinator parsing", using recursion following the structure of the grammar rules. Traditionally parser combinators have struggled to handle all features of context-free grammars, such as left recursion.

Previous work introduced novel parser combinators that could be used to parse all context-free grammars. A parser generator built using these combinators was proved both *sound* and *complete* in the HOL4 theorem prover. Unfortunately the performance was not as good as other parsing methods such as Earley parsing.

In this paper, we build on this previous work, and combine it in novel ways with existing parsing techniques such as Earley parsing. The result is a sound-and-complete combinator parsing library that *can handle all context-free grammars*, and *has good performance*.

1   Introduction

In previous work [13] the current author introduced novel parser combinators that could be used to parse all context-free grammars. For example, a parser for the grammar E -> E E E | "1" | ϵ can be written in OCaml as:

```
let rec parse_E = (fun i -> mkparser "E" (
  (parse_E **> parse_E **> parse_E) ||| (a "1") ||| eps) i)
```

In [4] Barthwal and Norrish discuss this work:

> [Ridge] presents a verified parser for all possible context-free grammars, using an admirably simple algorithm. The drawback is that, as presented, the algorithm is of complexity $O(n^5)$.

Existing techniques such as Earley parsing [5] take time $O(n^3)$ in the length of the input in the worst case. Therefore, as far as performance is concerned, [13] is not competitive with such techniques. In this work, we seek to address these performance problems. We have three main goals for our parsing library.

B. Combemale et al. (Eds.): SLE 2014, LNCS 8706, pp. 261–281, 2014.

- The library should provide an interface based on parser combinators.
- The library should handle all context-free grammars.
- The library should have "good" performance.

The challenge is to improve on our previous work by providing Earley-like performance: $O(n^3)$ in the worst case but typically much better on common classes of grammar. Our main contribution is to show how to combine a combinator parsing interface with an efficient general parsing algorithm such as Earley parsing. We list further contributions in Section 11. We now briefly outline our new approach, and then give an overview of the rest of the paper.

Consider the problem of parsing an input string s, given a grammar Γ (a finite set of rules) and a nonterminal start symbol S. In general, we will work with substrings $s_{i,j}$ of the input s between a low index i and a high index j, where $i \leq j$. In symbols we might write the parsing problem as $\Gamma \vdash S \to^* s_{i,j}$. Suppose the grammar contains the rule $S \to A\ B$. Then one way to derive $\Gamma \vdash S \to^* s_{i,j}$ is to derive $\Gamma \vdash A \to^* s_{i,k}$ and $\Gamma \vdash B \to^* s_{k,j}$:

$$\frac{\Gamma \vdash A \to^* s_{i,k} \qquad \Gamma \vdash B \to^* s_{k,j}}{\Gamma \vdash S \to^* s_{i,j}} \ (S \to A\ B) \in \Gamma$$

This rule resembles the well-known *Cut* rule of logic, in that it introduces an unknown k in the search for a derivation. The problem is that there is no immediate way to determine the possible values of k when working from the conclusion of the rule to the premises. Put another way, a top-down parse of the substring $s_{i,j}$ must divide the substring into two substrings $s_{i,k}$ and $s_{k,j}$, but there is no information available to determine the possible values of k. Attempting to parse for all k such that $i \leq k \leq j$ results in poor real-world performance.

The traditional combinator parsing solution is to parse *prefixes* of the substring $s_{i,j}$. Since $s_{i,j}$ is trivially a prefix of itself, a solution to this more general problem furnishes a solution to the original. Moreover, this approach gives possible candidates for the value k: We first attempt to find all parses for nonterminal A for prefixes of input $s_{i,j}$; the results will be derivations for $s_{i,k}$ where $k \leq j$. We can then attempt to parse nonterminal B for prefixes of $s_{k,j}$, since possible values of k are now known.

We propose a different solution: assume the existence of an oracle that can provide the unknown values of k. As we show later, this allows one to solve the problem of parsing context-free grammars using combinator parsing. However, in the real world we must also provide some means to construct the oracle. Our answer is simple: use some other parsing technique, preferably one that has good performance. In this work we use Earley parsing, but *any* other general parsing technique would suffice.

There are several technical problems that must be addressed. For example, to handle arbitrary grammars, including features such as left-recursion, we adapt the notion of parsing contexts originally introduced in [13]. A central new challenge is to reconcile the implementation of Earley parsing with that of

combinator parsers. For example, consider the following parser[1] for the grammar
E -> E E E | "1" | ϵ.

let rec $parse\_E$ = (fun $i \to mkntparser$ "E" (
  $((parse\_E \otimes parse\_E \otimes parse\_E) \gg$ (fun $(x, (y, z)) \to x + y + z))$
  $\oplus (a1 \gg$ (fun $\_ \to 1)) \oplus (eps \gg$ (fun $\_ \to 0))) i$)

This parser uses parsing actions to count the length of the parsed input. The
parsing code *implicitly* embodies the grammar. However, implementations of
Earley parsing require *explicit* representations of the grammar, such as:

let g = [("E", [NT "E"; NT "E"; NT "E"]); ("E", [TM "1"]); ("E", [TM "eps"])]

In this representation of the grammar (a finite set of rules, here represented
using a list), rules are pairs, where the left-hand side is a nonterminal (identified
by a string) and the right-hand side is a list of symbols, either nonterminal
symbols such as NT "E" or terminal symbols such as TM "eps".

Our solution to this challenge requires interpreting the parsing combinators in three different ways. The first interpretation embeds a symbol with a
given parser. With this we can define a function *sym_of_parser* which takes
a parser as an argument and returns the associated symbol. For example,
sym_of_parser parse_E evaluates to NT "E". The second interpretation builds
on the first to associate a concrete representation of the grammar with each
parser. With this we can define a function *grammar_of_parser* which takes a
parser as an argument and returns the associated grammar. For example, evaluating *grammar_of_parser parse_E* returns a record with a field whose value is
the following[2]:

[("(E*E)", Seq (NT "E", NT "E")); ("(E*(E*E))", Seq (NT "E", NT "(E*E)"));
("((E*(E*E))+1)", Alt (NT "(E*(E*E))", TM "1"));
("(((E*(E*E))+1)+eps)", Alt(NT "((E*(E*E))+1)", TM "eps"));
("E", Atom (NT "(((E*(E*E))+1)+eps)"))]

This is a *binarized* version of the previous grammar. Note that nonterminals
now have unusual names, such as (E*E). Right-hand sides are either atoms,
binary sequences (of symbols, not nonterminals cf. Chomsky Normal Form), or
binary alternatives. The function *grammar_of_parser* allows us to inspect the
structure of the parser, in order to extract a grammar, which can then be fed
to an Earley parser. The Earley parser takes the grammar, and a start symbol,
and parses the input string s. The output from the Earley parsing phase can be
thought of as a list of Earley productions of the form $(X \to \alpha.\beta, i, j, l)$. Here X

---

[1] In the following sections we have lightly typeset the OCaml code. The sequencing
combinator *****>** is written $\otimes$ and associates to the right; the alternative combinator
|||| is written $\oplus$; and the action function **>>>>** is written $\gg$. The notation $s.[i]$
denotes the ith character of the string s. Records with named fields are written e.g.
$\langle f1 = v1; f2 = v2 \rangle$. Functional record update is written $\langle r$ with $f1 = v1; f2 = v2 \rangle$.
Otherwise the OCaml syntax we use should be readily understandable by anyone
familiar with functional programming.
[2] A second field records the terminal parsers that are used, such as *a1* and *eps*.

is a nonterminal, α and β are sequences of symbols (β is non-empty), and i, j, l are integers. The meaning of such a production is that there is a rule $X \to \alpha \; \beta$ in the grammar such that the substring $s_{i,j}$ could be parsed as the sequence α, and moreover the substring $s_{j,l}$ could be parsed as the sequence β. These productions can be used to construct an oracle.

The oracle is designed to answer the following question: given a grammar Γ, a rule $S \to A \; B$ in Γ, and a substring $s_{i,j}$, what are the possible values of k such that $\Gamma \vdash A \to^* s_{i,k}$ and $\Gamma \vdash B \to^* s_{k,j}$? To determine the values of k we look for Earley productions of the form $(S \to A.B, i, k, j)$. Such a production says exactly that the substring $s_{i,j}$ could be parsed as the sequence $A \; B$ and that $s_{i,k}$ could be parsed as A and $s_{k,j}$ could be parsed as B.

The third interpretation of the parsing combinators follows the traditional interpretation, except that *we do not parse prefixes*, but instead *we use the oracle* to determine where to split the input string during a parse. In fact, all necessary *parsing* information has already been deduced from the input s during the Earley phase, so this phase degenerates into using the oracle to apply *parsing actions* appropriately, in the familiar top-down recursive manner. During this phase we make use of a parsing context to handle features such as left recursion, and memoization for efficiency.

In outline, our algorithm cleanly decomposes into 3 phases. Given a parser p and an input string s we perform the following steps.

1. Extract grammar Γ and start symbol S from the parser p and feed Γ, S and s to the Earley parser, which performs a traditional Earley parse.
2. Take the Earley productions that result and construct the oracle.
3. Use the oracle to guide the action phase.

Earley parsing is theoretically efficient $O(n^3)$ and performs well in practice. The construction of the oracle involves processing the Earley productions, which have the same bound as the Earley parser itself, $O(n^3)$. Parsing actions involve arbitrary user-supplied code, so it is not possible to give an *a priori* bound on the time taken during the action phase, however, in Section 9 we argue that the performance of this stage is close to optimal. Thus, we argue that our approach overall results in close-to-optimal (i.e. "good") asymptotic performance. In Section 9 we also provide real-world evidence to support these claims.

In this paper we present a version of our code, called mini-P3, that focuses on clarity for expository purposes, whilst preserving all important features. The full P3 code follows exactly the structure we outline here with only minor differences[3]. Our implementation language is a small subset of OCaml, essentially the simply-typed lambda calculus with integers, strings, recursive functions, records and datatypes. Apart from memoization, the code is purely functional. It should be very easy to re-implement our approach in other functional languages such as Haskell, Scheme and F♯. The full code for mini-P3 and P3 can be found in the online resources at http://www.tom-ridge.com/p3.html.

---

[3] Footnotes describe how mini-P3 differs from P3.

The structure of the rest of the paper is as follows. In Section 2 we give two key examples, and discuss some common misunderstandings concerning our approach. In Section 3 we introduce the basic types such as those for substrings and grammars, and discuss the types related to the parser combinators. The subsequent sections modularly introduce different aspects of our approach. We start by defining the sequencing and alternative combinators in Section 4. In Section 5 we introduce our running example, which we develop further in Section 7. In Section 6 we describe the Earley parsing phase and the construction of the oracle. In Section 8 we discuss the role of parsing context and the use of memoization to make the action phase efficient. In Section 9 we report on various experiments to measure performance. In Section 10 we discuss related work, and in Section 11 we conclude.

An extended version of this paper appears in the online resources. This includes further sections discussing motivation, mathematical preliminaries, further examples, parsing context, memoization and soundness and completeness. For space reasons this material cannot be included here.

2   Example

We introduce some example parsers to illustrate our approach, and clarify aspects of our approach that are commonly misunderstood. An efficient parser for the grammar E -> E E E | "1" | ϵ is:

```
let tbl = Hashtbl.create 0
let rec parse_E = (fun i → memo_p3 tbl (mkntparser "E" (
  ((parse_E ⊗ parse_E ⊗ parse_E) ≫ (fun (x,(y,z)) → NODE(x,y,z)))
  ⊕ (a1 ≫ (fun _ → LEAF(1))) ⊕ (eps ≫ (fun _ → LEAF(0)))))) i)
```

Our approach is complete in that it returns all "good"[4] parse trees. There are an exponential number of such parse trees. For example, for input length 19, there are more than $4 * 10^{17}$ parse trees, but as with most exponential behaviours it is not feasible to actually compute all these parse trees. The following parser is identical except that, rather than returning parse trees, it computes (in all possible ways) the length of the input parsed:

```
let tbl = Hashtbl.create 0
let rec parse_E = (fun i → memo_p3 tbl (mkntparser "E" (
  ((parse_E ⊗ parse_E ⊗ parse_E) ≫ (fun (x,(y,z)) → x + y + z))
  ⊕ (a1 ≫ (fun _ → 1)) ⊕ (eps ≫ (fun _ → 0))))) i)
```

Naively we might expect that this also exhibits exponential behaviour, since presumably the parse trees must all be generated, and the actions applied. *This expectation is wrong.* Running this example parser on an input of size 19 returns in 0.02 seconds with a single result 19. For an input of size 100, this parser returns a single result 100 in 5 seconds, and over a range of inputs this parser exhibits polynomial behaviour rather than exponential behaviour. As far as we

---

[4] The notion of "good" parse tree is defined in [13].

type (α, β) fmap $= (\alpha \times \beta)$ list   type substring $=$ SS of string $\times$ int $\times$ int
type term $=$ string   type nonterm $=$ string   type symbol $=$ NT of nonterm | TM of term

type rhs $=$ Atom of symbol | Seq of symbol $\times$ symbol | Alt of symbol $\times$ symbol
type parse_rule $=$ nonterm $\times$ rhs   type grammar $=$ parse_rule list

type raw_parser $=$ substring $\to$ substring list
type ty_oracle $=$ (symbol $\times$ symbol) $\to$ substring $\to$ int list
type local_context $=$ LC of (nonterm $\times$ substring) list

let *empty_fmap* $=$ []   let *empty_context* $=$ (LC [])
let *empty_oracle* $=$ (fun $(sym1, sym2) \to$ fun $ss \to$ [])

Fig. 1. Basic types and trivial values

are aware, *no other parser can handle such examples.* To make such examples
possible requires: careful engineering of the backend parser (here based on Earley
parsing) so that it is $O(n^3)$ in the length of the input; a *compact* representation
of parse results (using an oracle) that does not require more than $O(n^3)$ time to
construct; a semantically-meaningful notion of action when there are an infinite
number of possible parse trees (handled by the parsing context); careful use of
the oracle to guide the action phase; and memoization during the action phase
so that exponentially many possible actions are reduced to a polynomial number
of actual actions. The code above combines all of these aspects whilst presenting
a standard combinator-parsing interface to the programmer. In the rest of the
paper we discuss the techniques and careful engineering that make this possible.

3   Types

Basic Types. In Fig. 1 we give types for finite maps (represented by association
lists), substrings, terminals, nonterminals, symbols, the right-hand sides of parse
rules, parse rules, and grammars. Note that the **rhs** type permits only unary rules
(e.g. E -> F) and binary rules (e.g. sequences E -> A B or alternatives E -> A
| B). This is a restriction on the *internal representation* of the rules and not on
the user of the library.

Raw parsers capture the set of substrings associated to a given terminal. They
can be more-or-less arbitrary OCaml code[5]. Given a substring $SS(s, i, j)$, a raw
parser returns a list of substrings $SS(s, i, k)$ indicating that the prefix $SS(s, i, k)$
could be parsed as the corresponding terminal. For example, the raw parser
raw_a1 consumes a single 1 character from the input:

let *raw_a1* $(SS(s, i, j)) = $ (if $i < j$ && $s.[i] = $ '1' then $[SS(s, i, i+1)]$ else [])

---

[5] A raw parser should behave as a pure function, and should return prefixes of its
argument. For a fully formal treatment of the parsers associated with terminals
see [13].

```
type (α, β, γ) sum3  =  Inl of α | Inm of β | Inr of γ
type inl = unit    type outl = symbol
```

```
type mid  =  ⟨ rules : parse_rule list; tmparsers : (term, raw_parser) fmap ⟩
type inm = mid    type outm = mid
```

```
type inr  =  ⟨ ss : substring; lc : local_context; oracle : ty_oracle ⟩
type α outr  =  α list
```

```
type input = (inl, inm, inr) sum3    type α output = (outl, outm, α outr) sum3
type α parser3  =  (input → α output)
```

```
let empty_mid  =  ⟨rules = []; tmparsers = empty_fmap⟩
```

Fig. 2. Parser types and trivial values

The oracle type captures the idea that an oracle takes two symbols $sym1$, $sym2$, and a substring $SS(s, i, j)$, and returns those integers k such that $SS(s, i, k)$ can be parsed as $sym1$, and $SS(s, k, j)$ can be parsed as $sym2$. Finally, the type local_context represents the parsing context, see Section 8.

Parser Types. The types related to parsers are given in Fig. 2. In our approach, a parser should be viewed as a collection of three separate functions[6]. We first discuss the sum3 type, and the function $sum3$ which converts three separate functions to a single function, and the function $unsum3$ which converts a single function of the appropriate form to three separate functions. Following this, we discuss the particular instances of the sum3 type that we use for our parsers.

The sum3 Type. The sum3 type generalizes the familiar binary sum to three components. Given three functions of type $α → δ$, $β → ε$ and $γ → ζ$, we can form a composite function of type $(α, β, γ)$ sum3 $→ (δ, ε, ζ)$ sum3. We can define this composite function explicitly, and moreover define an inverse:

```
let dest_inl (Inl x)  =  x ...
```

```
let sum3 (f, g, h)  =  (fun i → match i with
  | Inl l → Inl(f l) | Inm m → Inm(g m) | Inr r → Inr(h r))
```

```
let unsum3 u  =  (
  let f  =  (fun x → dest_inl (u (Inl x))) in
  let g  =  (fun x → dest_inm (u (Inm x))) in
  let h  =  (fun x → dest_inr (u (Inr x))) in
  (f, g, h))
```

We use the functions $sum3$ and $unsum3$ extensively when defining the parser combinators. In particular, as a function from inputs to outputs, a parser satisfies

---

[6] This implementation of the combinators is just one of those we have experimented with, and alternatives are certainly possible.

the extra conditions (not explicit in the type): given an argument of the form Inl x, the parser produces a result of the form Inl x', and similarly for Inm and Inr. Parsers p of type input $\rightarrow \alpha$ output should be thought of as the sum of three functions, i.e. $p = sum3\ (f, g, h)$.

Left Component, Extracting a Symbol from a Parser. The left component of a parser consists of a function of type inl $\rightarrow$ outl, that is, from unit to symbol. If $parse\_E$ is a parser for the nonterminal E, then the expression $parse\_E$ (Inl ()) should evaluate to Inl (NT "E"). We define the following auxiliary function:

let $sym\_of\_parser\ p = (dest\_inl\ (p\ (\text{Inl}\ ())))$

Middle Component, Extracting a Grammar from a Parser. The middle component of a parser consists of a function of type inm $\rightarrow$ outm, where inm and outm are both equal to type mid. The middle component of a parser is therefore of type mid $\rightarrow$ mid. The mid type represents the grammar associated with a parser. The middle component of a parser such as $parse\_E$ is a grammar transformer, that takes a grammar and extends it with extra rules. The type mid is a record type with two fields. The first is a list of parse rules. The second is a finite map from terminals to raw parsers. If $parse\_E$ is a parser for the nonterminal E, then the expression $parse\_E$ (Inm m) will evaluate to a value of the form Inm m', where m' is m augmented with rules for the nonterminal E (and all nonterminals reachable from E), and the terminal parsers involved in the definition of $parse\_E$ (and all terminal parsers involved in the definition of nonterminals reachable from E). We can then define $grammar\_of\_parser$:

let $grammar\_of\_parser\ p = (dest\_inm\ (p\ (\text{Inm}\ empty\_mid)))$

Right Component, Recursive Descent Parser. The right component is a function of type inr $\rightarrow \alpha$ outr, where α outr $= \alpha$ list. This resembles the traditional type of a combinator parser: a function from a string to a list of possible values. We work with substrings rather than strings, so an input i of type inr contains a component $i.ss$ of type substring. Two additional fields are present: $i.oracle$ is an oracle that indicates how to split the input when parsing a sequence of symbols, and $i.lc$ is a parsing context that allows combinator parsers to handle all context-free grammars. We discuss these additional fields further in the following sections. The output type α outr is simply a list of values at an arbitrary type α.

4   Parsing Combinators

In the previous section we discussed the α parser3 type and related types. In this section we give the definition of the sequencing combinator $p1 \otimes p2$. The definition of the alternative combinator $p1 \oplus p2$ follows the sequencing combinator *mutatis mutandis*. The following section illustrates the use of these combinators on a simple example.

Consider the left component of the sequencing combinator. This takes two parsers $p1$ and $p2$ and produces the left component (a function from unit to symbol) of the parser $p1 \otimes p2$:

let *seql p1 p2* = (fun () → let (*f1*, _, _) = *unsum3 p1* in
  let (*f2*, _, _) = *unsum3 p2* in let *rhs* = Seq(*f1* (), *f2* ()) in *mk_symbol rhs*)

The left component is a function from unit argument () to a symbol representing the sequential combination of the two underlying parsers. We use the auxiliary function *mk_symbol* to generate new symbols for possible right hand sides. These new symbols are always nonterminals. The requirement on *mk_symbol* is simply that it should be injective on its argument: if *mk_symbol rhs'* = *mk_symbol rhs* then *rhs'* = *rhs*[7]. For example, with the current implementation, evaluating *mk_symbol* (Seq(NT "E", NT "E")) returns (NT "(E*E)")[8].

The middle component for the combination $p1 \otimes p2$, of type mid → mid, transforms a list of rules by adding a new rule representing the sequencing of *p1* and *p2*. It should also call the underlying parsers so that they in turn add their rules.

let *seqm p1 p2* = (fun *m* → let NT *nt* = *seql p1 p2* () in
  if List.*mem nt* (List.*map fst m.rules*) then *m* else (
    let (*f1*, *g1*, _) = *unsum3 p1* in
    let (*f2*, *g2*, _) = *unsum3 p2* in
    let *new_rule* = (*nt*, Seq(*f1* (), *f2* ())) in
    let *m1* = ⟨ *m* with *rules* = (*new_rule* :: *m.rules*) ⟩ in
    let *m2* = *g1 m1* in let *m3* = *g2 m2* in *m3*))

Note that the code first checks whether the nonterminal *nt* corresponding to $p1 \otimes p2$ is already present in the rules. If so, this nonterminal has already been processed, and there is no need to continue further. This check also prevents nontermination of *seqm* when dealing with recursive grammars. If the nonterminal is not present, then the new rule is constructed, added to the list of rules, and then the middle components *g1* and *g2* of the parsers *p1* and *p2* are invoked in turn, to add their rules.

The right component of the sequencing combinator takes two parsers *p1* of type α parser3, and *p2* of type β parser3, and produces the right component of the parser $p1 \otimes p2$, of type inr → ($\alpha \times \beta$) outr.

---

[7] Related to this is the requirement that users do not annotate two *different* parsers with the *same* nonterminal; the following must be avoided:

let rec *parse_E* = (fun *i* → *mkntparser* "E" ... *i*)
  and *parse_F* = (fun *i* → *mkntparser* "E" ... *i*)

There seems no way to enforce this constraint using types. An alternative is to use a *gensym*-like technique to construct arguments to *mkntparser* automatically. This ensures uniqueness of names, but requires non-purely-functional techniques.

[8] Generated names should not clash with user names. The traditional solution is to incorporate a "forbidden" character, not available to users, into generated names. A better approach would use a more structured datatype than strings for the names of nonterminals. For simplicity, we stick with strings and assume the user does not use symbols such as * in the names of nonterminals.

```
let seqr p1 p2  =  (fun i0 →
  let sym1  =  sym_of_parser p1 in let sym2  =  sym_of_parser p2 in
  let ks  =  i0.oracle (sym1, sym2) i0.ss in
  let SS(s, i, j)  =  i0.ss in
  let f1 k  =  (
    let rs1  =  dest_inr (p1 (Inr ⟨ i0 with ss = (SS(s, i, k)) ⟩)) in
    let rs2  =  dest_inr (p2 (Inr ⟨ i0 with ss = (SS(s, k, j)) ⟩)) in
    list_product rs1 rs2) in
  List.concat (List.map f1 ks))
```

The function *seqr* first determines the symbols *sym1* and *sym2* corresponding
to the two underlying parsers. It then calls the oracle with the appropriate symbols and substring $i0.ss = \mathsf{SS}(s, i, j)$. The resulting values for k are bound to
the variable *ks*. For each of these values k, parser *p1* is called on the substring
$\mathsf{SS}(s, i, k)$ and *p2* is called on the substring $\mathsf{SS}(s, k, j)$. The results are combined
using the library functions *list_product* (which takes two lists and forms a list
of pairs) and List.*concat*. The corresponding right component *altr* for the alternative combinator is much simpler: as with traditional combinator parsers, the
results of the parsers *p1* and *p2* are simply appended.

We can now define the sequential combination $p1 \otimes p2$. This uses *seql*, *seqm*
and seqr to construct a new parser of type $(\alpha \times \beta)$ parser3 from a parser *p1* of
type α parser3 and a parser *p2* of type β parser3.

```
let p1 ⊗ p2  =  (fun i0 → let f  =  seql p1 p2 in
  let g  =  seqm p1 p2 in let h  =  seqr p1 p2 in sum3 (f, g, h) i0)
```

The alternative combination $p1 \oplus p2$ is identical, except that *seql* becomes
altl and so on. We also define the "semantic action" function, which takes a
parser p of type α parser3 and a function f from α to β and returns a parser
of type β parser3, by mapping the function f over the list of values in the right
component. Apart from the fact that we now have three components to deal
with, this is the approach taken by traditional parser combinators.

```
let p ≫ f  =  (fun i → match i with | Inl _ → (Inl (dest_inl (p i)))
  | Inm _ → (Inm (dest_inm (p i))) | Inr _ → (Inr (List.map f (dest_inr (p i)))))
```

Finally, we turn to the auxiliary function *mkntparser*. This function allows the
user to introduce concrete *names* for nonterminals, to label the corresponding
code for parsers: let *parse_E* = (fun i → *mkntparser* "E" ... i). At this stage,
we introduce a version of *mkntparser* that does not deal with context. In Section
8 we add the ability to handle context.

```
let mkntparser' nt p  =  (fun i → match i with
  | Inl () → Inl (NT nt)
  | Inm m → (if List.mem nt (List.map fst m.rules) then Inm m else (
      let sym  =  sym_of_parser p in
      let new_rule  =  (nt, Atom sym) in
      p (Inm ⟨ m with rules = (new_rule :: m.rules) ⟩))))
  | Inr r → (let Inr rs  =  p i in Inr (unique rs)))
```

For the left component, *mkntparser'* simply returns a symbol NT *nt* corresponding to the user supplied label *nt*. For the middle component, the parser *p* has a corresponding symbol *sym*. In terms of the grammar, we should add a new rule *nt* → *sym*. Thus, when passed an argument lnm *m* we add this new rule before recursively invoking the underlying parser *p*. The right component is unchanged except that as an optimization we return only unique results.

As well as *mkntparser'*, we have an auxiliary function *mktmparser* whose purpose is similar: to introduce concrete names for terminals. This is necessary because the middle component *m*, as well as accumulating the grammar rules in the field *m.rules*, also accumulates named terminal parsers in the field *m.tmparsers*.

5   Example

We can now define an example parser. At this stage, we have no way to construct an oracle automatically, so we will hand-code this aspect of the parser. In addition, we have not dealt with the parsing context, so we will not be able to handle grammars such as E -> E E E | "1" | ϵ. We will make use of the raw parser *raw_a1* from Section 3. First, we define our terminal parser:

let *a1* = *mktmparser* "1" *raw_a1*

A parser for the grammar E -> E E E | "1", where the actions count the number of 1s, is:

let rec *parse_E* = (fun *i* → *mkntparser'* "E" (
  $((parse\_E \otimes parse\_E \otimes parse\_E) \gg (\text{fun } (x, (y, z)) \to x + y + z))$
  $\oplus (a1 \gg (\text{fun } \_ \to 1))) \, i)$

In order to run our parser on some input, we need to supply an oracle. At this point, we simply hand-code the oracle. The role of the oracle is to determine, given two symbols $sym1, sym2$, where to cut an input substring $SS(s, i, j)$ into two pieces $SS(s, i, k)$ and $SS(s, k, j)$, so that the first can be parsed as $sym1$ and the second can be parsed as $sym2$.

let *oracle* = (fun $(sym1, sym2)$ → fun $(SS(s, i, j))$ → ...)

For *parse_E* there are two uses of the sequencing combinator: one corresponding to the expression $parse\_E \otimes parse\_E$, and one to the first occurence in the expression $parse\_E \otimes (parse\_E \otimes parse\_E)$[9]. The two nonterminals that can occur as arguments to the sequencing combinator are E (corresponding to inputs which are non-empty sequences of the character 1) and (E*E) (corresponding to sequences of length at least two). We introduce an auxiliary function *upto'* such that $upto' \, i \, j = [i+1; \ldots; j-1]$ and code the oracle as:

let *oracle* = (fun $(sym1, sym2)$ → fun $(SS(s, i, j))$ → match $(sym1, sym2)$ with
  | (NT "E", NT("(E*E)")) → $(upto' \, i \, (j-1))$
  | (NT "E", NT("E")) → $(upto' \, i \, j))$

We can then run a parser on an input, assuming the existence of the oracle:

---

[9] Recall that the sequencing combinator associates to the right.

```
let run_parser3' oracle p s = (let i0 = ⟨ ss = (SS(s, 0, String.length s));
    lc = empty_context; oracle = oracle ⟩ in
let rs =  dest_inr (p (Inr i0)) in unique rs)
```

This simply evaluates the right component of the parser and returns unique results. We can run the example parser in the OCaml top-level, and OCaml responds with the expected result:

```
let _ = run_parser3' oracle parse_E "1111111"
− : int list = [7]
```

We can also examine the left and middle components of our example parser. Most interesting is the middle component:

```
let m = grammar_of_parser parse_E
val m: mid = ⟨rules =  [("(E*E)", Seq (NT "E", NT "E"));
    ("(E*(E*E))", Seq (NT "E", NT "(E*E)"));
    ("((E*(E*E))+1)", Alt (NT "(E*(E*E))", TM "1"));
    ("E", Atom (NT "((E*(E*E))+1)"))];
  tmparsers =  [("1", < fun >)]⟩
```

The result is a record m. The $m.rules$ field contains a concrete representation of the grammar, with nonterminals corresponding to every use of the sequencing and alternative combinators. In addition, the $m.tmparsers$ field represents a finite map from terminals to the corresponding raw parsers. In this example, there is only one entry for the terminal "1".

In this section we have worked through the definition of a simple parser, and seen how the machinery introduced in previous sections allows us to extract a concrete representation of the grammar from code such as *parse_E*. With a concrete representation of the grammar, we can use a method such as Earley parsing to determine the information necessary to construct an oracle, and then finally use the oracle to guide the action phase of the parse.

6   Earley Parsing and Construction of the Oracle

We feed the concrete representation of the grammar, with the input string and start symbol, to an Earley parser. The resulting Earley productions can then be processed to form an oracle. As described in Section 1 an Earley production is of the form $(X \to \alpha.\beta, i, j, l)$, where $(X \to \alpha.\beta, i, j)$ is an Earley item, β is non-empty, and l indicates that β could be parsed between input positions j and l. We introduce a function *earley_prods_of_parser* of type α parser3 $\to$ string $\to$ production list, which takes a parser and an input and returns a list of productions. We process these productions using a function *oracle_of_prods* of type production list $\to$ ty_oracle. For a given parser and input, these two functions produce a parsing oracle which we use to guide the action phase. Further details of our approach to Earley parsing are included in the extended version of this paper, available in the online resources.

7   Example, with Earley Parsing

We continue the example from Section 5. Deriving the productions for a given input and constructing the oracle is straightforward:

let *ps* = *earley_prods_of_parser parse_E* "1111111"
let *oracle* = *oracle_of_prods ps*

We can query the oracle, for example, to find out where to split the input if we wish to parse a sequence of two symbols:

let _ = *oracle* (NT "E", NT "(E*E)") (SS("1111111", 0, 7))
− : int list = [1; 3; 5]

The resulting list $[1; 3; 5]$ reveals that the sequence of two nonterminals E (E*E) can be used to parse an input "1111111" by splitting the input at positions 1, 3 and 5. In Section 5 we hand coded the oracle. We can now improve on this by automatically constructing the oracle from the parser itself.

let *run_parser3 p s* = (let *ps* = *earley_prods_of_parser p s* in
   let *oracle* = *oracle_of_prods ps* in *run_parser3' oracle p s*)

We can then run our parser in the OCaml top-level as before:

let _ = *run_parser3 parse_E* "1111111"
− : int list = [7]

8   Context and Memoization

Parsing context, introduced in [13], forces all top-down parse attempts to terminate, which means that *arbitrary* context-free grammars, such as those including direct and indirect left recursion, can be handled by combinator parsers. In addition, it can be shown that using parsing context preserves the *completeness* of parsing. The technical development involves the definition of the concept of a "good" parse tree, and all good parse trees are guaranteed to be returned by our parsers. In the current setting, we use parsing context *only when applying actions*. The function *mkntparser'* of Section 4 associates a concrete symbol with a parser, but does not otherwise take parsing context into account. We also define the function *mkntparser* (used in the example in Section 2), which is identical except that it takes parsing context into account. With this change, we can handle all context-free grammars. Fully formal mechanized definitions are given in [13], and further discussion on the integration of parsing context in the current setting is given in the extended version of this paper.

Memoization is a standard technique that involves storing the results of a function. When invoking the function on an input that has already been seen, the stored result is returned without re-executing the function. We use memoization in the action phase to avoid recomputing parse results for parts of the input for which the results have already been computed. Since this material is standard, we omit further details, which can be found in the extended version of the paper.

9   Experiments and Performance

In this section we discuss performance, mainly by comparing our approach to the popular Haskell Happy parser generator [1]. We assess the performance of P3 and Happy across 5 different grammars. P3 outperforms Happy on all of these grammars, often by a large margin. There are clear opportunities to improve the performance of P3 even further, so these initial results are extremely encouraging[10].

Why Happy? We should compare P3 against a parser that can handle all context-free grammars: On restricted classes of grammar, we expect that P3 has good asymptotic performance, but absolute performance will not compare favourably with specialized parsing techniques. We carried out preliminary experiments with general parsers such as ACCENT[11], Elkhound[12] and SPARK[13], but encountered problems that were seemingly hard to resolve. For example, the author of SPARK confirmed that SPARK cannot directly handle grammars such as E -> E E | "1" | ϵ. The underlying reason appears to be that SPARK does not make use of a compact representation of parse trees, but works instead with abstract syntax trees, which is problematic in this case because a single input can give rise to a possibly infinite number of parse trees. On the other hand, it was relatively straightforward to code up example grammars in Happy, and extract the results using a compact representation. We believe Happy represents a demanding target for comparison because it is mature, well-tested and extensively optimized code. For example, the authors of the Parsec library take Happy performance to be the definition of efficiency[14].

What to Measure? We measure the time taken for each of the three phases separately. First we compare the time to compute a compact representation of all parses. This involves comparing our core implementation of Earley's algorithm with the core GLR implementation in Happy. Second, we examine the overhead of constructing the oracle. Third, we examine the cost of applying parsing actions. As a very rough guide, we expect the Earley parsing phase to be $O(n^3)$. The construction of the oracle essentially involves iterating over the list of productions, which is $O(n^3)$ in length, so we might expect that this phase should also take time $O(n^3)$. The time taken to apply the actions depends on the actions themselves, but we can analyse particular actions on a case-by-case basis to check that the observed times for this phase are reasonable.

Earley Implementation. P3 relies on a back-end parser. P3 terminal parsers are effectively arbitrary *functions*, whereas existing Earley implementations expect non-epsilon terminal parsers to parse a single character. For this reason,

---

[10] Details of the test infrastructure can be found in the online resources.

[11] http://accent.compilertools.net/

[12] http://scottmcpeak.com/elkhound/

[13] http://pages.cpsc.ucalgary.ca/~aycock/spark/

[14] "[Our real-world requirements on the combinators]...they had to be efficient (ie. competitive in speed with happy and without space leaks)" [10]

Table 1. Grammars and identifiers

Identifier	Grammar
aho_s	S -> "x" S S | ϵ
aho_sml	S -> S S "x" | ϵ
brackets	E -> E E | "(" E ")" | ϵ
E_EEE	E -> E E E | "1" | ϵ
S_xSx	S -> "1" S "1" | "1"

it was necessary to extend Earley's algorithm to treat corresponding "terminal items". We implemented an Earley parser from scratch in OCaml, emphasizing both functional correctness and performance correctness (i.e. the implementation should have worst-case $O(n^3)$ performance). For our implementation we plan to *mechanize* correctness proofs for functional correctness (the traditional target of verification) and performance correctness (which as far as we are aware has not been tackled by the verification community for non-trivial examples). The implementation is purely functional, but is parameterized by implementations of sets and maps. The sets and maps are used linearly, so it is safe for the compiler to substitute implementations which use mutable state and in-place update. The OCaml compiler does not support this optimization currently, so we introduce mutable set and map implementations manually. The timings we give here are for the default configuration which uses mutable state in cases where the input length is less than 10000, and purely functional datastructures otherwise. Falling back on purely-functional datastructures results in worst-case $O(n^3 \lg n)$ performance, but has the advantage that space consumption is typically *much reduced*, which allows us to tackle much bigger inputs than would be possible with a solely imperative implementation. Of course, for the user the library always behaves as though it is purely functional.

Grammars and Inputs. We selected 5 grammars as representative examples of general context-free grammars, see Table 1. The grammars aho_s and aho_sml are taken from a well-known book on parsing [2]. They were used to assess parser performance in related work [7]. The grammar brackets is a simple grammar for well-bracketed expressions. The grammar E_EEE is the example grammar we have used throughout the paper. The final grammar S_xSx is an example of a non-ambiguous grammar that cannot be handled using Packrat parsing, taken from [6]. These grammars attempt to cover different points in the grammar space: aho_s favours parsers which produce left-most derivations; aho_sml favours those that produce right-most derivations (e.g. GLR parsers such as Happy); E_EEE is the simplest highly-ambiguous grammar with no "left-right" or "right-left" bias. S_xSx parses unambiguously, and also favours parsers that produce right-most

Table 2. aho_s: time to compute compact representation

Size	Happy	Earley
20	0.10	0.10
40	3.18	0.10
60	28.88	0.11
80	144.50	0.13
100	512.09	0.17

Table 3. aho_sml: time to compute compact representation

Size	Happy	Earley
100	0.22	0.19
200	2.22	0.53
300	9.75	1.24
400	28.56	2.61
500	71.08	4.42

Table 4. E_EEE: Earley parse time and oracle construction time

Size	Earley	Oracle
100	0.21	0.35
200	0.67	2.33
300	1.84	6.68
400	3.68	15.21

Table 5. aho_s: Earley parse time, oracle construction time, and time to apply actions

Size	Earley	Oracle	Action
100	0.19	0.05	0.22
200	0.49	0.50	2.18
300	1.15	2.19	6.25
400	2.49	4.60	15.4
500	4.35	9.10	31.4

derivations. brackets is a standard grammar which tends to expose bugs in general parsers[15].

We used binarized versions of these grammars when measuring the performance of our Earley parser, because the P3 library feeds only binarized grammars to the Earley parser. We tried to check whether binarized versions of the grammars improved the performance of Happy, but at least with a binarized version of the grammar E_EEE, Happy appeared to hang on non-empty input strings.

For inputs, we simply used strings consisting of the characters x or 1, or well-bracketed expressions, of varying lengths. For S_xSx all inputs were of odd length.

Results: Computation of Compact Representation. Our Earley parser clearly outperformed Happy across *all* grammars. For the grammars aho_s and E_EEE the results are dramatic. For example, Table 2 gives the results for aho_s[16]. For the grammars aho_sml and S_xSx which favour the GLR approach of Happy, Earley clearly outperforms Happy, but the results are within an order of magnitude or two. For example, the results for aho_sml are given in Table 3. Finally

---

[15] One criticism of these grammars is that they are all "small". We also experimented with a large real-world grammar, the current ocamlyacc grammar for OCaml. For a sample 7,580 byte OCaml program, parsing takes about 1s, whereas ocamlyacc can parse this file in a fraction of a second. ocamlyacc has several features, such as precedence and associativity annotations, which make parsing deterministic. Our Earley implementation does not have such features, and thus produces all possible parses ignoring precedence and associativity. Future work should investigate supporting these sorts of annotation in Earley parsing. Importantly, Earley parsing using the OCaml grammar over a range on inputs resulted in almost-linear behaviour.

[16] All times in this section are measured in seconds. All sizes are measured in characters.

the grammar `brackets` caused Happy to appear to loop when parsing input, possibly due to a bug in Happy[17]. In addition to absolute performance, we can also check whether our Earley parser has the expected time complexity. Across all grammars we observe that our Earley implementation has worst-case performance $O(n^3)$ with mutable set and map implementations, and $O(n^3 \lg n)$ with purely functional set and map implementations. In conclusion, Earley clearly outperforms Happy on all grammars, sometimes dramatically so. On several grammars, Happy appeared to loop when attempting to parse inputs.

Results: Oracle Construction. How long should we expect the construction of the oracle to take? One way to construct the oracle is by iterating over the $O(n^3)$ Earley productions. We expect that oracle construction should be $O(n^3)$, and this is what we observe in practice. For example, for the grammar E_EEE, the times for the Earley phase, and the times to construct the oracle, are given in Table 4. We note that even when oracle construction time is included in the parse time, our approach outperforms Happy across all grammars.

Results: Applying Parsing Actions. We now examine the overhead of applying parsing actions. Our approach restricts to good parse trees, which are finite in number. Parsers such as Happy do not restrict to good parse trees, and so attempting to construct parse trees, or apply actions to, parsing results for a grammar such as E -> E E E | "1" | ϵ will result in non-termination. Thus, *it is not possible to compare the performance of P3 and Happy*, but we can look at the behaviour of P3 itself.

How long should we expect the action phase to take? Consider the aho_s grammar S -> "x" S S | ϵ, where the actions count the number of characters parsed. Without memoization we expect the action phase to take an exponential amount of time. With memoization we can argue as follows. Suppose the time to apply the actions is dominated by the non-memoized recursive calls, so that we can ignore the time taken for memoized calls. There are $O(n^2)$ non-memoized calls to parse an S (corresponding to different spans (i, j) of the input string). For each call, the input must be split in $O(n)$ places, and the single result from each subparse combined. Thus, each call takes $O(n)$ time, giving an overall $O(n^3)$ execution time for the action phase. In practice, the time taken to look up a precomputed value in the memoization table cannot be ignored, thus we observe slightly worse than $O(n^3)$ performance. In Table 5 we include times for all phases to give an idea of the relative costs. Using a naive estimation technique puts the action phase at $O(n^{3.2})$. For the grammars aho_sml, E_EEE and brackets one can reason similarly. Finally, consider the following code for the grammar S_xSx:

```
let rec parse_S_xSx = (fun i → memo_p3 tbl (mkntparser "S" (
  ((a1 ⊗ parse_S_xSx ⊗ a1) ≫ (fun (_,(x,_)) → 2 + x))
  ⊕ (a1 ≫ (fun _ → 1)))) i)
```

For an input of length $n+1$ there should be $n/2$ recursive calls when applying the actions, each of which takes a constant time to execute, giving expected

---

[17] Reported to the authors of Happy on 2013-06-24.

$O(n)$ cost for applying the actions. In practice, the time to apply the actions is negligible compared to the other two phases.

Conclusion. The Earley parser outperforms Happy across all grammars, often dramatically so. Even though these results are very good, we note that the performance of our Earley parser is not critical: our approach can be adapted to use any general parsing implementation as a back end, so we can take advantage of faster, optimized back-end parsers if they become available.

Constructing the oracle currently involves processing all productions from the Earley stage. A more intelligent approach would be to process only those productions that contribute to a valid parse. For example, for the grammar S_xSx there are only $O(n)$ such items. This optimization should reduce the oracle construction time significantly for many grammars.

Finally, the observed cost of applying the actions for our chosen grammars agrees with a basic complexity analysis, but there is some scope for reducing the real-world execution time further e.g. by using more sophisticated memoization techniques.

Overall, our implementation meets the expected worst-case bound of $O(n^3)$ for parsing and oracle construction, and has very good real-world performance when compared to Happy. For the action phase, the asymptotic performance also appears optimal. For all phases, there is scope for improving the real-world performance still further.

10   Related Work

Research on parsing has been carried out over many decades by many researchers. We cannot hope to survey all of this existing work, and so we here restrict ourselves to consideration of only the most directly related work. The first parsing techniques that can handle arbitrary context-free grammars are based on dynamic programming. Examples include CYK parsing [9] and Earley parsing [5]. The popular GLR parsing approach was introduced in [16]. Combinator parsing and related techniques are probably folklore. An early approach with some similarities is [12].

The extension of combinator parsing to handle all context-free grammars using a parsing context, as in this paper, appears in [13]. The performance of this approach is $O(n^5)$, which is not competitive with the approach presented here (as confirmed by real-world experiments, which we omit for space reasons). Experiments showed that this previous approach outperformed Happy on the grammar E_EEE, but it seems clear that Happy has poor real-world performance on many such grammars. As described in that paper, the use of a parsing context is related to a long line of work that uses the length of the input to force termination [8]. Grammar extraction from combinator parsers, and the use of a separate back-end parser, was first described in [11]. Our approach improves on this by providing an efficient back-end, using an oracle (rather than parse trees), context (to provide meaningful semantics via the notion of "good" parse trees), and memoization to make the action phase efficient.

Our work is motivated by the desire to provide a combinator parsing interface with performance competitive with $O(n^3)$ general algorithms such as Earley parsing. In [14] the authors "develop the fully general GLL parsing technique which is recursive descent-like, and has the property that the parse follows closely the structure of the grammar rules". The desire is to improve on the shortcomings of GLR: "Nobody could accuse a GLR implementation of a parser for, say, C++, of being easy to read, and by extension easy to debug." This work is very similar in its aims to ours. Prototype hand-coded implementations of recognizers for several grammars, based on the GLL algorithm, are described in [14]. These do not provide a combinator parsing interface. An implementation of GLL in Scala that provides the desired combinator parsing interface can be found online[18] but the author admits "at the moment, performance is basically non-existent." However, we believe that the GLL algorithm represents the main competition to our approach and we eagerly await future efficient implementations which provide a combinator parsing interface.

11   Conclusion

We presented an approach to parsing that provides a flexible interface based on parsing combinators, together with the performance of general approaches such as Earley parsing. The contributions of our work are:

- We introduced the idea of using an oracle as a compact, functional representation of parse results. This contrasts with traditional representations such as shared packed parse forests [3], which are essentially state-based representations. The idea of using an oracle as the basis of a parsing implementation is novel.
- We introduced the design of a parsing library split into a front-end combinator parsing library, and a back-end parser (here based on Earley's algorithm), connected via the oracle. This combines the well-known benefits of combinator parsing with the efficiency of general-purpose parsing algorithms such as Earley. This separation has many benefits, for example, the combinator parsers are very simple to implement, and the back-end parser can be swapped, potentially increasing performance without altering the combinator interface. This split also allows examples, such as those in Section 2, that are not possible with any other parser currently available.
- To allow arbitrary functions (of the correct type) to be used as terminal parsers, we extended Earley parsing to deal with "terminal items".
- We engineered a back-end Earley implementation. This implementation is functionally correct, and is observed to fit the worst-case time bound of $O(n^3)$ across all our example grammars. As a general parser, it has very good real-world performance, outperforming the Haskell Happy parser generator[19]

---

[18] http://www.cs.uwm.edu/ dspiewak/papers/
generalized-parser-combinators.pdf

[19] ACCENT, Elkhound and SPARK are not competitive here, see Section 9.

across all our example grammars, often dramatically so. In future work, we intend to give mechanized proofs of functional and performance correctness for this back-end parser.

- We provided the results of real-world experiments that support our performance claims.
- We showed how to define front-end parsing combinators which allow a concrete representation of the grammar (and terminal parsers) to be extracted in order to be fed to the Earley parser. These combinators then use the results of Earley parsing to guide the action phase. We argued that the performance of the action phase, when memoized, was asymptotically close to optimal. No other parsers (apart from [13] which is $O(n^5)$) support applying actions when working with *arbitrary* context-free grammars, so a real-world comparison is unfortunately not possible.
- We showed how to integrate cleanly many different techniques, including combinator parsing, Earley parsing, the oracle, memoization, and parsing contexts. In addition the online distribution integrates the technique of boxing, allowing the input type to be arbitrary. This permits both scannerless parsing, and parsing with an external lexer. Even with all these different techniques, the code is extremely concise and simple.
- We showed how to combine semantic action functions with an Earley parser. For example, using our approach it is trivial to define parsers that return parse trees, see Section 2. For other techniques, such as GLL, the construction of parse trees can itself be a significant research contribution [15].
- We developed extensive examples, available in the online distribution, that demonstrate the power of our approach.

References

1. Happy, a parser generator for Haskell, http://www.haskell.org/happy/
2. Aho, A.V., Ullman, J.D.: The theory of parsing, translation, and compiling. Prentice-Hall, Inc. (1972)
3. Atkey, R.: The semantics of parsing with semantic actions. In: LICS 2012, pp. 75–84. IEEE (2012)
4. Barthwal, A., Norrish, M.: A mechanisation of some context-free language theory in HOL4. Journal of Computer and System Sciences (2013)
5. Earley, J.: An efficient context-free parsing algorithm. Commun. ACM 13(2), 94–102 (1970)
6. Ford, B.: Packrat parsing: simple, powerful, lazy, linear time, functional pearl. In: ICFP 2002, pp. 36–47. ACM (2002)
7. Frost, R.A., Hafiz, R., Callaghan, P.: Parser combinators for ambiguous left-recursive grammars. In: Hudak, P., Warren, D.S. (eds.) PADL 2008. LNCS, vol. 4902, pp. 167–181. Springer, Heidelberg (2008)
8. Hafiz, R., Frost, R.A.: Lazy combinators for executable specifications of general attribute grammars. In: Carro, M., Peña, R. (eds.) PADL 2010. LNCS, vol. 5937, pp. 167–182. Springer, Heidelberg (2010)
9. Kasami, T.: An efficient recognition and syntax analysis algorithm for context-free languages. Tech. Rep. AFCRL-65-758, Air Force Res. Lab., Massachusetts (1965)

10. Leijen, D., Meijer, E.: Parsec: A practical parser library. Electronic Notes in Theoretical Computer Science 41(1), 1–20 (2001)
11. Ljunglöf, P.: Pure functional parsing. Göteborg University and Chalmers University of Technology, Gothenburg (2002)
12. Pratt, V.R.: Top down operator precedence. In: Proceedings ACM Symposium on Principles Prog. Languages (1973)
13. Ridge, T.: Simple, functional, sound and complete parsing for all context-free grammars. In: Jouannaud, J.-P., Shao, Z. (eds.) CPP 2011. LNCS, vol. 7086, pp. 103–118. Springer, Heidelberg (2011)
14. Scott, E., Johnstone, A.: GLL parsing. Electronic Notes in Theoretical Computer Science 253(7), 177–189 (2010)
15. Scott, E., Johnstone, A.: GLL parse-tree generation. Science of Computer Programming 78(10), 1828–1844 (2013)
16. Tomita, M.: LR parsers for natural languages. In: Proc. of the 10th Int. Conf. on Computational linguistics, pp. 354–357. ACL (1984)

Origin Tracking in Attribute Grammars

Kevin Williams and Eric Van Wyk

Department of Computer Science and Engineering
University of Minnesota, Minneapolis, MN, USA
kwill,evw@cs.umn.edu

Abstract. Origin tracking is a technique for relating the output of a transformation back to its input. In term rewriting systems, where this notion was developed, it relates subtrees in the resulting normal form term to the original term. The technique is useful in several settings, including program debugging and error reporting.

We show how origin tracking can be integrated into higher-order attribute grammars, which construct new syntax trees during attribute evaluation. Furthermore, we extend origins with additional information to track sub trees that correspond to the redex and contractum of rewrite rules when implemented using attribute grammars. The computation of origins and their extensions is formally defined using big-step operational semantics. Finally we describe a program transformation framework as an example use of origin tracking in attribute grammars.

1 Introduction and Motivation

Transformations on syntax trees have many applications, ranging from optimizations which aim to reduce execution time to translating human-readable code down into low-level languages. Such transformations can output trees with non-obvious relations to the transformation's input. Without making explicit relations between the trees, it can be difficult to perceive how the two trees are related. The transformation's output may have been copied from a subtree of the transformation's input or constructed by a transformation based on a specific subtree of the input, but these connections are lost in the transformations.

Origin tracking [5] constructs links from each node in the output tree of a transformation to a node in the transformation's input. In many cases a series of transformations is made to achieve some goal, such as optimization, and origins are traced across multiple steps. Simply put, origins connect a node to the node which introduced it to the tree. Consider a transformation which replaces every negation node *negate* with subtraction from zero. An example of this is shown in Fig. 1. Intuitively, *const*(0) and the *sub* node were introduced to the tree because the original *negate* node acted as a transformational catalyst. Other nodes in the output tree were not modified by the transformation, and thus have origins pointing back to the nodes they were copied from (the origin of *const*(3) in the output tree has an origin pointing to the *const*(3) node in the input tree).

Van Deursen [4] added origin tracking to primitive recursive schemes (PRS), in which evaluation by term rewriting is done in two phases, but we focus on the

B. Combemale et al. (Eds.): SLE 2014, LNCS 8706, pp. 282–301, 2014.

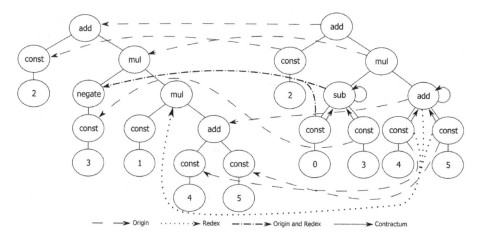

Fig. 1. Input and output for rewrite rules replacing negation with subtraction and removing the multiplicative identity. Links are shown for origins, redex, and contractum.

second here for the purpose of discussing origin tracking and connecting it to attribute grammars. In PRS evaluation, an unordered set of left-linear rewrite rules are applied nondeterministically and exhaustively to a given input tree. For example, the following rewrite rules replace negation with subtraction from zero and reduce multiplication by one on the left:

$$negate(X) \rightarrow sub(const(0), X), \quad mul(const(1), X) \rightarrow X$$

Per the notion of origins in PRS [4], origins for individual nodes are constructed based on where the node is located related to the contractum and if it was explicitly constructed from a (non-variable) term on the right hand side of the rewrite rule. If the node is either disjoint from or above the contractum, then it is given an origin based on the *context* case which points to the node from which it was duplicated in the input tree. For example, this holds for the *add* and *mul* nodes in Fig. 1. If the node is explicitly constructed by the rewrite rule (such as the *sub* and *const* (of 0) nodes in the figure), then it is given an origin based on the *auxiliary symbols* case which points to the root of the redex. Finally, nodes which are copied based on variable bindings in the rewrite rule are given an origin based on the *common variables* case which points to the node from which it was duplicated in the input tree; see the *const*(4) node in the figure. Note the similarity between origins constructed by the *context* and *common variables* cases: these are origins on nodes copied from the input tree.

In this paper, we migrate this notion of origins into attribute grammars (AGs) [10]. During tree construction, we annotate trees with a path to their origin. We use annotations to hold origins in AGs. Annotations are similar to attributes except they are set on undecorated trees when the tree is built and before its attributes are evaluated or it is used as sub-tree in some other tree construction operation. Annotations are accessed in the same way as attributes (e.g. *t.anno* where *anno* is an annotation on tree *t*). The operational semantics of this evaluation are presented in Section 2 without origins and in Section 3 with origins.

With origins and without the rewrite rules themselves, it can still be difficult to determine what caused the changes resulting in the *const*(4) node in Fig. 1. By adding a reference for the redex (dotted and dash-dotted lines), it is clear that it was affected by a reducing transformation catalyzed by the lower *mul* node in the input tree, which is not clear with only origin edges. Similarly, adding the contractum arrow for *const*(0) shows that it was not the only node modified by the transformation which constructed it; because its contractum points to its parent, it can assume that its parent is also new. Beyond redex and contractum, we found two additional properties which are useful in exploring transformations: a boolean flag which shows whether the node was newly constructed by the transformation (nodes constructed by the *auxiliary symbols* case in a PRS) and a set of labels which describe the applied transformation. While these four properties have simple implementations within PRS, they are not straightforward to define these within AGs. This is partly due to the abundance of attributes which construct the unmodified nodes and are unnecessary in PRS. The combination of these four new properties with origins are called extended origins and are discussed in Section 4.

In Section 2, we define a simple attribute grammar calculus and the big-step operational semantics of attribute evaluation. The effort to define this operational semantics pays off in Section 3 where it is extended to precisely show how origins can be added to attribute grammars and computed during attribute evaluation, the first contribution of this paper. The second contribution is the definition and specification of *extended* origins in Section 4. This extension adds to each node whether the node was newly constructed by a transformation, the node's redex, the node's contractum, and a set of descriptive labels. Section 5 contains the third contribution, an application to a program transformation specification language based on Halide [12], a transformation tool for optimizing matrix computations. We close with related work in Section 6 and conclude in Section 7.

2   Attribute Grammars

In this section we provide a specification of attribute grammars that is used throughout the paper. After a description of the structure of an attribute grammar we provide a big-step operational semantics for evaluation of expressions in attribute equations without origins. This semantics is then extended in Sections 3 and 4 to compute origins and their extensions during attribute evaluation. Typing rules for expressions are also provided to aid in understanding the distinction between undecorated and decorated trees.

2.1 Definition of the Formalism

In this formulation of attribute grammars we assume a set of primitive types, PT, used in all attribute grammars, where PT includes types $Bool$, Int, Str.

An attribute grammar AG has the form $\langle G, A, O, D \rangle$ where $G = \langle N, P, sig, S \rangle$ is the underlying context free grammar. N is the set of nonterminals. $X = N \cup PT$, and denotes the symbols that appear on the right hand side of productions. P is finite set of production names, each with a signature $sig(p \in P) = x_0 :: N_0 \ ::= \ x_1 :: X_1 \ ... \ x_{n_p} :: X_{n_p}$ where $n_p \geq 0$. In this formalism, as in our attribute grammar system Silver [13], production signatures provide names for the symbols in a production; these names are then used in attribute equations to refer to nodes in the syntax tree. A function $type_P$ extracts just the type from a production signature such that $type(x_0 :: N_0 \ ::= \ x_1 :: X_1 \ ... \ x_{n_p} :: X_{n_p}) = N_0 ::= X_1 ... X_{n_p}$. $S \in N$ is the type of the root node of a tree representing, for example, a complete program or compilation unit.

The set of attributes $A = \langle A_{syn}, A_{inh}, A_{loc}, type_A \rangle$, contains the finite disjoint sets of names of, respectively, the synthesized, inherited, and local attributes and a mapping of attribute names to types in X. Note that $type_A(a \in A_{syn} \cup A_{inh}) \in X$ since we limit synthesized and inherited attributes to hold only undecorated trees and primitive values. This can easily be generalized to support reference [6] or remote [2] attributes (decorated trees) but we keep things simple in this formalism. $type_A(a \in A_{loc}) \in N$ so that local attributes only hold syntax trees. In the original work on HOAGs [14], this was the case and local attributes were called non-terminal attributes. Note that in Silver and other AG systems, we generalize this to allow local attributes to hold any type, but restrict them here to trees to simplify the discussion.

The "occurs-on" relation $O = \langle O_{attr}, O_{loc} \rangle$ indicates which attributes occur on which nonterminals and which local attributes occur on which productions: $O_{attr} \subseteq (A_{syn} \cup A_{inh}) \times N$ and $O_{loc} \subseteq A_{loc} \times P$. Note that a local attribute has the same type on each production. Though not formalized here, there are no inherited attributes on S.

Attribute equations and functions are specified in $D = \langle EQ, \sigma_f \rangle$. EQ is the set of set of equations indexed by P and have the form $lhs = e$. Expressions e are defined below, and the left hand side lhs, for a production $p \in P$ with $sig(p) = x_0 :: N_0 \ ::= \ x_1 :: X_1 \ ... \ x_{n_p} :: X_{n_p}$, has the form

$$
\begin{aligned}
lhs ::= \ & x_0.a \text{ where } (a, N) \in O_{syn} \\
\mid \ & x_i.a \text{ where } i > 0, (a, X_i) \in O_{attr}, a \in A_{inh} \\
\mid \ & \ell_i.a \text{ where } (a, type_A(\ell_i)) \in O_{attr}, a \in inh \\
\mid \ & \ell_i \quad \text{ where } (\ell_i, p) \in O_{loc}
\end{aligned}
$$

F is finite set of function names, $F = dom(\sigma_f)$, where σ_f maps function names to lambda-expressions of the form $\lambda y_1 : T_1, ..., y_n : T_n.e$, where y ranges over variables bound in expressions and T ranges over types, defined below.

Fig. 2 shows an attribute grammar, written in Silver, that computes the transformations described in Section 1. Note that here, the process is deterministically driven by a root production $root$ which defines its $doExpd$ local attribute

```
nonterminal Root, Expr;

synthesized attribute expd::Expr
  occurs on Expr;
synthesized attribute simp::Expr
  occurs on Expr;

abstract production negate
e::Expr ::= ne::Expr
{ e.expd = sub(const(0), ne.expd);
  e.simp = negate(ne.simp);  }

abstract production mul
e::Expr ::= l::Expr r::Expr
{ e.expd = mul(l.expd, r.expd);
  e.simp
    = case l of
      | const(1) -> r.simp
      | _ -> mul(l.simp, r.simp)
      end;  }
```

```
abstract production root
r::Root ::= e::Expr
{ local doExpd :: Expr = e.expd;
  local doSimp :: Expr =
    doExpd.simp;  }

abstract production add
e::Expr ::= l::Expr r::Expr
{ e.expd = add(l.expd, r.expd);
  e.simp = add(l.simp, r.simp);  }

abstract production sub
e::Expr ::= l::Expr r::Expr
{ e.expd = sub(l.expd, r.expd);
  e.simp = sub(l.simp, r.simp);  }

abstract production const
e::Expr ::= i::Integer
{ e.expd = const(i);
  e.simp = const(i);  }
```

Fig. 2. Silver syntax specification which replaces negation with subtraction from zero and removes the multiplicative identity

as the expanded tree which replaces negation with subtraction. Similarly, the *doSimp* local attribute removes multiplicative identities from *doExpd*. Two of the attribute equations have obvious connections to the original rewrite rules: *negate*'s *expd* equation resembles the negation expansion rule, and *mul*'s *simp* equation resembles the rule conducting the removal of the multiplicative identity. The remaining attributes serve to reconstruct the tree outside where the rewrite rule would have been applied; in the PRS, this reconstruction is conducted automatically behind the scenes.

Many attributes have dependencies on other attributes on the same production or on its children. Thus attributes without any dependencies are evaluated first, followed by attributes whose dependencies have been evaluated. Thus, for well-defined attribute grammars, evaluation never runs into the case where needed attributes are not defined. Note that references to parent (left hand side), child, and local attribute trees are seen as decorated in attribute equations; this is reflected in the typing rules found in the following section.

2.2   Static and Dynamic Semantics of Expression Evaluation

Here we first discuss the form of expressions (e), values (v), and types (T), as shown in Fig. 3, and present typing and big-step operational semantics evaluation rules for expressions without origins. These rules are relatively straightforward; the only potentially unexpected aspect is that we treat decorated and undecorated syntax trees as having different types and, thus, value representations.

$$e ::= \textbf{if } e \textbf{ then } e \textbf{ else } e$$
$$| \quad \textbf{case } e \textbf{ of}$$
$$\quad q_1(y_1^1, ..., y_{n_{q_1}}^1) \Rightarrow e_1$$
$$\quad ...$$
$$\quad q_n(y_1^n, ..., y_{n_{q_n}}^n) \Rightarrow e_n$$
$$| \quad f(e, ..., e)$$
$$| \quad var$$
$$| \quad var.attr$$
$$| \quad p(e, ..., e)$$
$$| \quad \textbf{new } var$$
$$| \quad v$$
$$var ::= x_0 \quad | \quad x_i, i > 0 \quad | \quad \ell_i \quad | \quad y$$

$$v ::= \textbf{true}$$
$$| \quad \textbf{false}$$
$$| \quad n$$
$$| \quad str$$
$$| \quad p(v, ..., v)$$
$$| \quad [n, ..., n]$$
$$| \quad \lambda y_1 : T_1, ..., y_n : T_n.e$$
$$T ::= PT$$
$$| \quad N$$
$$| \quad N ::= X...X$$
$$| \quad T...T \rightarrow T$$
$$| \quad Ref \ N$$

Fig. 3. The form of expressions e, variables var, values v, and types T

The primary reason for the formality here is to be provide a precise means for specifying the computation of origin, redex, and contractum information in the later, extended version of these evaluation rules.

Expressions include if-then-else expressions, case-expressions, and function application that behave as one would expect in a functional language; these are listed first in the productions over e. Case expressions also introduce variable bindings which again are denoted by y_i. Expressions also include variable references, var, of which there are four varieties: references to the tree constructed by a production and named by the variable on the root/left-hand side (x_0) and child trees ($x_i, i > 0$). Local attributes (ℓ_i) and bound variables y round out the types of variables, all denoted by var.

Attributes may be referenced on decorated syntax trees, denoted $var.attr$. The restriction of $var.attr$, and not allowing $e.attr$, ensures that attributes are only accessed of the production root, children, locals or variables bound by functions or case-expressions. The restriction is removed in Silver and most AG systems but it keeps things simple here. Tree construction, $p(e_1, ..., e_{n_p})$, constructs new undecorated syntax trees. Synthesized attributes cannot be accessed on such trees; the process of decorating the root node of an undecorated tree with its inherited attributes converts it to decorated tree.

Expressions also include the values, v, to which which expressions evaluate, also shown in Fig. 3. These include boolean, numeric (n), and string (str) literals. Tree literals $p(v, ..., v)$ are undecorated trees; they are simply terms in the language of the grammar G. Paths, $[n_1, ..., n_k]$, are sequences of integers describing a path to a subtree. The empty path $[\ ]$ refers to the root node of the original syntax tree, $[1]$ refers to the first child of that root node, and the path $[1, 2]$ refers to the second child of that first child. For example, the *negate* node in Fig. 1 is referenced by the path $[2, 1]$. Finally, lambda expressions are also values.

Types include primitive types PT, undecorated trees with nonterminal of type N at the root, production types $N ::= X...X$, function types $T...T \rightarrow T$ and path types, $Ref \ N$, for paths to trees of type N.

Fig. 4 contains the big-step operational semantics of the evaluation of expressions, these rules have the form $\sigma, t \vdash e \to v$ indicating that for an environment σ mapping bound variables y to values, and expression e that is part of an equation for the production that constructed the tree t, evaluates to value v.

The figure also has typing rules to assisting in understanding evaluation. These have the form $AG, p, \Gamma \vdash e \colon T$ indicating that an expression e in an equation associated with production p in AG has type T where Γ maps bound variables to their types.

Before beginning, we note one additional form of type rule for production, function, and attribute names of the form $AG \vdash e \colon T$ since these are done independently of any production or equation. Specifically, $AG \vdash p \colon T$, $AG \vdash f \colon T$, and $AG \vdash a \colon T$ indicate that, respectively, a production p, function f or attribute a has the indicated type. These are straightforward and not formalized here, they simply refer to the appropriate components of AG.

Variable references: Inside of equations for a production we consider the variables representing the root, child nodes, and local attributes to be decorated trees, and thus their type is *Ref N* and their values are paths to the appropriate nodes. For example, in Fig. 4 the rule T-ROOT indicates that the root node variable x_0 is a reference to the nonterminal on the left hand side of the production p. Rule E-ROOT indicates that x_o evaluates to the path t on the left hand side of the turnstile — this is the path to the tree on which this expression is being evaluated. Child node variables x_i are typed similarly and evaluate to the path to the tree t extended to denote their sub-tree. Local attributes are declared to have the type of a nonterminal, just like child trees in productions and similarly the production has equations defining the inherited attributes on each local attribute. Thus their type in expressions are decorated trees, represented by paths. The negation of the index i for the local ℓ_i is used in specifying the path to this local decorate tree. Bound variables are bound to types and values and are found in Γ and σ, respectively.

Attribute access: The type rule T-SYNINH checks that attributes are accessed on decorated trees only, and that the attribute decorates the tree and thus determines its type. The rule E-SYNINH indicates that because the parent node, each child node, and local variables are typed as decorated trees, synthesized and inherited attributes can be accessed from them. (Note that local attributes are accessed by name directly, without the "dot" notation shown above.)

Tree construction: Productions are used like functions to build undecorated trees of some nonterminal type N, and are essentially just terms in the language of G. Child expressions are evaluated to values that match the production's type.

When an equation copies an undecorated tree value into a higher order synthesized or inherited attribute (of the same type), it is simply that same undecorated tree that is stored in the attribute. On the other hand, when an equation copies such a value into a local attribute, then that undecorated tree becomes a decorated tree in the sense that it can now be given inherited attributes and then have synthesized attributes computed on it.

$$\frac{AG \vdash p: N ::= X_1...X_n}{AG, p, \_ \vdash x_0: Ref\ N}\ \text{(T-ROOT)}$$

$$\sigma, t \vdash x_0 \to t \quad \text{(E-ROOT)}$$

$$\frac{AG, p, \Gamma \vdash var: Ref\ N \quad (attr, N) \in O_{attr} \quad AG \vdash attr: T}{AG = \langle G, A, \langle O_{attr}, \_ \rangle, p, \Gamma \vdash var.attr: T}\ \text{(T-SYNINH)}$$

$$\frac{\sigma, t \vdash var \to h}{\sigma, t \vdash var.attr \to h.attr}\ \text{(E-SYNINH)}$$

$$\frac{i > 0 \quad AG \vdash p: N ::= X_1...X_n}{AG, p, \_ \vdash x_i: Ref\ X_i}\ \text{(T-CHILD)}$$

$$\frac{i > 0}{\sigma, t \vdash x_i \to t \cdot [i]}\ \text{(E-CHILD)}$$

$$\frac{AG \vdash p: N ::= X_1, ..., X_n \quad \forall i_n^1(AG, p, \Gamma \vdash e_i: X_i)}{AG, p, \Gamma \vdash p(e_1, ..., e_n): N}\ \text{(T-TREE)}$$

$$\frac{AG \vdash \ell: N}{AG, p, \_ \vdash \ell_i: Ref\ N}\ \text{(T-LOCAL)}$$

$$\frac{\forall i_n^1(\sigma, t \vdash e_i \Rightarrow v_i)}{\sigma, t \vdash q(e_1, ..., e_n) \Rightarrow q(v_1, ..., v_n)}\ \text{(E-TREE)}$$

$$\sigma, t \vdash \ell_i \to t \cdot [-i]\ \text{(E-LOCAL)}$$

$$\frac{AG, p, \Gamma \vdash var: Ref\ X}{AG, p, \Gamma \vdash \mathbf{new}\ var: X}\ \text{(T-NEW)}$$

$$\frac{(y, T) \in \Gamma}{AG, p, \Gamma \vdash y: T}\ \text{(T-BVAR)}$$

$$\frac{\sigma, t \vdash var \to h}{\sigma, t \vdash \mathbf{new}\ var \to *h}\ \text{(E-NEW)}$$

$$\frac{(y, v) \in \sigma}{\sigma, t \vdash y \to v}\ \text{(E-BVAR)}$$

$$\frac{AG, p, \Gamma \vdash e: Ref\ N \quad \forall i_n^1(AG \vdash q_i: N ::= X_1^i...X_{n_{q_i}}^i) \quad \forall i_n^1(AG, p, \Gamma[r_1^i \mapsto Ref\ X_1, ..., r_{n_{q_i}}^i \mapsto Ref\ X_{n_{q_i}}] \vdash e_i: T)}{AG, p, \Gamma \vdash \mathbf{case}\ e\ \mathbf{of}\ q_1(y_1^1, ..., y_{n_{q_i}}^1) \Rightarrow e_1\ ...\ q_n(y_1^n, ..., y_{n_{q_n}}^n) \Rightarrow e_n: T}\ \text{(T-CASE)}$$

$$\frac{\sigma, t \vdash e \to h \quad q_i = prod(*h) \quad \sigma[y_1^i \mapsto h \cdot [1], ..., y_{n_{q_1}}^i \mapsto h \cdot [n_{q_i}]], t \vdash e_i \to v}{\sigma, t \vdash \mathbf{case}\ e\ \mathbf{of}\ q_1(y_1^1, ..., y_{n_{q_1}}^1) \Rightarrow e_1\ ...\ q_n(y_1^n, ..., y_{n_{q_n}}^n) \Rightarrow e_n \to v}\ \text{(E-CASE)}$$

$$\frac{AG, p, \Gamma \vdash e_1: Bool \quad AG, p, \Gamma \vdash e_2: T \quad AG, p, \Gamma \vdash e_3: T}{AG, p, \Gamma \vdash \mathbf{if}\ e_1\ \mathbf{then}\ e_2\ \mathbf{else}\ e_3: T}\ \text{(T-IF)}$$

$$\frac{\sigma, t \vdash e_1 \to \mathbf{true} \quad \sigma, t \vdash e_2 \to v}{\sigma, t \vdash \mathbf{if}\ e_1\ \mathbf{then}\ e_2\ \mathbf{else}\ e_3 \to v}\ \text{(E-IFTRUE)}$$

$$\frac{\sigma, t \vdash e_1 \to \mathbf{false} \quad \sigma, t \vdash e_3 \to v}{\sigma, t \vdash \mathbf{if}\ e_1\ \mathbf{then}\ e_2\ \mathbf{else}\ e_3 \to v}\ \text{(E-IFFALSE)}$$

$$\frac{AG \vdash f: T ::= T_1, ..., T_n \quad \forall i_n^1(AG, p, \Gamma \vdash e_i: T_i)}{AG, p, \Gamma \vdash f(e_1, ..., e_n): T}\ \text{(T-FUNCAPP)}$$

$$\frac{\sigma_f(f) = \lambda y_1: T_1, ..., y_n: T_n.e \quad \forall i_n^1(\sigma, t \vdash e_i \to v_i) \quad \sigma[y_1 \mapsto v_1, ..., y_n \mapsto v_n], t \vdash e \to v}{\sigma, t \vdash f(e_1, ..., e_n) \to v}\ \text{(E-FUNCAPP)}$$

Fig. 4. Typing and evaluation rules for expressions without origins

New: As described by rule E-NEW, the *new* operator extracts the value (an undecorated tree or primitive value) that a path refers to. (confirmed by the type rule T-NEW). It uses a dereference operator * to do this. A path refers to a decorated tree or a primitive value, the dereference operator extracts a new undecorated tree from that path. In the case of a primitive value it just returns it. Note that in this formulation only variable accesses evaluate to references.

Case: The type rule T-CASE requires that the expression to be matched, e, be a reference to a tree with type N, each production to be matched, p_i, must have n_{p_i} children, and each expression e_i has the same type. Note that the types added to Γ for evaluation of the case clause expression are converted to *Ref* types. This is the same process used in the type rules of parent, child, and local variables since all of these will be seen as decorated (*Ref*) trees in the evaluation of the expression. The rule E-CASE matches the result of evaluating e with one of the given productions p_i, binds each y_j^i to the jth child of the value of e, and evaluates the ith expression e_i.

Other constructs: The typing and evaluation rules for if-then-else expressions and function application are the same as in simple functional languages.

3   Origin Tracking in Attribute Grammars

In Section 2, we defined how attributes are evaluated within AGs without origins. In this section, we define how attributes are evaluated with origins. The semantics in that section were defined so that only a few key modifications need to be made to compute origins during expression evaluation, as described below.

As discussed above, the origin is defined as an annotation which contains a reference to the node's origin. In the case of initial trees, the origin is defined as $\perp$. We redefine the language of values v to replace the tree value $p(v, ..., v)$ with the tree value with an origin with a vertical bar to divide it from the node's children: $p(v, ..., v|o)$. None of the typing rules require modification, but two evaluation rules must be updated. These two rules (E-TREE and E-NEW) are replaced by the two rules shown in Fig. 5. The rule E-O-TREE is only different from E-TREE in that it gives the constructed tree an origin pointing to the tree on which the attribute is defined.

Where E-NEW used *h, the rule E-O-NEW uses *duplicate(h)*, the function *duplicate* is defined in Fig. 6. If *duplicate* is passed a path to a primitive value, then it returns that value. If *duplicate* is passed a path to a (decorated) tree it constructs an undecorated copy of the tree with origins on the new tree pointing to the corresponding nodes on the original tree. Note that *duplicate* mimics the *common variables* case of PRS origins discussed in Section 1 in that a subtree is copied into the result of the transformation's output such that its origins point back to the transformation's input.

If we replace the expression for the *simp* equation on production *mul* in Fig. 2 with *simplify(l, r)* where *simplify* is a function whose body is the **case** expression

$$\frac{\forall i_n^1(\sigma, t \vdash e_i \to v_i)}{\sigma, t \vdash q(e_1, ..., e_n) \to q(v_1, ..., v_n | t)} \qquad \text{(E-O-Tree)}$$

$$\frac{\sigma, t \vdash var \to h}{\sigma, t \vdash \mathbf{new}\ var \to duplicate(h)} \qquad \text{(E-O-New)}$$

Fig. 5. New rules required to add origins to AGs. The "E-O-" prefix in the name of each of the above rules means that the rule replaced the similarly named rules from Fig. 4 with the "E-" prefix. Note that adding origins does not affect the typing relations.

$duplicate(h) =$
    $if\ type(*h) \in PT\ then\ *h$
    $else\ case\ *h\ of$
        $q(t_1, ..., t_k |\_) \to\ q(\ duplicate(h \cdot [1]), ..., duplicate(h \cdot [k])\ |\ h\ )$

Fig. 6. Definition of duplicate with origins using pseudo code

currently in the figure, then the origin computed for any tree now constructed or duplicated in that function is the same as if the function *simplify* was not called and the original specification was used. This is because the evaluation rule E-FuncApp in Fig. 4 uses the same tree t in the context of evaluating $f(e_1, ..., e_n)$ as in the context of evaluating the body of f. Thus, origins are dependent on the attribute being evaluated, not the functions used in that evaluation.

To simplify interaction with the generated origins, we define the function *getOrigin* such that $getOrigin(p(t_1, ..., t_k | o)) = o$. A tree's origin *path* is generated by repeatedly calling *getOrigin* on its output until it returns $\bot$ (signifying the initial tree has been reached). Note that origin paths and paths are different: *origin paths* are ordered sequences of trees, and paths $[n, ..., n]$ as seen in v are ordered sequences of integers used to locate decorated trees. This function will be added to the interface defined in the next section.

4   Extending Origin Tracking with Transformation Information

Origins are useful for constructing paths from the result of a set of transformations to the initial tree. However, the information provided by origins does not always provide all of the information that we may want from a transformation. Specifically, the answers to the following four questions are missing:

- Was the tree newly constructed by the transformation in question?
- What is the root of the transformation's input (its redex)?
- What is the root of the transformation's output (its contractum)?
- Why did the transformation happen?

We define a set of functions to provide an interface for answering these questions. The first question is answered by a function *getIsContractum* that returns true on subtrees which were not just copied from the previous tree (i.e. *true* for nodes with *auxiliary symbols* origins). The second question is answered by *getRedex* which returns a path to the redex of the transformation, and the third is answered by a function *getContractum* which returns a path to the contractum of the transformation. The fourth question is answered by a function *getLabels* which returns a set of *labels* for a given subtree where each *label* contains a characterization of the transformation which constructed the subtree.

These four functions, along with origins, make our interface for extended origins. Two of these functions (*getIsContractum* and *getLabels*) directly return annotations pulled off of their argument while the others compute their results from new annotations.

4.1   The Extended Origins Interface

In this section, we define the interface functions and state some invariants on their behavior.

The function *getIsContractum* returns whether a node was newly introduced by the last applied transformation, and requires a new annotation of type *bool* called *isContractum* such that $getIsContractum(t) = t.isContractum$. This annotation is set so that the nodes with *context* or *common variables* origins in the PRS setting define *isContractum* to be *false* and those nodes with *auxiliary symbols* origins define *isContractum* to be *true*.

To set *isContractum* we must be able distinguish between attribute equations that implement a rewrite rule and set *isContractum* to *true* (such as the definition of *expd* on *negate* and *simp* on *mul* in Fig. 2) and those that direct the transformation and set *isContractum* to *false* (such as the both attributes on *sub*). The expression $p(e_1, ..., e_n)$ is evaluated with *isContractum* = *true* unless three conditions hold, indicating that *isContractum* should be set *false*. These are:

- p matches the production of the tree the attribute is evaluated on,
- each e_i is either x_i or $x_i.attr$ for some attribute *attr*, and
- the constructed tree will be the root (not some subtree) of the tree eventually computed as the value of the attribute whose equation is being evaluated.

The first two conditions are simple to validate, and the third is determined by a new boolean flag *er* which is added to the left of the turnstile in the evaluation relation defined below. In our running example, in the *expd* attribute on *negate*, the *sub* node is evaluated where *er* = *true* and the *const*(0) node is evaluated where *er* = *false*.

getLabels requires a new finite set L with type *labels* $\times P \times A$ which statically defines labels for each attribute on each production. Calling *getLabels(t)* returns the set of labels associated with the production p and attribute *attr* which constructed t, denoted L^p_{attr}. These labels may be different for every application, but possible labels for AGs include "translation", "rephrasing", "local", "inherited", and "synthesized". Other customizable labels refer to the task completed

$$getRedex(t) =$$
$$\quad if\ t = \bot\ then\ \bot$$
$$\quad else\ if\ t.redex \neq \bot\ then\ t.redex$$
$$\quad\quad else\ getRedex(parent(t))$$
(a)

$$getContractum(t) =$$
$$\quad if\ t = \bot\ then\ \bot$$
$$\quad else\ if\ t.redex \neq \bot\ then\ t$$
$$\quad\quad else\ getContractum(parent(t))$$
(b)

Fig. 7. Definitions of getContractum and getRedex using pseudo code

by a given attribute, such as "replace negation with subtraction". Though these labels are strings, we do not exclude the possibility for labels of other types.

$getRedex$ and $getContractum$ require a single new annotation called $redex$ which contains either a path to the redex of the tree the annotation resides on or $\bot$, indicating that there is no redex. Both $getContractum$ and $getRedex$ are defined using a helper function $parent$ which returns the parent node of its given subtree or $\bot$ if it does not have a parent. $getRedex$ is defined in Fig. 7(a), and $getContractum$ is defined in Fig. 7(b).

Consider the following nodes in the output tree in the example from Section 1: sub, the inner add, and mul. The sub node, t_s, was constructed by the $expd$ attribute on $negate$ and $getIsContractum(t_s) = true$, $getRedex(t_s)$ returns a path to the $negate$ node, and $getContractum(t_s)$ returns a path to t_s. The add node, t_a, was copied by the inner mul in the input tree using a new $copy$ which defines t_a's redex as a path to the inner mul in the input tree. Also, $getIsContractum(t_a) = false$ and $getContractum(t_a)$ returns a path to t_a. The mul node, t_m, was unchanged by the transformation and is not new, so $getIsContractum(t_m) = false$, and $getRedex(t_m) = getContractum(t_m) = \bot$.

Below are invariants relating the above functions and origins on a tree t with children $t_1, ..., t_n$. Each invariant is followed by a brief description.

$$getOrigin(t) = \bot \implies \neg getIsContractum(t) \land getRedex(t) = \bot \land$$
$$getContractum(t) = \bot \land getLabels(t) = \{\}$$

If the origin is undefined (which only occurs on initial trees) then the above are default values for each of the properties.

$$getIsContractum(t) \implies getOrigin(t) \neq \bot \land getRedex(t) \neq \bot \land$$
$$getContractum(t) \neq \bot$$

If the tree was constructed by a transformation, then its origin, redex, and contractum are defined.

$$getOrigin(t) \neq \bot \implies \forall t_i(getOrigin(t_i) \neq \bot)$$

If the origin is defined, then the origin of every child of t is defined.

$$(getRedex(t) \neq \bot \land getContractum(t) \neq \bot) \implies$$
$$\forall t_i(getRedex(t_i) \neq \bot \land getContractum(t_i) \neq \bot)$$

If a tree defines both its redex and contractum, then each of its children define their redexes and contractums.

$$getRedex(t) \neq \bot \iff getContractum(t) \neq \bot$$

The redex is defined if and only if the contractum is defined. This is should be clear from each of their definitions.

4.2   Evaluating Extended Origins in Attribute Grammars

As seen above, extending origins requires three new annotations: $isContractum$, $redex$, and $labels$. Thus the tree value form $p(v_1, ..., v_n|v)$ in v is replaced by $p(v_1, ..., v_n|v, v, v, v)$ where the first annotation is the node's origin, the second holds $isContractum$, the third holds $redex$, and the last holds $labels$.

Also, two items are added to the left of the turnstile in the evaluation rules: er (used for setting $isContractum$) and the name of the attribute being evaluated, a, to find the correct set of labels. Thus evaluation rules have the form

$$\sigma, t, a, er \vdash e \to v.$$

Many of the evaluation rules used for origins are only changed to use this extended form and thus are not shown. Some only require the addition of the two variables in the consequent, as shown here:

$$\frac{i > 0}{\sigma, t, a, er \vdash x_i \to t \cdot [i]} \qquad \text{(E-EO-CHILD)}$$

This applies to E-EO-ROOT, E-EO-LOCAL, and E-EO-BVAR. Others, including E-EO-IFTRUE, E-EO-IFFALSE, E-EO-CASE, and E-EO-FUNCAPP, simply use the new form in the antecedent, passing along the new values a and er in the evaluation of their component expressions. Recall that function application with origins constructs origins based on the tree on which the attribute is being evaluated. Similarly, the annotations introduced in extended origins are constructed independently of the function being evaluated as they are also passed along as values to the left of the turnstile.

The rule for attribute access requires a notable modification. Consider the reducing transformation conducted by mul in the example in Fig. 1. If the left child of mul is $const(1)$, then the node's $simp$ attribute returns a copy of the $simp$ attribute on the node's right child. If tree copying remains unchanged and copies every annotation on the tree, then the resulting attribute might not define the correct redex. In our example, it would not define any redex. This is inconsistent with the description of $getRedex$ which should define a redex because a transformation has changed the tree. We explicitly define the $copy$ functionality for attribute access for extended origins. The $copy$ is shown in Fig. 8(a), and the new rules are shown here:

$$\frac{\sigma, t, a, true \vdash var \to h}{\sigma, t, a, true \vdash var.attr \to copy(h.attr, t)} \qquad \text{(E-EO-SYNINHR)}$$

$$copy(t', r') =$$
$$\quad if\ type(t') \in PT\ then\ t'$$
$$\quad else\ case\ t'\ of$$
$$\quad\quad q(t'_1, ..., t'_k | o, n, r, l) \rightarrow$$
$$\quad\quad\quad q(copy(t'_1, \bot), ..., copy(t'_k, \bot)),$$
$$\quad\quad\quad | \ o, n, if\ r' \neq \bot\ then\ r'\ else\ r, l))$$

$$duplicate(h, r', l') =$$
$$\quad if\ (type(*h) \in PT\ then\ *h$$
$$\quad else\ case\ *h\ of$$
$$\quad\quad q(t'_1, ..., t'_k | o, n, r, l) \rightarrow$$
$$\quad\quad\quad q(duplicate(h \cdot [1], \bot, l'), ...,$$
$$\quad\quad\quad duplicate(h \cdot [k], \bot, l')$$
$$\quad\quad\quad | \ h, false, r', l')$$

(a) (b)

Fig. 8. Definitions of *copy* and *duplicate* for extended origins using pseudo code. *copy* only modifies the redex if r' is not $\bot$, and *duplicate* specifies every annotation.

$$\frac{\sigma, t, a, false \vdash var \rightarrow h}{\sigma, t, a, false \vdash var.attr \rightarrow copy(h.attr, \bot)} \ \text{(E-EO-SynInhNR)}$$

In E-EO-SynInhR, the expression will return a value which is the root of the value computed for attribute a, so the value of the attribute $attr$ on h is modified to have a redex pointing to t. In E-EO-SynInhNR, the expression will not be the root of the value on attribute a, so it is copied with an undefined local redex.

The rules for *new*, and thus the *duplicate* function, must be modified to construct correct values for new annotations *isContractum*, *redex*, and *labels* for duplicated trees. Our original example does not include any such *common variables* cases, for example if in the *simp* equation on *mul* we replaced $r.simp$ with just r. In this case the new tree should have *isContractum* set to *false* and *redex* set to a path to the *mul* node. We define a new *duplicate* which modifies the one in Fig. 6 and inserts the new annotations. The new definition of *duplicate* is shown in Fig. 8(b), and the new rules that replace E-New are shown here:

$$\frac{\sigma, t, a, true \vdash var \rightarrow h}{\sigma, t, a, true \vdash \mathbf{new}\ var \rightarrow duplicate(h, t, L_a^{prod(t)})} \ \text{(E-EO-NewR)}$$

$$\frac{\sigma, t, a, false \vdash var \rightarrow h}{\sigma, t, a, false \vdash \mathbf{new}\ var \rightarrow duplicate(h, \bot, L_a^{prod(t)})} \ \text{(E-EO-NewNR)}$$

In E-EO-NewR, *new* is evaluated such that the given path is duplicated and given t as a new redex if $er = true$ and $\bot$ if $er = false$.

This last set of rules demonstrates the greatest difference between the evaluation of origins and extended origins. Since we need to determine if a tree is part of the contractum to set *isContractum* and set its *redex* annotation the single rule E-O-Tree is replaced by three rules shown in Fig. 9. Rule E-EO-NotCntr defines the case in which the constructed tree has a *context* or *common variables* type of origin and is not a constructed as part of the contractum (abbreviated Cntr in rule names). In this case the constructed tree does not have a redex and sets *isContractum* to *false*. The *mul* node in the

$$\frac{q = prod(*t) \quad \forall i_n^1(e_i = \textbf{new } x_i \vee e_i = x_i.attr) \quad \forall i_n^1(\sigma, t, a, false \vdash e_i \Rightarrow v_i)}{\sigma, t, a, true \vdash q(e_1, ..., e_n) \Rightarrow q(v_1, ..., v_n | t, false, \bot, L_{attr}^{prod(t)})}$$
$$\text{(E-EO-NotCntr)}$$

$$\frac{\neg(q = prod(*t) \wedge \forall i_n^1(e_i = \textbf{new } x_i \vee e_i = x_i.attr)) \quad \forall i_n^1(\sigma; t, a, false \vdash e_i \to v_i)}{\sigma; t, a, true \vdash q(e_1, ..., e_n) \to q(v_1, ..., v_n | t, true, t, L_a^{prod(t)})}$$
$$\text{(E-EO-CntrRoot)}$$

$$\frac{\forall i_n^1(\sigma; t, a, false \vdash e_i \to v_i)}{\sigma; t, a, false \vdash q(e_1, ..., e_n) \to q(v_1, ..., v_n | t, true, \bot, L_a^{prod(t)})} \text{(E-EO-CntrChild)}$$

Fig. 9. Tree construction rules for extended origins

original example's output is an example of this. E-EO-CNTRROOT defines the case where the tree being constructed may be the root of the computed attribute value and is part of the contractum, resulting in a node which defines its redex to be t and $isContractum = true$. This resembles the *auxiliary symbols* origin case, and the *sub* node in the original example's output is an example of this. The final rule, E-EO-CNTRCHILD, the constructed tree sets $isContractum$ to *true* and has no redex since it is not the root of the value of the computed attribute. This resembles the *auxiliary symbols* origin case, and *const(0)* in the original example's output is an example of this. Recall, setting *redex* to $\bot$ does not mean that the *getRedex* function will not be able to find the root of the redex on a parent node.

5   Applying Extended Origins

This section explores an application of extended origins to a language extension built using Silver. This extension is for parallel matrix programming [15] based on ideas from Halide [12], a tool intended for writing high-performance image processing code which separates the "algorithm" (the operations to be evaluated) from the "schedule" (the transformations which specify the order in which the operations are evaluated). The schedules in Halide are designed to not affect the semantics of the algorithm and only modify where and when operations take place (e.g. by tiling, parallelizing, or vectorizing loops).

As an example of this, the code in Fig. 10(a) constructs a 2-dimensional gradient matrix *grad* based on indexes x and y. The result of applying the two schedules is shown in Fig. 10(b). The two schedules have parallelized the y dimension (`parallelize y`) and designated the y loop as the outermost loop (`reorder y, x`). These are the only schedules discussed in this paper, but we do not claim that these two schedules are sufficient for high performance computing; instead, they were selected based on their transformations and how they interact with extended origins.

In this small example, many relations are obvious. The OpenMP pragma must have been generated in some way by the *parallelize* schedule and the y iteration occurs outside of the x iteration due to the *reorder* schedule. Consider if this

```
grad(x,y) = x + y {          #pragma omp parallel for ...
   parallelize y;            for y from 0 to yMax {
   reorder y, x;                for x from 0 to xMax {
}                                  grad[x][y] = x + y;
                                }
                             }
        (a)                            (b)
```

Fig. 10. Example's input and output

example included more schedules which closely interacted with each other and were more invasive, thereby obfuscating relationships between the output code and the initial schedules and algorithm. Such a set of schedules would output code without any simple connection back to the original code.

By adding extended origins to this implementation, we can connect each node of the output tree to the schedules which affected it. Intuitively, each OpenMP pragma should be connected to a parallelize schedule, and each reorder schedules should be connected to the nodes they rearrange.

Here, we briefly describe how an AG transforms the input code shown in Fig. 10(a) into the code in Fig. 10(b). First, the algorithm is expanded into nested for loops, each of which is encapsulated within its own *forMarker* node. The expression nested in the deepest loop is a transformed version of the assignment statement in the original code: grad[x][y] = x + y under a *bodyMarker*. The marking nodes are used to mark where the tree should be cut when applying the reorder schedule. This simplifies the reorder schedule because other schedules which add new nodes must decide whether the added nodes should stay inside a given loop (inside a loop and above the nested marker) or outside a given loop (below a marker and above its loop). The first schedule is transformed into its *ScheduleAsRoot* variation which has the remaining schedules and the current state of the algorithm as its children. After applying its transformation, it replaces itself with the next schedule's *ScheduleAsRoot* node. After all schedules have been applied, the markers are removed and the final tree is returned.

The *parallelize* schedule inserts an OpenMP pragma immediately before the loop iterating over the given variable. To do this, a new higher-order synthesized attribute *parallel* is defined on all nonterminals which replicates constructs not affected by the transformations using equations similar to those on the *add* production in the running example. On the loop which iterates over the variable to be parallelized, the *parallel* attribute holds the sequence of the new pragma followed by a copy of the original loop. Initially, the for-loop compared its iterating variable against an inherited attribute *parWith* which held the variable to be parallelized and, if the two variables matched, constructed the new pragma. However, this gave the pragma an origin pointing to the loop, and therefore cannot connect the pragma to the *parallelize* schedule.

We define *parWith* to have type *ParWith*, a nonterminal which defines the new pragma as one of its attributes and with only one production which contains the variable to be parallelized as a child. The *ParWith* node is constructed by the *parallelizeAsRoot* node, which was in turn constructed by the *parallelize*

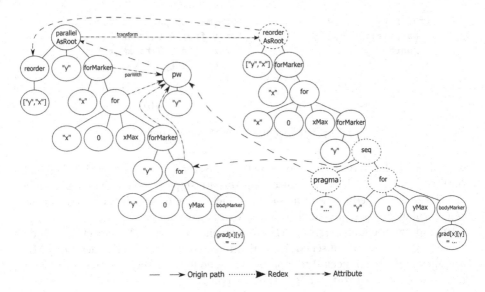

Fig. 11. Diagram showing the result of applying the parallelization schedule using *parWith* where the type of *parWith* is *ParWith*. Origins are shown with dashed arrows, attributes are shown with dot-dash arrows, and new nodes are shown with dashed ovals. Note that the pragma's origin path includes both the *pc* and *parallelizeAsRoot* nodes, and therefore also includes the *parallelize* node.

schedule; thus the *parWith* tree's origin path includes the *parallelize* schedule. In the loop's definition of *parallel*, the loop copies the pragma attribute from its *parWith* attribute. Thus the origin path of the pragma leads through the *parWith* tree to the *parallelizeAsRoot* node and the *parallelize* schedule. This relation is depicted in Fig. 11. Had we instead defined *parWith* to be a string instead of a tree, this origin path would not exist and we would lose the relationship between the parallel loop and the parallel schedule.

The reorder schedule acts as one would expect: it splits the loops into fragments rooted at *forMarker*s or *bodyMarker* nodes, rearranges the fragments, and re-nests the fragments in the new order. Note that this transformation outputs nodes which are duplicates of the input nodes, so none of the output tree's nodes have the *reorder* schedule in their origin path. Instead, the connection to the schedule is facilitated by the *redex* property. The reordering of the schedules is conducted within local attributes on *reorderScheduleAsRoot*, so the nodes in the ordered list of fragments have redexes pointing to it. Thus, each of the output nodes are connected to the schedule via origins to the ordered list, a redex to *reorderScheduleAsRoot*, and an origin to the *reorder* schedule. Though this connection seems hard to find, the local attribute holding the reordered fragments can be given a label which suggests following the redex property to find the schedule which conducts the reordering.

6   Related Work

The example in Section 1 is based on van Deursen's description of origin tracking in primitive recursive schemes (PRS) [4]. In our addition of redex and contractum information to origins in attribute grammars we designed the evaluation rules for tree construction to distinguish the equations which correspond directly to rewrite rule transformations (whose origins correspond to the *auxiliary symbols* case in a PRS) from those that simply reconstruct the tree (whose origins correspond to the *context* and *common variables* cases). The reason we focus on the rewrite rules from the second phase of a PRS is that the first phase includes rewrite rules that more closely resemble attribute grammar equations. The expansion of *negate* would be specified by the following rules:

$$expd(negate(X)) \to sub(const(0), expd(X))$$
$$expd(mul(X, Y)) \to mul(expd(X), expd(Y))$$
$$expd(sub(X, Y)) \to sub(expd(X), expd(Y))$$
$$expd(const(N)) \to const(N)$$

Here, *expd* corresponds to a synthesized attribute in attribute grammars; the rules above can be easily transcribed into attribute grammar equations.

In fact, this is done in previous work [11] in which bidirectional transformations are specified as rewrite rules and then implemented in attribute grammars. In that work, the translation of rewrite rules to attribute equations defines a similar notion of origins, called "links-back", but these are not implemented on general attribute equations. "Links-back" are only generated from rewrite rules, significantly simplifying the process.

PRSs and AGs can be encoded in the other formalism [3], but adding origins to attribute grammars by encoding a PRS with origins as an AG is not as intuitive as a direct approach. Additionally, the translation approach does not support the extension of redex and contractum information to origins.

Various language processing systems have implemented origins tracking. These include Spoofax [8], based on strategic term rewriting; CENTAUR [1], implemented in Lisp and Prolog with some notion of attributes similar to annotations as described here; and in the meta-programming language Rascal [9].

The annotations for origins and redexes are implemented in Silver as reference [6]/remote [2] attributes; these allow graph structures to be defined on top of syntax trees using attributes that point to other nodes in the syntax tree. They are useful in many settings such as linking variable uses to their declarations.

7   Discussion and Conclusion

In Silver, many of the above restrictions imposed by the simple attribute grammar calculus in Section 2 are removed since the restrictions can easily be generalized. In addition to the generalizations mentioned earlier, the **new** construct is not used in Silver because Silver uses the context of a reference to a tree such as x_i to determine if it should be seen as a decorated or undecorated tree. For example, it is decorated on the right hand side of an attribute equation for attribute evaluation and case expressions, but undecorated otherwise.

One concern regarding this definition of evaluation is that two transformations which result in the same output without origins can result in trees with different annotations. When inserting the OpenMP pragma in the application given in Section 5, the designer has a choice to either define the *parallel* attribute on the loop as $seq(pragma(...), for(...))$ or $seq(pragma(...), x_0)$. The former constructs a new tree for the loop which defines $isContractum = true$, while the latter duplicates the original tree such that $isContractum = false$. This is inconsistent, and one could argue that $isContractum = false$ is the best result for this transformation. However, such a decision would disagree with the currently held correlation between PRS origin cases in Section 1 and the *isContractum* annotation. Currently, nodes with origins constructed by either *context* or *common variables* cases define $isContractum = false$, and nodes with origins constructed by the *auxiliary symbols* case define $isContractum = true$. This is a classic case of two unique transformations which construct the same tree (excluding annotations). We expect to find no issues with allowing some nodes with *auxiliary symbols* origins to define $isContractum = false$, but more research is required before any further claim can be made.

One area of future work is to determine how best to use the information tracked by extended origins. How can we effectively present the data collected in the Halide-inspired language extension to the programmer? This is beyond the scope of this paper, but we can be assured that we have the raw data required.

Extended origins may also be useful in debugging attribute grammars. Algorithmic debugging [7] is a search technique applied to attributed syntax trees, following the structure of the tree and (local) higher order attributes. Extended origins provide additional "edges" that may be traversed during debugging in searching for the errant attribute equation, but more research into this is needed to determine how useful that would be in practice.

We have not yet analyzed how tracking origins affects the amount of memory Silver uses. More trees are kept in memory and not garbage collected due to the origin and other references. In many applications using origins such as debugging and transformation visualization we may run Silver in a "debug" mode to track origins and pay the memory cost, but then turn it off for other applications.

To conclude, in this paper we defined origin tracking in attribute grammars according to core themes shown in their construction in PRS. After showing that origins provide little context, four additional properties and their accessors were defined and added to define extended origins. These properties were shown to provide meaningful connections between nodes and schedules through complex transformations. Future work includes applying other complex transformations and analyzing how they interact with extended origins.

Acknowledgments. We thank the anonymous reviewers for their helpful comments. This work is partially supported by NSF Awards No. 0905581 and 1047961.

References

1. Borras, P., Clement, D., Despeyroux, T., Incerpi, J., Kahn, G., Lang, B., Pascual, V.: Centaur: The system. SIGPLAN Not 24(2), 14–24 (1988)
2. Boyland, J.T.: Remote attribute grammars. J. ACM 52(4), 627–687 (2005)
3. Courcelle, B., Franchi-Zannettacci, P.: Attribute grammars and recursive program schemes I and II. Theoretical Computer Science 17(2), 163–191, 235–257 (1982)
4. van Deursen, A.: Origin tracking in primitive recursive schemes. In: Conf. Proc. Computing Science in the Netherlands. pp. 132–143, available as technical report CS-R9401. Centrum voor Wiskunde en Informatica, Amsterdam, The Netherlands (1993)
5. van Deursen, A., Klint, P., Tip, F.: Origin tracking. Journal of Symbolic Computation 15, 523–545 (1992)
6. Hedin, G.: Reference attribute grammars. Informatica 24(3), 301–317 (2000)
7. Ikezoe, Y., Sasaki, A., Ohshima, Y., Wakita, K., Sassa, M.: Systematic debugging of attribute grammars. In: Proc. 4th Int. Workshop on Automated Debugging, pp. 235–240 (2000)
8. Kats, L.C.L., Visser, E.: The Spoofax language workbench. Rules for declarative specification of languages and IDEs. In: Proc. of ACM Conf. on Object Oriented Programming, Systems, Languages, and Systems (OOPSLA). ACM (2010)
9. Klint, P., van der Storm, T., Vinju, J.: Rascal: a domain specific language for source code analysis and manipulation. In: Proc. of Source Code Analysis and Manipulation, SCAM 2009 (2009)
10. Knuth, D.E.: Semantics of context-free languages. Mathematical Systems Theory 2(2), 127–145 (1968), corrections in 5 (1971)
11. Martins, P., Saraiva, J., Fernandes, J.P., Van Wyk, E.: Generating attribute grammar-based bidirectional transformations from rewrite rules. In: Proc. of the ACM SIGPLAN 2014 Workshop on Partial Evaluation and Program Manipulation (PEPM), pp. 63–70. ACM (2014)
12. Ragan-Kelley, J., Barnes, C., Adams, A., Paris, S., Durand, F., Amarasinghe, S.: Halide: A language and compiler for optimizing parallelism, locality, and recomputation in image processing pipelines. In: Proc. of ACM Conf. on Programming Language Design and Implementation (PLDI), pp. 519–530. ACM (2013)
13. Van Wyk, E., Bodin, D., Gao, J., Krishnan, L.: Silver: an extensible attribute grammar system. Science of Computer Programming 75(1–2), 39–54 (2010)
14. Vogt, H., Swierstra, S.D., Kuiper, M.F.: Higher-order attribute grammars. In: Proc. of ACM Conf. on Programming Language Design and Implementation (PLDI), pp. 131–145. ACM (1989)
15. Williams, K., Le, M., Kaminski, T., Van Wyk, E.: A compiler extension for parallel matrix programming. In: Proc. of the International Conf. on Parallel Programming (ICPP) (September 2014)

Dynamic Scope Discovery
for Model Transformations

Māris Jukšs[1], Clark Verbrugge[1], Dániel Varró[3], and Hans Vangheluwe[2,1]

[1] School of Computer Science, McGill University
Montréal, Québec, Canada
{mjukss,clump,hv}@cs.mcgill.ca
[2] Department of Mathematics and Computer Science
University of Antwerp, Belgium
hans.vangheluwe@uantwerp.be
[3] Department of Measurement and Information Systems
Budapest University of Technology and Economics, Hungary
varro@mit.bme.hu

Abstract. Optimizations to local-search based model transformations typically aim at effectively ordering the traversal of pattern edges to reduce the search space. In this paper we propose a dynamic approach to on-line discovery of rule application areas. Our approach incorporates tracking transformation progress in the input model using temperature-based coloring of model elements. The resulting heat map is used to discover possible rule application scopes ahead of rule execution. Further refinement of scopes is achieved by applying a Naive Bayes (NB) classifier to predict a set of possible match candidates. NB is well suited for the computationally intensive environment of model transformations due to its incremental training phase and low classification overhead. Our design is intended to take a runtime, black-box approach to observing and learning from the transformations as they are executed. Finally, we demonstrate a prototype evaluation of the approach in our transformation tool AToMPM [24] and address the benefits, limitations as well as future applications.

Keywords: model transformations, learning from transformations, model transformation optimization, supervised learning, scope.

1 Introduction

Local search based techniques [32,6,12,28,27,7] frequently serve as the execution strategy of model (or graph) transformation systems. These strategies start pattern matching from some initial node(s) and gradually extend the match candidate along edges in the neighborhood of already matched nodes in accordance with some search plan. Search plans provide an efficient ordering on pattern edges calculated mostly in a preprocessing phase [32,6,12] or adaptively at runtime [27,7,9].

B. Combemale et al. (Eds.): SLE 2014, LNCS 8706, pp. 302–321, 2014.

In this paper, we present a dynamic, black-box approach to runtime search space reduction of graph pattern matching in model transformations, which is complementary to existing search plan based approaches. Our design passively observes the transformation process to collect nodes which will likely constitute a match of the next transformation rule. For this purpose, we make use of two techniques. First, we incorporate a temperature-inspired coloring of the input model elements into the transformation engine. We observe model elements as they are "touched" by the transformation, and color the nodes according to a simple temperature schema. The resulting heat-map can then be used to construct an initial, reduced search space that is passed on to the pattern matcher.

Further refinement of this search scope is then achieved by applying a variant of a supervised machine learning technique, based on a Naive Bayes classifier [16]. At runtime, successful matches are used incrementally as positive training examples to help with further prediction. The training examples reference the heat-map in addition to domain specific properties of the model elements that contribute to matches, and may include structural graph information as well. The classifier is then used to decide whether the node should be included in the refined search scope. Our approach is primarily intended for long-running, simulation-oriented transformations, where transformation evolves in the neighborhood. The benefit and applicability of our approach to other types of transformations need to be investigated in the future work.

To validate and assess our process for model simulation transformations, we experimentally examine two non-trivial graph transformations. We show the effect of different parametrization of scoping on both transformations. Through this, we demonstrate that the temperature-based approach in itself and also combined with NB are effective at reducing the search scope. We achieve a high overall success rate of 90 percent in case of single resource mutual exclusion benchmark and reduce the size of the search scope at least 10 times in case of forest-fire simulation. Specific contributions of this paper include:

- We describe a temperature-based system for tracking and predicting the scope of rule matches in model transformation. This runtime technique provides heuristic information that helps identify possible matches without explicit reference to rule content or scheduling information.
- Improvement to the scope discovery is further facilitated by incorporating machine learning into the search process. A Naive Bayes classifier is trained at runtime, filtering "warm" nodes to more accurately identify model elements that have a high probability of being part of a successful match.
- Feasibility and performance of our design is evaluated by experimenting with both a mutual exclusion benchmark [29] and a forest fire simulation [14] using the research oriented tool AToMPM [24]. This work demonstrates effectiveness in both graph-modifying and pure simulation contexts, and illustrates the impact of different parametrization of our technique.

In Section 2 we give some necessary background of graph pattern matching. Section 3 then presents our approach, explaining both the temperature and NB scope refinement mechanisms. Experiments are discussed in Section 4. Section 5 discusses related work, and finally, section 6 gives conclusions and future work.

2 Background

As relevant background information, we overview the concepts of graph pattern matching, which is a key component of many model transformation engines based on local search based techniques. To illustrate the basic terminology, a distributed mutual exclusion algorithm (with full specification in [10] and proposed as a transformation benchmark in [29]) will be used as a running example.

We assume that the main concepts of a domain are captured by an associated metamodel MM together with their attributes and relationships thus defining the abstract syntax of a corresponding domain-specific language. Domain concepts are specified as *classes* which may have attributes that define some kind of properties of the specific class. *Associations* define connections between classes. Both ends of an association may have a *multiplicity* constraint attached to them, which declares the number of objects that, at run-time, may participate in an reference. The most typical multiplicity constraints are the at most one (0..1), and the arbitrary (denoted by *) designations. An *instance model M* describes a concrete system defined in a modeling language and we assume that it is a well-formed instance of the metamodel (thus additional well-formedness constraints are also respected). Typically instance models are represented as graphs, class instances correspond to nodes and associations to edges.

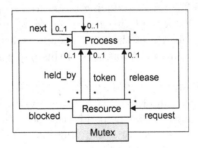

Fig. 1. Metamodel for the mutual exclusion problem [29]

A metamodel of the mutual exclusion problem is depicted in Fig. 1, which contains only two classes called Process and Resource. These classes are connected by references of type next, request, held_by, release, token, and blocked.

2.1 Graph Transformation Rules

Rule-based model transformations are frequently captured by means of graph transformation rules $r = (LHS, NAC, RHS)$, which consists of a left hand side

(*LHS*) pre-condition pattern (with optional negative application condition (*NAC*) pattern) and the right hand side (*RHS*) post-condition pattern.

The *application* of a rule *r* to an *instance model M* replaces a match of the *LHS* in *M* by an image of the *RHS*. This is performed in a graph pattern matching and a rewrite phase. (1) In the graph pattern matching phase, a transformation engine needs to find a match $m : LHS \mapsto M$ of *LHS* in *M* and then consecutively check the negative application conditions *NAC* which prohibit the presence of certain nodes and edges in the instance model. In the rewrite phase, (2) the engine removes a part of the model *M* that can be mapped to *LHS* but not to *RHS* yielding the context model and then glues the context model with an image of the *RHS* by creating new objects and links (that can be mapped to the *RHS* but not to the *LHS*) to obtain *M'* as result of the transformation step.

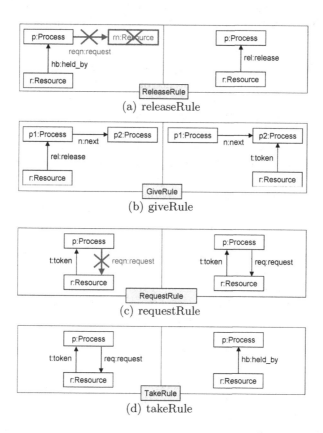

Fig. 2. A subset of rules describing the mutual exclusion algorithm [10,29]

In Fig. 2 the four rules of the mutual exclusion algorithm used in Varró *et al.*'s benchmark [29] are presented (out of the total 13 rules in [10]). For instance, releaseRule (Fig. 2(a)) prescribes by its *LHS* that a resource r needs to be held_by a process p, while its RHS contains the same nodes p and r connected by an edge of type release. The releaseRule also has a negative application condition which expresses that the process p is not allowed to have any requests issued for any resources. Furthermore, releaseRule captures that if a process p requests a resource r which is eventually granted by a respective token, then process p can grab resource r .

2.2   Graph Pattern Matching

In this work, we are interested in improving the pattern matching process for *LHS*, which is the most computationally intensive task for local-search based approaches. Any local search based technique starts graph pattern matching from an initial set of nodes of the instance model (called *initial seed*), and then tries to match each edge of the graph pattern in the instance model one by one. For this purpose, two main match operators are defined in the VF2 algorithm framework [5] as follows:

- **Check:** This operator takes two nodes in the graph pattern which are already matched, and checks for the existence of a specific type of edge between the two nodes. As a result, *check* is a cheap operation assuming the existence appropriate indexes on the source and target nodes.
- **Extend:** This operator takes one node in the graph pattern which is already matched, then selects an unmatched outgoing edge from the node (or incoming edge to this node), and tries to extend the match along a corresponding edge in the instance model. For this purpose, all potential model edge candidates need to be investigated one by one. If there are many edge candidates for extending the match then the extend step can be complex, which is normally the case when navigating along edges with to-many multiplicities.

In the current paper, we assume that edges can be navigated in both directions (*i.e.* from its source node to its target node or vice versa). If this is not the case for a specific modeling framework (*e.g.* reverse navigation can be inefficient in EMF), then it can be reflected by assigning navigation costs accordingly.

The cost of graph pattern matching can be defined as the size of the search tree, *i.e.* the number of model elements visited during the pattern matching step, which depends on the size of the graph pattern and the branching factor at each decision point. For a graph pattern with k elements and n_i branching factor (*i.e.* the number of potential instance nodes to match) at decision point i, the size of the search tree is calculated as the sum-product $ST = \sum_{j=1}^{k} \prod_{i=1}^{j} n_i$. A smaller search tree means more efficient execution, and thus estimating the cost of graph pattern matching has been central to many existing graph pattern matching approaches, *e.g.* [28,7,27,9].

Existing approaches (see also Section 5) focus on defining a good ordering on the edges of the graph patterns either statically in a preprocessing phases or dynamically at runtime. The main idea of these approaches is to start matching cheap edges of the pattern, *i.e.* those with small branching factor. For instance, navigating along an edge with an at most one multiplicity guarantees to either succeed or fail, thus its branching factor is 1. As a consequence, the search process for matching rule releaseRule would start with matching edge token (with at most one multiplicity) before matching edge request (with arbitrary multiplicity).

In many cases, the most critical decision is where to start the pattern matching as the first pattern node can typically be matched to many possible instance model nodes. For instance, assuming the search order (1) extend: token(r,p); (2) check: request(p,r) in case of releaseRule, we need to consider (and enumerate) all model nodes of type Resource before starting navigation along the first token edge.

Our paper proposes a complementary optimization technique to existing approaches in order to *reduce the branching factor at each decision point* dynamically at execution time independently from the search plan (*i.e.* the edge ordering) of a graph pattern. We aim at filtering match candidates by giving priority to (1) recently touched nodes (calculated using a heat map) and (2) nodes which constitute a match with higher probability (estimated by Naive Bayes classifier).

3 Dynamic Scope Discovery

Our overall design for dynamic scope discovery builds on two main components. Below we first give an overview of how the process is integrated into a transformation system, followed by details of the temperature and the Naive Bayes classifier components.

3.1 Overview

Our approach to scope discovery is embedded within the graph pattern matching process of a typical model transformation system. Fig. 3 presents a general overview of this integration with rectangles representing the major steps carried out in the pattern matching phase model of a transformation system.

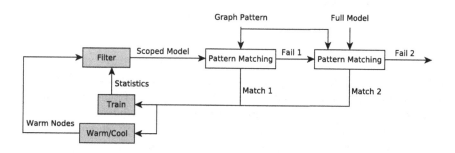

Fig. 3. Dynamic scope discovery and matching (new components are shaded)

- **Operation phase:** During main operation, our basic design carries out graph pattern matching in two phases using any existing matcher component. First, a reduced (scope) graph is computed by filtering, and pattern matching is initiated on this reduced graph (middle pattern matching box in Fig. 3). A valid match on this reduced graph is guaranteed to be a valid match of the full graph. But since this approach is optimistic, we retain the pattern matching of the full graph as a fallback (right box) when pattern matching on the reduced graph fails.
- **Filtering phase:** The filtering of nodes for obtaining the reduced scope graph is carried out by a combination of two techniques. (1) First, *a heat map of model nodes is calculated*: if a transformation rule touches (matches, modifies) a model node then it becomes a warm node. Several subsequent matches heat up a node, which gradually cools down if it is no longer part of a match. The number of warm nodes in the system, and subsequently the size of the scoped model, is directly dependent on parameters of the warming and cooling process, which will be described in Section 3.2. (2) The exact population of the warm set is also reduced by a Naive Bayes classifier. This classifier is trained using the matches produced during the pattern matching phase, and is then used to further filter the warm set. Note that is a simplified view, and the filtering step can more generally contain an arbitrary chain of filters that refine the warm node input.
- **Initialization and Training phase:** Initial pattern matching is performed on the full model when all nodes are cold in the system. The scoped model is thus initially empty, and the scoped pattern matching fails. As we observe the matches of the transformation rules, warm nodes are discovered, populating the Scoped Model subset, and scoped pattern matching may succeed. The training of the Naive Bayes classifier can be carried out either in a preprocessing phase (i.e. prior to a transformation run), or during transformation execution.

As a result, matching a pattern on a scope graph will probabilistically reduce the complexity of matching by reducing the branching factor. We expect that this can be a significant reduction for simulation kind of model transformations, which may exploit the strong locality of subsequent execution steps.

3.2   Warming the Nodes

Coloring input graph nodes with temperature values is a straightforward way of representing frequency of access to the graph nodes and thus the temporal locality of transformations: high temperature nodes are frequently accessed (or near to ones that are), and so likely to be part of a future, successful match and/or rewrite, while low temperature nodes are outside the current locus of activity, and so less likely to be part of a match.

Node temperature is maintained by augmenting the transformation engine with the ability to color/heat the nodes belonging to a match. At rewrite time, every node in a match chosen by the engine for a rewrite will be tagged with a temperature value. In our system this means updating temperature attribute of a node. This temperature attribute is created at runtime, transparent to the language engineer and is not part of the attributes specified in the metamodel for the language being transformed.

Node temperature is expected to increase on frequent access, and decrease if not accessed over time. We track the temperature changes of a node using a global timer that counts the number of rule executions during transformation. References to warm nodes and the time of the last temperature change are kept in the *temperature list*, which defines the temperature scope. Nodes that are not participating (not matched and/or colored) in the transformation for a number of rule executions will be cooled down. We call the number of rule executions that must occur before a node begins cooling as the node's *warm time*. The decision to cool down nodes is made at every transformation step. Reference to a node is removed from the temperature list once the temperature of the node cools down to zero.

Temperature values in our system range from 0 to 100 (temperatures exceeding maximum value are scaled back to 100), with increments occurring in discrete steps. For simplicity we chose to decrease the node temperature to zero after its warm time expires. However, temperature decrease step can be equal to a discrete value similar to temperature increase step. For each node in the match the temperature is increased by 40 degrees. Nodes in the neighborhood of a match are also colored with a temperature, although with a smaller increase to indicate less confidence; we used a step of 20. In our case we consider only immediate neighborhood, using single hop distance, and exploring the effects of variable-size neighborhoods on our approach is future work. All temperature related values were specifically chosen for the purpose of this paper and their variation needs to be explored in the future work as well.

Once temperature is updated, we compose the warm set as a subgraph of the instance model where all nodes have temperature higher than 0, without making any distinction of the temperature values. Diversity in temperature steps is intended primarily for the NB classifier described in the next section. Without NB, it would be sufficient to use two values for the temperature: 0 or 100, cold or hot.

Heat map example: Mutex. Fig. 4 illustrates the basic heating process, showing the application of releaseRule on a model of a ring of processes with a single resource. Note that we omit labels on the connections between processes; they are of type *next*. Here nodes participating in the current rule application are shaded, and all nodes in the model initially have temperatures equal to zero (we only show temperatures of the elements participating in the rule application and their neighbors). The right side of the figure shows the result after the matching; as described above, matched nodes are warmed up to 40 degrees, and immediate neighbors are warmed up to 20.

Heat map example: Forest-fire. A finer-grain example of temperature is shown in Fig. 5, showing a stage in the forest-fire simulation transformation we will

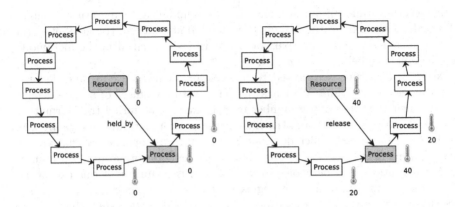

Fig. 4. Application of releaseRule on a model (left) results in warmed up nodes (right)

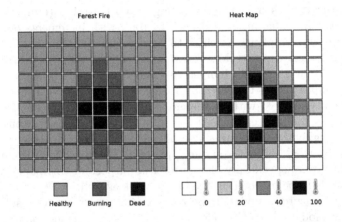

Fig. 5. Forest-fire simulation rendering (left) with burned out, black cells in the middle and the model heat map over the cells (right)

evaluate with our approach in Section 4. Note that we omit the metamodel and the transformation rules of this example for brevity; full details are available in earlier work [14]. In this simulation a fire spreads across a 2D grid of neighboring cells starting in the center. Each cell in a grid represents a forested area which may catch fire if any neighboring cells are on fire. Once fully burned, a cell represents a barrier to further fire spreading. The simulation terminates when no burning cells remain. Assuming all cells are exactly the same and in the absence of wind effects, fire will spread in a circular fashion (discretely represented).

In Fig. 5 on the left, there are dead, burned out cells in the middle of a fire ring of width of 2. On the right is the heat map over the input model of the cells on the left. We can see that white nodes in the middle of the heat map are cold (0 degrees). These nodes correspond to dead trees on the left, they are not touched by transformation anymore and therefore cool down. Black nodes are the hottest, they were matched several times recently. Going outwards the temperatures of the nodes decrease, as some rules are yet to match these nodes in the process of spreading fire. The least warm, outer nodes have the temperature of 20 degrees, they are immediate neighbors of match nodes and are likely to be touched in the next iteration transformation.

A subgraph created from the temperature list is then passed to a matcher for the initial match attempt. Note that temperature scope approach does not guarantee a match especially for the transformations with random behavior, and correlation of the heat-map with match success strongly depends on the degree of locality in matching. Our design also depends on rule application mainly being interested in finding *any* match, rather than *all possible* matches. Contexts where all possible matches are necessary are not suitable for the heuristic filtering enabled by temperature based matching.

3.2.1 Complexity of Dynamic Heatmaps.

Maintaining match scope through temperature allows for a reduced search space, but requires non-trivial bookkeeping to track the warm set. Depending on the warm time of the nodes and the transformation process, warm set can grow at most to the size of the input model. Therefore it is important to handle the warm set efficiently. For this we use an ordered set data-structure, with node ordering based on the time the temperature of a node was last changed.

The first heating of a given node implies inserting it into the tree, while reheating a node requires removing and reinserting. Node cooling requires searching the tree, with possible removals from the tree if nodes were cooled down to 0. A simple minimum-temperature value can be used to avoid processing cool-downs until necessary, but identifying the nodes needed for cooling requires searching for the n nodes at minimum temperature. By using an augmented red-black tree that allows interval search, we can perform inserts and deletions in $O(log\ n)$ worst case time, and find the now-cold nodes in time $O(log\ n)$. The efficiency of this approach thus depends on the trade-off between performing these additional data-structure operations and the corresponding reductions in search cost. Investigation of this trade-off is planned in future work.

3.3 Scope Refinement by Naive Bayes Classifiers

The temperature scope described in previous subsection may be larger than necessary to find a match. This is especially apparent when nodes cool down slowly and the temperature scope grows correspondingly large. More aggressive cooling would mitigate this, but requires a cool-down threshold well tuned to the transformation. Our design thus instead makes use of a Naive Bayes classifier to learn from features describing the nodes involved in the transformation at runtime, including temperature, and so further refine the subset of relevant nodes fed to the matcher.

A Naive Bayes classifier is a simple machine learning technique that makes an independence assumption on the training data [16]. With a training vector of features for a given class, we assume that each feature is independent and does not affect the conditional probabilities of these features given a class. This approach is simplistic of course, but NB is known to perform well in many classification applications, and speed in our design is important—an independence assumption greatly simplifies the calculations necessary. The incremental training phase for NB is also an advantage.

Training is performed after each rewrite, with each node that is part of a successful match participating in training before being changed in the rewrite step. We consider each node in the pattern as an independent entity disregarding relationships between nodes. This simplifies training and the classification. The class or the label of the training example is the identifier of the rule, and the training features of the nodes are the domain specific attributes, node type and the temperature. For example in the case of the mutual exclusion transformation described in Section 2, nodes may have domain attributes such as name of the process and resource, process priority, *etc.* Each of the domain specific attributes including the temperature constitutes an independent training feature. Graph structure also carries a lot of information that can be harnessed, and we plan in future work to also consider structural graph attributes such as node degree, number of incoming or outgoing edges, *etc.*

Training consists of keeping track of the number of distinct feature values encountered for each rule identifier. At this stage, features with continuous values such as temperature require discretization for efficient training [31]. Here we use a simple binning approach, based on 10 bins of equal size. Other approaches are possible, such as to assume the numerical value to be part of normal (Gaussian) distribution [31].

In NB, the probability $P(Y|X)$ of a class Y given set of features $X = \langle X_1, X_2, .., X_n \rangle$ is calculated as:

$$P(Y|X) = P(Y) \prod_{i=1}^{n} P(X_i|Y) \tag{1}$$

In Fig. 6, we show the application of giveRule on a portion of the model shown in Fig. 4. The match is shaded on the left, and the effect of the rule is shown on the right with updated temperatures according to rules described earlier. Before rewriting, the match is used for training NB. We have three feature vector corresponding to the three nodes in the match on the left. We only use type of the node and its temperature to demonstrate the concept. $X_1 = \langle \text{process}, 40° \rangle$, $X_2 = \langle \text{process}, 20° \rangle$, $X_3 = \langle \text{resource}, 40° \rangle$. The label for training is the giveRule identifier. Thus statistics accumulated for giveRule is two processes, one resource, two 40-degree and one 20-degree temperatures. At the filtering step given a node described by the feature vector $X = \langle \text{process}, 20° \rangle$ and the upcoming execution of requestRule from the mutual exclusion running example, the probability that the node will be part of a match (or should be included in the scoped model) is $P(\text{requestRule}|X) = P(\text{requestRule})P(\text{process}|\text{requestRule})P(20°|\text{requestRule})$.

Knowing the probability, a decision is then made whether to include the node in the refined scope or not. Essentially, there are two ways we can approach the classification of nodes using NB. One is by calculating the probability of

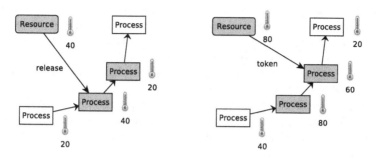

Fig. 6. Application of giveRule on a portion of model (left) and the result (right)

nodes belonging to all possible rules (classes), using a competition approach in which the class with highest probability "wins". Another is through judging the probability of one class, choosing a threshold for accepting the probability as a description of the class. The higher computational cost of the former (competition) approach makes it less appealing in our performance-oriented context, and so we use the latter approach with a threshold of zero.

4 Experiments

In our experimental evaluation we investigate if our concept is feasible in the context of long-running, simulation-oriented transformations. Feasibility in our context implies two research questions:

- **RQ1:** Does our dynamic scoping technique effectively reduce the search space?
- **RQ2:** Does dynamic scoped matching provide satisfactory success rate?

In order to answer RQ1, we compare the size of the scoped graph wrt. the size of the entire instance graph. In order to address RQ2, the failure of our scoped matching technique is when the original rule has a match on the entire graph, but a scoped matching fails to detect it. We consider scoped matching a success when scoped matching produces a match or when the fallback matching on the full input model fails. We evaluate our approach using two non-trivial transformations: a mutual exclusion problem from the transformation benchmark suite [29], and a forest-fire simulation from our previous work on scope [14] and introduced in 3. The latter constitutes a pure simulation benchmark, mainly modifying node attributes, while the former requires some amount of node creation and destruction in representing changing edge relations in the model (model edges are represented in AToMPM using graph nodes). First we present the benchmarks in more detail, explain the experimental setup, followed by results presentation.

4.1 Benchmarks and Measurements

Both mutual exclusion and forest-fire transformations were executed with three different node warm times of 10, 50, and 300. These represent short, medium and long node warm times. We used a simple model for cooling, immediately reducing node temperature to zero and removing it from the temperature list. Each benchmark was executed using temperature scope matching (Temp), followed by additional filtering using NB (Temp+NB). For evaluation purposes we maintain several metrics at each transformation step. Metrics have global and individual rule resolutions. We track: success rate of scoped matching, size of temperature scope, size of scope resulted after additionally using NB filtering. We report these in the following section (individual rule results are omitted). Evaluation was performed on x64 i7 mobile quad-core processor with 16Gb RAM running Ubuntu 12.10.

Experimental setup for mutual exclusion simulation. Mutual exclusion experiments were executed on two types of the input models each containing 1000 processes in accordance with the benchmark setup published in [29]. First input model contained single resource (similar to model in Fig. 4) and second input model contained multiple resources (one resource for each process). In single resource case, the size of the graph underlying the input model was 2002 nodes and the multiple resource model contained 4000 nodes (counting model associations represented as nodes). Transformation applicable to both input models was executed in an *as long as possible* fashion, using the sequence of rules, in the following order: releaseRule, giveRule, requestRule, and takeRule specified in Fig. 2. Each rule was scheduled to execute exhaustively as long as the matches were found, followed by the next rule scheduled in the same fashion. Each model was simulated for several cycles after which transformation terminates. One transformation cycle is defined by sequential execution starting from releaseRule and terminating at takeRule. The multiple resource model was transformed for 4 cycles, resulting in approximately 20000 rule executions. The single resource model was simulated for 100 cycles with close to a 1000 rule executions. We observed that this is quite sufficient to demonstrate the stability of the success rate of scoped matching in the system *i.e.* transient effects (such as initialization and training) are no longer visible.

Experimental setup for forest-fire simulation. Forest-fire simulation was executed on a grid of 100 by 100 cells with one cell burning to start the simulation. The number of nodes in the underlying graph is 29800 (including the nodes representing association edges). Simulation ran until all cells burned out. We observed that the success rate in the forest-fire simulation stabilizes after 15000 iterations.

4.2   Results

In this section we present results, demonstrating the overall success rate and the size of scopes with respect to the iterations of transformation, where iteration is equal to a single rule execution. All figures in this section contain legends that are following the order of the graphs in the plot: the top line in each graph corresponds to the top entry in the legend list.

Mutual exclusion results. Overall success rate of our single resource mutex benchmark with node warm time (WT) of 10 is presented in Fig. 7 on the left. On the right in Fig. 7 sizes of scopes are shown for node warm times of 300 and 10 (log scale on y axis).

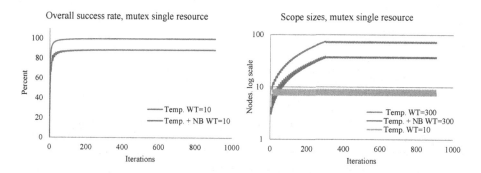

Fig. 7. Single resource model. Overall success rate and scope sizes

We observed that success rate does not improve after increasing WT, and a short WT of 10 is sufficient to demonstrate a good success rate. It is evident that NB filtering reduces success rate by about ten percent. On the right in Fig. 7, warm scope at WT equal to 10 is presented to contrast the long WT. With a long WT the reduction of warm scope by NB is more evident. After the system stabilizes, warm scope is reduced by approximately 30 nodes with NB, equivalent to 30 percent of the warm scope. NB filtering does reduce the scope size, however, it reduced the success rate due to exclusion of some of the match candidates.

In Fig. 8 we present the success rates of Temp (left) and Temp+NB (right) scope matching in the multiple resource mutex model. Highest success rate in both filtering situations is achieved at WT equal to 300. Success rate with temperature filtering is at 50 percent in the worst case with WT of 10. We observe a similar reduction in success rate to the one seen in the single mutex

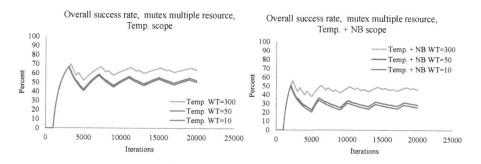

Fig. 8. Overall success rate, multiple resource model

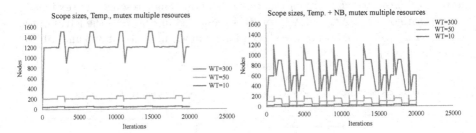

Fig. 9. Scope sizes, multiple resource model

benchmark, by applying NB filtering. NB filtering reduces the overall success rate by approximately 10 percent compared to warm scope matching.

Scope sizes for multiple resource model are shown in Fig. 9. Temperature filtering is on the left and NB filtering on the right. The peaks on the left plot are due to the increased number of nodes in the graph after repeatedly executing requestRule, which adds an extra node corresponding to the *request* association. Temperature based filtering reduced the scope to sizes ranging from 100 nodes (WT=10) to 1400 nodes (WT=300) (full model 4000 nodes). Consider the area under the graph for WT of 300 in the left and right plots. NB filtering does reduce the temperature scope even though there are peaks to 1200 nodes. When the number of nodes in the temperature scope peaks on the left and remains flat, NB scope size does not follow the trend closely.

Forest-fire results. Fig. 10 presents overall success rates for temperature scope matching (left) and additional NB filtering (right). We observe satisfactory and equivalent success rates with WT of 300 for both filtering cases. This is likely because we use more data for NB training compared to the mutex example, such as the "burning" state of the forest cell. On the right in Fig. 10 we can clearly see a gradual rise in success rate for WT 300. This is due to the initial NB training as well as the increase of the warm scope. The success rate in both plots is high at the beginning because a small portion of the graph is active. As the active region grows, the rate reduces and stabilizes sometime after 10000 rule executions.

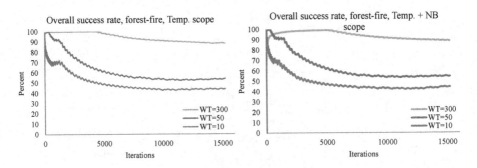

Fig. 10. Overall success rate, forest-fire simulation

Table 1. Forest-fire scope sizes (nodes), full input graph 29800 nodes

	Temp		Temp+NB	
WT	Ave.	Std. Dev.	Ave.	Std. Dev.
300	1110	319	357	415
50	357	415	157	155
10	77	17	37	36

Table 1 shows the average scope sizes in nodes and standard deviation for different warm times. Temp+NB scope is three times smaller on average than Temp scope. Average Temp scope is close to 20 times smaller than number of nodes in the forest-fire graph.

Result summary. After running both benchmarks we learned that scoped matching in our approach is promising based on success rates of 30 to 90 percent. This depends on the warm time of the nodes and the additional filtering, such as NB in our example. In certain cases such as for the single resource mutex model, the success rate was over 90 percent with a significant reduction to the search space, reducing it to just 10 nodes compared to 2000 nodes for the full input graph. NB filtering does reduce the search scope further at the slight expense of success rate. NB filtering performed best in the case of the forest-fire simulation both in terms of success rate and in reducing search scope. It is important to note that these results were achieved using the initial prototype. Even though we observe interesting results, deeper investigation of performance, parameter values and applications is necessary in future work.

5   Related Work

Pattern matching techniques used in different graph and model transformation tools for supporting query evaluation can be categorized in different ways.

Our technique is classified as a *local-search based approach* which constructs a search plan (i.e. an ordering on node and edge traversal in the graph pattern) which drive the search process. This search plan can be constructed *statically* as a preprocessing step (like in [12,32,6,17]), constructed *dynamically* during execution time [9,5], or selected *adaptively* from preprocessed search plan candidates [28,27].

Heuristics used for constructing efficient search plans rely upon different sources of information. *Metamodel-specific* heuristics like [32,6,9,13,2] exploit the containment and cardinality constraints of a metamodel e.g. by navigating first along edges with at most one multiplicity. *Model-specific search plans* [28,7,27] evaluate statistical information of the underlying instance model (e.g. the number of edges of a certain type) to start the search from promising candidate nodes. In fact, initial bindings can be explicitly provided to the pattern matching process by *pivot* (or input) nodes as in [6,12,30,27].

Our technique is unique and complementary to these approaches in the sense that it aims to exploit the *transformation process* as heuristics by reducing the scope of the candidates to those elements touched by recent transformation rules. Our approach is also complementary (and thus applicable) to both *compiled* [26,6,3] and *interpreted* [2,13,15,26] model transformation approaches. An overview of tools supporting local-search based pattern matching is provided in Table 2.

Table 2. Overview of tools with local-search based pattern matching

Tool	Execution		Search Plan			Heuristics			
	Comp. (C)	Interp. (I)	Stat (S)	Adapt (A)	Dyna (D)	Meta Model (MM)	Model (M)	Pivot (P)	Transf. (T)
ATL [13]		I	S			MM		P	
Epsilon [15]		I	S			MM		P	
eMOFLON [27,26]	C	I		A			M	P	
Fujaba [6]	C		S			MM		P	
GReAT [30,1]	C	I	S			MM		P	
GrGEN [7]	C			A			M	P	
GROOVE [20]		I	S				M		
Henshin [2]		I	S			MM		P	
MoTif [23]	C	I	S			MM		P	
MoTE [7]		I			D		M	P	
PROGRES [22,32]	C	I	S			MM		P	
VIATRA [28,11,3,12]	C	I	S	A		MM	M	P	
VMTS [17]	C	I	S	A		MM	M	P	
Our approach	(C)	I		A	D			P	T

Topological activity [18,19] computation in *MGS* [8] explores the active and inactive regions in the model. Active regions are exclusively used to find the pattern matches. Nodes that are hot, in our application, can be considered activity region in *MGS* language terms. However, our approach takes a temperature node coloring approach instead of treating trajectory of system states to compute active regions. In addition nodes in our concept "cool down" at specified rate, in MGS case, topological areas become inactive at next iteration.

GXL [21] a graph transformation language with rule-based scoping and graph parameters. Scoping in GXL means that scope produced by one rule application can be passed by value and used by other rules, and so on. *Stratego/XT* [4], a program transformation, term rewriting language, allows scoping of rewrite rules by limiting their lifetime to a specific rewriting strategy. Rewriting strategy places application of a rewrite rule to a part of a abstract syntax tree being transformed. Stratego explores the natural hierarchy of an underlying model. Scope in our approach is dynamic and is driven by transformation process.

Our previous work on scope in model transformations [14,25] concentrated on constraining model transformation to explicitly specified scope within the input model. It was up to domain specialist to decide the scope of the transformations at design time (i.e. as part of the transformation rules themselves). The presented technique aims to automatically determine scope of rule application before executing it. Specifically we are interested in dynamically constraining pattern matching to a reduced portion of the input model.

6 Conclusions and Future Work

In this paper we investigated the approach to reducing search scope of model transformations by tracking transformation process within the input model. For this we used temperature inspired underlying graph node coloring. Temperature regions constitute the likely rule application areas that we explored in pattern matching during runtime. In addition to temperature filtering we investigated additional filtering based on Naive Bayes classifier. In the context of simulation oriented transformations we demonstrated that our approach works well in certain situations: the success rate of matching within the scope defined by our filtering was over 90 percent in single resource mutex benchmark. We also observed the reduction of search scope by using our filtering approaches. NB application further refined the search area, however in some instances at the expense of the matching success rate.

In future work we would like to explore the cost of the warm scope maintenance and the runtime effects of our concept. We believe that deeper investigation of temperature scope related parameters, with addition of structural graph information for NB training will be beneficial to the performance and accuracy of the approach. Temperature scope in the context of search plans could in the future provide dynamic information to search plan generation at runtime. Incremental matching technique is another area of model transformation that could possibly incorporate our approach. Another area to investigate is a NB classifier trained at runtime that could be saved and used as static filter in future transformation applications offloading the training expense.

References

1. Agrawal, A., Karsai, G., Kalmar, Z., Neema, S., Shi, F., Vizhanyo, A.: The design of a language for model transformations. SoSym 5(3), 261–288 (2006)
2. Arendt, T., Biermann, E., Jurack, S., Krause, C., Taentzer, G.: Henshin: Advanced concepts and tools for in-place EMF model transformations. In: Petriu, D.C., Rouquette, N., Haugen, Ø. (eds.) MODELS 2010, Part I. LNCS, vol. 6394, pp. 121–135. Springer, Heidelberg (2010)
3. Balogh, A., Varró, G., Varró, D., Pataricza, A.: Compiling model transformations to ejb3-specific transformer plugins. In: Haddad, H. (ed.) Proceedings of the 2006 ACM Symposium on Applied Computing (SAC), Dijon, France, April 23-27, pp. 1288–1295. ACM (2006)

4. Bravenboer, M., van Dam, A., Olmos, K., Visser, E.: Program transformation with scoped dynamic rewrite rules. Fundam. Inf. 69(1-2), 123–178 (2005)
5. Cordella, L.P., Foggia, P., Sansone, C., Vento, M.: A (sub)graph isomorphism algorithm for matching large graphs. IEEE Transactions on Pattern Analysis and Machine Intelligence 26(10), 1367–1372 (2004)
6. Fischer, T., Niere, J., Torunski, L., Zündorf, A.: Story diagrams: A new graph transformation language based on UML and Java. In: Ehrig, H., Engels, G., Kreowski, H.-J., Rozenberg, G. (eds.) Graph Transformations 1998. LNCS, vol. 1764, pp. 296–309. Springer, Heidelberg (2000)
7. Geiß, R., Batz, G.V., Grund, D., Hack, S., Szalkowski, A.: GrGen: A fast SPO-based graph rewriting tool. In: Corradini, A., Ehrig, H., Montanari, U., Ribeiro, L., Rozenberg, G. (eds.) ICGT 2006. LNCS, vol. 4178, pp. 383–397. Springer, Heidelberg (2006)
8. Giavitto, J.L., Godin, C., Michel, O., Prusinkiewicz, P.: Computational models for integrative and developmental biology (2002)
9. Giese, H., Hildebrandt, S., Seibel, A.: Improved flexibility and scalability by interpreting story diagrams. ECEASST 18 (2009)
10. Heckel, R.: Compositional verification of reactive systems specified by graph transformation. In: Astesiano, E. (ed.) ETAPS/FASE 1998. LNCS, vol. 1382, pp. 138–153. Springer, Heidelberg (1998)
11. Horváth, Á., Bergmann, G., Ráth, I., Varró, D.: Experimental assessment of combining pattern matching strategies with viatra2. STTT 12(3-4), 211–230 (2010)
12. Horváth, Á., Varró, D., Varró, G.: Generic search plans for matching advanced graph patterns. Electronic Communications of the EASST 6 (2007), selected papers of GT-VMT 2007: Graph Transformation and Visual Modelling Techniques (2007)
13. Jouault, F., Allilaire, F., Bézivin, J., Kurtev, I.: ATL: A model transformation tool. Sci. Comput. Program. 72(1-2), 31–39 (2008)
14. Jukša, M., Verbrugge, C., Elaasar, M., Vangheluwe, H.: Scope in model transformations. Tech. Rep. SOCS-TR-2013.4, McGill University (January 2013)
15. Kolovos, D.S., Paige, R.F., Polack, F.A.C.: The Epsilon Transformation Language. In: Vallecillo, A., Gray, J., Pierantonio, A. (eds.) ICMT 2008. LNCS, vol. 5063, pp. 46–60. Springer, Heidelberg (2008)
16. Maron, M.E., Kuhns, J.L.: On relevance, probabilistic indexing and information retrieval. J. ACM 7(3), 216–244 (1960)
17. Mészáros, T., Mezei, G., Levendovszky, T., Asztalos, M.: Manual and automated performance optimization of model transformation systems. STTT 12(3-4), 231–243 (2010)
18. Muzy, A., Touraille, L., Vangheluwe, H., Michel, O., Hill, D.R., Traoré, M.K.: Activity regions in discrete-event systems. In: Symposium on Theory of Modeling and Simulation - DEVS Integrative M&S Symposium (DEVS 2010), Spring Simulation Conference, Orlando, FL, pp. 176–182. Society for Computer Simulation International, SCS (April 2010)
19. Potier, M., Spicher, A., Michel, O.: Topological computation of activity regions. In: Proc. of the 2013 ACM SIGSIM Conference on Principles of Advanced Discrete Simulation, SIGSIM-PADS 2013, pp. 337–342. ACM, New York (2013)
20. Rensink, A.: The GROOVE simulator: A tool for state space generation. In: Pfaltz, J.L., Nagl, M., Böhlen, B. (eds.) AGTIVE 2003. LNCS, vol. 3062, pp. 479–485. Springer, Heidelberg (2004)
21. Sarkar, M.S., Blostein, D., Cordy, J.R.: GXL - a graph transformation language with scoping and graph parameters (1998)

22. Schürr, A., Winter, A.J., Zndorf, A.: Graph grammar engineering with PRO-GRES. In: Botella, P., Schäfer, W. (eds.) ESEC 1995. LNCS, vol. 989, pp. 219–234. Springer, Heidelberg (1995)
23. Syriani, E., Vangheluwe, H.: A modular timed graph transformation language for simulation-based design. Software and Systems Modeling (SoSyM) 12(2), 387–414 (2013)
24. Syriani, E., Vangheluwe, H., Mannadiar, R., Hansen, C., Mierlo, S.V., Ergin, H.: AToMPM: A web-based modeling environment. In: Demos/Posters/StudentResearch@MoDELS. pp. 21–25. CEUR (2013)
25. Varró, D., Balogh, A.: The model transformation language of the VIATRA2 framework. Science of Computer Programming 68(3), 214–234 (2007)
26. Varró, G., Anjorin, A., Schürr, A.: Unification of compiled and interpreter-based pattern matching techniques. In: Vallecillo, A., Tolvanen, J.-P., Kindler, E., Störrle, H., Kolovos, D. (eds.) ECMFA 2012. LNCS, vol. 7349, pp. 368–383. Springer, Heidelberg (2012)
27. Varró, G., Deckwerth, F., Wieber, M., Schürr, A.: An algorithm for generating model-sensitive search plans for emf models. In: Hu, Z., de Lara, J. (eds.) ICMT 2012. LNCS, vol. 7307, pp. 224–239. Springer, Heidelberg (2012)
28. Varró, G., Friedl, K., Varró, D.: Adaptive graph pattern matching for model transformations using model-sensitive search plans. Electr. Notes Theor. Comput. Sci. 152, 191–205 (2006)
29. Varró, G., Schürr, A., Varró, D.: Benchmarking for graph transformation. In: VL/HCC, pp. 79–88 (2005)
30. Vizhanyo, A., Agrawal, A., Shi, F.: Towards generation of efficient transformations. In: Karsai, G., Visser, E. (eds.) GPCE 2004. LNCS, vol. 3286, pp. 298–316. Springer, Heidelberg (2004)
31. Yang, Y., Webb, G.I.: Discretization for naive-Bayes learning: Managing discretization bias and variance. Mach. Learn. 74(1), 39–74 (2009)
32. Zündorf, A.: Graph pattern-matching in PROGRES. In: Cuny, J., Engels, G., Ehrig, H., Rozenberg, G. (eds.) Graph Grammars 1994. LNCS, vol. 1073, pp. 454–468. Springer, Heidelberg (1996)

Streamlining Control Flow Graph Construction with DCFlow

Mark Hills

East Carolina University, Greenville, North Carolina, USA
http://www.cs.ecu.edu/hillsma, http://www.ecu.edu

Abstract. A control flow graph (CFG) is used to model possible paths through a program, and is an essential part of many program analysis algorithms. While programs to construct CFGs can be written in meta-programming languages such as Rascal, writing such programs is currently quite tedious. With the goal of streamlining this process, in this paper we present DCFLOW, a domain-specific language and Rascal library for defining control flow rules and building control flow graphs. Control flow rules in DCFLOW are defined declaratively, based directly on the abstract syntax of the language under analysis and a number of operations representing types of control flow. Standard Rascal code is then generated based on the DCFLOW definition. This code makes use of the DCFLOW libraries to build CFGs for programs, which can then be visualized or used inside program analysis algorithms. To demonstrate the design of DCFLOW we apply it to Pico—a very simple imperative language—and to a significant subset of PHP.

1   Introduction

A control flow graph [2] (CFG) is used to model all possible paths (the flow of control) through a program. Nodes in the graph either represent individual constructs in the program, such as individual statements or expressions (referred to collectively as *instructions* below), or are synthesized based on program information. An example of the latter is nodes created to provide a unique exit from a function in languages with **return** statements that can occur anywhere in the function body. Edges in the graph represent the actual flow of control through the program, taking account of the evaluation order and the impact of various control constructs, such as conditionals, loops, and gotos.

Programs to build CFGs can be written in meta-programming languages such as Rascal [15,16]. However, the process of writing such programs, especially for larger languages, can be quite tedious. For example, the code currently used to extract control flow graphs from PHP programs, developed as part of the PHP AiR project [7], is 1,583 lines of Rascal,[1] including a large amount of boilerplate

---

[1] This is calculated using the cloc tool, and is based on counting lines of Rascal code of all modules under lang::php::analysis::cfg, available at
https://github.com/cwi-swat/php-analysis/tree/master/src/lang/php/analysis/cfg

B. Combemale et al. (Eds.): SLE 2014, LNCS 8706, pp. 322–341, 2014.
© Springer International Publishing Switzerland 2014

code to handle similar cases and keep track of information needed to properly build the graph. For actively evolving languages, such as PHP, this code also needs to be kept up to date to support new language features.

With the goal of streamlining the process of defining the control flow rules for a programming language and extracting control flow graphs from individual programs, in this paper we present a declarative, domain-specific language for specifying the control flow rules for programming languages—DCFLOW, short for **Declarative Control Flow**. In DCFLOW, control flow is defined at the level of the language's abstract syntax, allowing DCFLOW to be used even in cases were a Rascal parser for the language under analysis is not available. Control flow rules are defined declaratively, specified in terms of the AST types and a number of operations representing different types of control flow and CFG nodes. DCFLOW definitions are then used to generate standard Rascal code—a combination of custom code based on the DCFLOW definition, calls to the DCFLOW libraries, and calls to some user-provided code, all written in Rascal. Since DCFLOW definitions are translated into standard Rascal code, it is possible to examine, debug, and extend the generated code.

DCFLOW makes use of a number of Rascal features, including algebraic data types, reified types, and string templates, described in Section 2. In Section 3 we then describe DCFLOW in detail, showing how specific language features in both Pico and PHP are supported. Section 4 then provides an evaluation of DCFLOW, comparing it to hand-written Rascal and the DEFACTO system [3]. Finally, Sections 5 and 6 present related work and a final discussion with ideas for future work, respectively. Additional information about Rascal and DCFLOW can be found online.[2]

2   Enabling Rascal Features

The DCFLOW languages makes use of several key Rascal language features: *algebraic data types* for creating user-defined types, including the abstract syntax types; *type literals* and *type reification* to allow meta-level access to Rascal types; *string templates* for code generation; and Rascal support for *custom, Eclipse-based IDEs*. Each of these features is described in more detail below.

2.1   The Rascal Type System

The Rascal type system provides a uniform framework including both built-in and user-defined types, with the latter including both abstract (algebraic) datatypes and grammar non-terminals (also referred to as *concrete* datatypes). The type system is based on a type lattice with **void** at the bottom and **value** (the supertype of all types) at the top. In between are the types for atomic values (**bool, int, real, rat, str, loc, datetime**), types for tree values (**node**, representing named nodes with zero or more children, and defined abstract and

---

[2] See http://www.rascal-mpl.org and http://www.cs.ecu.edu/hillsma

```
data TYPE = natural() | string();
alias PicoId = str;
data PROGRAM = program(list[DECL] decls, list[STATEMENT] stats);
data DECL = decl(PicoId name, TYPE tp);

data EXP = id(PicoId name)
  | natCon(int iVal)
  | strCon(str sVal)
  | add(EXP left, EXP right)
  | sub(EXP left, EXP right)
  | conc(EXP left, EXP right) ;

data STATEMENT
  = asgStat(PicoId name, EXP exp)
  | ifElseStat(EXP exp,list[STATEMENT] thenpart,list[STATEMENT] elsepart)
  | whileStat(EXP exp, list[STATEMENT] body) ;
```

Fig. 1. The Pico AST in Rascal, Defined with Algebraic Data Types

concrete datatypes), and composite types with typed elements. Examples of the latter are **list[int]**, **set[str]**, **tuple[str,int]**, **rel[int,bool]**, **lrel[loc,int]**, and, for a given non-terminal type Stmt, **map[Stmt,int]**. The **node** datatype is a supertype of both abstract and concrete datatypes, while concrete datatypes are also all subtypes of the **Tree** datatype. Sub-typing is always covariant with respect to these typed elements; with functions, as is standard, return types must be covariant, while the argument types are instead contravariant. For example, for sets, **set[str]** is a subtype of **set[value]**, while for functions, **str(value)** is a subtype of **value(str)**.

2.2   Algebraic Datatypes

Algebraic datatypes (ADTs) in Rascal are defined using the **data** keyword, with one or more constructors defining the alternatives available for building new values of the user-defined type. An example with several related ADTs is shown in Figure 1, which gives the definition of the abstract syntax for the Pico language. Figure 1 defines five new datatypes: TYPE, PROGRAM, DECL, EXP, and STATEMENT.[3] These datatypes then each include one or more constructors. TYPE includes two, **natural** and **string**, that are used to indicate the type of data being declared in a Pico program. These constructors are a form of constant – neither contains any fields. EXP defines the different types of expressions in Pico, with fields corresponding to values for identifiers or constants (e.g., **natCon** has field **iVal** which contains a Rascal **int**) or to subexpressions (e.g., **add** has fields **left** and **right** for the left and right operands of a plus expression). ADTs in Rascal are open to extension, allowing new constructors to be added by other modules, and are also inherently recursive. Rascal includes extensive support for pattern matching

---

[3] PicoId is a type alias—PicoId is another name for str, the Rascal string type.

and term traversal over both built-in and user-defined datatypes, features used extensively in DCFLOW to work with program ASTs defined using types like those in Figure 1.

2.3   Type Literals and Reified Types

Reified types make it possible to manipulate types as first-class values that can be passed around, returned, queried and manipulated. Rascal's reification operator creates *self-describing* type values that contain both the reified type and all datatypes used in this type's definition. A type can be reified using the prefix reification operator (#), resulting in a value called a *type literal*. A reified type value contains a symbol to represent the type and a map of definitions for any abstract or concrete datatype dependencies. It is given the type **type[&T]**, where the type parameter **&T** is bound to the type that was reified. For example:

- #str produces a literal value type(\str(),()) of type type[str].
- #rel[int,loc,str] produces type(\rel([\int(),\loc(), \str()]),()) of type type[rel[int,loc,str]].

The **type** data constructor used to build type literals is built in to Rascal; the representations for type symbols and their definitions are defined as Rascal datatypes in a library module, **Type**. Above, the map of definitions was empty: (). For abstract or concrete datatypes this map will contain the complete (possibly recursive) abstract datatype or grammar. Given the EXP type shown in Figure 1, and focusing just on the **add** constructor:

```
data EXP = ... | add(EXP left, EXP right) | ...;
```

the reified type #EXP will produce the following term of type **type[EXP]** (again focusing just on **add**, and with some details elided):

```
type(adt("EXP"),
    (adt("EXP"):choice(...,cons(label("add"),adt("EXP"),
    [label("left",adt("EXP")),label("right",adt("EXP"))]),...)))
```

Type literals allow the implementation of DCFLOW to work *generically* over different AST definitions for different programming languages. The implementation of DCFLOW uses the type information for the AST being processed to generate correct code for CFG construction, while the IDE support uses this same type information to detect errors in the DCFLOW definition.

2.4   String Templates

Rascal provides string templates for code generation, a frequently occurring operation in meta-programming. String templates are multi-line string literals with a left-margin (given with a single quote character), interpolation of arbitrary expressions, auto-indentation, and structured control flow. An example from

```
res = "public tuple[<p.astType>,LabelState] labelAST(LabelState ls, <p.astType> ast) {
     '    Lab incLabel() {
     '        ls.counter += 1;
     '        return lab(ls.counter);
     '    }
     '    labeledAst = bottom-up visit(ast) {
     '        <for (n <- gs.annotatedTypeNames) {> case <n> n => n[@lab = incLabel()]
     '        <}>
     '    };
     '    ls.cfgNodes = ( n@lab : cfgNode(n,n@lab) | /node n := labeledAst, (n@lab)?);
     '    return < labeledAst, ls >;
     '}";
```

```
public tuple[PROGRAM,LabelState] labelAST(LabelState ls, PROGRAM ast) {
    Lab incLabel() {
        ls.counter += 1;
        return lab(ls.counter);
    }
    labeledAst = bottom-up visit(ast) {
        case PROGRAM n => n[@lab = incLabel()]
        case STATEMENT n => n[@lab = incLabel()]
        case EXP n => n[@lab = incLabel()]

    };
    ls.cfgNodes = ( n@lab : cfgNode(n,n@lab) | /node n := labeledAst, (n@lab)?);
    return < labeledAst, ls >;
}
```

Fig. 2. String Templates in Rascal

DCFLOW is shown in Figure 2. The top of Figure 2 shows a string template from the `GenerateLabeler` module. Rascal code given between angle brackets, such as `<p.astType>`, is evaluated, with the results inserted into the string at that position (string interpolation); an embedded **for** loop generates a **case** (used in the Rascal **visit** construct, which is used for structure-shy traversal) for each element **n** in the set `annotatedTypeNames`, which holds the names of the abstract syntax types that should be labeled, and are thus "linkable", in the control-flow graph. The code generated by this string template, specifically for labeling Pico ASTs, is shown at the bottom of Figure 2.

2.5   Custom Eclipse IDE Support

Rascal provides built-in support for creating Eclipse-based IDEs for languages defined in Rascal. Features supported include configurable syntax highlighting, foldable code sections, user-defined code outlines displayed using a standard Eclipse outline view, user-defined annotators that can register messages that display in the IDE and the Eclipse problem view (e.g., for reporting errors), automatic checking (invoking user-provided Rascal functions) of code during editing, and the addition of menu items to trigger user-provided functions. A number of these features have been used to create an IDE for DCFLOW, with error checking to ensure that common mistakes (such as misspelling a field name) are visible in the IDE even before code generation occurs.

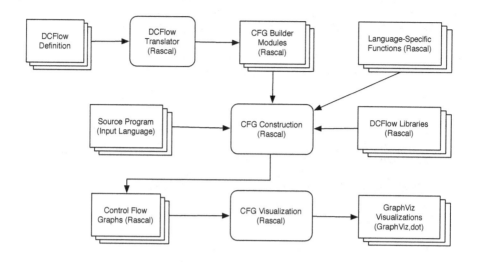

Fig. 3. DCFlow Architecture

3   DCFlow

DCFLOW is a declarative, domain-specific language and supporting libraries for defining the control flow rules for a programming language (referred to below as the *input language*). The architecture of DCFLOW is shown in Figure 3. Once a DCFLOW specification is created, the DCFLOW translator converts the specification into a collection of Rascal modules. These modules handle the labeling of the AST, which assigns unique IDs to each instruction, and the creation of a control flow graph for an input program, based on the DCFLOW rules specifying the control flow for the input language. The CFG construction process uses the generated modules, language-specific functions provided by the user (discussed more below), and DCFLOW libraries to actually perform the control flow graph generation, giving one or more control flow graphs for an input program. These graphs can be used in analysis algorithms (see Section 4 for an example), and can also be visualized using DCFLOW visualization functionality, which generates GraphViz diagrams using the dot language. Examples of these diagrams can be seen in Figures 6 and 7.

The rest of this section describes the DCFLOW language in detail. First we discuss control flow graphs and their representation in the Rascal DCFLOW libraries. We then describe the DCFLOW language, illustrating features of the

```
begin
    declare x : natural,
            y : natural;
    x := 3;
    if x then
        y := 10
    else
        y := 15
    fi
end
```

Fig. 4. Sample Pico Program

```
map[loc, CFG]: (|pico+program://CFG/src/programs/pico/condition.pico|:cfg(
    |pico+program://CFG/src/programs/pico/condition.pico|,
    (
        lab(4):cfgNode( natCon(10), lab(4)),
        lab(5):cfgNode( asgStat( "y", natCon(10) ), lab(5)),
        ...
    ),
    {
        flowEdge( lab(5), lab(11), {}), flowEdge( lab(4), lab(5), {}),
        flowEdge( lab(7), lab(11), {}), flowEdge( lab(1), lab(2), {}),
        flowEdge( lab(2), lab(3), {}), flowEdge( lab(10), lab(1), {}),
        flowEdge( lab(3), lab(4), {conditionTrue()}),
        flowEdge( lab(3), lab(6), {conditionFalse()}),
        flowEdge( lab(6), lab(7), {})
    },
    ( ":exit":exitNode(lab(11)), ":entry":entryNode(lab(10)) )))
```

Fig. 5. DCFLOW CFG Representation, in Rascal

language with a number of example control flow definitions from Pico and PHP. We end with a brief discussion of some additional features in DCFLOW, as well as of what is currently not supported.

3.1 DCFlow Control Flow Graphs

Figure 4 shows an example of a simple program in Pico. After setting x to 3, a conditional checks the value of x. The true branch, which sets y to 10, is taken when x is not 0, while the false branch, which sets y to 15, is taken when x is 0. The control flow graph for this program, extracted using a DCFLOW CFG builder and given as a Rascal term, is then shown in Figure 5. A CFG is a directed graph, with nodes representing instructions or synthesized information (e.g., a synthesized exit node for a function) and

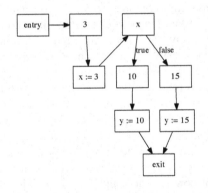

Fig. 6. CFG for Program in Figure 4

directed edges showing how control flows between the nodes.

Rascal provides built-in support for source location literals (values of type loc) that are Uniform Resource Identifiers[4] (URIs) optionally followed by text coordinates that allow the identification of specific text ranges in the information the URI points to. Location literals are quoted with bars, such as |http://www.rascal-mpl.org|. Since, in many languages, a program can yield

---

[4] See http://www.ietf.org/rfc/rfc3986.txt.

multiple control flow graphs (e.g., in PHP each function will have its own graph), DCFLOW returns a map from source locations to control flow graphs. The location points to the location in the source code associated with the graph, for instance, to the function represented by the graph, and is created by a user-defined function specific to the input language. We intentionally use locations like those used in M3 [10], a model for source code artifacts. The ADT defining the control flow graph contains the location, a map from unique node labels to the actual control flow graph nodes (some of which are elided here), a set of directed flow edges (given with node labels as the from and to endpoints), and finally a map from special labels to specific nodes, in this case marking the designated entry and exit nodes for the program.

A visualization of this CFG is shown in Figures 6 and 7. The graphs clearly encode the order of evaluation: starting at the **entry** to the program, first 3 is evaluated, then the assignment to x is performed. After this, x is evaluated, with control then following either the **true** branch or the **false** branch. Along the **true** branch 10 is evaluated, followed by the assignment to y; along the **false** branch 15 is evaluated, again followed by the assignment to y. Both branches rejoin at the unique **exit** node, which represents the end of the program. Figure 6 shows a CFG with each node in its own block, while Figure 7 shows a CFG where blocks have been merged into *basic blocks* using the DCFLOW **BasicBlocks** library module. A basic block is a sequence of instructions where control has to enter with the first instruction and must leave only at the end (e.g., an instruction in the middle of

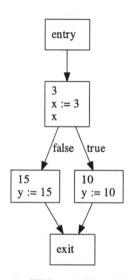

Fig. 7. CFG with Basic Blocks

the block cannot transfer control to anything other than the next instruction). We still show the order of evaluation in each block, so (for instance) we still see that 15 is evaluated before the assignment y := 15—this is more verbose, but makes the evaluation order explicit.

3.2 DCFlow Definitions and Sequential Control Flow

Figure 8 shows the DCFLOW definition for the straight-line part of the Pico language (i.e., the entire language except for **if** and **while** statements). Since DCFLOW is designed to be used with Rascal, DCFLOW modules have a similar structure to Rascal modules. A DCFLOW module is named using **module** (in this case, **Pico**); the name used here is then also used to name the generated files. While a number of DCFLOW modules are automatically added as imports in the generated code, additional modules can be added using the **ast** and **import** commands. Additionally, one module must be imported using **ast**, which

```
module Pico

ast demo::lang::Pico::Abstract;
import lang::pico::CFGBase;
context PROGRAM::program;
astType PROGRAM;

rule PROGRAM::program = entry(exit(stats));
rule EXP::add = entry(left) --> right --> exit(self);
rule EXP::sub = entry(left) --> right --> exit(self);
rule EXP::conc = entry(left) --> right --> exit(self);
rule EXP::id = entry(exit(self));
rule EXP::strCon = entry(exit(self));
rule EXP::natCon = entry(exit(self));
rule STATEMENT::asgStat = entry(exp) --> exit(self);
```

Fig. 8. The DCFLOW Definition for Straight-Line Pico

indicates where the AST types, used extensively in DCFLOW, are declared. Since a program could result in multiple control flow graphs, `context` indicates the constructors for which control flow graphs should be created. These may be nested: in PHP, control flow graphs are created for the script, representing the entire file, and for each individual function and method contained inside. Finally, `astType` actually names the "top" type of the AST, generally the type representing an individual program or compilation unit; the assumption is that there is one unique type. DCFLOW loads the reified representation of this type, which also includes all types on which this depends, during code generation.

Following this initial information, `rule` is used to define the control flow rules for individual language constructs, based on the abstract syntax for the language. The general structure of a rule is:

rule `typename::consname = flow;`

where typename is the name of the type, as given in the `data` declaration; `consname` is the name of the constructor; and `flow` describes the control flow for the construct, given using DCFLOW operations, names of special CFG nodes, and the field names of the constructor. Looking at Figure 8, the `entry` and `exit` operations indicate where flow enters the construct and where it exits the construct, while the special name `self` stands for the construct as a whole.[5] Each rule triggers the generation of three functions: `entry`, `exit`, and `internalFlow`. `entry` returns the label of the first instruction that is executed as part of the construct, while `exit` returns a set of possible final instructions for the construct. `internalFlow` builds edges to represent the flow of control inside the construct.

For instance, looking at the rule for the `id` constructor of `EXP`, the flow is given as `entry(exit(self))`. `entry` and `exit` mark where control flow enters

---

[5] If a field in the constructor is also named self, or any other DCFLOW keyword, it can be used by prefixing it with a backslash, i.e., as \self.

and exits the construct—nesting one inside the other indicates that both mark the same construct. Since this is given as `self`, the generated `entry` and `exit` functions will return the label (for `exit`, a set containing just the label) for the `id` expression. Since the rule does not reference any fields, the construct has no internal control flow. Thus, the generated `internalFlow` function adds no edges.

A more complex case is that for the `add` constructor of `EXP`. Here, the control flow is given as `entry(left) --> right --> exit(self)`. The arrows signify the flow of control between the named items. Here, this means that control enters at the left operand, flows into the right operand, and then finally to self, modeling the evaluation of the left operand, followed by evaluation of the right, and then finishing with evaluation of the addition expression as a whole. Since the left operand is, itself, an expression (a fact determined by the DCFLOW generator by consulting the reified representation of the `EXP` type), the generated code will determine the entry label for an occurrence of `add` by recursing on the first operand and finding its entry label, which could lead to additional recursive calls. For instance, to find the entry label for `(a+b)+c` one would find the entry label for `a+b`, which is the entry label for `a`, which (as stated above) is the same as the label for `a` itself. Since the exit label is determined by checking `self`, no recursion takes place—the entry label for `self` is always that of the item as a whole. The internal flow function generated for `add` links the exit labels of `left` to the entry label of `right`, and the exit labels of `right` to the entry label for `self`. This "wires up" the expressions representing `left`, `right`, and `left + right`, ensuring the flow in the CFG mirrors that in an executing program.

A final example is the first rule in Figure 8. The control flow for a program is based on field `stats`, which represents the list of statements making up the program. Since this is a list, DCFLOW will generate code to compute the internal flow for each statement in the list and to link the `exit` and `entry` labels of the statements together in sequence. DCFLOW also contains a `foreach` operations that can be used to iterative over lists, allowing this to be done manually, but this is a common enough occurrence that the typical behavior is the default.

This definition can be condensed using several shorthands, as shown in Figure 9. First, if the type of the AST is not provided explicitly using `astType`, DCFLOW assumes it is the type of the first context list item. Second, constructs with the same control flow can be defined in the same rule, with whitespace

```
module Pico

ast demo::lang::Pico::Abstract;
import lang::pico::CFGBase;
context PROGRAM::program;

rule PROGRAM::program = ^$stats;
rule EXP::add EXP::sub EXP::conc = ^left --> right --> $self;
rule EXP::id EXP::strCon EXP::natCon = ^$self;
rule STATEMENT::asgStat = ^exp --> $self;
```

Fig. 9. The DCFLOW Definition for Straight-Line Pico, Condensed

```
tuple[FlowEdges,LabelState] internalFlow(EXP item:add(EXP left,EXP right), LabelState ls) {
  FlowEdges edges = { };
  < edges, ls > = addEdges(edges, ls, left);
  < edges, ls > = addEdges(edges, ls, right);
  for(exlab <- exit(left,ls)) {
    < edges, ls > = linkItemsLabelLabel(edges, ls, exlab, entry(right,ls) );
  }
  for(exlab <- exit(right,ls)) {
    < edges, ls > = linkItemsLabelLabel(edges, ls, exlab, item@lab );
  }
  return < edges, ls >;
}
```

Fig. 10. Generated Rascal Code, Control Flow for Addition in Pico

separating the names. Third, entry and exit can be replaced with ˆ and $, respectively—the operators are intentionally the same as those used to match the start and end of a string in regular expression syntax. While we may take advantage of more defaults in the future, we currently prefer having more explicit information in DCFLOW specifications, since this creates less "magic" that the user is then required to understand, making definitions less cryptic.

To get an idea of the code generated by DCFLOW, Figure 10 shows the code generated to handle the internal flow of the Pico addition expression. The input to the function is the addition expression and the label state, which, at runtime, tracks information needed to properly label the AST and build the control flow graph. An empty set to hold the generated edges is created, then **addEdges** is called twice, first on the left operand, then on the right. After this the two are linked, with all exits from the left operand (in languages with constructs such as the ternary conditional expression, there could be multiple exits) linked to the entry to the right. This same operation is then performed again, in this case linking the right operand to the add expression itself. Finally, this set of generated edges, along with the current state, are returned.

3.3 Defining Basic Decisions and Loops

The definition of the **if** and **while** statements in Pico is shown in Figure 11. Both are defined using the same building blocks shown above, with some minor additions. First, it is possible for a rule to have multiple, distinct operations, separated by commas. The first rule shown, for **if**, has three, while the second has two. Second, one or more labels can be given on an arrow by writing them inside the arrow body (after at least one dash, and also followed by at least one dash). So, the rule for **if** states that the condition (**exp**) is the entry, and that there are then two edges, one from **exp** to the then branch when the condition is true, and one from **exp** to the else branch when the condition is false. Third, **exit** can appear multiple times, marking multiple possible exits from the construct. Finally, **entry** and **exit** can contain a list of names instead of just a single name. In this case, the names will be tried, in order, during CFG construction, stopping when a usable label or set of labels, respectively, is found. This handles the situation where **thenpart** or **elsepart** may be empty, in which case the final instruction evaluated on that path would actually be the condition **exp**.

```
rule STATEMENT::ifElseStat = ^exp,
                             exp -conditionTrue-> exit(thenpart,exp),
                             exp -conditionFalse-> exit(elsepart,exp);
rule STATEMENT::whileStat = ^$exp -conditionTrue-> body -backedge-> exp,
                             exp -conditionFalse-> create(footer);
```

Fig. 11. Pico Decisions and Loops Modeled in DCFLOW

The `while` statement has a similar definition: the condition is tried and, if true, the body is executed. Here, we explicitly mark the edge from the body back to the condition as a loop backedge. When the condition is false, we instead need to exit the construct. We could link to the following instruction using the keyword `following`, but instead create a new footer node for the entire loop, linking to that instead. This will cause all exits from the loop (here, through `exp`, which is marked as the exit) to pass through this footer node, and will cause the footer node to be used as the `exit` when linking this to any statements following this in the program. Finally, note that, once a name has been marked as an entry or exit point, other uses of the name do not need to be so marked again.

3.4 Defining Unstructured and Structured Jumps

DCFLOW distinguishes between *unstructured* and *structured* jumps. Unstructured jumps, such as `goto` statements, essentially ignore other control flow constructs, transferring control to an arbitrary instruction. In PHP, a `goto` will jump to a label defined on a statement, and cannot transfer control out of the current context (e.g., from inside a function back to the top-level script) or into a loop or switch.[6] Structured jumps, such as `break` and `continue`, work in tandem with language constructs such as `while`, `for`, and `switch` statements, with the target of the jump depending on the semantics of the associated statement. In PHP, a `continue`[7] in a `while` loop will jump back to the loop condition, while a `break`[8] will instead transfer control to the first instruction after the loop. To work with nested control constructs, both `break` and `continue` accept an optional numeric argument—if given inside a loop nested inside another loop, `break 2` would jump to the instruction following the outer loop. Other languages, such as Java and Rascal, provide similar functionality by instead allowing loops to be labeled, similarly to how statements are labeled for `goto` in PHP.

The DCFLOW definitions of `goto`, `while`, `break`, and `continue` for PHP are shown in Figure 12. These rules introduce several new DCFLOW constructs, and also assume that several Rascal functions have been defined. To support unstructured jumps, calls to user-provided function `findUnstructuredJumpTargets` are generated; this function identifies all unstructured jump targets—for PHP, statement labels—in the current context. The `jump` construct then specifies a jump in the control flow to a destination identified by the operand—here, the `label`

---

[6] http://www.php.net/manual/en/control-structures.goto.php
[7] http://www.php.net/manual/en/control-structures.continue.php
[8] http://www.php.net/manual/en/control-structures.break.php

```
rule Stmt::goto      = jump(\label),^$self;

rule Stmt::\while    = create(footer), jumpTarget(cond,\continue),
                       jumpTarget(footer,\break),
                       ^$cond -conditionTrue-> body -backedge-> cond,
                       cond -conditionFalse-> footer;
rule Stmt::\break    = entry(breakExpr,self) --> $self,
                       jump(breakExpr,\break);
rule Stmt::\continue = entry(continueExpr,$self) --> self,
                       jump(continueExpr,\continue);
```

Fig. 12. PHP Jumps Modeled in DCFLOW

field of the goto statement. This is looked up using user-provided function getTargetsForJump and, for unstructured jumps, must be one discovered by findUnstructuredJumpTargets. The code for jump will then create flow edges from the exit labels of the instruction to these target labels.

The definition for while shows how structured jump targets are defined. An explicit footer is created for the loop first. Two jump targets are then registered with the jumpTarget operation—a target for continue, which will jump back to the condition, and a target for break, which will jump to the loop footer.[9] DCFLOW generates calls to user-provided function createJumpTarget to actually perform this registration. The definition of the loop itself is then very similar to that given for Pico in Figure 11. The structured jumps to these targets then occur in the break and continue statements, which both have very similar definitions. In both cases the entry to the construct is the optional argument, with the construct itself serving as the default if this argument is empty. Flow then goes to the actual break or continue statement. The jump is again specified with the jump operation; the first argument gives information on the target, while the second identifies the type of jump target, which must match the type given in the jumpTarget command. This will result in flow edges from the exit labels of the instruction (here, just one) to the entry label of the target instruction—for while, either to the condition (for continue) or to the added footer (for break).

3.5   Other Features and Limitations

There are several other features of DCFLOW that support less common cases, including list operations such as first, next, and last; an is operation to check to see if a field is constructed using a specific constructor; and foreach and if operations that can be used to describe more complex control flow.

There are also some control constructs DCFLOW cannot currently support, the most common being exceptions. In the PHP definition, we instead define support for exceptions directly in Rascal, indicating in the DCFLOW definition that

---

[9] Targets break and continue are available by default. DCFLOW operations also allow defining new types of targets.

the code generator should ignore the `throw`, `try/catch`, and `try/catch/finally` statements. While it would be useful to expand DCFLOW to support such features, it may be quite challenging to define them generically—error handling features of languages can differ in fairly significant and sometimes subtle ways. Given this, it may be the case that using such generic features to define the control flow in DCFLOW would take roughly the same amount of effort as defining the control flow directly in Rascal, in which case this would provide little benefit (as discussed in Section 4, the amount of code to handle these features for PHP is a fraction of the total code, most of which can now be generated directly from a DCFLOW definition) while risking an increase in conceptual complexity.

4   Evaluation

As stated in Section 1, the purpose of DCFLOW is to streamline the process of defining the control flow rules for programming languages, with the goal of generating Rascal code that can extract control flow graphs from programs in that language. In this section, we evaluate the effectiveness of DCFLOW using three techniques. First, we compare DCFLOW definitions to definitions given directly in Rascal. Second, we compare DCFLOW definitions to definitions given using DEFACTO [3], a fact extraction framework developed for ASF+SDF [26,25] and RScript [14], a precursor to Rascal. Finally, we illustrate use of DCFLOW-generated control flow graphs in a standard data flow analysis for Pico programs.

4.1   Comparison with Rascal Definitions

Since the main motivation for creating DCFLOW was to simplify the process of creating control flow graphs and graph extractors in Rascal, we first compare the results of using DCFLOW with custom Rascal solutions. The control flow for Pico, discussed first, has been completely defined, while the control flow for PHP, discussed second, is complete except for the definitions for a handful of features implemented directly in Rascal.

Pico: Module `demo::lang::Pico::ControlFlow`, part of the standard Rascal library, contains the definition for the control flow graph for Pico as well as all code to extract this graph from Pico ASTs. In total, this consists of 45 lines of code: 11 giving the module header, imports, and definitions of control flow nodes and graphs, and 34 defining the rules used to extract the control flow. The DCFLOW definition for Pico is 10 lines of code: 4 header lines and 6 rules. The DCFLOW generator converts this into 408 lines of Rascal code—it is much larger than the custom Rascal solution because the generator is language generic, so it cannot take advantage of the simplicity of the Pico control flow rules.

PHP: As mentioned in Section 1, the PHP AiR definition of PHP control flow is 1,583 lines of Rascal. The DCFLOW definition is currently 66 rules (some handling multiple constructs) and 6 header lines, generating 2,714 lines of Rascal.

User-provided functions to compute jump targets add another 57 lines of code, while code used to handle features such as exceptions is another 169 lines.

4.2 Comparison with DeFacto

In DEFACTO, fact extraction is performed using *fact annotations, annotation functions,* and *selection annotations.* Fact annotations are added to the production rules of a grammar, and state a named fact that can be computed for the given language construct. For instance, a production that defines a new identifier as having a certain type can be annotated with a `typeOf` fact stating that this identifier has the defined type. The fact is represented using a relation, with a single instance of the fact represented as a tuple in the relation. Annotation functions and selection annotations are then used to deal with lists and optional elements of productions, allowing list iteration (e.g., to get the first or last element of a list, or to get pairs of elements representing the next relation) and selection based on the presence or absence of list elements or optional subterms. DEFACTO annotations can be given in separate modules which are "woven" in as needed, allowing different facts to be extracted based on the needs of the analysis. Non-local facts can then be computed using RScript, which allows relational algebra operations to be performed over these relations.

DEFACTO and DCFLOW share many similarities: both work by defining rules over language constructs, and both include support for handling commonly occurring constructs such as lists and optional data. There are also a number of differences between the two approaches. DCFLOW is designed specifically to specify control flow rules, versus more general program facts, so it supports more specialized notation (e.g., the name decorations used in Figure 9, arrows to represent edges) and can make more default assumptions about how common constructs (e.g., a list representing the body of a block) are handled. DCFLOW also works at the level of the abstract syntax, instead of concrete syntax, allowing it to be used in cases where a Rascal parser definition is not available (but also requiring an abstract syntax to be defined even if it is not otherwise needed). The underlying language is also different: RScript can be seen as a subset of Rascal, specifically focused on relational operations and fixpoint computation, but lacking the broader support for string manipulation, code generation, IDE creation, and visualization that is used in DCFLOW.

Specifically focusing on Pico, the DEFACTO and RScript control-flow graph extraction consists of 11 fact annotations over 3 relations and one relational expression, giving a total of 12 statements and 13 lines of code. In DCFLOW, a rule is defined for each AST constructor used to define the program, expressions, and statements, 10 in total, although these are collapsed 6 distinct rules since several have identical control flow. The entire module has a total of 10 lines of code, the 6 rules, the module name, two imports (one for the AST type, one for a language-specific function used to create a Rascal location representing Pico programs), and the definition of the context, specifying the scope of the control flow graph (here, the entire program). The module containing the language-specific function is a total of 4 lines of code: the module header, two imports, and a one-line function definition. The comparison for Pico thus shows a very similar level of effort using both DEFACTO and DCFLOW. DEFACTO is no longer maintained, so it is hard to determine if this would hold with larger languages and/or languages with more complex control flow, such as PHP.

4.3   Reaching Definitions with DCFlow CFGs

As part of our evaluation, we have defined a standard reaching definitions analysis for Pico using the CFG created by DCFLOW. An alternate version [15], working directly over relations of control flow facts, is in the Rascal standard library in module `demo::ReachingDefs`. Figure 13 shows an example Pico program, with the instruction labels shown at the end of several lines (e.g., the first assignment to x is labeled 2). The implementation of the reaching definitions algorithm is then shown in Figure 14. Function `computeDefs` computes a relation over the entire program, from Pico identifiers to the labels where these identifiers are defined (here, using assignment statements). `gen` computes the set of all labels corresponding to definitions introduced by the instruction— assignments introduce the label of the assignment statement, while all other instructions introduce the empty set (indicated with

```
begin
declare x : natural,
        y : natural;
x := 1; // 2
y := 2; // 4
if x then
  y := y + 1 // 9
else
   while y do
     x := x + 1; // 14
     y := y - x // 18
   od
fi;
y := x // 22
end
```

Fig. 13. Reaching Definitions Example, in Pico

`default`, meaning this function handles all other cases). `kill` also treats assignment as a special case—a new assignment into a name will remove all defs of that name except for the current one. Function `computeReach` then uses these to compute the `in` and `out` sets for each instruction, returned as relations from instruction labels to definition labels. `in` will contain all definitions that may reach the start of the labeled instruction, while `out` contains all definitions that reach the end. Starting with empty relations, and the definitions for the program given by `computeDefs`, a fixpoint computation (indicated using `solve`) iteratively computes the `in` and `out` sets for each label. The `in` set is the result of the `out` sets for all predecessors (computed with `pred`, a DCFLOW library function), while the `out` set is the result of the `in` set, minus anything killed by the current instruction, plus anything generated—basically, any definitions that come in to the instruction that are not killed by it, plus any definitions the instruction generates itself. When the fixpoint completes the relations are returned.

Looking at several points of interest in Figure 13, running the algorithm shows that no definitions reach instruction 2, since at the start of the instruction no definitions have occurred yet; the definition at 2 reaches 4; and the definition of

```
rel[PicoId,Lab] computeDefs(CFG c) =
  { < name, 1 > | cfgNode(asgStat(PicoId name, _),1) <- c.nodes<1> };

set[Lab] gen(cfgNode(asgStat(PicoId name, _),1)) = { 1 };
default set[Lab] gen(CFGNode n) = { };

set[Lab] kill(cfgNode(asgStat(PicoId name, _),1),rel[PicoId,Lab] defs) = defs[name]-1;
default set[Lab] kill(CFGNode n, rel[PicoId,Lab] defs) =  { };

tuple[rel[Lab,Lab] reachIn, rel[Lab,Lab] reachOut] computeReach(CFG c) {
  rel[Lab,Lab] reachIn = { };
  rel[Lab,Lab] reachOut = { };
  defs = computeDefs(c);
  solve(reachIn,reachOut) {
    reachIn  = { < l, r > | l <- c.nodes, r <- reachOut[pred(c,l)] };
    reachOut = { < l, r > | l <- c.nodes,
                            r <- (gen(c.nodes[l]) + (reachIn[l] - kill(c.nodes[l],defs))) };
  }
  return < reachIn, reachOut >;
}
```

Fig. 14. Reaching Definitions Algorithm, in Rascal

x at 2 reaches 14, but not 18, since 14 redefines x and is always run before 18. The definition of y at instruction 18 can also reach itself, since an assignment to y made in one iteration of the loop will reach the next iteration. Any of the definitions before 22 can reach 22, since control may have flowed through either the true or false branch of the conditional.

5   Related Work

In this section we look at two areas of related work. First, we look at general fact extraction techniques, such as DeFacto. Second, we look specifically at recent research on specifying control flow declaratively, and on using domain-specific languages to specify program properties which can be used in analysis.

Fact Extraction: Basic fact extraction can be performed using tools such as Lex [17] and languages such as AWK [1], Perl, or Python, using regular expressions to match patterns in the code and then record the associated facts. These approaches are language specific—different patterns would be needed for each language—and cannot naturally handle the nested constructs common in programming languages. Murphy and Notkin [20,21] have extended this approach to include additional contextual information, allowing regular expressions to be given in a hierarchy where some expressions only match after others have already matched (e.g., an expression matching a function call may match only after an expression matching a function definition has already matched). Extracted facts can also be organized in relations, allowing additional facts to be computed after scanning is complete.

Approaches based on grammars can more naturally handle the nested constructs common to programming languages, but also generally require the source code to be syntactically correct. The most basic example of a grammar-based extractor would be one that used the semantic actions in Yacc [11] or other parsing systems to record and compute facts. More complex tools include the Rigi system [19], which provides fixed fact extractors for several languages, representing extracted facts as tuples in a format named RSF (Rigi Standard Format), and systems that use attribute grammars [12,22,6,23,29], which use synthesized attributes to specify facts and inherited attributes to propagate these through the parse tree.

Other approaches have focused on using queries to build relations, with relational operations then used to combine facts and perform the analysis. Rigi, mentioned above, uses tuples given in the RSF format and a language, the Rigi Command Library (RCL), to manipulate these tuples. GROK [9] and Croco-Pat [4,5] (using a notation called RML) instead use relational algebra, with GROK supporting binary relations and CrocoPat supporting n-ary relations. The DEFACTO system [3], discussed in Section 4, uses RScript [14], which also supports n-ary relations and relational algebra, as a query language for extracted facts, as does Vankov's work on formulating program slicing using relational techniques [27]. Rascal [15,16] has n-ary relations as a native datatype, while relational operations, such as transitive closure, are built in to the language.

DSLs and Declarative Control Flow: Other than DEFACTO, the most closely related work to DCFLOW uses JastAdd [6] to declaratively define control flow rules and dataflow analysis algorithms based on abstract syntax trees [24]. Reference attributes are used to represent the control flow edges in the AST; collection attributes allow the specification of inverse relations (such as the predecessor relation, given an existing successor relation between control flow nodes); and higher order attributes allow the synthesis of new AST nodes, such as standard entry and exit nodes for methods. In contrast, DCFLOW focuses just on the declarative specification of control flow rules, and uses Rascal functionality, instead of attribute grammars, to create the control flow graph. For instance, computing pred can either be performed by inverting the flow relationship, given as a graph, or by pattern matching over the control flow edges.

DCFLOW is also similar, conceptually, to other work on using focused domain-specific languages to support program analysis tasks. This includes the DHAL language [18] and its variants, for data flow analysis, and an approach for performing incremental name and type analysis [28], implemented as part of the Spoofax language workbench [13], which includes a task language with a number of instructions related to name and type analysis (e.g., to lookup or cast a type) and a number of combinators to combine the results of subtasks.

6 Discussion and Future Work

In this paper we presented DCFLOW, a domain-specific language for declaratively specifying the control flow rules for a programming language based on its abstract syntax. DCFLOW can specify the control flow for a large number of typical language constructs, generating the Rascal source code needed to construct control flow graphs for programs using these features. As shown in Section 4, these specifications are much shorter than a custom Rascal solution, especially for larger languages. For features that are not currently supported, such as exceptions, Rascal code can be written directly, extending the code generated by DCFLOW and taking advantage of DCFLOW library modules.

In the future, we plan to continue development of DCFLOW, extending it to handle features that are not currently supported in cases where a general form, reusable across multiple languages, can be defined without adding too much additional complexity. We also want to improve the visualization support provided by the DCFLOW library, allowing control flow graphs to be visualized directly in Rascal as well as using GraphViz. Finally, we would like to explore enabling DCFLOW to be used as part of the Rascal resources framework [8], allowing code generation and import of the CFG builder to be triggered by importing DCFLOW specifications into Rascal modules.

References

1. Aho, A., Kernighan, B., Weinberger, P.: Awk - A Pattern Scanning and Processing Language. Software–Practice and Experience 9(4), 267–280 (1979)
2. Allen, F.E.: Control Flow Analysis. In: Proceedings of a Symposium on Compiler Optimization, pp. 1–19. ACM, New York (1970)
3. Basten, H.J.S., Klint, P.: DeFacto: Language-Parametric Fact Extraction from Source Code. In: Gašević, D., Lämmel, R., Van Wyk, E. (eds.) SLE 2008. LNCS, vol. 5452, pp. 265–284. Springer, Heidelberg (2009)
4. Beyer, D., Noack, A., Lewerentz, C.: Simple and efficient relational querying of software structures. In: Proceedings of the 10th Working Conference on Reverse Engineering, pp. 216–225 (2003)
5. Beyer, D., Noack, A., Lewerentz, C.: Efficient relational calculation for software analysis. IEEE Transactions on Software Engineering 31(2), 137 (2005)
6. Ekman, T., Hedin, G.: The JastAdd system - modular extensible compiler construction. Science of Computer Programming 69(1–3), 14–26 (2007)
7. Hills, M., Klint, P.: PHP AiR: Analyzing PHP Systems with Rascal. In: Proceedings of CSMR-WCRE 2014, pp. 454–457. IEEE (2014)
8. Hills, M., Klint, P., Vinju, J.J.: Meta-language Support for Type-Safe Access to External Resources. In: Czarnecki, K., Hedin, G. (eds.) SLE 2012. LNCS, vol. 7745, pp. 372–391. Springer, Heidelberg (2013)
9. Holt, R.: Binary Relational Algebra Applied to Software Architecture. CSRI 345. University of Toronto (March 1996)
10. Izmaylova, A., Klint, P., Shahi, A., Vinju, J.J.: M3: An Open Model For Measuring Code Artifacts. Technical Report arXiv-1312.1188, CWI (December 2013)
11. Johnson, S.C.: Yacc: Yet Another Compiler-Compiler. Technical Report CS TR 32, Bell Labs (1975)
12. Jourdan, M., Parigot, D., Julié, C., Durin, O., Bellec, C.L.: Design, Implementation and Evaluation of the FNC-2 Attribute Grammar System. In: Proceedings of PLDI 1990, pp. 209–222 (1990)
13. Kats, L.C.L., Visser, E.: The Spoofax Language Workbench. In: OOPSLA 2010 Companion, pp. 237–238. ACM (2010)
14. Klint, P.: Using Rscript for Software Analysis. In: Working Session on Query Technologies and Applications for Program Comprehension, QTAPC 2008 (2008)

15. Klint, P., van der Storm, T., Vinju, J.: EASY Meta-programming with Rascal. In: Fernandes, J.M., Lämmel, R., Visser, J., Saraiva, J. (eds.) Generative and Transformational Techniques in Software Engineering III. LNCS, vol. 6491, pp. 222–289. Springer, Heidelberg (2011)

16. Klint, P., van der Storm, T., Vinju, J.J.: RASCAL: A Domain Specific Language for Source Code Analysis and Manipulation. In: Proceedings of SCAM 2009, pp. 168–177. IEEE (2009)

17. Lesk, M.: Lex - a lexical analyzer generator. Technical Report CS TR 39, Bell Labs (1975)

18. Moonen, L.: Data Flow Analysis for Reverse Engineering. Master's thesis, University of Amsterdam (1996)

19. Müller, H., Klashinsky, K.: Rigi – a system for programming-in-the-large. In: Proceedings of ICSE 1988, pp. 80–86 (April 1988)

20. Murphy, G., Notkin, D.: Lightweight source model extraction. In: Proceedings of FSE 1995, pp. 116–127. ACM Press, New York (1995)

21. Murphy, G.C., Notkin, D.: Lightweight Lexical Source Model Extraction. ACM TOSEM 5(3), 262–292 (1996)

22. Paakki, J.: Attribute grammar paradigms - a high-level methodology in language implementation. ACM Computing Surveys 27(2), 196–255 (1995)

23. Sloane, A.M.: Lightweight Language Processing in Kiama. In: Fernandes, J.M., Lämmel, R., Visser, J., Saraiva, J. (eds.) GTTSE 2009. LNCS, vol. 6491, pp. 408–425. Springer, Heidelberg (2011)

24. Söderberg, E., Ekman, T., Hedin, G., Magnusson, E.: Extensible intraprocedural flow analysis at the abstract syntax tree level. Science of Computer Programming 78(10), 1809–1827 (2013)

25. van den Brand, M., Bruntink, M., Economopoulos, G., de Jong, H., Klint, P., Kooiker, T., van der Storm, T., Vinju, J.: Using The Meta-environment for Maintenance and Renovation. In: Proceedings of CSMR 2007, pp. 331–332. IEEE (2007)

26. den van Brand, M.G.J., van Deursen, A., Heering, J., de Jong, H.A., de Jonge, M., Kuipers, T., Klint, P., Moonen, L., Olivier, P.A., Scheerder, J., Vinju, J.J., Visser, E., Visser, J.: The ASF+SDF Meta-environment: A Component-Based Language Development Environment. In: Wilhelm, R. (ed.) CC 2001. LNCS, vol. 2027, pp. 365–370. Springer, Heidelberg (2001)

27. Vankov, I.: Relational approach to program slicing. Master's thesis, University of Amsterdam (2005)

28. Wachsmuth, G.H., Konat, G.D.P., Vergu, V.A., Groenewegen, D.M., Visser, E.: A Language Independent Task Engine for Incremental Name and Type Analysis. In: Erwig, M., Paige, R.F., Van Wyk, E. (eds.) SLE 2013. LNCS, vol. 8225, pp. 260–280. Springer, Heidelberg (2013)

29. Wyk, E.V., Bodin, D., Gao, J., Krishnan, L.: Silver: An extensible attribute grammar system. Science of Computer Programming 75(1-2), 39–54 (2010)

Test-Data Generation for Xtext
Tool Paper

Johannes Härtel, Lukas Härtel, and Ralf Lämmel

Software Languages Team
University of Koblenz-Landau, Germany
http://softlang.wikidot.com/

Abstract. We describe a method and a corresponding tool for grammar-based test-data generation (GBTG). The basic generation principle is to enumerate test data based on grammatical choices. However, generation is broken down into two phases to deal with context-sensitive properties in an efficient and convenient manner. The first phase enumerates test data (i.e., parse trees) with placeholders. The second phase instantiates the placeholders through post-processors. A DSL for grammar transformation is used to customize a given grammar, meant for parsing, to be more suitable for test-data generation. Post-processors are derived from a corresponding object-oriented framework. The actual tool, XTEXTGEN, extends the XTEXT technology for language development.

Keywords: Grammars. Test-data generation. Test-data enumeration. Grammar transformation. Grammar customization. Context sensitivity. XTEXT. XTEND. XTEXTGEN.

1   Introduction

Test-data generation is generally an important method in software engineering and specifically in software *language* engineering; see, e.g., [3,17,18]. In this paper, we are interested in *grammar-based test-data generation* (GBTG) [16,14,8] such that the grammar structure is interpreted for systematic generation of positive and possibly negative examples. Such data can be used to test compilers, interpreters, virtual machines, object serializers, and other language processing components whose input is meant to conform to a given grammar. Scenarios of regression, stress, and identity testing are often addressed in this manner. Based on testing hypotheses for regularity and independence [14], the resulting data sets help revealing issues of language processing components.

In this paper, we advance the field of GBTG.

Contributions of This Paper

- We enhance an existing language modeling technology, XTEXT[1], seamlessly with GBTG. XTEXT readily supports a number of language implementation

---

[1] http://www.eclipse.org/Xtext/

B. Combemale et al. (Eds.): SLE 2014, LNCS 8706, pp. 342–351, 2014.

aspects related to syntax, e.g., parser generation, model derivation, and error marking, but GBTG was not supported so far.

- We use grammar transformation [5,15] to describe transparently the customization of a grammar meant for parsing to become sufficiently controlled for test-data generation. This approach improves grammar reuse and separation of grammar concerns.
- We treat context-sensitive properties during test-data generation in a systematic manner. To this end, we designate placeholders to the relevant language elements (e.g., identifiers) and instantiate them eventually by postprocessors that take a global view on test data (i.e., parse trees).

The paper's website[2] provides access to GBTG resources including XTEXTGEN.

Road-Map of This Paper. §2 provides an illustrative example in terms of a simple sample language and an associated testing objective. We also discuss relevant challenges in GBTG. §3 describes our GBTG method and the architecture of XTEXTGEN which implements GBTG for the XTEXT technology. §4 describes a transformation-based form of grammar customization, thereby controlling test-data generation. §5 describes a post-processing approach for test data with placeholders so that context-sensitive properties can be handled both efficiently and conveniently. §6 discusses related work. §7 concludes the paper.

2   Illustrative Example

We pick a simple example here: test-data generation for a finite-state machine (FSM) language (FSML). Fig. 1 illustrates FSML with a sample FSM for a turnstile for use in a metro system. Fig. 2 shows a grammar for FSML in XTEXT's EBNF-like notation with extra hints at model construction. We want to test language processing components that depend on FSML for their input. Basic examples of such components are an interpreter, a code generator, and a textual-to-visual syntax translation; see [13] for some examples for FSML.

Test-data generation should enumerate fine state machines of increasing complexity while exercising all grammatical choices systematically. One challenge with the basic idea of GBTG is that the combinatorial complexity of the grammar needs to be controlled, e.g., in terms of restricting depth of parse trees or length of lists. Otherwise, the generated sets are simply too large or do not reach syntactical structures of 'interest' before running out of scale. We address this challenge by a designated test-data generation algorithm and grammar transformation-based customization.

Another challenge is that generated test data may need to meet context-sensitive properties because language processing components under test may assume validity with regard to these properties. For instance, FSML readily comes with well-formedness constraints as follows; see [13] for a precise description:

---

[2] http://softlang.uni-koblenz.de/xtextgen/

```
initial state Locked {
  Ticket / Collect −> Unlocked;
}
state Unlocked {
  Pass −> Locked;
  Ticket / Eject −> Unlocked;
}
```

Fig. 1. A finite state machine sample in both textual and visual syntax

```
grammar sle.fsml.FSML with org.eclipse.xtext.common.Terminals

generate fSML "http://www.fsml.sle/FSML"

// A FSM as a collection of multiple states
FSM: states+=FSMState*;

// A possibly initial state with a name and multiple transitions
FSMState:
  (initial?="initial")? 'state' name=ID
  '{' transitions+=FSMTransition* '}';

// A transition with input, optional action and (new) target state
FSMTransition:
  input=ID
  ('/' action=ID)?
  '−>' target=[FSMState|ID] ';';
```

Fig. 2. XTEXT grammar of the running example

- There is exactly one initial state.
- The names of all declared states are distinct.
- All states referenced by transitions are also declared.
- The FSM is deterministic.

We handle context-sensitive properties with the help of placeholders for the related parse-tree parts, e.g., identifiers. These placeholders are rewritten to suitable instances in a post-processing phase. A framework of suitable tree-rewriting functions is provided.

3   Method Overview

Consider Fig. 3 for the work and data flow of GBTG according to our method and tool. A test engineer supplies two artifacts: an .xtext file, which (semantically, as

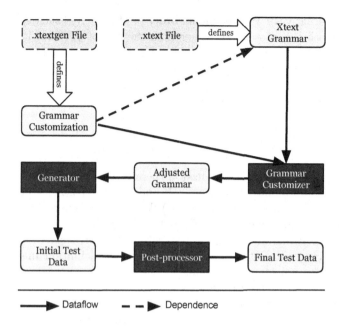

Fig. 3. GBTG with XTEXTGEN

per XTEXT) defines an XTEXT grammar model, and an `.xtextgen` file, which (semantically, as per XTEXTGEN) defines a customization of the grammar at hand. Customization sets up placeholders and limits multiplicities. XTEXTGEN processes the grammar and its customization and returns an 'adjusted grammar' which, in turn, is the foundation for test-data generation. 'Initial test data' may contain placeholders to be instantiated by post-processing to yield 'final test data'. Essentially, XTEXTGEN operates on the XTEXT grammar notation except that arbitrary multiplicities can be expressed and there is a special form $<p>$ to denote placeholder symbols.

The basic generation algorithm *enumerates* test data (parse trees) along the grammatical choices such that we map each grammatical expression to a possibly infinite *sequence*. A case discrimination follows:

- ϵ (epsilon): We use a singleton sequence ['].
- t (terminal): We use a singleton sequence $[t]$
- n (nonterminal): We assume that n is defined in terms of alternatives; see the case for alternatives below.
- $<p>$ (placeholder): Treat as a terminal; see above.
- $x\,y$ (sequence): The juxtapositions of all combinations of elements from x and y are enumerated in a certain order. We use *Cantor pairing*[3] rather than a "nested loop" over the sequences of x and y. In this manner, different elements from the two sequences are more quickly exercised.

---

[3] `http://en.wikipedia.org/wiki/Pairing_function`

- $x \mid y$ (alternatives): We assume an order of alternatives such that the minimum depth [14] of x is not larger than the one of y. (That it, it is easier to instantiate x than y.) The sequences for x and y are combined by *zipping* them together; x goes first. For instance, ['1','2','3',...] and ['a','b','c',...] are combined as ['1','a','2','b','3','c',...].
- Finite repetitions are mapped as follows:
  - $x? = x^{0,1}$
  - $x^{0,k} = \epsilon \mid x^{1,k}$
  - $x^{1,k} = x \mid x\,x \mid x\,x\,x \mid x \cdots x$ (up to k operands)

There can be infinite sequences indeed, if there is any recursion in the grammar or if there are any infinite repetitions ('*' and '+') left past customization. We use one of two strategies in such a case: a) We impose a generic limit on infinite repetitions and recursive depth. b) We only request a finite prefix of some user-specified length, when executing the test-data generator.

The validity constraints in an XTEXT language definition may deal with context-sensitive aspects of the language. The constraints are not generally in a form that they can be used to guide the test-data generation process for valid models. That is, the constraints can be applied to complete parse trees, but they cannot generally be applied to subtrees which arise during generation. It is impractical to filter invalid complete trees afterwards, as too many invalid candidates would be generated. Thus, we generate parse trees with placeholders in a first phase and we apply custom post-processors to instantiate the placeholders. The placeholders deal with identifiers and other syntactic structures that are directly related to the context-sensitive properties.

4   Grammar Customization

In previous work on GBTG [14,9,8], various controls have been investigated, e.g., limits of the depth of parse trees or elimination of combinations according to pairwise testing. Our method uses grammar customization (i.e., transformation) for controlling test-data generation. These transformation operators suffice for the running example:

- "n/i : replace e/k by e'" — In the i-th alternative of nonterminal n, replace the k-th occurrence of grammar symbol (expression) e by e'. If an index (i or k) is omitted, then the first (i.e., the 0−th) alternative or occurrence is assumed.
- "n/i : limit e/k to $b..b'$" — In the i-th alternative of nonterminal n, in the k-th occurrence of e, limit the multiplicity of e to the range $b..b'$. Here, we assume that e is of multiplicity '?' (i.e., 0..1), '+' (i.e., 1..*), or '*' (i.e., 0..*) and $b..b'$ is a proper constraint on the existing lower and upper bound. If '$..b'$' is omitted, then we assume that $b = b'$.

In Fig. 4, we exercise XTEXTGEN's grammar customization by transformation for the FSML example. In line 1, the customization links to the underlying XTEXT

```
 1   customize sle.fsml.FSML
 2
 3   // Use a more specific name for state names
 4   FSMState : replace ID by <state name>;
 5
 6   // Use more specific names for transition parts
 7   FSMTransition :
 8     replace ID/0 by <input value>;
 9     replace ID/1 by <action value>;
10     replace ID/2 by <state reference>;
11
12   // Require bounds for the number of states
13   FSM : limit FSMState* to 1..6;
14
15   // Limit the number of transitions
16   FSMState : limit FSMTransition* to 1..6;
17
18   // Replace optional "initial" keyword by placeholder
19   FSMState : replace "initial"? by <initial>;
```

Fig. 4. Grammar customization for the running example

grammar. In line 4, we introduce a placeholder *state name* for the occurrence of *ID* in the position of the name of a declared state. In this manner, a post-processor can control the introduction of state names. Likewise, in lines 7-10, we designate specific placeholders to the constituents of a transition, which would otherwise all be generated according to a general notion of *ID*. In line 13, we require that only FSMs with 1 to 6 states are generated. In line 16, we require that the number of transitions per state is between 1 and 6. Here, we assume that we want to limit the combinatorial complexity per state. Finally, in line 19, we replace the optional 'initial' keyword by a mandatory 'initial' placeholder. Thereby, we turn off the combinatorial choice of whether or not to have an 'initial' keyword and we delegate it to post-processing to enforce the constraint of a single initial state.

5   Test-Data Postprocessing

Conceptually, a post-processor is a parse-tree rewriting function. The typical rewrite step is the replacement of a placeholder by a suitable instance. Post-processors may require state, e.g., a custom symbol table, to handle context-sensitive properties. A post-processor may perform branching (by returning multiple output trees per input tree). In principle, a post-processor may also act like a filter (by rejecting input trees). A test-data generator usually combines several post-processors through function composition.

Fig. 5 shows the composition of several post-processors for the running example. Post-processors are programmed in XTEND, which is the Java-like language used with XTEXT. The individual post-processors are also described in XTEND

```
// Prepare the individual post-processors
val pickInitial = new PickInitial // Pick an initial state
val removeInitials = new RemoveInitials // Remove remaining placeholders
val nameStates = new NameStates // Assign names to declared states
val useStates = new UseStates // Use valid names in transitions


// Compose the post-processors
val fsmlPP = pickInitial
  .andThen(removeInitials)
  .andThen(nameStates)
  .andThen(useStates)
```

Fig. 5. XTEND post-processors for FSML

```
// A new branch for each match
class PickInitial extends ForEachBranch {
  override protected match(Leaf leaf) {
    return leaf.value == "<initial>"
  }
  override protected build(Leaf leaf) {
    return new Leaf(leaf.label, "initial")
  }
}

// Replace by match by epsilon
class RemoveInitials extends RemoveAll {
  override protected match(Leaf leaf) {
    return leaf.value == "<initial>"
  }
}
```

Fig. 6. Two iterators for treating initial states

while taking advantage of XTEXTGEN's framework of tree-rewriting functions. For instance, Fig. 6 shows the post-processors dealing with the constraint for a single initial state. The first post-processor branches on each possible choice of an initial state and replaces the placeholder by the keyword. The second post-processor removes the placeholders which were not picked in any given branch. In this manner, all options for a single initial state are effectively enumerated.

For brevity, we do not show the XTEND code for the remaining post-processors. Conceptually, *nameStates* generates a new state name for each declared state. The parse tree rewritten by *nameStates* is annotated with the set of generated names so that *useStates* can pick from it by random selection. Thus, both *nameStates* and *useStates* are non-branching (1:1) post-processors. Generally, the ability to pass data between post-processors is an important technique for handling context-sensitive properties.

Test-Data Statistics for the Running Example. To give an idea of the size of test-data sets and execution time of test-data generation we report on two runs of XTEXTGEN for the FSML example. In the first configuration, we have fully constrained all cardinalities to 1..1. In the second configuration, we have allowed up to 6 states with up to 6 transitions per state; all actions are required.

The measurements were taken on a Windows 8.1 machine with an Intel Core i7-3632QM CPU at 2.20 GHz, 12.0 GB of RAM and a 750 GB harddrive with 8GB of SSD cache. The Java 8 Update 5 runtime environment was used. The generation was executed on Eclipse Luna with DSL developer platform installed, including XTEXT 2.6.1. Persistence of test data set was achieved by serializing the parse trees and appending them to a text file using UTF-8 encoding.

Configuration	1	2
# of generated test-cases	1	324726
Size of test-data set	85B	0.257GB
Time for test-data set generation	606.1ms	2403.9s
Time for post-processing	545.6ms (90.0%)	354.0975s (14.7%)
Time for persistence	7.1ms	2049.8s

6 Related Work

Some forms of grammar-based test-data generation have been used in compiler testing for many years; see [3,12] for surveys. In more recent work [16,14,9,8], domain-specific languages for test-data generators have been proposed. These efforts differ in the underlying generation algorithms, the available control mechanisms, (e.g., depth control or pairwise testing) and the linguistic style (e.g., annotation versus custom grammars).

For instance, the YouGen tool [9,8] generates test data by depth while relying on annotations of the nonterminal rules. Annotations control pairwise testing, derivation limits for depth control and Python methods to be applied for global as well as local pre- and post-processing. XTEXTGEN favors grammar transformation over annotation. Also, placeholders combined with composable post-processors support an effective global view on test data with context-sensitive properties. XTEXTGEN is fully integrated with XTEXT.

The LPTL language [11,10] for test-data specification supports test-driven development with designated IDE support for the language engineer. To this end, the language under test is embedded into the language for test-data specification. Test-data generation is readily mentioned as an excellent complementary approach to LPTL for catching corner cases that the language engineer did not think of.

Our approach is inspired by our previous work [14] in terms of assuming systematic, controlled enumeration of test data. However, there are several important differences. Firstly, we use an enumeration algorithm including Cantor pairing and mandatory multiplicity control as opposed to combinatorial coverage by depth. Secondly, grammars can be reused such that they are customized by separate transformations. Thirdly, the treatment of context-sensitive properties is more standardized by dedicating an extra phase to placeholder handling on the grounds of a framework of tree-rewriting functions. In previous work, context-sensitive properties were addressed by either complicated formalisms and algorithms limiting scalability of test-data generation [7] or more ad-hoc means of post-processing [14]. Our approach is deeply integrated with XTEXT and the corresponding ecosystem; this includes Eclipse.

XTEXT bridges between grammarware (text-based concrete syntax) and modelware (EMF-based abstract syntax). This sort of bridging is not completely straightforward [1]. Formalization problems caused by the tree structure of the abstract syntax tree lead to a restriction of the metamodel classes that can be transformed back into the grammar. This relates to the property of (for example) EMF metamodels to provide a containment structure.

In the areas of metamodeling and model transformation, the issue of test-data generation arises, too [2,6]; metamodels are instantiated in a way similar to our approach of using a grammar in generative mode. When testing model transformations, e.g., in model-driven engineering [19,4], test-data generation could be based on both the metamodels of the source models and the transformation description itself. The latter aspect goes beyond our approach and tool.

7   Concluding Remarks

We have described a method and a tool (XTEXTGEN) for grammar-based test-data generation (GBTG). This effort has been informed by our earlier work on GBTG, specifically [14]. Our main objective is to create a GBTG method and tool that is open-source, well-integrated with an existing technology for language definition (XTEXT), suitable for large-scale test-data generation, transparent in terms of achieved grammar coverage, amenable to customization (controls) and handling of context-sensitive properties.

In our experience, practical grammar-based test-data generators tend to treat context-sensitive properties in an ad-hoc manner. In our approach, we aim at leveraging developer knowledge of well-formedness or validity to identify syntactical positions by means of placeholders, which can be instantiated subsequently so that valid test data is obtained.

Several topics remain for future work. We would like to incorporate negative test-data generation into our method. To this end, mutations could be applied systematically to the grammar or to positive test cases directly; see also [20]. We would like to fully enable the level of EMF models as opposed to the XTEXTGEN-specific parse trees for user interaction with test-data generation, e.g., in the context of post-processing. Finally, we plan to research more deeply on reusing existing validity constraints (as in XTEXT's model checkers) for test-data generation. A symbolic execution approach, such as the one used by the Java Pathfinder tool, may help in reusing existing constraints for test-data generation.

References

1. Alanen, M., Porres, I.: A Relation Between Context-Free Grammars and Meta Object Facility Metamodels. Technical report, Turku Centre for CS (2003)
2. Brottier, E., Fleurey, F., Steel, J., Baudry, B., Traon, Y.L.: Metamodel-based test generation for model transformations: An algorithm and a tool. In: ISSRE, pp. 85–94. IEEE (2006)
3. Burgess, C.J.: The Automated Generation of Test Cases for Compilers. Software Testing, Verification and Reliability 4(2), 81–99 (1994)
4. Burgueño, L., Wimmer, M., Troya, J., Vallecillo, A.: TractsTool: Testing Model Transformations based on Contracts. In: Demos/Posters/StudentResearch@MoDELS. CEUR Workshop Proceedings, vol. 1115, pp. 76–80 (2013)
5. Dean, T.R., Cordy, J.R., Malton, A.J., Schneider, K.A.: Grammar Programming in TXL. In: SCAM, p. 93. IEEE (2002)
6. Ehrig, K., Küster, J.M., Taentzer, G.: Generating instance models from meta models. Software and System Modeling 8(4), 479–500 (2009)
7. Harm, J., Lämmel, R.: Two-dimensional Approximation Coverage. Informatica, 24(3) (2000)
8. Hoffman, D., Ly-Gagnon, D., Strooper, P.A., Wang, H.-Y.: Grammar-based test generation with YouGen. Softw. Pract. Exper. 41(4), 427–447 (2011)
9. Hoffman, D., Wang, H.-Y., Chang, M., Ly-Gagnon, D., Sobotkiewicz, L., Strooper, P.A.: Two case studies in grammar-based test generation. Journal of Systems and Software 83(12), 2369–2378 (2010)
10. Kats, L.C.L., Vermaas, R., Visser, E.: Integrated language definition testing: Enabling test-driven language development. In: OOPSLA, pp. 139–154. ACM (2011)
11. Kats, L.C.L., Vermaas, R., Visser, E.: Testing domain-specific languages. In: OOPSLA Companion, pp. 25–26. ACM (2011)
12. Kossatchev, A.S., Posypkin, M.A.: Survey of Compiler Testing Methods. Programming and Computing Software 31, 10–19 (2005)
13. Lämmel, R.: Another DSL primer, 2013. Technical Documentation. Version 0.00003 as of (December 25, 2013),
https://github.com/slebok/slepro/blob/master/docs/fsml/paper.tex.
14. Lämmel, R., Schulte, W.: Controllable Combinatorial Coverage in Grammar-Based Testing. In: Uyar, M.Ü., Duale, A.Y., Fecko, M.A. (eds.) TestCom 2006. LNCS, vol. 3964, pp. 19–38. Springer, Heidelberg (2006)
15. Lämmel, R., Zaytsev, V.: Recovering grammar relationships for the Java Language Specification. Software Quality Journal 19(2), 333–378 (2011)
16. Maurer, P.: Generating Test Data with Enhanced Context-free Grammars. IEEE Software 7(4), 50–56 (1990)
17. McKeeman, W.M.: Differential Testing for Software. Digital Technical Journal of Digital Equipment Corporation 10(1), 100–107 (1998)
18. Sirer, E.G., Bershad, B.N.: Using Production Grammars in Software Testing. SIGPLAN Notices 35, 1–13 (1999)
19. Vallecillo, A., Gogolla, M., Burgueño, L., Wimmer, M., Hamann, L.: Formal Specification and Testing of Model Transformations. In: Bernardo, M., Cortellessa, V., Pierantonio, A. (eds.) SFM 2012. LNCS, vol. 7320, pp. 399–437. Springer, Heidelberg (2012)
20. Zelenov, S.V., Zelenova, S.: Automated Generation of Positive and Negative Tests for Parsers. In: Grieskamp, W., Weise, C. (eds.) FATES 2005. LNCS, vol. 3997, pp. 187–202. Springer, Heidelberg (2006)

Author Index